A COMPREHENSIVE HISTORY OF JAINISM

[up to 1000 A.D.]

BY

ASIM KUMAR CHATTERJEE,
M.A. D. PHIL. (CAL.)

Department of Ancient Indian History and Culture,
Calcutta University

FIRMA KLM PRIVATE LIMITED
CALCUTTA ★ ★ ★ 1978

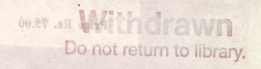

First Edition, 1978.

Printed in India

By Kalidas Munshi at The Pooran Press, 21, Balaram Ghose Street, Calcutta 700 004, and Published by Firma KLM Private Ltd. Calcutta 700 012

DEDICATED

To The Sad

Memory of my elder brother Dr. Amiya Kumar Chatterjee (1936-1974), M.R.C.P. (Edin), a Cancer Specialist, who himself became a victim of that deadly disease.

PREFACE

Jainism, which is definitely older than Buddhism, originated some 800 years before the birth of Christ. Pārśvanātha, the 23rd Tīrthaṅkara, but in reality the founder of this religion, belonged to Vārāṇasī, India's most sacred city. It is exceedingly significant that the first genuine protest against the Brāhmaṇical religion came from a person who hailed from the strongest citadel of that religion. The religious system, established by Pārśva, gradually spread towards the east, and by the time, Lord Mahāvīra was born, became one of the dominating forces in the religious life of Eastern India. The *Ācārāṅga Sūtra*, which is one of the oldest Jain religious texts, informs us that even the parents of Mahāvīra, who lived near Vaiśālī in Northern Bihar, were followers of Pārśva.

Lord Mahāvīra, who was a somewhat junior contemporary of Buddha (as we have shown in this work), made Jainism one of the the most popular religious systems of Northern India. For thirty years after his enlightenment, he spared no pains to make the Nirgrantha religion an all-India religious system. If we have to believe in the evidence of the *Bhagavatī*, he personally preached even in Western India. His rival Buddha never went farther than the Kuru country. However, both these great Masters, it appears, spent the major part of their lives in modern Bihar and Uttar Pradesh, Magadha and Kosala being the *janapadas*, receiving their maximum attention.

After Mahāvīra his devoted followers made every effort to carry the message of Pārśva and Mahāvīra to millions of Indians living in different parts of this sub-continent. The immediate disciples of Mahāvīra were all Brahmins, but at a later stage some non-Brahmin disciples gradually made the Nirgrantha religion a thoroughly anti-Brāhmaṇical rellgious system. Even the great Bhadrabāhu, who was a native of Northern Bengal, was a Brahmin and the first genuine Jain philosopher viz. Umāsvāti, also belonged to that caste. However from the 1st century B.C., persons belonging to the business community started patronising this religion. The present author stroughly believes that it was this community, who were responsible for moulding it as an anti-Brāhmaṇical religious system.

In the present volume we have outlined the history of this religion from the earliest times to 1000 A.D. In the next volume we will endeavour to cover the period between 1000 A. D. and 1500 A.D. This volume will also contain chapters on Jain Iconography and Philosophy.

Our work is mainly based on the original sources and the views expressed are entirely those of the Author. This is the first systematic historical study of Jainism, and it is hoped that this work will be generously rceived by the academic world. For the misprints, and other errors, the Author can only crave the indulgence of the readers.

CALCUTTA
14. 3. 1978

Asim Kumar Chatterjee
'Meghdoot'
24 E Jyotish Roy Road.
P. O. New Alipore
Calcutta-53

By the same Author—

1. The Cult of Skanda-Kārttikeya in Ancient India, Calcutta, 1970.
2. Ravindranath, Calcutta, 1970.
3. Ancient Indian Literary and Cultural Tradition, Calcutta, 1974.

LIST OF ABBREVIATIONS

A.B	—	Aitareya Brāhmaṇa.
A.B.O.R.I.	—	Annals of the Bhandarkar Oriental Research Institute, Poona.
A.S.I.A.R.	—	Archaeological Survey of India, Annual Report.
B.I.	—	Bibliotheca Indica.
C.H.I.	—	Cambridge History of India
C.I.I.	—	Corpus Inscriptionum Indicarum.
D.H.N.I.	—	Dynastic History of Northern India (by H. C Ray).
E.C.	—	Epigraphia Carnatica
E.I.	—	Epigraphia Indica.
G.O.S.	—	Gaekwad's Oriental Series.
H.I.L.	—	History of Indian Literature (by M. Wintenitz).
I.A.	—	Indian Antiquary.
I.C.	—	Indian Culture, Calcutta.
I.H.Q.	—	Indian Historical Quarterly.
J.A.	—	Journal Asiatique.
J.A.H.R.S.	—	Journal of the Andhra Historical Research Society.
J.A.O.S.	—	Journal of the American Oriental Society.

J.A.S.B.	—	Journal of the Asiatic Society, Bengal.
J.B.B.R.A.S.	—	Journal of the Bombay Branch of the Royal Asiatic Society.
J.B.O.R.S.	—	Journal of the Bihar and Orissa Research Society.
J.D.L	—	Journal of Department of Letters, Calcutta.
J.I.H.	—	Journal of Indian History.
J.I.S.O.A.	—	Journal of the Indian Society of Oriental Art.
J.O.I.	—	Journal of the Oriental Institute.
J.R.A.S.	—	Journal of the Royal Asiatic Society, London.
J.S.B.I.	—	Jaina Sāhitya kā Bṛhad Itihāsa in 6 volumes.
M.A.R.	—	Mysore Archaeological Report.
Mbh.	—	Mahābhārata.
M.D.J.M.	—	Maṇikcandra Digambara Jaina Granthamālā.
N.I.A	—	New Indian Antiquary.
P.H.A.I.	—	Political History of Ancient India by H. C. Raychaudhuri.
P.I.H.C.	—	Proceedings of the Indian History Congress.
P.H.N.I	—	Political History Northern India by G. C. Chowdhury.
Q.J.M.S.	—	Quarterly Journal of the Mythic Society.

RV.	—	Ṛgveda.
Ś.B.	—	Śatapatha Brāhmaṇa
S.B.E.	—	Sacred Books of the East.
Sel. Ins.	—	Select Inscriptions etc. by D.C. Sircar.
Z.D.M.G.	—	Zeitschrift Deutschen Morgenländischen Gesellschaft.

CONTENTS

CHAPTER I

Tīrthaṅkaras from Ṛṣabha to Ariṣṭanemi

(1) Ṛṣabhanātha :

The canonical texts like the *Kalpasūtra*[1] and *Samavāyāṅga*[2] give us some idea about the life of the first Jain Tīrthaṅkara. He is regarded as the first Tīrthaṅkara of the current *osappiṇī* and is uniformly described as belonging to Kosala (*Kosalie*). His father was Kulakara Nābhi of Vinītā (Ayodhyā) city and his mother was called Marudevī. He belonged like Mahāvīra to the Kāśyapa lineage. The canonical texts would have us believe that his height was 500 *dhanusas*[3] (bow-lengths). A few vague and indistinct details are given about him in the texts and it is extremely difficult to get a connected account of his life from the early Jain works. The *Āvaśyakaniryukti*,[4] a work written after the first century A.D., gives us the information that Ṛṣabha, in course of his wanderings, visited countries like Jonaga and Suvaṇṇabhūmi. The same text[5] also mentions his two wives Sumaṅgalā and Sunandā and his hundred sons including Bharata. He lived for 2 million *pūrva* years as a prince and six million and 3 lakh *pūrva* years as a king. During his reign, we are told, he taught for the benefit of his people, 72 *kalās*, 64 *mahilā-guṇas*, one hundred arts and 3 occupations of man. Ṛṣabha, after anointing his 100 sons as kings of various kingdoms, renounced the world and attained omniscience outside the town of Purimatāla, which was near his home-town[6]. According to the *Samavāyāṅga*[7], his first disciples were Ṛṣabhasena and Baṁbhī. The same texts tells us the name of the tree associated with his viz. *nyagrodha*[8]. Ṛṣabha had under him 84 groups of Ganas, 84 Gaṇaharas (group-leaders), 84,000 monks with Ṛṣabhasena at their head, 3 lakh nuns with Baṁbhī and Sundarī as heads. His chief lay disciples were Sejjaṁsa and Subhaddā[9]. He total life-span, according to the texts, was 84 lakh years. He died on the summit of Aṭṭhavāya which has tentatively been identified with Kailash[10]. According to the 7th century text the *Āvaśyakacūrṇī*, Ṛṣabha's son constructed a shrine on this mountain.

We have tried above to give readers some idea about Ṛṣabha's life and activities as given in the early canonical texts. In the well known Vaiṣṇava work viz. the *Bhāgavata Purāṇa*[11] a fairly detailed account about the first Jain path-finder has been given. We should remember in this connexion that this work was known to the author of the *Nandīsūtra*[12] which was surely in existence before the Valabhī council (circa 525 A.D.). In that text this work is mentioned along with *Bhārata*, *Rāmāyaṇa*, Kauṭilya and Patañjali. The *Bhāgavata* account also depicts Ṛṣabha as the son of Nābhi and Marudevī (spelt *Merudevī*). But the most vital piece of information given in the *Bhāgavata* regarding Ṛṣabha is that he was regarded as an incarnation (*avatāra*) of Viṣṇu[13]. Since this work was in existence before the compilation of the *Nandīsūtra*, its evidence has some real importance. It shows that the first Jain Tīrthaṅkara was accepted as an incarnation of Viṣṇu by the Hindus in the early centuries of the Christian era, if not earlier, probably at the time when the founder of Buddhism was accepted as an *avatāra* of the same god.

The life and activities of Ṛṣabha as given in the *Bhāgavata*, tally in all major details, with that given in Jain texts. According to this account also, Ṛṣabha had 100 sons including Bharata. It has nothing but praise for Ṛṣabha's activities as an able monarch. It also records the fact, that after his abdication, he went about naked with dishevelled hair (*gaganaparidhānaḥ prakīrṇakeśaḥ*, V. 5 28). Just like Mahāvīra he too, had to suffer a lot in the hands of ignorant people (V.5.30). We are further told that he visited places like Koṅka, Veṅka, Kuṭaka and South Karṇāṭaka (V.6.7). The *Bhāgavata* further refers to his followers in those countries (V.6.9 ff.).

The *Bhāgavata*, however, has no word of praise for Ṛṣabha's followers who are emphatically called *pākhaṇḍas* (V.6.8). It also, criticizes them for their 'habits'. Most of Ṛṣabha's followers, according to that text, used to indulge in disparaging the Veda, Brāhmaṇa and *yajña* (*BrahmaBrāhmaṇayajñapuruṣaloka-vidūṣakāḥ prāyeṇa bhaviṣyanti*, (V.6.10). One thing that strikes a scrupulous and careful student of Jain history in this connexion is that, the author of the *Bhāgavata*, who has nothing but deference for Ṛṣabha, is extremely critical about his followers i.e. the Jains. There is nothing surprising in it. The Jains, from the very early times, indulged freely in blind anti-Brāhmaṇism. We would like to invite the attention of our readers to that oft-quoted passage of the *Kalpasūtra*[14], according to which no Tīrthaṅkara, Cakravartin or Baladeva (and Vāsudeva) can be born in a Brāhmaṇa family. This anti-Brāhmaṇical attitude is found uniformly in the canonical and non-canonical texts of both the Śvetāmbaras and Digambaras[15].

The Vedic texts[16] know one king Ṛṣabha, who is described as a performer of the Aśvamedha sacrifices. Another Ṛṣabha appears in the *Aitareya Brāhmaṇa* (7.17) as a son of Viśvāmitra. The *Mahābhārata* not only knows one ancient king Ṛṣabha (VI.9.7.) but also an ascetic of that name, who is represented in one place[17] as asking king Sumitra of Haihaya dynasty to give up desire or false hope which, in fact, is one of the fundamental teachings of Jainism. It is highly interesting to note that a certain Ṛṣabha-tīrtha is mentioned in the *Mahābhārata* (III.85. 10-11) as situated in the Ayodhyā region, the home-country of the first Tīrthaṅkara. This *tīrtha* is apparently mentioned in the Gunji Rock inscription of Kumāravīradatta which has been assigned to the 1st century A.D.[18]

Although neither the two epics, nor the Vedic texts, connect Ṛṣabha with a heretical religion, there is little doubt that a king or ascetic called Ṛṣabha was known from very early times. He was, in all probability, a historical personage and the Jains a century or two after the demise of Mahāvīra conceived the idea of making this ancient Ṛṣi their earliest path-finder. There is little doubt that the account of Ṛṣabha as given in the *Bhāgavata* was composed only after Jainism came to be regarded as one of the principal religions of India. The present writer is of the opinion that the *Bhāgavata* account of Ṛṣabha was composed after 100 B.C., but probably before the Kuṣāṇa period.

It is somewhat interesting to note that even a few mediaeval Jain commentarors were acquinted with the Hindu Purāṇic references to Ṛṣabha. Śāntisūri in his *Uttarādhyayana-vṛtti*[19] tells us that according to the *Brahmāṇḍa Purāṇa* Ṛṣabha belonged to the Ikṣvāku lineage and he was the son of Nābhi and Marudevī.

Inscriptions of Mathurā definitely prove that Ṛṣabha was regularly worshipped as a Tīrthaṅkara in the Mathurā region from the 1st century A.D. We have already observed he was made a Tīrthaṅkara probably a century or two after Mahavīra's demise. Since the *Kalpasūtra*, which was not improbably composed before 100 B.C., refers to him and describes his life, we will not be far wrong if we assume that he was inducted into the Nirgrantha religion around 300 B.C.

In the *Rāmāyaṇa* (VII. 111. 10) there is a reference to one king Ṛṣabha of Ayodhyā in whose reign the city once more rose to eminence. It is tempting to identify this Ṛṣabha with the the first Jain Tīrthaṅkara since both are connected with Ayodhyā. But in the absence of more positive evidence we cannot afford to be dogmatic on this point.

(2) Ajitanātha : Like the first Tīrthaṅkara, the second also according to the Jains, was a Kosalan. Ajita (Ajiya) was the son of Jitaśatru of Ayodhyā. His mother's name was Vijayā. His height was 50 *dhanusas* less then that of Ṛṣabha i.e. 450 *dhanusas*. He lived for 72 lakh years and the sacred tree associated with him was *saptaparṇa*. He died on the summit of Pareshnath hill (Sammeya). Sīhasena and Phaggu were his first disciples.[20] There is nothing to indicate that he was a historical figure.

(3) Sambhavanātha : The third Tīrthaṅkara Sambhava (Saṁbhava), like the first two, was a Kosalan. He was the son of king Jitāri and Senā of Śrāvastī. Since he is the third Tīrthaṅkara, he should be of lesser height ; and we are told that he was only 400 *dhanusas* in height ! His life-span was also not much, only 60 lakh years ! His sacred tree was *śāla*. Like the second, he too, attained liberation on the summit of Sammeya

hill.[21] His prominent disciples were Cāru and Sāmā. He is mentioned in a Mathurā inscription of Huviṣka[22] dated in the Kaniṣka year 48 corresponding to 126 A.D.

(4) Abhinandana : The fourth Tīrthaṅkara was also a Kosalan according to the Jains and was born at Vinītā. His parents were Samvara and Siddhārthā. His height, as expected, was 350 *dhanusas* and he lived 10 lakh years less than the third Tīrthaṅkara. Vajranābha and Ajitā were his chief disciples. His sacred tree was *priyaka*.[23]

(5) Sumati : The fifth Tīrthaṅkara was also born at Vinītā in the Kosala country. His parents were king Megha and queen Maṅgalā. His height was 300 *dhanuṣas* and life-span 40 lakh years. His sacred tree was *priyaṅga* and his chief disciples Camara and Kāsavī. He attained liberation on mount Sammeya.[24]

Like Ṛṣabha, this Tirthaṅkara also finds a place in the *Bhāgavata Purāṇa* (V.15.1.). This Purāṇa informs us that Sumati will be worshipped in the Kali age by irreligious and non-Aryan peoples as their god. It further tells us that Sumati followed the path of Ṛṣabha. There can be little doubt that the author of the *Bhāgavata* here has the fifth Jain Tīrthaṅkara in mind, who however, according to him, was the grandson of Ṛṣabha.

(6) Padmaprabha or Suprabha : This Tīrthaṅkara, unlike the first five, was not a Kosalan but was born in the adjoining Vatsa territory in the famous city of Kauśāmbī. His parents were king Dhara and queen Susīmā. His sacred tree was *chatrābha* and his disciples were Suvrata and Rati. He lived for 30 lakh years and had a height of 250 *dhanusas*. Nirvāṇa on Sammeya.[25]

(7) Supārśva : The seventh Tīrthaṅkara Supārśva was born at Vārāṇasī and his parents were king Pratiṣṭha and queen Pṛthvī. Height-200 *dhanusas* ; life-span-20 lakh years. Chief disciples—Vidarbha and Somā. *Śirīṣa* was his sacred tree. Death on the Sammeya mountain.[26]

(8) Candraprabha . The 8th Tīrthaṅkara Candraprabha is also known as Śaśī and was born at Candrapura. Scholars identify it with Candrāvatī, a modern village near Kāśī.[27] This Tīrthaṅkara had a height of 150 *dhanusas* and life-span of one

million years. He was the son of Mahāsena and Lakṣmaṇā of that town. His sacred tree was *nāgavṛkṣa* and he died on the Sammeya mountain. Diṇṇa and Sumanā were his chief disciples.[28]

(9) Puṣpadanta or Suvidhi : The ninth Tīrthaṅkara was the son of Sugrīva and Rāmā of Kākandī. It is identified with Kakan in the Monghyr district, Bihar.[29] Here is his statistics-height—100 *dhanusas*, life-span-2 lakh years, sacred tree *māli* or *mallī ;* disciples—Varāha and Vāruṇī ; Nirvāṇa—Sammeya mountain.[30]

(10) Śītalanātha : He was the son of Dṛḍharatha and Nandā of Bhaddilapura. This place has tentatively been identified with Bhadia, a village in the Hazaribag district, Bihar.[31] His sacred tree was *pilaṅka* and chief disciples Ānanda and Sulasā. He attained liberation on mount Sammeya at the age of one lakh years.[32]

(11) Śreyāṁsa : The 11th Tīrthaṅkara was the son of Viṣṇu and Viṣṇā of Siṁhapura (identified with Siṁhapurī near Benares).[33] His chief disciples were Gothubha and Dhāriṇī. He reached liberation on mount Sammeya.[34] He lived for 84 lakh years.

(12) Vāsupūjya : The 12th Tīrthaṅkara Vāsupūjya was the son of Vasupūjya any Jayā of Campā. He had a height of 70 *dhanusas* and his sacred tree was *pāṭala*. He had a life-span of 72 lakh years, and unlike most of his predecessors, did not die on mount Sammeya. According to the canonical texts, he breathed his last at Campā. Suhamma and Dharaṇī were his chief disciples.[35]

(13) Vimala : He was the son of Kayavamma and Sāmā of Kaṁpillapura. He had a height of 60 *dhanusas* and a life-span of six million years. His sacred tree was *jambu* and chief disciples Mandara and Dharaṇidharā. He attained liberation on mount Sammeya.[36]

(14) Ananta : He was the son of Siṁhasena and Sujasā of Ayodhyā. He had a height of 50 *dhanusas* and a life-span of 3 million years. His sacred tree was *aśvattha*. His first disciples were Yaśa and Padmā. He also died on mount Sammeya.[37]

(15) Dharmanātha: This Tīrthaṅkara was the son of Bhānu and Suvratā of Rayaṇapura. He had a height of 45 *dhanusas* and his sacred three was *dadhiparṇa*. Ariṣṭa and Śivā were his chief disciples. He had a life of 1 million years and his death took place on mount Sammeya.[38]

(16) Śāntinātha: This Tīrthaṅkara was the son of Viśvasena and Avirā of Gajapura (=Hastināpura). His chief wife was Vijayā. His sacred tree was *Nandī* and he had a height of 40 *dhanusas*. He attained liberation on Sammeya mountain at the age of one lakh years. His chief disciples were Cakkāha and Suī.[39] He is mentioned in a Mathurā inscription.[40]

(17) Kunthu: He was the son of Śūra and Śrī of Hastināpura. His height was 35 *dhanusas* and his sacred tree *tilaka*. His disciples were Svayambhū and Aṁjuyā. He attained liberation on mount Sammeya after living for 95,000 years.[41]

(18) Aranātha: He was the son of Sudarśana and Devī of Hastināpura. His height was 30 *dhanusas* and his sacred tree was mango. Kumbha and Rakkhiyā were his chief disciples. He attained liberation on mount Sammeya at the age of 84,000 years.[42] He is referred to in the well-known Mathurā inscription of the year 79 (=157 A.D.) which mentions the *devanirmita* Buddhist *Stūpa*.[43]

(19) Malli: This Tīrthaṅkara, unlike all others, was a woman.[44] She was the daughter of Kumbha and Prabhāvatī of Mithilā. A detailed account of her life and activities is preserved in the *Ṇāyādhammakahāo*.[45] She was exceedingly beautiful and had a height of 25 *dhanusas*. Kings of six leading cities of Northern India, we are told, demanded her hand for marriage. When refused, they all attacked Mithilā at the same time. But before long, they were all converted by her and became good Jains. Her sacred tree was *aśoka* and she had a life-span of 45,000 years. Indra and Bandhumatī were her chief disciples. This woman Tīrthaṅkara died on mount Sammeya.[46]

(20) Suvrata: He was the son of Sumitra and Padmāvatī of Rājagṛha. His sacred tree was *campaka* and he had a life-span of 30,000 years. His height was 20 *dhanusas* and Kumbha and Puṣpavatī were his chief disciples. He died on mount Sammeya..[47]

(21) Naminātha ; Like Malli, this Tīrthaṅkara also belonged to Mithilā. We are told that he was the son of Vijaya and Vappā of that city. He had a height of 15 *dhanusas* and a life-span of 10,000 years. Śubha and Amalā were his chief disciples. He died on mount Sammeya ; *bakula* was his sacred tree.[48]

(22) Ariṣṭanemi (Neminātha)—The immediate predecessor of Pārśva was Tīrthaṅkara Ariṣṭanemi, also known as Neminātha. According to the Jains, he was an exact contemporary of the great Vāsudeva Kṛṣṇa ; he too, we are told, belonged to the Yādava tribe. His parents were Samudravijaya and Śivā or Soriyapura. He had a height of only 10 *dhanusas* and his sacred tree was *vetasa*.

According to the sacred texts of the Jains, Ariṣṭanemi's marriage was settled with Rāimaī, a daughter of Uggasena. While goint to marry, he saw a good number of animals kept in cages and enclosures. On knowing that they were kept there for slaughter, in view of his impending marriage ceremony, he decided to renounce the world.

The name 'Ariṣṭanemi' is known to the poet of the *Mahābhārata*,[49] but he cannot be identified with the Jain Tīrthaṅkara. In the Udyogaparvan of the *Mahābhārata* Kṛṣṇa is once called by this name.[50] The Vaiṣṇava works have no knowledge of an Ariṣṭanemi belonging to Hari—Vaṁśa. Although he is referred to in a Mathurā inscription,[51] we cannot, in the absence of more positive evidence, call him as historical figure. It is also interesting to note that both Kṛṣṇa and Neminātha are given life-span of 1,000 years in the Jain canonical texts.

Asiṣṭanemi's chief disciples were Varadatta and Yakkiṇi and he died on the summit of mount Ujjaṁta (Girnar), one of the holiest *tīrthas* of the Jains.[52] The Buddhist texts know a certain 'Aranemi',[53] but he cannot be identified with the 22nd Jain Tīrthaṅkara.

We have given above the Jain account of their first twenty-two Tīrthaṅkaras. With the possible exception of Ṛṣabha none of them has any claim to historicity. Regarding Ṛṣabha's historicity, we have already given our opinion. But there is little doubt that he was accepted as a Tīrthaṅkara of the Jains, only after the demise of Mahāvīra.

NOTES

1 205 ff.
2 157.
3 *Kalp.*, 210 ; *Sam.*, 108 ; *Sthā ;* 435 etc.
4 336-7.
5 191, 383, 398.
6 *Kalp.*, 212.
7 157.
8 *Loc. cit.*
9 *Kalp.* 213-7 ; *Sam.*, 84.
10 N. L. Dey, *Geographical Dictionary* etc., p. 83.
11 V, chs. 3 ff.
12 42.
13 V. 3. 18 ; and 20.
14 See Jacobi's translation in *SBE,* Vol. 22, p. 225.
15 See the present author's *Ancient Indian Literary and Cultural Tradition* (Calcutta, 1974), pp. 101, 185-6.
16 See *ŚB,* 13.5.4.15 ; and *Śāṅkh Śrau Sū,* 16.9.8.20.
17 XII, chs. 125 ff ; also XII 128. 24.
18 Sircar, D. C. *Select Inscriptions* etc., p. 223.
19 P. 525.
20 See *Samavāyāṅga,* 71, 90, 157.
21 *Ibid.*, 59, 106, 157.
22 See Janert, K. L. (ed), *Mathurā Inscriptions,* pp. 45f.
23 See *Sam.*, 105, 157 ; *Sthā,* 730.
24 *Sam.*, 104, 157 ; *Sthā,* 664. *Kalp.*, 200.
25 *Sam.*, 103, 157 ; *Sthā,* 411.
26 *Kalp.*, 198 ; *Sam.*, 95, 101, 157.
27 See Jain, J. C. *Life In Ancient India,* p. 276.
28 See *Kalp.*, 197 ; *Sam.*, 93, 101, 157 ; *Sthā.* 520, 735.
29 Jain, J. C., *op. cit.*, p. 291.
30 *Sam.*, 75, 86, 100, 157 ; *Sthā,* 411 ; *Kalp.*, 196.
31 Jain, J. C. *op. cit.*, p. 272.
32 *Sam.*, 83, 157, *Kalp.*, 196.
33 Jain, J. C. *op. cit.*, p. 334.
34 *Sam,* 66, 80, 157.
35 *Sam.*, 62, 157 ; *Kalp.*, 193 ; *Sthā,* 520.
36 *Sam.*, 56, 157 ; *Kalp.*, 192 ; *Sthā,* 411.
37 *Sam.*, 50, 54, 157 ; *Sthā,* 411.

38 *Sam.*, 45, 48, 157 ; *Kalp.*, 190 ; *Sthā*, 735.

39 *Sam.*, 40, 75, 90, 93, 157, 158 ; *Kalp.*, 157 ; *Sthā*, 228.

40 See *EI*, Vol. I, no. 43(3).

41 *Sam.*, 32, 35, 37, 81, 91, 95, 157-8 ; *Kalp.*, 188 ; *Sthā*, 411, 718.

42 *Kalp.*, 187 ; *Sam.*, 157.

43 *El*, Vol. II, No. 14(20).

44 The Digambaras, however, regard this Tīrthaṅkara as a male; according to them, the highest knowledge is beyond the reach of any woman.

45 See 70ff.

46 *Sam.*, 25, 55, 39, 157 ; *Sthā*, 229, 777, *Nandīsūtra*, V. 19 ; Kalp., 186.

47 *Nandīsūtra*, V. 19 ; *Sam.* 20, 50, 157, *Kalp.*, 185 ; *Sthā*, 411 ; *Bhagavatī*, 576, 617.

48 *Nandī*, V. 19 ; *Sthā*, 411, 735 ; *Sam.*, 39, 41, 157 ; *Kalp.*, 184.

49 See I. 65. 40 ; III. 184.8 ; III. 184. 17-22 ; XII. 288. 5-86.

50 71.5.

51 See *E.I.*, Vol. II, No. 14(14).

52 See *Kalp.*, 174-83 ; *Sam.*, 10, 18, 40, 54, 104, 110, 157 ; *Nandī*. V. 19 ; *Sthā*, 381, 626, 651, 735 ; *Uttarādhyayana*, ch. XXII ; see also Jacobi, *SBE*. Vol. 45, pp. 112 ff ; *Nirayavalikā*, 5.1 ; *Ṇāyā*, 53, 129 ; *Antagaḍadasāo*, 8-9.

53 *Aṅguttara* (tr. E. M. Hare), Vol III, p. 264.

CHAPTER II

Pārśvanātha

The penultimate Jain Tīrthaṅkara Pārśva was, in all probability, the real founder of Jainism. The *Kalpasūtra* (149-69)[1] has given a brief history of his life ; but even this brief account, like all other Jain writings, is full of stereotyped words and sentences. According to this account, he was the son of Aśvasena, king of Vārāṇasī by his wife Vāmā. Charpentier writing in the *Cambridge History of India*[2] observes that "no such person as Aśvasena is known from Brāhman records to have existed". But we need not accept the Jain account that Aśvasena was really a king of Kāśī. He probably belonged to an aristocratic Kṣatriya family ; let us not forget that the Jains have uniformly depicted all their Tīrthaṅkaras as kings' sons. The modern historian cannot help condemning this affected attitude of the early Jain canonical authors. Such type of vanity is also discernible in the writings of the Buddhists, who leave no stone unturned to prove that their founder really belonged to the most angust and aristocratic family of those days[3]. It is. therefore, quite reasonable to infer that Pārśva, like the Buddha or Mahāvīra, was a scion of a well-to-do Kṣatriya family.

But the most significant fact about Pārśva is that he hailed from Vārāṇasī, the cultural and religious centre of India from time immemorial. As a citizen of this great city, he probably came in contact with some men of vision. That even Kṣatriyas of this city were men of learning and intuition is proved by the fact that king Ajātaśatru, lauded in the Upaniṣadic texts[4], is described as belonging to this city. He (not to be confused with his Buddhist namesake) is delineated as expounding to Dṛpta Bālāki Gārgya, a Brahmin Ācārya, the real nature of Ātman. His son Bhadrasena Ajātaśatrava too, was a man of wisdom and a rival of the great Uddālaka[5]. It is no wonder therefore, that Pārśva, as a scion of an aristocatic family of this marvellous metropolis, should receive some serious training in religion and philosophy in his early youth. We are told that he led the householder's life upto the age of 30 and then renounced the world. Nothing more is indicated in the canonical texts regarding his early life. Only from some late texts we learn that he married a woman named Prabhāvatī[6].

The *Kalpasūtra* then goes on to say that after practising penance for 83 days Pārśva obtained omniscience. After that he, we are told, remained a *Kevalin* for 70 years dying at the age of 100 on the summit of the Sammeya mountain. The round figure of 100 also looks suspect. We should remember that the *Kalpasūtra*, which contains the earliest biography of this great prophet, was in all probability, written 500 years after his death. Even then we are prepared to believe that Pārśva had a fairly long life and died at a ripe old age.

The *Kalpasūtra* does not give us any idea regarding Pārśva's doctrine. But we have enough information in some other canonical texts about his teachings. And quite a few of these canonical texts were composed before the *Kalpasūtra.*

In the famous *Uttarādhyayanasūtra* (ch. 23) is recorded a very beautiful conversation between Keśin a follower of Pārśva's church and Indrabhūti, a disciple of Mahāvīra. From Keśin's words here we learn that Pārśva enjoined only four vows and allowed an upper and under-garment. This conversation took place in the city of Śrāvastī where Keśin arrived, we are told, with a large number of his associates. We further learn from this conversation between the two monks that there was no fundamental difference between the two Teachers, Pārśva and Mahāvīra. The only difference was that the law of Mahāvīra recognised 5 vows one more than that of Pārśva. And while Pārśva allowed the use of cloths, Mahāvīra himself went about naked. That Pārśva's followers (called Samaṇas) were almost everywhere during Mahāvīra's life-time is proved by some other references to his followers in the older texts. The *Bhagavatī* more than once[7] refers to Pārśva's followers. In the 9th Uddeśaka of the 1st Śataka of that work we are confronted with a follower of

Pārśva called Kālasavesiyaputta who at first expressed grave doubts regarding Mahāvīra's teachings. The Master, however, before long, succeeded in converting him to his religion of 5-fold vows. In the 5th Uddeśaka of the 2nd Śataka of the same text we are told that the city of Tuṅgiyā was often visited by Pārśva's followers. In this connexion we came across the names of 4 monks belonging to Pārśva's school. They are Kāliyaputta, Mehila, Kāsava and Ānaṁdarakkhıya. The *Bhavavatī* records another interesting conversation (9.32) between a follower of Pārśva called Gaṁgeya (Gāṅgeya) and Mahāvīra at Vāṇiyagāma (near Vaisālī). This further proves that even northern Bihar came under the influence of Pārśva. This is also proved by the fact that according to the famous *Ācāraṅga Sūtra*[8] even Mahāvīra's parents, who lived near Vaiśālī, were themselves followers of Pārśva. The importance of this statement of the *Ācāraṅga* can hardly be overemphasized. This shows that Mahāvīra himself grew up under the umbrella of Pārśva's religion.

The *Ṇāyādhammakahāo*[9] makes mention of one Puṁḍariya, a prince of Puṣkalāvatī, who became a follower of Pārśva's religion of 4 vows. The same text[10] refers to a number of lay women who became followers of Pārśva's religion. The *Ṇāyādhammakahāo*[11] also tells us the story of one old maiden called Kālī who joined the ascetic order of Pārśva. The *Nirayavalikā*[12], an Upāṅga text, gives us the story of the conversion of one Bhūyā, the daughter of a merchant of Rājagṛha called Sudarśana, to the religion of Pārśva. She was converted by Pupphacūlā, the principal lady-disciple of Pārśva. So the combined testimony of the two texts viz. *Ṇāyādhammakahāo* and *Nirayavalikā* proves that women were freely admitted into the order of Pārśva. Pārśva, who was a great rationalist, naturally had no affected towards the weaker sex. Unlike the Buddha, he never hesitated to allow women to embrace the ascetic-life. In his boyhood Pārśva probably had seen nuns belonging to various Brāhmaṇical schools at Kāśī. Therefore no Ānanda was required to plead before him in favour of admitting women into the new order.

One of the earliest canonical texts viz. the *Sūtrakṛtāṅga*[13] records a highly interesting discussion between Indrabhūti and a follower of Pārśva called Udaya Peḍhālaputta. Like Keśin and Gāṅgeya he too, afterwards accepted the doctrine of Mahāvīra.

The above discussion abundantly shows that Pārśva, who preached his new religion around 800 B.C. (250 years before Mahāvīra)[14], succeeded to a large extent in popularising his teachings in different parts of Northern India. We have very strong reason to believe that the term 'Nirgrantha' was first invented by him and laer came to denote his followers. The evidence of the Buddhist texts also fully supports our contention. The *Sāmaññaphala Sutta* of the *Dīgha Nikāya* actually shows acquaintance with Pārśva's religion of 4 vows and not with Mahāvīra's doctrine of 5 restraints. Elsewhere in the Pāli *Tripiṭaka*[15] there are references to the Nirgrantha religion of 4 vows although, to our eternal regret, the Buddhists have not mentioned him by name. But it appears from their writings that Mahavīra was an ascetic belonging to the Nirgrantha order and nothing more.

Pārśva was the first historical prophet of ancient India to understand clearly the real significance of *Ahiṁsā*. The concept of non-violence is, no doubt, to be found in the earlier Upaniṣadic works and also the *Mahābhārata*. But to Pārśva *Ahiṁsā* meant something more concrete. It was his whole existence His other teachings (viz. not to lie, not to steal and not to have external possessions) are no doubt to be found in all schools of thought.

We have already referred to Pārśva's attitude towards women. He had also, unlike some later Jain thinkers, no affected attitude towards Brāhmaṇas. The *Nirayavalikā* (3.3) contains the story of Brahmin Soma's conversion to Pārśva's order. This Brāhmaṇa was, like Pārśva, a citizen of Vārāṇasī. That the doctrine of Pārśva had great appeal even for kings is proved by the elaborate story of the conversion of Paesi, king of Seyaviyā by Keśin, the famous follower of Pārśva, told in the *Rāyapaseṇīya*[16], an Upāṅga text. We have very little doubt that the *Pāyāsi Suttanta* of the *Dīgha Nikāya* was composed in imitation of this Upāṅga text. We must remember that Keśin was also known by the name 'Kumārasamaṇa'. And in the abovementioned Buddhist work a certain Kumārasamaṇa is delineated as engaged in conversation with king Pāyāsi of Setavyā, which is evidently the same as Seyaviyā. As a matter fact, there is reason to believe that Pārśva's followers were also generally known as Kumārasamaṇas. P. C. Bagchi[17] thinks that in a particular *Sūtra* of Pāṇini (II. 1.69) these Kumāraśramaṇas have been referred to. Although we cannot be dogmatic on this point, there may be some truth in his assertion.

According to the *Samavāyāṅga* (157) Diṇṇa was the principal male-disciple and Pupphacūlā the female-disciple of Pārśva. Pupphacūlā, as we have already noticed, is also mentioned in the *Ṇāyādhammakahāo*. His principal male lay-votary was Suvvaya[18] and female lay-votary Sunaṁdā[19].

Regarding the date of Pārśva, it may here be pointed out, that is is only from two late texts that we learn that his liberation took place 250 years before Mahāvīra's emancipation. In the concluding lines of Mahāvīra's and Pārśva's biography in the *Kalpasūtra* which were obviously added during the council of Valabhī (circa 525 A.D.), and in the *Āvaśyakabhāṣya*(17), another text of practically the same date, we are told about this figure of 250 years. It is quite possible that the time-gap separating Mahāvīra from Pārśva was less than 250 years. But since we have no other evidence, we have to assign provisionally a date around 800 B.C. to Pārśva.

NOTES

1 See also Jacobi's translation, in *SBE* (Vol. 22), pp. 271 ff.
2 P. 154.
3 See specially in this connexion the *Ambaṭṭha Sutta* included in the *Dīgha Nikāya*.
4 See *Bṛhadāraṇyaka Up.*, 2.1.1; also *Kauṣītaki Up.*, 4.1.
5 See *Śatapatha*, 5.5.5. 14.
6 See *Kalpasūtravṛtti* by Samayasundra, pp. 164-5.
7 I. 9; II.5; IX.32 etc.
8 See Jacobi's translation in *SBE* (Vol. 22), p. 194.
9 See 141 ff.
10 10th chapter of the second part.
11 Para 148 (II.I).

13 See Jacobi's translation (SBE, 45), pp. 420 ff.
14 For a discussion on the date of Pārśva, see *infra.*
15 See under 'Nāthaputta' and 'Nirgrantha' in Malalasekera's *Dictionary of Pāli Proper Names.*
16 See 157 ff.
17 See Sir Asutosh Mukherjee Silver Jubilee Volume (III), p. 74.
18 See *Kalpasūtra*, 163.
19 *Ibid.*, 164.

CHAPTER III

Life of Mahāvīra

The last or the twenty-fourth Tīrthaṅkara Vardhamāna Mahāvīra was born, according to some late non-canonical texts, 250 years after the emancipation of Pārśva. The earliest non-canonical text that mentions this figure, is the *Āvaśyakabhāṣya,*[1] a work written probably after 300 A.D. The same figure of 250 is obained from concluding passages of lives of Pārśva and Mahāvīra given in the *Kalpasūtra*[2], which were obviously added to that work during the council of Valabhī held during the reign of Dhruvasena 1 (c.525 A.D.), who was a feudatory of an imperial Gupta ruler. From the Pāli texts we learn that he died a year or two before the demise of the Buddha. And since he had a total life-span of 72 years, he was in all probability a somewhat junior contemporary[3] of the Śākyan prophet, who definitely died at the age of 80.

Unlike his predecessors, Mahāvīra's life has received extensive treatment in the early Jain canonical texts. The earliest work that throws considerable light on his life is the famous *Ācārańga Sūtra,* the first Aṅga and probably the earliest canonical work of the Śvetāmbara Jains. There is very little doubt that the *Ācārańga* account of the life of Mahāvīra was composed a century or two after the demise of the Teacher and is therefore tolerably reliablc. But it should also be remembered that the *Ācārańga* gives the details of Mahāvīra's life upto his 42nd year (the date of enlightenment) and gives no information about his last 30 years.

Both the *Ācārańga*[4] and *Kalpasūtra*[5] inform us that when the moon was in conjunction with the Hatthuttarā constellation (Uttaraphalgunī), Mahāvīra descended from the Puṣpottara celestial abode on the expiry of his period of life as a God.

Then he took the form of an embryo in the womb of the Brahmin lady Devānandā of the Jālandhara lineage, wife of the Brāhmaṇa Ṛṣabhadatta of the Koḍāla lineage (*Koḍālasagottassa*) belonging to the Brāhmaṇical part of Kuṇḍagrāma town (*Māhaṇakuṁḍaggāme nayare*). According to the *Kalpasūtra*[6] Devānandā saw the following 14 objects in her dream-an elephant, a bull, a lion, an anointment, a garland, the moon, the sun, a flag, a vase, a lotus lake, the ocean, a celestial abode, a heap of jewels and a flame.

Then the following idea struck the mind of Śakra (Indra), the king of gods. "It never has happened, nor does it happen, that Arhats, Cakravartins, Baladevas or Vāsudevas, in the past, present or future, should be born in low families, mean families, degraded families, poor families, indigent families, beggars' families or Brāhmaṇical families . . . . (they) are born in high families, noble families, royal families, noblemen's families, in families belonging to the race of Ikṣvāku, or of Hari or in other such families of pure descent on both sides".[7] Then he asked Hariṇegamesi, commander of the infantry (obviously another name of Skanda, who is also known as Naigameya or Naigameśa) to transfer the embryo from the womb of Devānandā to that of Triśalā of the Vāsiṣṭha *gotra* wife of Kṣatriya Siddhārtha of the Kāśyapa *gotra* belonging to the Kṣatriya part of the Kuṇḍapura town. This Siddhārtha, we are further told, was a scion of the clan of Jñātṛs (Prakrit Ṇāya). The order was soon carried out. This event, according to the above-mentioned texts, took place on the 83rd day after Mahāvīra's descent from heaven into the womb of Devānandā, when the moon was once more in conjunction with Uttaraphalgunī.[8] It was the 13th day of the dark half of the month of Āśvina. The *Kalpasūtra*[9] further informs that in that night (83rd) Devānandā dreamt that the 14 objects of her dream were taken from her by Triśalā. At the same time, the Kṣatriya lady Triśalā saw those 14 objects entering into her own dream.

No modern historian can accept the transfer of embryo story, whatever may be its antiquity.[10] It is more probable that Devānandā was the real mother of Mahāvīra and afterwards accepted by Kṣatriya Siddhārtha as his adopted son. In this connexion we would like to draw the attention of readers to the story told in the *Bhagavatī*[11] regarding Devānandā's meeting with Mahāvīra. This meeting took place at the Brāhmaṇical part of Kuṇḍagrāma. We are told that at that time (i.e. when Devānandā saw Mahāvīra when the latter was already a *Kevalin*) milk oozed from the breasts of that Brahmin lady. When enquired by Gautama, his chief disciple, Mahāvīra explained that she was his mother and because of motherly affection it had happened so. We are quoting here the original words of Mahāvīra "*Devāṇaṃdā māhaṇī mamaṁ ammagā, ahaṁ ṇaṁ Devānaṁdāe māhaṇīe attae*; *taeṇaṁ sā Devāṇaṁdā māhaṇī teṇaṁ puvvaputtasiṇeharāgeṇaṁ agayapaṇhayā, jāva samūsaviyaromakūvā mamaṁ animisāe diṭṭhīe pehamāṇī pehamāṇī ciṭṭhai*". We should particularly take note of the expression *puvvaputtasiṇeharāgeṇam*. This beautiful incident narrated in such an early text as the *Bhagavatī* abundantly explodes the popular Jain belief that Mahāvīra was the son of the Kṣatriya lady Triśalā. The transfer of embryo story probably originated a century or two after the demise of Mahāvīra (circa 300 B.C.), when Jainism was firmly established in India and assumed a thoroughly anti-Brāhmaṇical stance. It has to be remembered that in ancient India an adopted son (*dattaka*) was looked upon simply as 'real son' and so was the case with a *kṣetraja* son (cf. the case of the Pāṇḍavas). Jacobi's conjecture that Devānandā was another wife of Siddhārtha should not be taken seriously[12]. We however, do not want to be dogmatic on this issue, but we do feel that the mystery surrounding Mahāvīra's birth has not yet been properly investigated. Probably the original Jain inventor of the embryo story had in mind the story of Kṛṣṇa's birth as told in the Vaiṣṇava devotional literature.

Now, Siddhārtha's wife Triśalā, according to the 7th century text the *Āvaśyakacurṇī*[13] of Jinadāsagaṇi Mahattara, was a sister of the illustrious Ceṭaka, a Kṣatriya chief of Vaiśālī. But in the original canon nothing has been said about her relationship with that prince. She, however gets here the significant name Videhadiṇṇā.[14] It should be remembered that Kūṇika-Ajātaśatru, who according to the original canon, was a son of Cellaṇā, a daughter of Ceṭaka,[14A] receives the title

Videhaputta in the *Bhagavatī*[15] and a similar epithet of him is also found in the Pāli canon. So it is permissible to conjecture that the author of the *Āvaśyakacurṇī*, so famous for his erudition, had definite access to some other source which is now lost. Another daughter of Ceṭaka, called Mṛgāvatī, according to the *Bhagavatī*[16], was the mother of the great Udayana of Kauśāmbī. The Jain works[17] unanimously bestow on Ceṭaka the title 'king' and according to the *Nirayavalikā*[18] an Upāṅga text, he was as powerful a monarch as Kūṇiya, the king of Magadha. It is exceedingly strange that this famous personality is entirely ignored in the Pāli canonical texts.

According to both the *Ācārāṅga*[19] and *Kalpasūtra*[20] Mahāvīra was born on the 13th day of the bright half of the month of Caitra when the moon was in conjunction with the Uttara-phalgunī. A scrupulous reader of the Jain texts is not expected to take such astronomical details seriously. These details are scattered everywhere in the Jain literature and specially in connexion with the description of the lives of the Tīrthaṅkaras. He was christened Vardhamāna 'the increasing one' because the family treasure went on increasing from the moment of his birth[21] He was also known by two other names Samaṇa and Mahāvīra. We are told that he was called Samaṇa by the people because he remained always engaged in penances, and Mahāvīra because he was not afraid of fears and dangers[22]. The canonical texts also call him by such names as Nāṭaputta[23], Vesālia[24] and Videhadiṇṇa[25]. The first name was evidently more popular since it is constantly referred to in the Buddhist texts. Mahāvīra was called 'Vesālia' because he was born in a suburb of that city. As his birthplace lay within the territory of Videha, he was given the name 'Videhadiṇṇa'.

We have seen, in connexion with our discussion of Pārśva, that Mahāvira's parents themselves were followers of Pārśva. Since this statement is found in the *Ācārāṅga*, one of the oldest texts of the Jains, its authenticity cannot be questioned. This implies that Mahāvīra himself grew up under the shadow of Pārśva's religion. There is little doubt that Siddhārtha and Triśalā scrupulously taught him in his boyhood the Nirgrantha doctrine of 4 principal restraints as preached by the great thinker from Kāśī. As his birthplace was near the great city of Vaiśālī, it is highly probable that Mahāvīra came in contact not only with the followers of Pārśva in his early youth, but also with other thinkers of that celebrated city. There is little doubt that this city was founded centuries before the birth of Mahāvīra and the Buddha. According to the *Rāmāyaṇa*[26] the kings of this city were known for their large-heartedness and religious disposition. The combined testimony of the Jain and Pāli texts prove that the city had a number of shrines, mostly dedicated to *Yakṣas*, in the 6th century B.C. In the famous[27] *Mahāparinibbāna Suttanta* of the *Dīgha Nikāya* a number of such shrines are mentioned viz. Sārandada, Cāpāla, Udena, Gotamaka, Bahuputta and Sattamba. From the *Pātika Suttanta*[28] of the same work we further learn that Udena was to the east of Vaiśālī, Gotamaka to the south, Sattamba the west and Bahuputta to the north of that city. The shrine of Bahuputta, it is useful to note, was once visited by Mahāvīra as is vouched for by the evidence of the *Bhagavatī*[29]. Another shrine of this city, mentioned in the *Bhagavatī*, was Koṁḍiyāyaṇa where Gośāla performed his sixth *pauṭṭaparihāra* (entering into another's dead body). We will elsewhere in this work discuss the nature of influence exercised by the *Yakṣa*-worship on early Jainism. But it should have to be emphasised here that not all the *ceiya-cetiyas* were dedicated to the *Yakṣas*. The shrine of Bahuputta, as is evident from the Upāṅga text the *Nirayavalikā*[30], was probably dedicated to the goddess Bahuputtiyā, who was connected with children's welfare. We are, however, aware of the fact that a certain Bahuputtiyā, elsewhere[31] in the Jain texts, is described as a spouse of *Yakṣa* Pūrṇabhadra. Regarding the Gotamaka shrine, we can say this much that Sabhāparvan[32] of the *Mahābhārata* speaks of the shrine of Gotamaka at Rājagṛha and connects it with Ṛṣi Gautama. There is no reason why the shrine of the same name, situated in Vaiśālī, should not be connected with the same Ṛṣi. Worship of ancient saints, like the worship of *devas* and *yakṣas*, was an integral part of ancient Indian religion. The worship of Ṛṣi Agastya is a well-known instance. What we are trying to drive at is that both Mahāvīra and the Buddha were considerably influenced by the popular religious systems of their time. In this connexion we would like to draw the attention of readers to the words spoken by Mahāvīra in the 18th Śataka of the *Bhagavatī*[33] where he says that he used to visit places like *sabhā*, *pavā*, *ārāma*, *ujjāṇa* and *devakulas*. That both Mahāvīra and the Buddha used to fraquent the popular *caityas* is clear from the Jain and Buddhist writings.

Turning once more to the life of Mahāvīra, we find him marrying a girl called Yaśodā (Jasoyā) of the Kauṇḍinya *gotra* and the couple had a daughter, who was christened Priyadarśanā. The Digambaras vehemently deny that Mahāvīra ever married, but we need not take their objection seriously. It should be remembered that the reference to Mahāvīra's marriage is found in a work like the *Ācārāṅga*[34] and supported by the *Kalpasūtra*[35] So, we have to acccept the fact of Mahāvīra's marriage, however distasteful it may appear to a Digambara Jain. Both the above-mentioned works refer to Mahāvīra's grand-daughter Yaśovatī, the daughter of Priyadarśanā, but do not mention the name of Mahāvīra's son-in-law. We, however learn from the *Ācārāṅga* that the son-in-law belonged to the Kauśika *gotra*[36]. From a few late works[37] we learn that Mahāvīra's son-in-law was Jamāli. It is strange that although this gentleman is prominently mentioned quite a few times in the original canon, nothing has been said about his marriage with Priyadarśanā. On the other hand, the *Bhagavatī*[38], which gives a detailed account of him and the story of his rebellion, refers to his eight wives. His parents are mentioned, but not named. We, however learn that he belonged to a highly prosperous family of Kṣatriya-Kuṇḍagrāma near Vaiśālī.

The next important event in Mahāvīra's life was his renunciation which took place on his attaining the age of thirty[39]. Siddhārtha and Triśalā were no longer then in the land of living. His elder brother Nandivardhana[40] and sister Sudarśanā[41] were there, but they apparently did not try to prevent Mahāvīra from embracing an entirely new life. It is probable that before his final departure, Mahāvīra gave his daughter in marriage to a person of Kauśika *gotra*.

At the age of 30, on the 10th day of the month of Mārgasīrṣa, when the moon was once more in conjunction with

Uttaraphalgunī, after taking permission from the elders,[42] Mahāvīra left for the park of Ṇāyasaṁḍa[43], which was situated near his home-town. There under an Aśoka tree[44] he took all his ornaments and finery and then plucked out his hair in five handfuls.[45] The *Kalpasūtra*[46] then informs us that Mahāvīra retained his cloth for 13 months and then wandered about naked.

The original canon gives us some idea about Mahāvīra's wanderings in his 12-year pre-*Kevalajñāna* period. The *Ācārāṅga* mentions a few places which he visited after his departure from home[47]. And the *Bhagavatī*, which is also an original canonical text, gives us some vital information about this period of Mahāvīra's life. And this information is to be found in the 15th Śataka of this work.

According to this account in the 2nd year of his wanderings, Mahāvīra came in contact with Maṅkhaliputta Gośāla at Nālandā, a famous suburb of Rājagṛha[48]. The author of this portion of the *Bhagavatī* would have us believe that Gośāla became a disciple of Mahāvīra and wandered with him for six years in a number of places. In this connexion the *Bhagavatī* mentions three viz. Kollāga *Sannivesa* (a small town near Nālandā), Siddhārthagrāma and Kūrmagrāma. All these places probably were situated near Rājagṛha. In the later texts, they are represented as visiting a number of places together[49].

A few places visited by Mahāvīra during his wanderings are mentioned in the *Ācārāṅga*. We are told that besides Kummāragāma[50], a place he visited in the very beginning of his wanderings, he travelled in the country of the Lāḍhas[51], and also went to Vajjabhūmi and Subbabhūmi. According to the commentaries[52], Vajjabhūmi and Subbabhūmi were the divisions of Lāḍha which is to be identified with West Bengal.

In the commentaries like the *Niryuktis* and *Cūrṇīs* a very good number of places are described as being visited by Mahāvīra[53]. But it is extremely doubtful whether all these places were ever visited by the Jain prophet. A reading between the lines of the relevant passages of the original canon would convince a discerning reader that he only toured in Bihar and Bengal in his 12-year pre-enlightenment period.

Both the works the *Ācārańga*[54] and the *Kalpasūtra*[55] have described in identical language the story of his final enlightenment. We are told that in the 13th year, in the month of Vaiśākha, when the moon was in conjunction with Uttaraphalgunī, Mahāvīra attained Nirvāṇa (enlightenment) outside the town of Jaṁbhiya-gāma. The exact place where he attained supreme enlightenment was on the bank of the river Ṛjupālikā and near the residence of a householder called Sāmāga; an old temple (*ceiya*) stood near the place of his Nirvāṇa.

Next comes the most important period of Mahāvīra's life viz. his life as a teacher and path-finder. We are extremely fortunate to possess a passage, included in the *Kalpasūtra*, which gives us a very good idea about his 42-year ascetic-life including his 12-year pre-Nirvāṇa period. The passage runs thus "...the venerable ascetic stayed the first rainy season at Aṣṭhikagrāma, three rainy seasons in Campā and Pṛṣṭhicampā, 12 in Vaiśālī and Vāṇijyagrāma, 14 in Rājagṛha and its suburb called Nālandā, 6 in Mithilā, 2 at Bhadrikā, 1 in Ālabhikā, 1 in Paṇitabhūmi, 1 in Śrāvastī, and 1 at the town of Pāpā in king Hastipāla's office of writers (*rajjūsabhā*)[56]". We have already observed that in his 12-year career as a learner Mahāvīra probably visited only a few places of Bihar and Bengal. The passage, quoted above, does not probably give any chronological sequence of Mahāvīra's wanderings as a learner and teacher. We must remember that the passage, in question, was composed probably 200 years after Mahāvīra's demise. Therefore, it was almost impossible for the writer of the *Kalpasūtra* to give a complete chronological account of Mahāvīra's entire career as an ascetic. But there is no doubt that the passage has given us a broad and general idea about his wanderings from the age of 30, upto his death at the age of 72.

A closer analysis of the above-quoted passage of the *Kalpasūtra* would show that barring a year in Śrāvastī, and a year probably in Western Bengal, Mahāvīra spent his life only in what at present is known as the state of Bihar. But he occasionally visited other places of India as is evident from the combined testimony of the passages scattered in the original canon. We have also to consider, in this connexion, the extremely valuable information given by the Pāli texts.

According to different original texts the Master visited during his career as a teacher the following places-Kāmpilypura[57], Śāketa[58] Mathurā[59], Hastināpura[60], Vardhamānapura[61], Āmalakappā[62], Purimatāla[63], Kākandī[64], Polāsapura[65], Vārāṇasi[66], Kauśāmbī[67], Seyaviyā[68], Kajaṅgalā[69] etc. The later texts and commentaries mention a large number of places visited by Mahāvīra. But it is extremely doubtful whether their evidence has any real value. The canonical account of Mahāvīra's visit to Hastināpura is probably based on imagination since this city, according to the Purāṇas[70] was destroyed by the Ganges during the reign Nicakṣus, a great-grandson of Janamejaya II. The Jain and Buddhist writers had some real weakness for cities of epic fame; and that is why, cities like Hastināpura and Indraprastha occur so freequently in their writings, although both these cities disappeared from the map of India long before the birth of the Buddha and Mahāvīra. Frequent references to the Kauravas and Ikṣvākus in the Jain and Buddhist texts also indirectly prove the influence of the two epics on these works.

The Pāli texts also directly confirm the evidence of the Jain canonical texts regarding the wanderings of Mahāvīra. The *Upālisutta* of the *Majjhima Nikāya*[71] refers to Nāthaputta's visit to Nālandā with a large company of Jain monks. Another Pāli text viz. the *Saṁyutta*[72] connects this place with Mahāvīra. We have already seen that according to the *Kalpasūtra* the Teacher spent 14 rainy seasons at Rājagṛha and Nālandā. It was at Nālandā, as we have already noticed, that Mahāvīra had met Gośāla for the first time. Mahāvīra's intimate association with Rājagṛha is proved by repeated references to this city everywhere in the Jain canon. The *Majjhima Nikāya* (No. 14) also mentions the fact that Rājagṛha was a popular centre of the Jains. It further informs us that there were numerous Jains residing on mount Isigili (Ṛṣigiri). The Pāli works also confirm the Jain account of Mahāvīra's close link with Vaiśālī. Both the *Majjhima*[73] and *Aṅguttara*[74] connect Mahāvīra with this place. It is extremely interesting to note that even among the Śākyas of Kapilavastu, there was one Vappa, who was a disciple of Mahāvīra. This is proved by the evidence of the *Aṅguttara*[75]. A place called Macchikāsaṇḍa, according to the *Saṁyutta*[76], was visited by Mahāvīra with a great company of the Jains.

The combined evidence of the Jain and Buddhist texts leaves no room to doubt the great success of Mahāvīra's missionary activities. The Nirgrantha religion founded by Pārśva around 800 B.C., slowly yet surely became a major religion of Eastern India during Mahāvīra's life-time. The Teacher, as we have already noticed, met with his greatest success in Bihar, although places outside this province like Śrāvastī region and Western Bengal came increasingly under the influence of the Jain religion.

Let us now take a brief notice of Mahāvīra's relation with contemporary political figures. The Magadhan king Śreṇika—Bimbisāra, who was almost a personal friend of Gautama Buddha, figures in the Jain texts as an admirer of Mahāvīra.[77] He is chiefly called by the name Seṇia or Seṇiya in the Jain canonical texts, although the name Bimbisāra (Bhaṁbhasāra) is not entirely unknown.[78] Although a few canonical texts depict him as a devotee of Mahāvīra, he is said to have gone to hell after his death.[79] This probably shows that he was not really at heart a true Jain. But there is little doubt that his eldest son Abhaya was a real admirer, if not a devotee of Mahāvīra.[80] That he was essentially a kind-hearted and liberal person, is proved not only by the Jain texts but the Buddhist texts as well. It was this prince, who by his kindness and love, converted an abandoned child of a prostitute into a world-renowned physician. We are referring here to Jīvaka Komāravacca, the son of the courtesan Sālāvatī, who was later brought up as his foster-son by Abhaya. The close connexion of Abhaya with the Jains is also proved by the evidence of the Pāli *Majjhima Nikāya.*[81] Regarding Bimbisāra's more well-known son Ajātaśatru, who succeeded him, it may be pointed out, that he was probably more inclined towards Jainism than any other religion. It is, however, a fact that the Buddhist texts, sometimes claim him to be their follower. As a matter of fact, the famous *Sāmaññaphala Sutta* of the *Dīgha Nikāya* was recited to him by the Buddha in the concluding parts of which he expresses repentance for his sin of parricide. But there is very great reason to suspect that his passion for Buddhist religion was never genuine. His earliest *guru* was probably Devadatta, but at a later period, because of his mother's influence he became a friend and patron of Mahāvīra. He is favourably painted almost everywhere in the Jain canon and especially in the *Aupapātika Sūtra*.[82] The Jain texts like the *Bhagavatī*[83] and *Nirayavalikā*[84] give detailed account of his war with his opponents, the 18 confederate kings, in which he finally came out victorious.

Kūṇika-Ajātaśatru's mother Cellaṇā, a cousin of Mahāvīra, and daughter of king Ceṭaka of Vaiśālī, was favourably inclined[84A] towards the religion of her cousin. Her father Ceṭaka, who was a brother of Kṣatriyāṇī Triśalā, is represented in later texts, as a devotee of Mahāvīra. But what about the illustrious Prasenajit (Pasenadi of the Pāli texts), king of Kosala? This great patron of Gautama Buddha has been almost totally ignored in the Jain canonical works.[85] The other influential contemporary royal personalities like Udayana and Caṇḍa Pradyota had little to do with either of the two great heretical religions.[86]

There were two main objectives before Mahāvīra when he started his missionary career. The first was to convert the existing Nirgrantha ascetics belonging to Pārśva's order to his religion of 5 vows; and the second was to recruit new monks who would be able to popularise his teachings. We have already referred to such conversion of monks belonging to Pārśva's order in the second chapter of this book. These instances show that almost all the monks belonging to Pārśva's order were slowly converted to the new and more vigorous Nirgrantha religion preached by Mahāvīra. Mahāvīra's second objective viz. to recruit new monks also met with success. Like Pārśva he too, had his Gaṇadharas (the head of a group of monks) and the *Kalpasūtra*[87] refers to his principal disciple Indrabhūti (Iṁdabhūi) who was a Brāhmaṇa of the Gautama *gotra*. This getleman was a highly learned person and appears in the famous 23rd chapter of the *Uttarādhyayana*.

His two brothers Agnibhūti and Vāyubhūti were also prominent Gaṇadharas.[88] Among other prominent disciples (Gaṇadharas) of Mahāvīra mention be made of Sudharman and Moriyaputta, the 5th and 7th Gaṇadharas respectively. The Jain canon is said to have been preached to Jambusvāmin by Sudharman.[89] We propose to identify Moriyaputta, the 7th Gaṇadhara with Tāmali Moriyaputta mentioned prominently in the *Bhagavatī,*[90] although the *Āvaśyakaniryukti*[91] would have us believe that they were different persons.

Mahāvīira had a large number of nuns under him headed by Candanā.[92] There was also no dearth of lay votaries, many of whom were quite prosperous.[93] Details about them are given in the *Upāsakadaśā,* the 7th Aṅga of the Jain canon. In this connexion we should at least mention Ānanda of Vāṇiyaggāma (a suburb of Vaiśālī) who was not only a very rich lay votary but also a very pious man. His role is almost similar to that of Anāthapiṇḍika of the Buddhist texts. The *Upāsakadaśā*[94] contains a story, according to which, even Indrabhūti was defeated in an argument with this lay votary of Mahāvīra.

But the Teacher's religious career was not a smooth affair. We have already briefly referred to Gośāla, who according to the Jain texts, was at first a disciple of Mahāvīra. This controversial religious parsonality appears also in the Buddhist works as one of the six great heretical Teachers of the Buddha's time. There is, nothing, however in the Pāli works to show that he was a disciple and subordinate of Nirgrantha Nāthaputra. But there is little doubt that Maṅkhaliputra Gośāla was a veritable thorn in the flesh of both Mahāvīra and the Buddha. An analysis of the relevant passages of the *Bhagavatī*[95] and *Upāsakadaśā*[96] show that he was an influential Ājīvika leader of Śrāvastī and had a large number of followers. He was however, not the founder of the Ājīvika school; this sect was probably founded at least a century before the birth of Gośāla. In this connexion we would like to invite the attention of readers to the story recorded in such an early Pāli text as the *Mahāvagga*[97] according to which, immediately after his enlightenment (at the age of 35), Buddha had met one Upaka who was a naked Ājīvika monk. We have already seen that Mahāvīra was a somewhat junior contemporary of the Buddha and there is little doubt that Mahāvīra at that time was probably in his late twenties and hence a householder at Kṣatriya-Kuṇḍagrāma. There was no question of his meeting Gośāla at that time. This Upaka, therefore became an Ājīvika long before Gośāla started preaching his doctrine (according to the *Bhagavatī* Gośāla[98] had left Mahāvīra when the latter was 36 and founded his Ājīvika school in Śrāvastī). There are also other indications[99] in the Pāli texts to show that Ājīvikism was founded long before the Buddha and Mahāvīra.

A few scholars believe[100] that it was Gośāla who had persuaded Mahāvīra to give up the habit of wearing cloth. There is however, nothing in the Jain canon to prove the veracity of this supposition. The *Kalpasūtra*[101] simply states, as we have already noticed, that Mahāvīra wore clothes for one year and a month and then went about naked. It is also a fact that Mahāvīra had met Gośāla in his 2nd year of renunciation. But there is no reason why should we connect these two events. As a matter of fact, the Ājīvikas were not the only naked ascetics of that time. Even in the later Vedic period, monks belonging to different sects, used to wander about naked.

From the relevant passages of the *Bhagavatī* it becomes clear that bitter rivalry continued between Gośāla and Mahāvīra till the time of the former's demise. Maṅkhaliputra was proably a victim of epilepsy and his unnatural and premature death proably inspired the writer of the 15th Śataka of the *Bhagavatī* to write his account of the death of this bitter rival of Mahāvīra. Any one who has taken the trouble of going through this Book of the *Bhagavatī* will, we believe, be able to comprehend, that the account was composed by a diehard Jain who had nothing but spite and hatred for the Ājīvikas. There is little doubt that this religion continued to flourish for a long time after the death of Gośāla which took place in Śrāvastī, 16 years before the demise of Mahāvīra.

A disciple of the Master called Jamāli, who was a scion of a rich Kṣatriya family of Mahāvīra's home-town,[102] and who according to late commentaries,[103] a son-in-law of Mahāvīra, publictly announced his difference with his teacher and founded his own school in Śrāvastī. From the very beginning, as it appears from the *Bhagavatī*,[104] Jamāli started behaving like a rival of Mahāvīra. The *Bhagavatī* further informs[105] us that immediately after embracing the ascetic-life, Jamāli started wandering alone with a few of his followers which was much against Mahāvīra's wish. Afterwards there developed further doctrinal difference between the two and Jamāli, like Gośāla, declared himself a Jina in Śrāvastī. Those who had express faith in him, remained with him in Śrāvastī and he, along with his disciples, stayed in the well-known Koṣṭhaka shrine of that town. But those who refused to acknowledge him as their teacher went to Mahāvīra, who was staying then in the Pūrṇabhadra shrine of Campā and reported the whole matter to him. Afterwards, we are told, Mahāvīra publicly defeated Jamāli in a debate which took place at Campā.[106] But Jamāli even after this, continued to defy Mahāvīra's authority till his death. According to the Jain texts[107] he was the first Niṇhava (propounder of wrong doctrines).

There is little doubt that Jamāli, like Devadatta, was a born rebel and had a distinct personality of his own. It is a pity that we have no chance of coming across works composed by their disciples. Therefore persons like Gośāla, Jamāli or Devadatta will continue to be treated merely as 'rebels' in the religious history of India.

For 30 years Mahāvīra preached his doctrine and in spite of all opposition made his religion the solace for thousands of people of Eastern India. The end came quietly at the town of Pāvā in the king Hastipāla's office of the writers on the 15th day of the dark fortnight of Kārttika while the moon was in conjunction with Svāti.[108] In that very night, we are told, his chief disciple Indrabhūti obtained Kevala-*jñāna*.[109] The *Kalpasūtra*[110] further informs us that in the night, the venerable ascetic died, the 18 confederate kings of Kāśī and Kosala instituted an illumination saying "since the light of intelligence is gone, let us make an illumination of material matter". Several Pāli canonical texts confirm the Jain account that Mahāvīra breathed his last at Pāvā[111] and also add that the Buddha died after the demise of the Jain Tīrthaṅkara. The writer in the

Cambridge History of India (Vol.I)[112] believes that the Buddha died before Mahāvīra, which is obviously against the available evidence. The present writer feels that the Buddhist account of the death of their founder after the demise of Nāthaputta is basically based on facts.

NOTES

1 Verse No. 17.

2 See SBE, Vol. XXII, pp. 270, 275.

3 Let us remember that both Mahāvīra and the Buddha died after the accession of Kūṇika-Ajātaśatru. The Buddhists hold that the Buddha died in the 8th year of Ajātaśatru's reign (see Raychaudhuri in *PHAI,* 6th ed., p. 214). Since the Buddha died at the age of 80 and Mahāvīra at 72, the latter was slightly younger in age. We should also remember that the rebellion of Devadatta, which coincided with the accession of Ajātaśatru was known to Mahāvīra (see *Majjhima,* No. 58.). Therefore, there is little doubt that Mahāvīra was the younger teacher.

4 See *SBE*, Vol. XXII, p. 189

5 *Ibid.,* p. 219.

6 *Loc. cit.*

7 *Kalpasūtra* (SBE, Vol. XXII), p. 225.

8 *Ibid.,* pp. 189, 229.

9 P. 230.

10 Let us remember that the story is found in such early texts as the *Ācārāṅga,* and *Kalpasūtra.* An early sculpture from Mathurā also supports the tradition of the transfer of embryo.

11 (Sailana ed.), Vol. IV, pp. 1690-1704.

12 See *SBE,* Vol. XXII, *Introd.,* p. XXXI, fn.2.

13 Vol. I, p. 245.

14 See SBE, Vol. XXII, p. 193.

14A See *Nirayavalikā* (Rajkot, 1960), pp. 25ff.

15 Vol. III, p. 1199.

16 Vol. IV, p. 1986.

17 *Loc. cit.* See also *Nirayavalikā* pp. 40 ff.

18 P. 44f.

19 P. 191.

20 P. 251.

21 *Ācārāṅga,* p. 192.

22 *Kalpasūtra,* pp. 255-56.

23 See Mehta and Chandra, *Prakrit Proper Names,* part II, p. 576.

24 *Loc. cit.*

25 *Loc. cit.*
26 Gītā Press ed., I. 47.18.
27 See Nālandā ed., Vol. II, pp. 92f.
28 Nālandā ed., Vol. III, p. 9.
29 Vol. VI, p. 2665.
30 See III, 4th Adhyayana.
31 See Mehta and Chandra, *op. cit.*, Vol. II, p. 503.
32 Gītā Press ed. 21.5-8.
33 See Vol. VI, p. 2759.
34 P. 193.
35 This text, however, does not mention her name.
36 *Ācārāṅga,* p. 194.
37 See *Āvaśyakacūrṇī*, Vol. I, p. 416 ; *Kalapasūtravṛtti* (of Dharmasāgara), p. 92 ; *Uttarādhyayanavṛtti* (Śāntisūri) p. 154.
38 Vol. IV, p. 1723.
39 *Ācārāṅga,* p. 194 ; *Kalpasūtra,* p. 256.
40 See *Ācārāṅga,* p. 193.
41 *Loc. cit.*
42 *Kalpasūtra,* p. 256.
43 *Ācārāṅga,* p. 199, *Kalpasūtra,* p. 259.
44 *Kalpasūtra,* p. 259.
45 *Ācārāṅga,* p. 199 ; *Kalpasūtra,* p. 259.
46 Pp. 259-60.
47 Pp. 84f.
48 Vol. V, pp. 2376 ff.
49 See Mehta and Chandra, *op. cit.*, part II, pp. 577 ff.
50 P. 200.
51 P. 85.
52 See p. 84 note 1.
53 See Mehta and Chandra, *op. cit.*, Part II, p. 580.
54 Pp. 201 f.
55 P. 263.
56 P. 264.
57 See *Ṇāyā*, 157 ; *Upā*, 35.
58 *Ant.*, 14.
59 *Vipāka*, 26.
60 *Aṇut.*, 6.
61 *Vipāka*. 32.
62 *Rāj*. 5 ff.
63 *Vipāka*, 16.
64 *Ant.*, 14 ; *Aṇut.*, 3.
65 *Upā*, 39-45 ; *Ant.*, 15.
66 *Upā*, 27, 30 ; *Ant.*, 15.
67 *Bhagavatī*, Vol. IV, p. 1987.
68 See *Āvaśyakaniryukti*, vs. 469.

69 See *Bhagavatī,* Vol. I, p. 391.
70 See *Viṣṇu Purāṇa,* IV. 21.8 ; see also *PHAI* (6th ed.), p. 43.
71 See Nālandā ed., Vol. II, p. 43.
72 Nālandā ed., Vol. III, p. 281.
73 Nālandā ed., Vol. I, p. 280.
74 Nālandā ed., Vol. III, pp. 293 ff.
75 Nālandā ed., Vol. II, pp. 210 f.
76 Nālandā ed. Vol. III, p. 265.
77 See *Daśa,* 10.1 ; also *Ṇāyā,* 148.
78 *Uvavāyiya,* 9 ; *Daśa,* 10.1 ; *Sthā.* 693.
79 *Sthā,* 693.
80 See Mehta and Chandra, *op cit.,* Vol. I, pp. 49 ff.
81 See Nālandā ed., Vol. II, pp. 67 ff.
82 See Sailana ed., pp. 56 ff.
83 See Vol. III, pp. 1199ff.
84 See pp. 45 ff.
85 For a somewhat late reference to him see *Uttarādhyayananiryukti,* p. 286.
86 The *Bhagavatī,* however, represents Udayana as honouring Mahāvīra, see Vol. IV, p. 1987.
87 Pp. 267, 286.
88 *Loc. cit.*
89 See Mehta and Chandra, *op. cit.,* Part I, p. 270.
90 Vol. II, p. 572.
91 See vss. 595, 623, 645, 648.
92 *Kalpasūtra,* p. 267.
93 See specially the various stories about them given in the *Upāsakadaśā.*
94 *Upā,* 16f.
95 See Śataka 15.
96 See N. A. Gore (ed), 1953, pp. 114ff.
97 Nālandā ed., p. 11.
98 See Vol. V, p. 2386.
99 See Nālandā ed. of *Majjhima* Vol. I, pp. 41 ff.
100 See Barua, *Pre-Buddhistic Indian Philosophy,* p. 300.
101 Pp. 259-60.
102 See *Bhagavatī,* Vol. IV, p. 1705.
103 See *Āvaśyakacūrṇī,* I, p. 416 ; *Kalpasūtravṛtti* by Dharmasāgara, p. 92.
104 Vol. IV, pp. 1752f.
105 *Ibid.,* pp. 1753f.

106 *Ibid.*, pp. 1758ff.

107 See *Sthā,* 587 ; *Āvaśyakaniryukti,* 780.

108 *Kalpasūtra,* p. 269.

109 *Ibid.,* p. 265.

110 *Ibid.,* p. 266.

111 See *Dīgha*, Vol. III, p. 91 ; *Majjhima*, Vol. III, p. 37.

112 P. 163.

CHAPTER IV

Spread of Jainism (Early Phase)

It is extremely difficult to have a correct idea about the progress of Jain religion during the centuries preceding the Christian era in different parts of India. The available inscriptions, it is true, give us some help regarding the condition of Jain religion in some parts of India. But with the exception of the Mathurā region and Orissa, very few pre-Christian inscriptions, connected with Jain religion, have been discovered.[1] But the early canonical texts give us some help about the progress of Jain religion in different parts of Northern India.

In our discussion on the career of Pārśva we have noticed that he was successful in popularising the Nirgantha religion in different parts of what is now known as U.P. This religion, as we have already pointed out, originated in all probability, at Kāśī and before the demise of that great prophet won a good number of converts in some prominent cities of U P. He himself personally visited places like Kauśāmbī,[2] Śāketa,[3] Kāmpilyapura,[4] Āmalakappā,[5] Mathurā[6] and a few other cities. We are also told that he carried out missionary activities in Rājagṛha.[7]

After the demise of Pārśva his close disciples undoubtedly continued his task of popularising the doctrine of 4-fold restraints. In the canonical literature we often come across his disciples. The city of Tuṅgiyā is specially mentioned in the *Bhagavatī*[8] as a centre of the disciples of Pārśva. We have already noticed that even Northern Bihar after Pārśva's death, came under the influence of his religion. Not only were the parents of Mahāvīra followers of Pārśva, but a prominent disciple belonging to his school lived at Vāṇiyaggāma[9] near Vaiśālī. The *Sūtrakṛtāṅga*[10] refers to another prominent disciple, belonging to Pārśva's school, whom Mahāvīra met and converted at Nālandā. A few other places connected with the missionary activities of monks of Pārśva's order (*Pāsā-vaccijja*) have already been noticed. It is exceedingly probable that before the birth of Mahāvīra the Nirgrantha religion founded by Pārśva was firmly established in U.P. and Bihar.

Under Mahāvīra Jain religion became one of the major religious sects of Eastern India. We have already noted that Mahāvīra visited a good number of places of Eastern India during his missionary career and converted a large number of people of different prominent cities. He, however, achieved his greatest success in Bihar where the Nirgrantha religion became almost as popular as the religion founded by Gautama Buddha. This is indirectly confirmed by Pāli canonical texts. Another interesting thing which a zealous student of these two great heretical religions will not fail to notice is that, whereas the Buddhist canonical writers take so much trouble in mentioning repeatedly Nāthaputta and his followers, the Jain counterparts do not almost take any notice of the Buddha and his monks. The only religious rival of Mahāvīra, who figures prominently in the Jain canon, is Gośāla. In the commentaries, however, the later Jain writers take some notice of the Buddha and his followers.

As a result of Mahāvīra's religious conquest western Bengal came under the influence of Jainism. We have already noticed in connexion with our discussion on the career of Mahāvīra that he undertook tours to that part of Eastern India. It is also permissible to believe that Bengal accepted Jainism before Buddhism as only a few places of this province figure in Pāli canonical texts. Some parts of western U.P. also were visited by Mahāvīra. And we should particularly take note of Mahāvīra's visit to the great city of Mathurā[11] which, as we have already noted, was visited by Pārśva. We will afterwards see how this city became gradually one of the biggest centres of Jain religion in Northern India.

The *Bhagavatī*[12] gives us the somewhat intriguing information that Mahāvīra visited the city of Vītībhaya, the capital of Sindhu-Sauvīra. We are told in this connexion that the

Master travelled all the way from Campā to Vītībhaya in order to meet king Udāyana of Sindhu-Sauvīra. We are further told that this king afterwards became a Nirgantha monk. The *Bhagavatī* account of Mahāvīra's visit to the country of Sindhu-Sauvīra cannot be dismissed as a product of imagination since the work itself was probably written a century or two after Mahāvīra's demise. And once we accept the *Bhagavatī* account of Mahāvira's visit to the country of Sindhu-Sauvīra, we have to admit that the message of the Nirgrantha religion reached India's western coast in the lifetime of the Teacher himself. And it was indeed no mean achievement!

It is not easy to trace the history of the spread of Jainism after the death of Mahāvīra. But a careful study of the relevant portions of the *Therāvalī,* which is a part of the *Kalpasūtra* will give us some positive idea about the history of the gradual spread of Jainism in different parts of India.

Among the four *śākhās* originating from Godāsa, a disciple of Bhadrabāhu, who flourished in the 4th century B.C., we have the following three significant names[13]—Tāmraliptikā *śākhā,* Koṭivarṣiyā *śākhā and* Puṇḍravardhaniyā *śākhā.* All the three *śākhās* were evidently connected with the three well known geographical units, all of which were situated in Bengal. The first name does not need any comment. The second name Koṭivarṣa, according to the *Paṇṇāpaṇṇā,*[14] a canonical text was the capital of Lāḍha country and the third, the present North Bengal. We have already noticed that Mahāvīra himself visited some places of Bengal during his missionary career. So it is natural that Jainism should flourish after his death in the countries where he taught his doctrine. But there was another more important factor behind the popularity of Jainism in Bengal in pre-Christian times. We have already seen that according to the *Therāvalī* all these *śākhās* originated from from Godāsa, who was a disciple of the great Bhadrabāhu. Now, this saint (i.e. Bhadrabāhu), according to the *Bṛhatkathākośa*[15] of Hariṣeṇa (931 A.D.), was born at the town of Devakoṭṭa situated in the Puṇḍravardhana country. There is no doubt that Hariṣeṇa was indebted to earlier works for this information about Bhadrabāhu's place of birth. It is natural therefore, that the *śākhās* founded by Godāsa, a disciple of Bhadrabāhu, should be connected with Bengal.

So far as Tāmralipta is concerned, it would not be unreasonable to note, that at the famous port of Tāmralipta lived the merchant Tāmali Moriyaputta, who became a Jain recluse apparently in Mahāvīra's lifetime. The story of how he renounced everything is beautifully told in the *Bhagavatī*.[16] Regarding Northern Bengal, we will afterwards see that this country produced true and devoted Jains in the Gupta period.

From Balisaha, who was a disciple of Ārya Mahāgiri (c. 300 B.C.), who himself was a disciple of the well known Sthūlabhadra, originated a number of *śākhās*. And among them the name Kauśāmbikā is conspicuous by its presence. This *śākhā* was evidently connected with the famous city of Kauśāmbī, the capital of the Vatsa country and which, according to the Purāṇas, rose to prominence after the destruction of Hastināpura by the Gaṅgā in circa 1300 B.C. During the lifetime of Mahāvīra and Śākyamuni, Kauśāmbi was a flourishing metropolis, and the capital of the celebrated Udayana, who did not hesitate to pay homage to Mahāvīra when he visited his city.[17] Jayantī, an aunt of Udayana became a Jain nun, according to the *Bhagavatī*.[18] Another Jain Aṅga text viz. the *Vipākaśruta*[19] tells the story of the love-affair of Bṛhaspatidatta, the priest of Udayana, and Padmāvatī, a queen of that famous king.

Among the *śākhās* originating from Ārya Rohaṇa[20] (*c.* 250 B.B.), a disciple of Suhastin, we have the very significant name Udumbarikā. This *śākhā* was surely connected with the Audambara tribe who lived in the Punjab and whose coins, dating from pre-Christian times, have been discovered in large numbers from the Punjab.[21] There is no doubt that by the time this *śākhā* originated (c.250 B.C.),[22] Jainism was firmly established in the Punjab. From another disciple of Suhastin viz. Bhadrayaśas originated a number of *śākhās,* apparently in the middle of the third century B.C. At least two *śākhās* originating from him, were connected with geographical names. They were Bhadrīyikā and Kākandikā.[23] These two *śākhās* were apparently connected with the towns of Bhadrikā and Kākandī, mentioned prominently in the Jain texts. From another disciple of Suhastin viz. Kāmardhi originated a number *śākhās,* among which Śrāvastikā *śākhā*[24] deserves special mention. As the name indicates, this *śākhā* was connected with the famous city of Śrāvastī which was more than once visited by Mahāvīra. It was in this famous city that persons like Gośāla and Jamāli preached their doctrines. It was in this town that the famous encounter between the two great teachers, viz. Mahāvīra and Gośāla, took place. From yet another disciple of Suhastin viz. Ṛṣigupta, originated a number of *śākhās* among which the most significant name is that of Saurāṣṭrika.[25] This shows that before the end of the third century B.C., Jainism reached the country of Gujarat, and as history proves, it has maintained its glorious existence in that country till our present time. Another interesting *śākhā* connected with a definite geographical name is that of Madhyamikā[26] which originated from another disciple of Suhastin. The town of Madhyamikā, it is interesting to note, is mentioned in the canonical texts.[27] And the creation of this *śākhā* before the end of the 3rd century B.C., proves that Jain religion reached Rajasthan before that time.

This rapid analysis of the names of the *śākhās* of the *Therāvalī* gives us some idea about the history of the spread of Jainism in different parts of India. A particular passage[28] of the *Bṛhatkalpa,* a *Chedasūtra* text, attention to which has already been drawn by previous scholars, seems to indicate the extent of the spread of Jainism at the time of its composition (c. 350 B.C.). We are told in this passage that a Jain monk must not go beyond Aṅga-Magadha in the east, Kauśāmbī in the south, Kuṇāla (N. Kosala) in the north and Thuṇā (Thaneswar) in the west. This passage was in all probability composed before the creation of the *śākhās* mentioned in the *Therāvalī.* The *Bṛhatkalpa* may not be a very old text, but the passage in question probably preserves a much older tradition.

In 1912 a stone inscription was discovered by Pandit G. H. Ojha from a place called Baḍalī in Ajmer district, Rajasthan.[29] This inscription, according to that celebrated palaeographist, contains the words 'eighty four' and 'Vīra'. Pandit Ojha argues that the palaeography of this inscription is older than those of

Aśoka and that is why he feels that the inscription should be referred to the year 84 of the Vīra Nirvāṇa era. In that case the inscription should be regarded as old as 400 B.C. Some orthodox Jain scholars have therefore, jumped to the conclusion that Jainism was introduced in Rajasthan before 400 B.C. Ojha further remarks[30] that his view, regarding the above-mentioned inscription has the support of MM. S. C. Vidyabhusan. D. C. Sircar, another noted epigraphist, however, assigns[31] the inscription to the close of the 2nd century B.C., although he does not offer any argument in favour of such a late date for this inscription. The present author has very carefully examined the letters of this inscription and strongly feels that its palaeography cannot be later than the palaeography of the inscriptions of Aśoka. Sircar's attempt at explaining '*caturasiti*' as meaning '84 villages', is to say the least, ludicrous. But even then we cannot accept totally Ojha's view regarding the terms 'Vīra' and '84'. As a matter of fact, in no prechristian record do we get any reference to the Vīra Nirvāṇa era. And if the tradition recorded in the *Therāvalī* has any value, then we have to accept that Jainism was introduced in Rajasthan only after 250 B.C. But we are ready to revise our opinion, if we come across fresh and more positive evidences.

We do not know much about the religious leaning of the Nandas. But the Jains claim that the first Mauryan emperor Chandragupta embraced their religion during the closing years of his life. Candragupta's name is absent in all early Śvetāmbara canonical and non-canonical texts, and it is only in some Bhāṣya and Cūrṇī text,[32] written after the Gupta period, that he is mentioned by name. But even in those works, he is not called a Jain. But the Digambara traditions, both literary and epigraphic, delineate this celebrated royal personality as a Jain devotee.[33] Some scholars believe that the earliest Digambara literary tradition regarding Candragupta's conversion is that recorded by Hariṣeṇa in the *Bṛhatkathākośa* (931 A.D.). But a much earlier Digambara literary work, viz. the *Tiloya-Paṇṇatī*, written around 600 A.D., represents Candragupta as a Jain devotee.[34] But even this work was composed some 900 years after the death of that great emperor. So we cannot accept, in the absence of some earlier evidence, the argument of scholars like Smith[35] and Raychaudhuri[36] who hold that Candragupta became a Jain *sādhu* before his death. The Greek and Roman historians, who definitely knew the Jains[37], have not said anything regarding Candragupta's conversion to that religion. On this other hand, there are indications in their writings that Candragupta was an orthodox Hindu, believing in the sacrificial religion. The famous play of Viśākhadatta, written before the *Tiloya-Paṇṇatī*, does never connect Candragupta with Jainism. It also looks a little fantastic that a stern and ruthless military conqueror like Candragupta Maurya, should in a fine morning, turn into a penniless Jain *muni* and end his life in so strange a manner.

We have another very significant passage[38] in the *Niśītha-viśeṣacurṇī* of Jinadāsagaṇi Mahattara (7th cent. A.D.), which also seems to go against the Digambara tradition. The passage compares the Maurya dynasty with a barley-corn emphasising that its middle portion, represented by the rule of Samprati, was only elevated. Had Candragupta been a Jain, Jindāsagaṇi would never have failed to notice it in this vital passage. This evidence probably goes far to destroy the contention of the Digambaras regarding Candragupta's conversion to Jainism.

Regarding Aśoka, the third Mauryan king, it can be said with certainty that he was a Buddhist. But as a liberal and magnanimous monarch he had respect for non-Buddhists, and the Ājīvikas and Jains have been mentioned in his records.[39] The Śvetāmbara commentaries mention him as a king of Pāṭaliputra[40]. His son Kuṇāla is also mentioned several times and a tragic story about the loss of his eyes has been told in the commentaries[41].Kuṇāla's son Samprati (Saṁpai), according to the Jain commentaries[42], was a devout Jain and left no stone unturned to make this religion popular in different parts of India. That Samprati is not a shadowy figure, is proved by the combined evidence of the Jain, Buddhist and Purāṇic texts[43]. Jinadāsagaṇi informs[44] us that Samprati constructed Jain shrines in countries like Andhra, Damiḷa, Marahaṭṭa etc. We are further told that he was a votary of Suhastin. We have already noticed that it was during the time of Suhastin that different *kulas* and *śākhās* were established in different places of India. So there is little doubt that the uniform Jain tradition regarding Samprati's leaning towards the Nirgrantha religion is based essentially on facts.

NOTES

1 The inscription from Baḍalī (Rajasthan), which is definitely a pre-Christian record, is, however, a doubtful case.

2 *Nāyā*, 158

3 *Ibid.*, 154, 157.

4 *Ibid.*, 157.

5 *Ibid.*, 148-9.

6 *Ibid.*, 156.

7 *Ibid.*, 158 ; *Nir.*, 4.1.

8 Sailana ed., p. 468.

9 *Bhag.*, p. 1614.

10 See *SBE*, Vol. 45, p. 420.

11 *Vip.* 26 ; see also the edition from Kota (1935), pp. 204 ff.

12 P. 2234.

13 See *SBE*, Vol. 22, p. 288.

14 37th paragaraph.

15 Edited A. N. Upadhye, 131. 1-4.

16 Pp. 572 ff.

17 *Bhag.*, p. 1987.

18 *Ibid.*, pp. 1987 f.

19 Kota, 1935, pp. 200 ff.

20 *SBE*, Vol. 22, p. 290.

21 See *The Age of Imperial Unity*, p. 162. note 4.

22 Since Rohaṇa's preceptor Suhastin was a disciple of Sthūlabhadra (c. 300 B.C.), Rohaṇa flourished in the middle of the 3rd cent B.C.

23 *SBE.*, Vol. 22 p. 291.

24. *Loc. cit.*

25 *SBE*, Vol. 22, p. 292.

26 *Loc. cit.*

27 See *Vipākaśruta* (Kota, 1935), p. 369 ; see also *Sukhavipāka Sūtra* (Sailana), p. 26.

28 I, 51-52.

29 See *Bhāratīya prācīn Lipimālā* in Hindi, pp. 2f ; for the original inscription see *JBORS*, Vol. XVI, pp. 67-8.

30 Ojha, *op. cit.*, p. 3 fn. 1.

31 Sircar, *Select Inscriptions* etc. p. 89.

32 See Mehta and Chandra, *Prakrit Proper Names,* Part I, p. 245.
33 See Raychaudhuri in *PHAI*, pp. 294 f.
34 See *Tiloya-Paṇṇatī*, IV. 1481.
35 See *Oxford Hist. of India*. p. 76.
36 *PHAI*, p. 295.
37 See Majumdar, *Classical Accounts of India*, pp. 425 ff.
38 See Vol. IV, pp. 128-31.
39 See *Select Inscriptions* etc., p. 63.
40 See Mehta and Chandra, *op. cit.*, Part I, p. 72.
41 *Ibid.*, p. 188.
42 *Ibid.*, Part II, p. 741.
43 See *PHAI*, pp. 350 ff.
44 *Niś. Cū*, Vol. IV, pp. 128 ff.

CHAPTER V

Jainism in Mathurā

According to Jain canonical accounts both Pārśva and Mahāvīra had visited Mathurā in course of their religious wanderings. The story of Pārśva's visit to this great city is recorded in the *Ṇāyādhammakahāo*[1] and that of Mahāvīra in the *Vipāka Śruta*[2]. It is however, extremely doubtful whether these visits had created any substantial enthusiasm among the sophisticated residents of this city.

The great city of Mathurā was under the occupation of the non-Aryan (Asura) chief Lavaṇa during the days of Rāma. At a later period of Rāma's reign at Ayodhyā, his younger brother Śatrughna had wrested this city from the above-mentioned barbarian chief[3]. The same text informs us that this city gradually became a celebrated centre of trade and commerce. The king of Mathurā, some fifty years before the Bhārata war, was Kaṁsa[4] who was a friend of the great Jarāsandha of Maghadha. As it well known, his nephew Kṛṣṇa, son of Devakī and Vasudeva, with the help of his elder brother Baladeva, had killed him in his own court. But the Vṛṣṇis, as we learn from the Sabhāparvan[5] of the *Mahābhārata*, were uprooted from Mathurā, lock, stock and barrel, by Jarāsandha. The Vṛṣṇis, who had fled to Dvārakā, once more returned to North India after the death of Vāsudeva and Baladeva. The *Mahābhārata* tells us that the Vṛṣṇis, under Kṛṣṇa's great-grandson Vajra, were rehabilitated by Arjuna at the town of Indraprastha[6]. They also got a foothold in the Punjab (Pañcanada country) as we learn from the *Viṣṇu Purāṇa*[7]. At a later stage, Mathurā became a centre of Bhakti cult, first propagated by Vāsudeva Kṛṣṇa[8]. Both the Buddhist and Jain canonical writers show their intimate acquaintance with this place. The story of the Buddha's visit to Mathurā is recorded in the *Aṅguttara Nikāya*[9]. But the Buddha himself looked upon this city with disfavour[10]. According to the Pāli texts, this city was infested with Yakṣas[11]. But soon after the demise of the Buddha, one of his great disciples Mahākaccāna started preaching the doctrine of his Guru in this city. We further learn that the king of Mathurā, after the death of Buddha, was one Avantīputta[12], who judging by his name, was probably connected with the ruling house in Avantī. One of the finest Sūtras of the Pāli literature viz *Madhurasutta* was recited by the above-mentioned disciple of the Buddha in this city. The meeting of the learned Brāhmaṇa Kaṇḍarāyaṇa with Mahākaccāna took place in this city at a place called Gundāvana near Mathurā[13]. This Gundāvana may or may not be identical with Vṛndāvana[14] of Sanskrit literature.

Regarding the actual introduction of Jainism in the Mathurā region, we have a story told in the *Paumacariyaṁ* of *Vimalasūri*, a text composed 530 years after the demise of Mahāvīra[15]. This date is supplied by the poet in the concluding verses of his poem. And there is nothing in the *Paumacariyaṁ* itself that stands against this date. We have therefore to accept it as a work of the 1st century A.D.[16] According to this poem the Śvetāmbara Jain religion was introduced in Mathurā by the following seven Jain saints—Suramantra, Śrīmantra, Śrītilaka, Sarvasundara, Jayamantra, Anilalalita and Jayamitra[17]. The *Paumacariyaṁ* contains a verse[18], the importance of which can hardly be overestimated for the early history of Jainism, which runs as follows :—

iha Bhārahammivāse volīne Nandanaravīkāle
hohī paviralagahano Jinadhamme ceva dusamāe

According to this verse the Jain religion had to encounter difficult days after the rule of the Nandas. The poet further informs us that the people of India during this period had become more interested in the religion of the Buddha and Śiva (Liṅga)[19]. But as a result of the missionary activities of the above mentioned Jain monks, the religion of Pārśva and Mahāvīra became once more popular in some parts of India. There is little doubt that the author of the *Paumacariyaṁ*, writing in the 1st century A.D., faithfully portrays the religious condition of pre-Christian India when Buddhism was all-dominant. Śaivism also, if we have to believe in the evidence of Patañjali[20], was quite popular in the Maurya period. The above mentioned seven Jain saints, we are told, were responsible for the introduction of Jainism not only in Mathurā but also Śāketa (Ayodhyā|.[21] In this connexion, we are informed by Vimala that there was a temple dedicated to Muni Suvrata, the 20th Tīrthaṅkara, at the town of Śāketa.[22] Apparently, this temple was built a few centuries before Vimala. This was surely one of the earliest Jain temples of Northern India. The Jain Ṛṣis, according to the account of the Paumacariyaṁ[23], went to Mathurā from Śāketa. And if this account be accepted, we must conclude that Jainism travelled to Mathurā from eastern India via Ayodhyā.

Since the earliest Jain inscription from Mathurā is as old as 150 B.C., it can easily be conjectured that Jainism got a foothold there by the beginning of the 2nd century B.C., if not earlier. The seven Jain monks, who are mentioned in the Paumacariyaṁ in connexion with the introduction of Jainism in Mathurā, probably flourished in that period. It is also possible that some of them were the teachers of a few Jain monks mentioned in the inscriptions. The account of the Paumacariyaṁ induces us to believe, that the monks responsible for the introduction of Jainism in Mathurā, originally hailed from the great country of Kosala, the metropolis of which, as we have already noticed in a previous chapter, was intimately connected with the activities of Mahāvīra, the last Tīrthaṅkara. Pārśva, the real founder of Jainism, according to the Ṇāyādhammakahāo[24] had paid a visit to Śāketa in course of his religious tour. The Jain canonical writers believe Kosala to be the homeland of most of their earlier Tīrthaṅkaras. It is also possible that cities like Śrāvastī had received their first dose of Jainism even before the birth of Mahāvīra. The Śrāvastikā śākhā, mentioned in the Therāvalī had originated in the 3rd century B.C., and its very name indicates that this śākhā originated in Śrāvastī, the capital of Kosala.

What we are trying to suggest is that the Jain monks of Kosala by 200 B.C., had started popularising their religion in the celebrated city of Mathurā, which was surely a great centre of Bhāgavata cult from a much earlier period. This city, according to both Jain and Buddhist sources, was also intimately connected with Yakṣa worship. We have already noted the evidence of the Pāli canon regarding Yakṣa worship in Mathurā. According to the *Vipāka Śruta*[25] there existed a shrine dedicated to Yakṣa Sudarśana in Mathurā. So the Jain monks had to meet the challenge of both the Vaiṣṇavas and Yakṣa worshippers. And it is needless to say, and as attested by scores of inscriptions, the Jain religion had received good support from the ordinary people of Mathurā.

In this connexion we would like to point out that not only Kosala, but the adjoining Vatsa territory also probably sent Jain missionaries to Mathurā. The *Bhagavatī*[26] records that Mahāvīra was very cordially received along with his disciples by the great king Udayana in his capital Kauśāmbī. The Kauśāmbikā *śākhā*, mentioned in the *Therāvalī*, as we have already noticed in a previous chapter, originated by the beginning of the 3rd century B.C. Two inscriptions[27] from Pabhosa near Kauśāmbī of the 2nd century B.C., prove that the Jain monks enjoyed royal patronage during the Śuṅga period in the Kauśāmbī region. So it is possible that like the monks of Kosala, the Jain *sādhus* of the Vatsa country took active interest in the propagation of Jainism in Mathurā.

An interesting fact told by Vimala in his description of the introduction of Jainism in Mathurā is that the images of Tīrthaṅkaras along with the images of the above-mentioned Jain *sādhus* gradually came to be installed in different residential buildings of Mathurā. Now, image-worship was an integral part of Yakṣa worship. Every important Yakṣa shrine in Northern India had images of Yakṣa, to which it was dedicated. In this connexion we can refer to the story of Yakṣa Moggarapāṇi of Rājagṛha told in the *Antagaḍadasāo*[28] where there is a definite and clear reference to the image of that Yakṣa. We further learn from the *Vipāka Śruta*[29] that the images of Yakṣas were worshipped with leaves, flowers etc., like the image of gods. The practice of worshipping from later Vedic times, Deva[30] and Yakṣa icons, in their respective shrines, naturally influenced the early Jain religion. We will afterwards see that the worship of icons of Tīrthaṅkaras was practised even in the 4th century B.C. It is also safe to conjecture that the temple of Muni Suvrata at Śāketa, built probably in the 3rd century B.C, had an image of that Tīrthaṅkara.

The earliest Jain inscription from Mathurā has been assigned to the middle of the 2nd century B.C. by Bühler.[31] We are referring to the stone inscription[32] which records the dedication of an arch for the temple (*pāsādotoraṇa*) by *sāvaka* Utaradāsaka (Uttaradāsaka), son of Vachī (Vātsī) and disciple (*aṁtevāsi*) of the ascetic (*samaṇa*) Māharakhita (Māgharakṣita). This monk Māgharakṣita surely flourished in the first half of the 2nd century B.C., and was one of the successful early Jain missionaries of Mathurā. This inscription further proves that the earliest Jain temple in Mathurā was already in existence in the present Kaṅkālī Ṭīlā area before 150 B.C. And this temple (*pāsāda*) was probably the *devanirmita stūpa* of a 2nd century Jain inscription about which we will have something more to say afterwards. And it is also tempting to conjecture that our Māgharakṣita was a disciple of one of those seven monks mentioned in the *Paumacariyaṁ*. But in the absence of more positive proof we cannot be dogmatic on this point.

Chronologically, the next Jain inscription from Mathurā is that which mentions a person called Gotiputra and his wife Śimitrā who belonged to Kauśika *gotra*.[33] This inscription records, after invocation of Arhat Vardhamāna, the setting up of a tablet of homage (*āyāgapaṭa*) by the above-mentioned lady. But the most important expression of this inscription is the epithet *poṭhayaśakakālavāḷa* given to her husband Gotiputra. Bühler translates it as 'black serpent to the Poṭhayas and Śakas'.[34] The Poṭhayas of this inscription, according to Bühler should be identified with the Prosṭhas mentioned in the *Mahābhārata*.[35] Now, that epic mentions this tribe along with a few other tribes including Trigarta, the well known Punjab tribe. So it proves that the Prosṭhas were in all probability their neighbours. It is therefore, not surprising to find them mentioned in an inscription of Mathurā of pre-Christian days.

It is also significant that Poṭhayas are mentioned along with the Śakas, who had started playing an important part in the politics of Northern India from a much earlier period. The Śakas are mentioned immediately after Gandhāras (Gadara) in the Behistun and Persepolis inscriptions[36] of Darius, the great Achaemenian emperor of Persia who flourished in the last quarter of the 6th century B.C. They are also mentioned in other inscriptions of the same monarch and the Persepolis inscription of Xerxes.[37] It is exceedingly likely, therefore, that by the closing years of the 6th century B.C., when Darius flourished, the Śakas were already in India, although politically they came into the limelight only after 100 B.C. Mathurā, as we will presently see, was under the Śakas from the closing years of the 1st century B.C. Probably our Gotiputra was one of those Kṣatriyas of Mathurā who had left no stone unturned to check the Śaka advance into the Mathurā region. Probably for a few years, as the inscription indicates, he successfully fought off the Śaka challenge. But before long he had to give in. Lüders[38] rejects the translation of Bühler of the expression mentioning Poṭhayas and Śakas. According to him Poṭhayaśaka is a proper name. But he obviously fails to interpret the term *kālavāḷa*. Now, such a proper name as Poṭhayaśaka is exceedingly rare in ancient India and there can absolutely be no basis for such an interpretation. The translation given by Bühler is eminently reasonable. And if there is any truth in the later Jain tradition, another valiant warrior of the Āryāvarta successfully fought with the Śakas in the middle of the first century B.C. We are referring to king Vikramāditya, who according to the Indian tradition reigned in the middle of the first century B.C.[39] In any case, our Gotiputra is one of those few Indians, who had tried to withstand the advance of foreign tribes into the heart of India, and for his great patriotic zeal he should be remembered by all lovers of Indian history. His wife who is called 'Kośikī' also probably belonged to an aristicratic Kṣatriya family. Both this gentleman and his wife, as this inscription indicates, were devoted worshippers of Tīrthaṅkara Vardhamāna. Another inscription, also written in Prakrit, mentions this gentleman and gives his real name as Indrapāla.[40]

This inscription contains the expression *arahatapūjāye* which once more proves Gotiputra's leaning towards the Jain religion. It is highly significant that, unlike most of the early Jain devotees, mentioned in the Mathurā inscriptions, this person was a Kṣatriya nobleman. Like Khāravela of Kaliṅga he was a valiant soldier, but his martial zeal did not prevent him from falling in love with a religious system which was basically based on the concept of non-violence. Non-violence is not cowardice, and the example of Gotiputra shows that a person believing in non-violence could, for the sake of his mother-land, convert himself into a much sterner stuff. Both the inscriptions mentioning Gotiputra are placed in the 2nd half of the 1st century B.C. by Bühler and Fleet.[41]

We will now discuss some other pre-Kuṣāṇa Jain inscriptions of Mathurā. Majority of such inscriptions are undated, although a few have dates in them. The most important is that inscription which mentions the Śaka Mahākṣatrapa Śoḍāsa[42] and gives us the date 72 which should be referred to the era of 58 B.C. It should therefore correspond to 14 A.D. This Mahākṣatrapa was the son of Mahākṣatrapa Rañjuvula who had apparently conquered Mathurā before the beginning of the Christian era. Gotiputra was probably one of his adversaries. Both Rañjuvula and Śoḍāsa are mentioned in the well known Mathurā Lion capital Inscriptions[43] and also the Mora well inscription[44] which refers to the Vṛṣṇi heroes. Both father and son had probably equal deference for Brāhmaṇical Hinduism, Buddhism and Jainism. The inscription under discussion records, after an invocation of the Arhat Vardhamāna, the setting up of an Āryavatī[45] by Amohinī, the Kochī (=Kautsī), a female lay disciple of the ascetics (*samanasāvikā*), together with her sons Pālaghoṣa, Poṭhaghoṣa and Dhanaghosa for the worship of Arhats.

Another interesting early inscription from Mathurā[46] records the setting up of a shrine (*devikula*) of the Arhat, an *āyāgasabhā*, a reservoir (*prapā*) and stone slabs (*śilapaṭa*) in the Arhat temple (*Arahatāyatana*) of the Nigathas (Nirgranthas) by a few courtesans (*gaṇikā*). Regarding the names of the prostitutes there is some confusion. According to Bhagwanlal Indraji at least four of them viz Nādā, Vāsā, Dandā and Leṇaśobhikā are mentioned in this inscription. But Lüders[47] reduces the number to two. The interpretation of Bhagwanlal seems more reasonable. But what is of much greater interest is that, even women leading immoral life, could be converted to the doctrine of dedication and love by a few zealous ascetics. The setting up of so many things proves, that the prostitutes metioned in this inscription, were quite rich. However there is nothing surprising to find prositutes taking an active part in religious affairs. Even a superficial acquaintance with the Buddhist canon would show how prominent prostitutes actively helped the Buddha and Saṅgha. One of the best lay-disciples of the Buddha was the son of a prostitute. We are referring to Jīvaka Komāravaccha, the physician who was a son of a prostitute called Sālāvatī, whose fee per night at Rājagṛha was 100 *kahāpaṇas*.[48] The fee of the courtesan Ambapālī at Vaiśālī was 50 *kahāpaṇas* per night.[49] The great Vasantasenā of Bhāsa's *Cārudatta* and Śūdraka's *Mrcchakaṭika* was not only an exceedingly rich lady but also one of the most accomplished persons of Ujjayinī. It seems that the *gaṇikās*, mentioned in the inscription under discussion, were prominent citizens of Mathurā. The reference to *devikula* (*devakula*) proves that this term was used freely to describe any type of shrine. Apparently the *devikula* built by these courtesans was a somewhat smaller one because it was built within the enclosure of the Arhat temple (*āyatana*).

Another pre-Kuṣāṇa inscription[50] found from Kaṅkālī Ṭīlā records the setting up of a tablet of homage by Śivayaśā, who has been described as the wife of a dancer (*nataka*) called Phaguyaśa. This inscription once more shows that persons of queer professions took active interest in the welfare of the Jain Church. Another inscription, which has been assigned to the pre-Kuṣāṇa period by Bühler, is that which refers[51] to Sihanādika, son of the *vānika* Sihaka and Kośikī. This Sihanādika according to this inscription set up a tablet of homage (*āyāgapaṭa*) for the worship of Arhats. Bühler observes that the epithet *vānıka* given to the father of Sihanādika proves that he was a representative of the merchant community. His mother, however, belonged to a superior caste which is indicated by the word *Kośikī*. In that case, this should be regarded as an instance of *pratiloma* marriage which is generally condemned in the Smṛti texts. But the epithet *vānika* given to Sihanādika's father Sihaka does not clearly prove that he belonged to the Vaiśya caste. There are many cases of persons of superior caste adopting the profession of lower classes. We have the classic example of Cārudatta, who was a *sārthavāha* but was at the same time a Brāhmaṇa. In the Buddhist canon we have at least fifty cases of a Brāhmaṇa adopting the profession of much lower classes. In the *Aṅguttara Nikāya*[52] we come across a Brāhmaṇa called Saṅgāvara who was a celebrated mason and built many houses at Vaiśālī.[53]

The fragmentary inscription[54] recording the dedication by Pūsā, the wife of Puphaka Mogaliputta is also a pre-Kuṣāṇa record according to Lüders.[55] But a more important pre-Kuṣāṇa inscription is that which mentions a Jain monk called Jayasena[56] and his female disciple (*āmtevāsinī*) Dharmaghoṣā. It further records the gift of a temple (*pāsāda*) by that lady. An inscription[57] found from Kaṅkālī Ṭīlā mentions according to Bühler, a Śrāvikā called Lahastinī. It records the dedication of an arch (*toraṇa*). Lüders,[58] however is of the opinion that *lahastinī* here is not a proper name. Another inscription, which appears to be pre-Kuṣāṇa record, is that which refers[59] to the setting up of a tablet of homage (*āyāgapaṭa*) by one Acalā, the daughter-in-law of Bhadrayaśas and wife of Bhadranadi. The gift of another *āyāgapaṭa* is recorded in an inscription[60] by a woman who is described as the wife of one Māthuraka (inhabitant of Mathurā).

Before we turn our attention to the Jain inscriptions of the Kuṣāṇa period, we must have to take note of the last important pre-Kuṣāṇa record that mentions Bhagavat Nemesa.[61] There is little doubt and as pointed out Bühler, the god Nemesa who is sculptured as a goat-headed deity here is Hariṇegamesī of the Jain canonical texts. This god, as we learn from the *Kalpasūtra,* transferred the embryo of Mahāvīra from the womb of Devānandā to that of Triśalā. The story of the transfer of embryo is almost repeated by the Jain artist of Mathurā.[62] The god Hariṇegamesī is not only mentioned in the *Kalpasūtra* but also in such works as the *Antagaḍadasāo,*[63] *Bhagavatī*[64] etc. This god is surely identical with Kārttikeya who is also known by the name Naigameya.[65] Bühler points out that four mutilated statues or statuettes of Mathurā museum refer to the same legend as told in the *Kalpasūtra*.[66] Two of these figures are goat-headed males and two are females, each holding an infant in a dish.[67] This infant is no other than the Lord Mahāvīra himself.

A very good number of Jain inscriptions of the Kuṣāṇa period found from Mathurā are dated. The earliest of such inscriptions is that which is dated in the year 4 corresponding to 82 A.D., which falls within the reign of the great Kuṣāṇa king Kaniṣka. It mentions a monk called Puśyamitra[68] and for the first time in the Jain records of Mathurā, the *gaṇa, kula* and *śākhā* of a particular monk are mentioned. We have already noticed that these *gaṇa, kula* and *śākhās* originated after Bhadrabāhu, who was in all probability, a contemporary of Candragupta Maurya. Not a single among the pre-Kuṣāṇa inscriptions, which we have noticed so far, contains any reference to them. According to the present inscription the monk Puśyamitra belonged to the Vāraṇa *gaṇa*, the Arya (*Ārya*)—Hāḷakiya *kula* and the Vajanagarī *śākhā*. It was formerly read as Arya-Haṭṭakiya *kula* by Bühler. But Lüders[69] in 1911 suggested that all the letters read as 'ṭṭa' should be read as 'ḷa' Now, according to the *Therāvalī* there is no *gaṇa* of the name of Vāraṇa. But the *śākhā* Vajanagarī, mentioned here, is included in the *gaṇa* called Cāraṇa. There is therefore, little doubt and as suggested long ago by Bühler, 'Cāraṇa' is evidently a mistake for 'Vāraṇa'. Now, this particular *gaṇa*, according to the same text, originated from Sirigutta (Śrīgupta) of the Hāriya (Hārita) *gotra*, who was one of the disciples of Suhastin, who flourished around 250 B.C., since he himself was a disciple of Sthūlabhdra, a junior contemporary of Bhadrabāhu. This particular *gaṇa* therefore, originated in the latter half of the 3rd century B.C., and judging by its occurrence in the Mathurā inscriptions, it was surely one of the most popular *gaṇas* of the Mathurā region. The *kula* Ārya-Hāḷakiya should be the correct reading for 'Hālijja' which according to the *Therāvalī* is a *kula* under Cāraṇa. The name of the *śākhā* viz. Vajanagarī is exactly the same here as in the *Therāvalī*. According to Bühler[70] this particular *śākhā* should be connected with the Vṛjji country. But in the absence of more definite evidence we cannot accept Bühler's stand. It is, however, a fact that most of the *śākhās* and *kulas* of the early Śvetāmbara Jains had something to do with geographical units. This we have already noticed in the previous chapter.

Now, this particular inscription not only mentions the monk Puśyamitra but also his female pupil (*śiśinī*) Sathisihā and also her pupil whose name cannot be read. There is however a reference to a monk called Sihamitra whose *saḍhacarī* (female companion) was this unnamed female disciple of Sathisihā and at whose request an unnamed lady along with two of her male relatives Grahaceṭa and Grahadāsa made a gift of an image.

A number of Jain image inscriptions[71] bearing the date of the year 5 of the reign of Kaniṣka have been found from the Kaṅkālī Ṭīlā mound. The earliest of which is a fragmentary inscription.[72] But there is a reference in it to the *gaṇa* called Koliya (which Bühler read as *Koṭṭiya*). It also mentions a preacher (*vācaka*) whose name cannot be read. The reference to *vācaka* undoubtedly proves that the Jain canon was already in existence before this date. It further indirectly proves that the canon was reduced to writing before the 1st century A.D. We will afterwards see in connexion with our discussion of the Jain canonical literature that the complete canon came into existence at least before 100 B.C. The Koḷiya *gaṇa*, mentioned in this inscription, was the most popular *gaṇa* of Mathurā. Majority of the inscriptions found from this region mention this particular *gaṇa*. Now, according to the *Therāvalī* this particular *gaṇa* originated from two monks called Suṭṭhiya (Susthita) and Suppaḍibuddha (Supratibuddha), who were like Śrīgupta, disciples of Suhastin. So there is little doubt that this particular *gaṇa* also originated like Vāraṇa in the latter half of the 3rd century B.C.

The second inscription[73] bearing the date of the year 5 pointedly mentions Devaputra Kaniṣka. It further records the gift of an image of Vardhamāna by a woman whose name cannot be read. Her father's name was Pāla and we are told that she made this gift at the request of Khudā, the female companion (*saḍhacarī*) of Sena, the female pupil (*śiśinī*) of Sethiniha. This particular monk belonged to Koḷiya *gaṇa*,

Bahmadāsika *kula* and Ucenāgarī *śākhā*. Bahmadāsika is evidently the same as Bambhalijja of the *Therāvalī,* mentioned as one of the four *kulas* under Koḷiya *gaṇa*. There is no doubt that 'Bahmadāsika' is the correct term. The name of the *śākhā* viz. Ucenāgarī is preserved in the *Therāvalī* in exactly the same form. This is one of the four *śākhās* under Koḷiya *gaṇa ;* the other *śākhās* also, as we will see later in this chapter, are mentioned in the epigraphs of Mathurā. Bühler[74] thinks that Ucenāgarī *śākhā* was named after the fort of Unchanagar, modern town of Bulandshahr. This suggestion may be correct; but it remains only a suggestion. The two other inscriptions[75] of the same date refer to the same *gaṇa, kula* and *śākhā*. But one of them[76] discloses the names of two monks viz. Mihila and his pupil Kṣeraka. These two monks, we will see afterwards, are also mentioned in a few other inscriptions of Mathurā. The next inscription[77] is dated in the year 7 and mentions *mahārāja rājātirāja devaputra Ṣāhi* Kaniṣka. This interesting image inscription mentions the nun Jayā (*Āryā Jayā*), sister of the *vācaka* Sandhika, the *śiṣya* of the *gaṇin* Buddhaśrī who belonged to the Ārya-Odehikiya (=Ārya Uddehikīya) *gaṇa,* the Nāgabhūtikiya *kula*. Now *this* particular *gaṇa* appears in the *Therāvalī* in an unchanged form. The name of the *kula* also appears as Nāgabhūya in the *Therāvalī* where it is mentioned as one of six *kulas* under Uddeha *gaṇa*. The same text further informs us that this *gaṇa* originated from Ārya Rohaṇa, one of the disciples of Suhastin. Therefore this *gaṇa* also like Koḷiya and Vāraṇa originated in the 2nd half of the 3rd century B.C.

One inscription,[78] of the year 9 mentions 'Mahārāja Kaniṣka'. It records the dedication of an image by Vikaṭā, wife of Bhaṭṭimita at the request of *vācaka* Nāganandi out of the Koḷiya *gaṇa,* Sthāniya *kula,* the Vairī *śākhā*. Now, Sthāniya is apparently a Sanskrit term. In Prakrit it should be Ṭhāṇijja which actually appears as *Vāṇijja*' in the *Therāvalī* under Koḷiya *gaṇa*. The name of the *kula* viz. Vairī appears unchanged in the *Therāvalī*. There is another inscription of the same date (i.e. the year 9) which was first edited by R. D. Banerji.[79] It was afterwards corrected by Lüders.[80] This inscription yields the name of the same *gaṇa, kula* and *śākhā* as we find in the previous inscription of the same date. It records the gift of Grahapalā, daughter of Grahamitra, daughter-in-law of Avaśiri, wife of Kaḷala, at the request of Ārya Taraka who belonged to the *gaṇa* etc., mentioned above. Another short inscription between the feet of the Jina mentions the female pupil (*śiśinī*) of Ārya Aghama. R. D. Banerji also edited another image inscription[81] of the year 12 which was supposed by him as an image discovered from Ramnagar, the ancient Ahicchatra. He evidently relied on the report of Führer[82] who probably discovered this image. But Lüders[83] is of the opinion that not a single Jina image was ever discovered from the site mentioned in the 'Reports' of Führer. The inscription under discussion mentions the Koḷiya *gaṇa*, Bambhadāsiya *kula* and Ucenāgarī *śākhā*[84]. According to R. D. Banerji a number of carpenters[85] jointly made a gift of an image. The person who inspired them to make this gift according to Lüders, is Deva,[86] the sister of Nāndi, the female pupil of Ārya Pūśila. Chronologically the next Jain inscription[87] is dated in the year 15 and records the dediction of a fourfold (*sarvatobhadrikā*) image of Bhagavat by Kumāramitā, wife of *Śreṣṭhin* Veṇi, mother of Bhaṭṭisena, at the request of Āryā Vasulā, the female pupil of Āryā Saṅgamikā, who was the female pupil of Ārya Jayabhūti of the Mehika *kula*. It is of very great interest to note that the same nun viz. Āryā Vasulā is mentioned in a Mathurā inscription[88] dated in the year 86 where the monk Jayabhūti and the nun Saṅgamikā are also mentioned. This lady Vasulā therefore, had an unusually long life. The *kula* of the monk Jayabhūti viz. Mahika appears as Mehiya in the *Therāvalī* as a *kula* belonging to Vesavāḍiya *gaṇa*, which according to it, was founded by Kāmiddhī, who also was a disciple of Suhastin. Bühler[89] translates the term *śreṣṭhin* as 'alderman' which will suggest that Veṇi, the husband of Kumāramitā was a very respectable gentleman of Mathurā. Lüders,[90] however takes it to mean a 'banker.' In any case, in ancient India a '*śreṣṭhin*[91] was regarded as an important person and his position was definitely superior to an ordinary merchant or *sārthavāha*. The inscription[92] of the 18 refers to a *sarvatobhadrikā* image and also mentions the Koḷiya *gaṇa* and Vacchaliya *kula*. This particular *kula* is mentioned in the *Therāvalī* under Koḷiya *gaṇa* as Vacchalijja. Another inscription[93] of the same date is more interesting since it yields the name of Ariṣṭanemi, the 22nd Tīrthaṅkara. We have already observed, in connexion with our discussion of Tīrthaṅkaras, that the cult of Tīrthaṅkaras originated a century or two after the demise of Mahāvīra. We will presently see that quite a few other Tīrthaṅkaras appear in the inscriptions of Mathurā. The image inscription[94] of the year 19 is also important since another Tīrthaṅkara viz. Śāntinātha is mentioned here. The Koḷiya *gaṇa*, Ṭhāniya *kula* and Verī *śākhā* are also mentioned. The 'Verī' here is the same as 'Vairī.' The dedication of this image was made at the request of *vācaka* Mātṛdina, who was a pupil (*śiṣya*) of *vācaka* Baladina. The *vācaka* Mātṛdina also appears in an inscription[95] of the year 22 as we will see soon.

We have two inscriptions[96] of the year 20. The first of which records the dedication of an image of Vardhamāna by the *Śrāvikā* Dinā, daughter of Dātila, wife of Mātila, mother of Jagavāla, Devadāsa, Nāgadina and Nāgadinā at the request of the *vācaka Ārya* Saṅghasiha who belonged to Koḷiya *gaṇa*, the Sthāniya *kula*, the Verī (Vairī) *śākhā*. The second inscription[97] of the same date records the dedication by Mitra, the first wife of Haggudeva, daughter-in-law of the ironmonger (*lohavāṇiya*) Vādhara, daughter of the jeweller (*māṇikara*) Khalamitta at the request of the *vācaka* Ārya Sīha, the pupil of the *vācaka* Ārya Datta, who was the companion (*śraddhacara*) of the *gaṇin* Ārya Pāla, who was the *śiṣya* (pupil) of Ārya Ogha, who was the pupil of the great preacher (*bṛhaṁtavācaka*) whose name begins with Ja and ends with mitra out of the Koḷiya *gaṇa*, Brahmadāsiya *kula* and Ucenāgarī *śākhā*. An undated inscription[98] contains the names of the monks Sīha and the *guru* Datta mentioned in this inscription.

There are two inscriptions bearing the date 22. The first of which records[99] the dedication by Dharmasomā, the wife of caravan-leader (*sarttavāhinī*) at the request of the *vācaka* Ārya Mātṛdina. As we have already noted, this monk is mentioned in an inscription of the year 19. A second inscription[100] of the same date records the dedication of an image of Vardhamāna. But its main interest lies in the fact that it refers to the Petavāmika *kula* of the Vāraṇa *gaṇa*. In the list of *kulas* under Cāraṇa (i.e. Vāraṇa) in the *Therāvalī* we have the *kula* called Piidhammiya. There is little doubt that this is the corrupt form of 'Petavāmika'. The inscription[101] of the year 25 records the dedication by Vusu(?), the wife of a dyer (*rayaginī*), daughter of Nādi, daughter-in-law of Jabhaka, wife of Jayabhaṭa. Two monks are also mentioned viz. Sadhi and his preceptor Ārya Balatrata who belonged to the Koliya *gaṇa*, Brahmadāsika *kula* and Ucenāgarī *Śākhā*. The monks Ārya Balatrata and his pupil Sadhi are also mentioned in an undated inscription of Mathurā.[102]

The inscription[103] of the year 28 is interesting, for it mentions, according to Fleet,[104] Lüders[105] and Vogel[106], the king Vāsiṣka,[107] the successor of Kaniṣka. There are two inscriptions of the year 29. In the first inscription[108] the name of the reigning king is given but it cannot be properly read. But he was surely Huviṣka,[109] the successor of Vāsiṣka. It records the dedication of an image of Vardhamāna by the married lady (*kuṭuṁbinī*) Bodhinadī, daughter of Grahahathi at the request of Gahapravika (?), pupil of Ārya Datta, a *gaṇin* belonging to the Vāraṇa *gaṇa* and Puśyamitriya *kula*. This *kula* is mentioned is Pūsamitti under Cāraṇa (i.e. Vāraṇa) in the *Therāvalī*. Another inscription of the same date[110] refers to *Mahārāja devaputra* Hukṣa i.e. Huviṣka. It also yields the name of a monk called Nagadata (Nāgadatta).

V. S. Agrawala in 1937 drew our attention to a Jain inscription bearing the date of the year 30;[111] but beyond the date there is nothing more in it. The inscription[112] of the year 31 refers to the dedication by Grahaśrī, daughter of Buddhi and wife of Devila. It refers to a monk called Godāsa who belonged to the Koḷiya *gaṇa*, Sthāniya *kula* and Verī *śākhā*. The interest of the inscription[113] of the year 32 lies in the fact that it refers to an unnamed perfumer (*gandhika*) and the monk Nandika of to the Koḷiya *gaṇa*, Sthāniya *kula* and Verī *śākhā*. More interesting is the inscription[114] of the year 35 that records the dedication of an image of Vardhamāna by the perfumer (*gaṁdhika*) Kumārabhaṭi, son of Kumāramitā, the *śiśinī* (female pupil) of Ārya Baladina who belonged to Koliya *gaṇa*, Sthāniya *kula* and Vairā *śākhā*. The name of the nun at whose request the gift was made, is given as Kumāramitā. It seems that this lady became a nun after leading married life for several years. The donor, mentioned in this inscription, was her son who naturally was anxious to help his mother, who became a nun in her old age. It is also tempting to identify this Kumāramitā with her namesake of the inscription of the year 24, described as the wife of *śreṣṭhin* Veṇi and mother of Bhaṭṭisena. If we accept this identification, we must regard the donor of the present inscription as another son of this lady. A few may suggest that the donor of the inscription under discussion was a natural son of the nun Kumāramitā. In that case, we have to believe that Jain monks and nuns of Mathurā led an immoral life. But unless and until we get more definite evidence, we are not ready to accept it.

The Jain elephant inscription[115] of the year 38 is of great interest. It mentions *mahārāja devaputra* Huviṣka and also records the setting up of elephant Naṁdiviśāla by the *śreṣṭhin* Rudradāsa., son of the *śreṣṭhin* Śivadāsa for the worship of Arhats. The reference to Nandiviśāla certainly proves that the donor Rudradāsa, in spite of his deference for Jain monks, was really a Śaiva devotee. His name and the name of his father also suggest this inference on our part. In the Pāli canonical texts[116] we find references to 'Nandivisāla' which certainly meant Śiva's Nandi. Lüders[117] does not succeed in his attempt to explain the relation of Nandiviśāla with Jainism. There is really no need for such an attempt. It is enough that the Jain monks of Mathurā allowed Śaiva devotees to build a typically Śaiva object of worship within the compound of their own shrine. Some elements of orthodox Hinduism found their way into both Jainism and Buddhism. Every dedicated student of the Pāli and Jain literature knows how deeply orthodox Hinduism influenced both these religious systems. It is quite likely that a number donors, mentioned in the Jain inscriptions of Mathurā, had equal respect and love for orthodox Hindu deities. As a matter of fact, most of such donors never felt that they were doing something for a different religious system. They only wanted to do some pious act and to them there was really not much difference between a Jaina *Sādhu* and a Śaiva or Vaiṣṇava ascetic. But this question we can discuss elsewhere, for in this type of work there is not much scope for such a discussion.

The next Jain inscription[118] is dated in the year 40 although Lüders[119] thinks that the reading '40' is not very clear. This inscription records the dedication of an image by a lady, the wife of *grāmika* (village headman or simply a villager) Jayanāga, mother of Sihadata. Two monks are mentioned viz. Mahānandin and Dantin (Dati) belonging to the Vāraṇa *gaṇa*, Ārya-Hāḷakiya *kula and* Vajanagarī *śākhā*. The inscription[120] of the year 44 mentions Mahārāja Huviṣka. It records the dedication at the request of Nāgasena, the pupil (śiṣa) of Haginaṁdi, a *vācaka* belonging to Vāraṇa *gaṇa*, Āryaceṭiya *kula* and Hāritamālakaḍhi *śākhā*. Both these *kulas* and *śākhās* are mentioned in the *Therāvalī* under the Cāraṇa (i.e. Vāraṇa) *gaṇa*. The Jain inscription[121] of the year 45 mentions two persons called Buddhi and Dharmavṛddhi. Probably the second person was a monk. The inscription of the year 47 (Lüders No. 45) mentions the monk Ohanadi (Oghanandin) and his disciple Sena belonging to the Petivāmika *kula* of the Vāraṇa *gaṇa*. Another undated inscription[122] that mentions some *Mahārāja rājātirāja* also refers to these two monks. R. D. Banerji edited an important inscription[123] of the year 48 of the time of Mahārāja Huviṣka. It records the gift an image of Sambhava, the 3rd Tīrthaṅkara by Yaśā, the daughter-in-law of Budhika, granddaughter of Śavatrata, at the request of Dhañaśiri (Dhanyāśrī), the female pupil (*śiśinī*) of Dhañavala (Dhanyavala) in the Koḷiya *gaṇa*, the Brahmadāsika *kula*, the Ucenāgarī *śākhā*. We have already noticed that a few other Tīrthaṅkaras are also mentioned in the Mathurā inscriptions. Another inscription[124] of the same year of Mahārāja Huviṣka mentions the Brahmadāsiya *kula* and the Ucenāgarī *śākhā*.

Probably the most important Jain inscription[125] of Mathurā is that of the year 49. The figure '49' was formerly read as 79 by Bühler;[126] but afterwards Lüders[127] read it as 49. It records the dedication of an image of the Arhat Nāndivarta (Nandyāvarta) at the 'Voḍva' *stūpa* which was built by gods (*devanirmite*) by *śrāvikā* Dinā at the request of the monk Vṛdhahasti who belonged to the Koḷiya *gaṇa* and Vairā *śākhā*. This monk, as we will see afterwards, is mentioned in an inscription of the year 60. Now, the Jain Tīrthaṅkara who has this symbol (Nandyāvarta) is Arhanātha, the 18th Tiirthaṅkara. But the most important expression of this inscription is the epithet *devanirmita* applied to the 'Voḍva' *stūpa* here. According to Bühler the expression means 'the *stūpa* built by gods.'

He further takes 'Voḍva' to mean 'Buddhist'. That there was a *devanirmita stūpa* in Mathurā in proved by the evidence of the Jain literature. In both the *Bṛhatkalpabhāṣya* and *Vyavahāra-bhāṣya* Saṅghadāsagaṇi Kṣamāśramaṇa (8th century) has referred to the '*devanirmita*' *stūpa* of Mathurā.[128] The great Jain saint Jinabhadragaṇi (6th century) lived in this *stūpa* and had rescued here a mutilated manuscript of *Mahāniśīthasūtra*.[129] Bühler argues on the basis of the testimony of the Tibetan historian Tāranātha that pre-Mauryan shrines were known by the term *devanirmita*. The Jain texts, mentioned above, record that there was a persistent dispute regarding this particular *stūpa*. The Buddhists, Jains and also the Vaiṣṇavas claimed this *stūpa* as their own. It is probable that originally it was either a Brāhmaṇical or a Buddhist shrine but from the days of the Kuṣāṇas it passed into the hands of the Jains. This particular *stūpa* is probably represented by the extensive ruins at Kaṅkālī Ṭīlā and it is also probable that this *stūpa* included Buddhist and Brāhmaṇical objects of worship.

There are a few Jain inscriptions[130] of the year 50. But only one of them is important. We are referring to the inscription that records the dedication of an image of Vardhamāna by Vijayaśrī, daughter of Bubu, wife of Rājyavasu, mother of Devila, grandmother of Viṣṇubhava. It also mentions a nun called Jinadāsī and a monk named Samadi (?) who belonged to the Vāraṇa *gaṇa*, Kaniyasata *kula* and Saṁkasiyā *śākhā*. Among the *kulas* mentioned in the *Therāvalī* this particular *kula* is mentioned as Kanahasaha. The Saṁkasiyā *śākhā* is also mentioned in this text under the same *gaṇa*. The two other Jain inscriptions with the year 50 are not so important, although one of them mentions *Mahārāja devaputra* Huviṣka.[131]

The inscription[132] of the year 52 records the dedication of an image by the worker in metal (*lohikākāraka*) called Śūra, the son of Śramaṇaka, at the request of Ārya Deva, the companion (*saḍhacara*) of the *gaṇin* Ārya Maṁguhasti, the pupil of Ārya Ghastuhasti of the Koḷiya *gaṇa*, Verā *śākhā* and Sṭānikiya *kula*. The great importance of this inscription lies in the fact that it mentions the monk Maṁguhasti who is prominently mentioned in the early Jain literature. In the *Nandīsūtra*, (vs. 30), a late canonical text of the Jains, probably composed around 350 A.D., the name of this monk is conspicious by its presence. In the *Āvaśyakaniryukti*,[133] another early Jain text, this monk is mentioned as a resident of Mathurā which fully proves that Ārya Maṁguhasti of this inscription is really the monk mentioned as Ārya Maṅgu in these two texts. Incidentally, Maṅgu is the only monk of early Jain literature to be mentioned in an inscription of Mathurā.

The image inscription[134] of the year 54 is also very interesting. It records the dedication of an image of Sarasvatī by the worker in metal (*lohikakāruka*) Gova (Gopa), the son of Sīha. The monks, mentioned in the inscription of the year 52, are also mentioned here with the exception of Maṁguhasti, who is replaced by Māghahasti. But it is probable that Māghahasti is another name of Maṅgu. But the importance of this inscription lies in the fact that it once more proves the close connexion of Hindu deities with Jainism. In our chapter on Jain Iconography we will discuss the importance of this particular icon of Sarasvatī. This inscription also has the word *raṅga* which proves the popularity of drama in Mathurā. The word *raṅga*, of course, means an auditorium. A much earlier reference to an auditorium will be found in the *Bhagavatī*[135] where we get the word *pecchāghara*. The same text also contains the word *raṅgasthāna*.[136] We will afterwards see that in another inscription of Mathurā there is a very clear reference to actors.

The next Jain inscription[137] is dated in the year 60. This inscription mentions *mahārāja rājātirāja devaputra* Huviṣka. It records the dedication of an image of Ṛṣabha at the request of Ārya Kharaṇṇa (?), pupil of Ārya Vṛddhahasti, who is mentioned in that well known inscription of the year 49. There are two inscriptions[138] of the year 62 and a monk called Karkuhastha and his disciple Grahabala are mentioned in both of them. One of these inscriptions[139] contains the significant words *catuvani saṁgha* (community of four classes). The next Jain inscription[140] is dated in the year 74 and it was edited by R. D. Banerji. It records the gift of Dharavalā at the request of Arhadāsī, the female pupil of Grahavi'ā. A monk whose name cannot be read but who belonged to the Vāraṇa *gaṇa* and Vajanakāri *śākhā* is also mentioned.

We have an interesting inscription[141] of the year 77 which records the dedication by one Devila at the temple of Dadhikarṇa (*Dadhikarṇadevakulika*). This Dadhikarṇa is also mentioned in an inscription[142] where he is called *bhagavat Nāgendra* i.e. the divine lord or serpents. This inscription records the dedication of a stone slab (*śilāpaṭṭa*) in the temple (*stāna*) of that god by the sons of actors (*śailālakas*), the Māthuras, who are praised as the Chāndaka brothers, chief of whom was Nandibala. This inscription, according to Führer was found near the brick *stūpa* adjoining Jain temples.[143] As pointed out by Bühler[144] Dadhikarṇa is mentioned as a prominent snake in the *Harivaṁśa*.[145] In the list of Nāgas in the *Abhidhānacintāmaṇi*[146]his name occurs. We should remember that the real founder of Jainism viz Pārśvanātha had snake as his emblem. The temple of Dadhikarṇa, mentioned here, was probably situated within the Jain temple-complex of Mathurā. However, there is no need to regard these two inscriptions as Jain records. The reference to actors (*śailālakas*) proves that drama was quite popular in Mathurā in the Kuṣāna period, if not earlier. Pāṇini's *sūtra* '*Pārāśarya-Śilālibhyāṁ bhikṣunaṭasūtrayoḥ* (4.3.110) definitely proves that drama in India is least as old as 500 B.C.[147] But even this problem cannot be discussed here in details. It is sufficient to note that even before Aśvaghoṣa the art of drama was already in a sophisticated stage in Mathurā.

The next inscription[148] is dated in the year 80 and mentions *Mahārāja* Vāsudeva. Beyond this there is nothing of much importance in this inscription. But the inscription[149] of the year 81 is slightly more interesting since it mentions a woman called Datā, the female pupil (*āṁtevāsikinī*) of Āryā Jivā. The image inscription[150] of the year 83 mentions Mahārāja Vāsudeva and also a woman called Jinadāsī, who is represented as the wife of a perfumer (*gandhika*). We have two important Jain inscriptions of the year 84, the first edited by R. D. Banerji and second by D. R. Sahni. The first inscription[151] mentions *mahārāja rājātirāja devaputra Ṣāhi Vāsudeva*. It records the setting up of an image of Ṛṣabha by several women at the request Kumāraka, pupil (*śiṣya*) of Gamikagutta. We have already noticed that the earliest Tīrthaṅkara Ṛṣabha appears in an inscription of the year 60. The second inscription[152] of the year 84, edited by D. R. Sahni, records the gift an image of

Vardhamāna by Okhārikā, the daughter of Damitra and Datā. Two monks Satyasena and Dharavṛddhi of the Koḷiya *gaṇa* are also mentioned. A woman called Okharikā is also mentioned in an inscription of the year 299, as we will notice afterwards. For the year 86 we have an inscription[153] which records the dedication by some woman, the daughter of Dasa, the wife of Priya, at the request of Āryā Vasulā, the *śiśinī* of Saṅgamikā of the Mehika *kula.* As we have already noticed, nuns Vasulā and Saṅgamikā are mentioned in a much earlier inscription dated in the year 15. Of the two inscriptions[154] of the year 87, the earlier one refers to Mitra, the pupil of Ārya Kumāranandin of the Ucenāgara *śākhā.* The second inscription only mentions king Vāsudeva with his full titles. The inscription[155] of the year 90 is interesting since if refers to the Praśnavāhanaka *kula* and Majhamā *śākhā* of the Koḷiya *gaṇa.* In the *Therāvalī* both these *kulas* and *śākhās* are mentioned.. However instead of Majhamā we get Majhimillā. The epigraph of the year 93 records[156] the setting up of an image of Vardhamāna by the daughter of *hairaṇyaka* ('treasurer' according to Bühler) Deva at the request of the *gaṇin* Nandi.

The inscription of the year 98 refers to *rājña Vāsudevasya*[157] and two monks Kṣema and Devadatta who belonged to Odehikiya *gaṇa*, the Paridhāsika *kula* and Petaputrikā *śākhā.* A certain perfumer (*gandhika*) called Varuṇa is also mentioned. The Paridhāsika *kula* is mentioned as Parihāsaya in the *Therāvalī.* For the *śākhā* called Petaputrikā we have a slightly different form in that text which was certainly due to the copyists' error. Another inscription[158] of the same date refers to the Ucenagarī *śākhā* of the Koḷiya *gaṇa.*

The inscription[159] with the year 299 is certainly puzzling; for it is difficult to think of a *mahārāja rājātirāja* ruling in 377 A.D. in Mathurā, other than a Gupta monarch. V. S. Agrawala,[160] in order to solve this riddle, has suggested that the the year 299 should be referred to an earlier era. Now even if we refer to this inscription to the era of 58 B.C., we have to find out, who was this great king ruling in the Mathurā region in the middle of the 3rd century A.D. This particular inscription records the setting up of an image of Mahāvīra in the temple of Arhats. A *devakula* is also mentioned in this inscription. As we have already noticed, a woman, called Okhārikā appears in this inscription. A woman of this name is mentioned, as already noted, in an inscription of the year 84.

We have several important undated Kuṣāṇa inscriptions bearing on the Jain religion. A few of them mention the ruling king but majority of them do not contain any royal name. One undated inscription,[161] mentioning Kaniṣka, was first edited by R. L. Mitra. But it does not contain any information. An undated inscription[162] of the time of *devaputra* Huviṣka also does not help us much. However the two inscriptions mentioning the monk Jeṣṭahasti of the Koḷiya *gaṇa,* Brahmadāsika *kula* and Ucenāgarī *śākhā* are of some value. One of them[163] records the dedication of an image of Ṛṣabha by Gulhā, the daughter of Varmā and wife of Jayadāsa, at the request of Āryā Śāmā, the *śiśinī* of Ārya Gāḍhaka, who was a pupil of Ārya Jeṣṭahasti. The second inscription[164] records the dedication a fourfold image (*savadobhadrikā*) by Sthirā, daughter of Varaṇahasti and of Devī, daughter-in-law of Jayadeva and and Moṣiṇī, wife of Kuṭha Kasutha, at the request of Ārya Kṣeraka, pupil of Ārya Mihila who was a pupil of Jeṣṭahasti. Let us not forget that monks Kṣeraka and Mihila are mentioned in an inscription of the year 5. So there is little doubt that the monk Jeṣṭahasti, who was the teacher of Kṣeraka's teacher flourished in the beginning of the 1st century A.D., if not earlier.

An undated Jain image inscription[165] of the Kuṣāṇa period mentions an image of Pārśva. It also refers to the *vācaka* Ghoṣaka, pupil of Uggahini of the Sthānikiya *kula.* No other inscription of Mathurā refers to this great Tīrthaṅkara and the real founder of Jainism. According to Bühler[166] this person Uggahini was probably a female. In this case, we will have to accept the fact that in Mathurā in those days, males accepted even females as their *gurus.* But Lüders,[167] it seems, takes Uggahini as a male. Another undated inscription[168] is of some importance since it mentions Kaniyasika *kula* of the Vāraṇa *gaṇa.* This particular *kula,* as we have already noted, is mentioned in an inscription of the year 50, although the reading there is not so clear. Another interesting inscription[169] records the dedication of an image of Vardhamāna by Jayā, daughter of Navahasti, daughter-in-law of Grahasena, mother of the brothers Śivasena, Devasena and Śivadeva. The monk Ārya Balatrata and his pupil Ārya Sandhi, belonging to the Ucenāgarī *śākhā* are also mentioned. These two monks, as we have already seen, are mentioned in an inscription of the year 25.

R. D. Banerji edited an interesting image inscription[170] which mentions a monk of Adhicchatra (i.e. Ahicchatra) belonging to Petavāmika *kula* and Vajanagarī *śākhā*. It was taken by him to be an inscription from Ramnagar, ancient Ahicchatra. But Lüders[171] is not prepared to believe it. In any case, this inscription certainly proves that Ahicchatra was not immune from Jain influence in the Kuṣāṇa period.

We have a few inscriptions of the post—Kuṣāṇa period found from the Mathurā region ; but we have to take note of them in another chapter. As a matter of fact, as V. S. Agrawala has pointed out,[172] hundreds of Jain sculptures belonging to Gupta and early mediaeval period have been discovered from Mathurā. Quite a few of them will have to be considered in our chapter on Jain Iconography.

The above analysis of the contents of most of the Mathurā inscriptions of the early period, abundantly proves the tremendous popularity of Jainism from the 2nd century B.C. onwards. We have already observed, on the basis of the evidence of Vimala--sūri's 1st century work the *Paumacariyaṁ*, that Jainism which had suffffered a setback after the Nandas, was revived by some Jain saints, who preached both at Śāketa and Mathurā. These inscriptions of Mathurā show that very few among Jain devotees came from the so-called aristocratic families. No inscription from Mathurā yields the name of any Brahmin patron of Jainism. It is exceedingly likely that members of this particular caste were much more interested in sacrificial cult and diverse theistic religions than in either Buddhism or Jainism. Mathurā, we should remember, was a stronghold of the Bhāgavata cult and even in the 2nd century A.D., when Jainism had reached a very high level of popularity, this city was known to a foreigner like Ptolemy as a 'city of gods'[173] There is nothing to show that Śaka or Kuṣāṇa kings themselves, had any particular weakness for this religion. On the other hand, they manifestly show their bias for Hinduism and Buddhism. But a few of the Kṣatriyas showed some regard for this religion. A few ladies of aristocratic families also had some affection for this religion which was basically based on non-violence. But as we have seen in our analysis of the inscriptions, ninety five percent of the admirers were common people. Even persons of questionable professions contributed liberally for the welfare of the religion of Pārśva and Mahāvīra. We should also particularly take note of the interest shown by the business community for Jainism in Mathurā. The canonical and non-canonical texts also abundantly show the weakness of the traders for this religion.

What now about the monks and nuns mentioned in the Mathurā inscriptions? Quite a good number of monks, belonging to different *gaṇas* and *kulas* are mentioned in these inscriptions. The following *gaṇas are* directly mentioned in these inscriptions—Koḷiya, Vāraṇa and Uddehikīya. All the *kulas* under Koḷiya, mentioned in the *Therāvalī*, appear in the incriptions. They are :—Brahmadāsika, Vacchaliya, Ṭhāṇiya and Pavahaka ; and so is the case with all the *śākhās* mentioned under this *gaṇa* in that text. The only *śākhā* under Koḷiya, not noticed by us viz. Vijjāharī actually appears in a Gupta inscription[174] of Mathurā which we will discuss elsewhere. Among the *kulas* under Vāraṇa, the following are mentioned in the Mathurā inscriptions—Petivāmika, Puśyamitra, Kaniyasika and possibly Ayyabhista and with the exception of Gavedhūyā all the *śakhas* under this *gaṇa* are referred to in the Mathurā inscriptions. A few of the *śakhas* and *kulas* under Uddehikīya are also mentioned in the inscriptions. But this *gaṇa* was not so popular as Koḷiya or Vāraṇa. Another *kula* viz. Mehika which is a *kula* under Vesavāḍiya in the *Therāvalī,* as we have already noticed, is mentioned twice.

In a previous chapter we had observed that *gaṇas, kulas* etc. appeared only a century or two after the demise of Mahāvīra. In the earlier canonical texts they are very rarely referred to. The three words *gaṇa, kula* and *saṅgha* (and not *śākhā*) are mentioned together in the *Bhagavatī*.[175] In one place of the *Ācārāṅga*[176] *gaṇa, kula* etc. are mentioned. If we believe in the evidence of the *Therāvalī*, *gaṇa, kula* etc. originated after Bhadrabāhu. So we should not be incorrect if we say that *gaṇa, kula* and *śākhā* etc., became a regular feature of the Jain religion from the beginning of the 3rd century B.C. And if we believe in the evidence suplied by the *Therāvalī*, most of the *śākhās* originated during the 3rd century B.C. For the benefit of students of Jain religion we are giving below a list of Jain monks and nuns mentioned in the inscription of Mathurā—

(A) MONKS

Name	*Gaṇa, Kula and Śākhā*	*Date* (approximate)
1. Māharakhita	— — —	150 B.C.
2. Jayasena	— — —	25 B.C.
3. Puśyamitra	Vāraṇa, Ārya-Hāḷkiya, Vajanagarī	25 A.D.
4. Sihamitra	-do-	75 A.D.
5. Sena	Koḷiya, Brahmadāsika, Ucenāgarī	75 A.D.
6. Sethiniha	-do-	50 A.D.
7. Buddhaśrī	Odehikīya, Nāgabhūtikiya	50 A.D.
8. Sandhika	-do-	75 A.D.
9. Nāganaṁdi	Koḷiya, Sthāniya, Vairī	-do-
10. Taraka	-do-	-do-
11. Puśila	Koḷiya, Bambhadāsiya Ucenāgarī	-do-
12. Jeṣṭahasti	-do-	25 A.D.
13. Mihila	-do-	50 A.D.
14. Kṣeraka	-do-	75 A.D.
15. Jayabhūtī	Mehika *kula*	25 A.D.
16. Baladina	Koḷiya, Ṭhāṇiya, Vairī	75 A.D.
17. Mātṛdina	-do-	100 A.D.

Name	*Gaṇa, Kula and Śākhā*	*Date* (approximate)
18. Saṅghasiha	-do-	100 A.D.
19. Ārya Ogha	Koḷiya, Brahmadāsiya Ucenāgarī	25 A.D.
20. Ārya Pāla	-do-	50 A.D.
21. Ārya Datta	-do-	75 A.D.
22. Ārya Sīha	-do-	100 A.D.
23. Balatrata	-do-	75 A.D.
24. Sadhi	-do-	100 A.D.
25. Ārya Datta	Vāraṇa, Puśyamitriya	75 A.D.
26. Gahaprakiva (?)	-do-	100 A.D.
27. Nāgadatta	- -	-do-
28. Godāsa	Koḷiya, Sthāniya, Vairī	-do-
29. Nandika	Vārana Sthāniya, Vairī	-do-
30. Baladina	Koloya, Sthāniya, Vairī	100 A.D.
31. Dati	Vāraṇa, Ārya-Hāḷakiya,	75 A.D.
32. Mahānandin	-do-	100 A.D.
33. Haginaṁdi	Vāraṇa, Āryaceṭiya, Haritamālakaḍhi	75 A.D.
34. Nāgasena	-do-	100 A.D.
35. Dharmavṛddhi	- -	120 A.D.
36. Ohanadi	Vāraṇa, Peṭavāmika	100 A.D.
37. Sena	-do-	125 A.D.
38. Dhañavala	Koḷiya, Brahmadāsika Ucenāgari	-do-
39. Vṛddhahasti	Koḷiya, Vairī, Sthānikīya	-do-
40. Samadi	Vārana, Ayyabhista, Saṁkasiyā	100 A.D.
41. Hastahasti	Koḷiya, Sthāniya, Vairī	75 A.D.
	-do-	-do-

Name	*Gaṇa, Kula and Śākhā*	*Date* (approximate)
43. Maṅguhasti	-do-	100 A.D.
44. Māghahasti	-do-	-do-
45. Deva	-do-	125 A.D.
46. Ārya Kharaṇṇa	Koḷiya, Sthānikīya Vairī	140 A.D.
47. Grahabala	—	140 A.D.
48. Karkuhastha	—	125 A.D.
49. Gamikagutta	—	140 A.D.
50. Kumāraka	—	160 A.D.
51. Satyasena	Koḷiya	160 A.D.
52. Dharavṛddhi	-do-	160 A.D.
53. Kumāranandin	Koḷiya Ucenāgarī	140 A.D.
54. Mitra	-do-	160 A.D.
55. Nandin	—	170 A.D.
56. Devadata	Odehikīya, Pāridhāsika, Petaputrika	170 A.D.
57. Kṣema	-do-	170 A.D.
58. Śivadiṇa	—	375 A.D. (?)
59. Datilācārya	Koḷiya, Vidyādharī	433 A.D.
60. Nāganandin	—	2nd cent.
61. Gāḍhaka	Koḷiya, Brahmadāsiya, Ucenāgarī	75 A.D.
62. Uggahini	Koḷiya, Sthānikīya	2nd cent.
63. Ghoṣaka	-do-	-do-
64. Goṣṭha	Odehikīya, Nāgabhūtikīya	75 A.D.

(B) NUNS

1. Dharmaghoṣā	—	25 B.C.
2. Sathisihā	Vāraṇa, Ārya-Hāḷakiya, Vajanagarī	75 A.D.

3. Khuḍā	Koḷiya, Brahmadāsika, Ucenāgarī	-do-
4. Jayā	Odehikīya, Nāgabhūtikīya	-do-
5. Devā	Koḷiya, Brahmadāsika, Ucenāgarī	-do-
6. Saṅgamikā	Mehika *kula*	-do-
7. Vasulā	-do-	100 A.D.
8. Kumāramitrā	Koḷiya, Sthāniya, Vairī	-do-
9. Dhānaśrī	Koḷiya, Brahmadāsika, Ucenāgarī	120 A.D.
10. Jinadāsī	Vāraṇa, Ayyabhyista Samkasiyā	125 A.D.
11. Akakā	Vāraṇa, Ārya-Hāḷakiya, Vajanagarī	120 A.D.
12. Nandā	-do-	-do-
13. Āryā Jīvā	—	150 A.D.
14. Āryā Sāmā	Koḷiya, Brahmadāsika, Ucenāgarī	75 A.D.

We have been able to identify at least one monk mentioned in the Jain inscriptions of Mathurā. It is possible that a few other monks and nuns, mentioned in the inscriptions, appear also in the literary texts. In this connexion we should remember that Jain literary texts also refer to the glorious state of Jainism in Mathurā. We have already discussed the evidence of the *Paumacariyaṁ* of Vimalasūri. According to the *Āvaśyaka-niryukti*[177] (circa 350 A.D.) the Jain monks had no trouble regarding alms in this city. The 8th-century Śvetāmbara commentator Saṅghadāsagaṇi at least in two places of his works refer to the great influence, the Jains exercised, in Mathurā. As we have alrady noted, he refers to the great *devanirmita stūpa* of Mathurā. He also describes the *stūpamaha*[178] festival of this place in his *Vyavahārabhāṣya.* It was in Mathurā that a council to collect and edit the Jain canon under the presidentship of Skandila[179] was held 827 years after the death of Mahāvīra. This corresponds roughly to 1st half of the 4th century A.D. The 14th-century Jain savant Jinaprabha is his monumental work the *Vividhatīrthakalpa* gives us a vidid idea about the glorious condition of the Jain religion in Mathurā. According to his testimony, the 6th-century Jain saint Jinabhadragaṇi lived and wrote his commentaries in Mathurā. We have already refered to the fact that this great saint had saved the manuscript of the *Mahāniśīthasūtra* from destruction at the *devanirmita stūpa* of Mathurā. We will afterwards take note of the evidence of the Digambara literary texts regarding the condition of Jainism in Mathurā. Quite a good number of Śvetāmbara and Digambara Jain saints lived and worked in Mathurā. Let us remember that even in the days of Hariṣeṇa (931 A.D.) the author of the *Bṛhatkathākośa,*[180] the city of Mathurā was known as a great centre of the Jain religion. The most popular *gaṇa* of Mathurā viz. the *Koṭiya* survived, as observed by Bühler[181] even upto the 14th century A.D.[182] Even in the days of Jinaprabha (14th century) Mathurā was known as a great Jain *tīrtha.*

NOTES

1 Para 156.
2. Para 26.
3 *Rām,* VII, chs. 60 ff.
4 *Mbh.,* XII. 339. 89-90.
5 14. 48 ff.
6 XVII. 1.9.
7 V. 38. 12.
8 See *Mbh.,* XII. 339. 89-90.
9 II. 57 ; III. 255.
10 II. 256.
11 See Malalasekera, *Dict. of Pāli Proper Names,* Vol. II, pp. 438-99.
12 *Loc. cit.*
13 *Aṅguttara,* I. 67f.
14 A very early reference to Vṛndāvana will be found in Bhāsa's *Bālacarita,* 3rd Act.

15 See Prakrit Text Society edition, Vol. II, ch. 118. 103.

16 See the present author's *Ancient Indian Literary and Cultural Tradition* (Calcutta, 1974), pp. 177f.

17 89. 2 ff.

18 89.42.

19 89. 43 ff.

20 *Mahābhāṣya* on Pāṇini, V. 3. 99.

21 See 89. 20 ff.

22 89.20

23 See ch. 89.

24 154, 157.

25 P. 204. (Kota, 1935).

26 P. 1987 (Sailana edition).

27 Lüders, *List of Brāhmī Inscriptions*, etc., Nos. 904-5.

28 (Tr. L. D. Barnett), pp. 86 ff.

29 P. 248.

30 The earliest reference to *devagṛha* will be found in the *Taittirīya Brāhmaṇa*, and to *devakula* in the *Śāṅkhāyana G.S.*; see M.M-Williams, *S. E. D*, pp. 492-93.

31 *EI*. Vol. II, p. 195.

32 *Ibid*., XIV (1) ; see also Lüders, *op. cit*. No. 93.

33 *EI*, Vol. I, p. 396, No. 33 ; Lüders, No. 94.

34 *EI*, I, p. 396.

35 VI. 9. 61.

36 See Sircar, D. C. *Select Inscriptions* etc., pp. 3ff, and 6 ff ; see also Sen, S. *Old Persian Inscriptions*, pp. 2-6.

37 Sircar, *op. cit*., pp. 11ff ; Sen, *op. cit*., pp. 148 ff.

38 *E.I*, Vol. 24, pp. 202 ff ; see also his *List*, p. 169.

39 See the summary of the present author's paper entitled 'Was there a pre-Gupta Vikramāditya ?' in *Summaries of Papers*, 27th All-India Oriental conference, pp. 199-200.

40 See *E.I*, Vol. II, XIV, No. 9 ; see also Lüders, No. 96.

41 *J.R.A.S*., 1905, pp. 635-655.

42 *E.I*, Vol. II, p. 199, No. 2 ; see also Sircar *op. cit*., pp. 120-21 ; and Lüders, No. 59.

43 See Sircar, *op. cit*., pp. 114 ff.

44 *Ibid*., p. 122 ; see also *E.I*, Vol. 24, p. 194.

45 *E.I*, Vol. II, p. 199, No. 2.

46 See *Actes du sixième Congrès International des Orientalists à Leide*, part III, pp. 142 ff.

47 *I.A*., Vol. 33, pp. 152 f., No. 30 ; see also his *List*, No. 102.

48 *Mahāvagga* (Horner), p. 380.

49 *Ibid*., p. 379.

50 *E.I*, Vol. II, p. 200, No. 5 ; Lüders, *List*, No. 100.

51 *E.I*, Vol. II, p. 207, No. 30 ; Lüders, *List*, No. 105.

52 *Aṅguttara* (tr. E. M. Hare), Vol. III, p. 171.
53 *Loc. cit.*
54 *I.A.*, Vol. 33, p. 151, No. 28.
55 *Loc. cit.*
56 Bühler, *E.I.*, Vol. II, p. 199, No. 4 ; Lüders, No. 99.
57 *E.I*, Vol. I, p. 390, No. 17 ; Lüders, No. 108.
58 *I.A.*, Vol. 33, pp. 153f.
59 *E.I*, Vol. II, p. 207, No. 32 ; Lüders, No. 107.
60 *E.I*, Vol. II, p. 200, No. 8 ; Lüders, No. 103.
61 *E.I*, Vol. II, p. 200, No. 6 ; Lüders, No. 101.
62. See Smith, *Muttra Antiquities*, pp. 25f ; see also Bühler in *E.I.* Vol. II, pp. 314 ff.
63 P. 67.
64 P. 803.
65 See the present author's *The Cult of Skanda-Kārttikeya* etc. pp. 103 ff.
66 *E.I.* Vol. II, pp 314 ff.
67 See Cunningham, *Reports* etc, Vol. 20, p. 36, plate IV.
68 *E.I.*, Vol. II, p. 201, No. 11 ; Lüders, No. 16.
69 *J.R.A.S.*, 1911, p. 1085.
70 See *E.I*, Vol. I, pp. 373 ff.
71 See Lüders, *List*, Nos. 17-20.
72 *E.I.*, Vol. II, p. 201, No. 12 ; Lüders, No. 17.
73 *E.I*, Vol. I, pp. 381f., No. 1, Lüders, No. 18.
74 See *E.I.*, Vol. I, pp. 378ff.
75 Lüders, Nos., 19-20.
76 Cunningham, *A.S.I.*, *Report*, Vol. III, p. 31, see Lüders, No. 20.
77 *E.I*, Vol. I, p. 391, No. 19 ; Lüders, No. 21.
78 See Bühler, *Vienna Oriental Journal*, Vol. I, pp. 173f., No. 2 ; Lüders, *List* No. 22.
79 *E.I.*, Vol. X, pp. 109f., No. 3 ; Lüders No. 22a.
80 *J.R.A.S.*, 1912, pp. 157 f.
81 *E.I*, Vol. X, pp. 110f, No. 4 ; see Lüders, No. 23a.
82 See *N.W.P and Oudh Provincial Museum Minutes*, Vol. V, p. 6, App. 6A ; see *E.I.*, Vol. X, p. 111.
83 See *J.R.A.S.*, 1912, pp. 153 ff.
84 See *E.I*, Vol. X, pp. 110f.
85 *Loc. cit.*
86. See No. 23a.
87 *E.I.*, Vol. I, p. 382, No. 2 ; Lüders, No. 24.
88 *E.I*, Vol. I, p. 388, No. 12 ; Lüders, No. 70.
89 *E.I.* Vol. I, p. 382.
90 See No. 24.

91 In the *Mṛcchakaṭika* the *śreṣṭhin* is eveidently an important person. In the Pāli canon also he holds a very high position.
92 *E.I*, Vol. II, p. 202, No. 13; Lüders, No. 25.
93 *E.I.* Vol. II, p. 202, No. 14; Lüders, No. 26.
94 E.I. Vol. I, pp. 382f., No. 3, Lüders, No. 27.
95 *E.I.* Vol. I, p. 391, No. 20, Lüders, No. 31.
96 Lüders, Nos, 28-29.
97 *E.I.* Vol. I, pp. 383f., No. 4.
98 Lüders, No. 123.
99 *E.I.* Vol. I, p. 395, No. 29; Lüders No. 30.
100 *E.I.* Vol. I, p. 391, No. 20; Lüders, No. 31.
101 *E.I.* Vol I, p. 384, No. 5; Lüders No. 32.
102 Lüders No. 119.
103 Lüders No. 33.
104 *J.R.A.S.*, 1905, p. 358.
105 Lüders *List*. p. 164 (No. 33).
106 *J.R.A.S.*, 1910, p. 1314.
107 See Raychaudhuri, *P.H.A.I.*, p. 476.
108 *E.I*, Vol. I, p. 385, No. 6; Lüders, No. 34.
109 See Raychaudhuri, *op. cit.*, pp. 476ff.
110 *E.I.* Vol. II, p. 206, No. 26; Lüders, No. 35.
111 *J.U.P.H.S.* Vol. 10, pt. 1, pp. 1ff, No. 2.
112 *E.I*, Vol. II, pp. 202f., No. 15; Lüders, No. 36.
113 *E.I.*, Vol. II, p. 203, No. 6; Lüders, No. 37.
114 *E.I*, Vol. I, p. 385, No. 7; Lüders, No. 39.
115 See *I.A.*, Vol. 33, pp. 40f., No. 10; Lüders, No. 41.
116 See *Saṁyutta*, Vol. I, p. 87.
117 *I.A.*, Vol. 33, pp. 40f.
118 *E.I.*, Vol. I, pp. 387f, No. 11; Lüders, No. 48.
119 *I.A.* Vol. 33, pp. 103f.; Sec. *E.I.*, Vol. IX, pp. 244f.
120 *E.I.* Vol. I, p. 387, No. 9; Lüders, No. 42.
121 *E.I.* Vol. I, p. 387 No. 10; Lüders, No. 44.
122 Lüders, No. 81.
123 *E.I.* Vol. X, p. 112, No. 5; Lüders, No. 45a.
124 *I.A.* Vol. 33, p. 103, No. 14; Lüders, No. 46.
125 *E.I.* Vol. II, p. 204, No. 20; Lüders, No. 47.
126 *E.I.* II, p. 204.
127 *E.I.* Vol. IV, pp. 244f.
128 See *Prakrit Proper Names*, Vol. II, p. 589.
129 See *Vividhatīrthakalpa*, p. 19.
130 Lüders, Nos. 49-51.
131 See *I.A.* Vol. 6, p. 219, No. 11; Lüders, No. 51.
132 *E.I.*, Vol. 2, pp. 203f. No. 18; Lüders, No. 53.

133 See *Prakrit Sāhitya kā itihāsa*, p. 207.
134 *E.I.*, Vol. I, p. 391, No. 21 ; Lüders No. 54.
135 P. 1948.
136 P. 1912.
137 *E.I.*, Vol. I, p 386, No. 8 ; Lüders, No. 56.
138 Lüdcrs, Nos. 57-58.
139 See Bühler, *Vienna Oriental Journal*, Vol. I, pp. 172f ; correction by Lüders *I.A.*, Vol. 33, pp. 105f ; No. 19 ; see his *List*, p. 166 (correction under No. 57).
140 *E.I.*, Vol. X, pp. 115f., No. 9, Lüders, No. 59a.
141 *I.A.* Vol. 33, p. 102, No. 13 ; Lüders, No. 63.
142 *E.I.*, Vol. I, p. 390, No. 18 ; Lüders No. 85.
143 See *E.I.*, Vol. I, p. 381.
144 *Loc. cit.*
145 II. 109.29 (Gītā Press).
146 Vs. 1311.
147 Pāṇini cannot be later than the 5th cent. B.C.
148 *E.I.*, Vol. I, p. 392, No. 24 ; see Lüders, No. 66.
149 *E.I.*, Vol. II, pp. 204f., No. 21 ; Lüders, No. 67.
150 *I.A.*, Vol. 33? p. 107, No. 21 ; Lüders, No. 68.
151 *Proc. J.A.S.B*, N.S., Vol. V. pp. 276f ; Lüders, No. 69a.
152 *E.I.*, Vol. XIX, p. 67, No. 4.
153 *E.I.*, Vol. I, p. 388, No. 12 ; Lüders, No. 70.
154 Lüders, Nos. 71-72.
155 *E.I.*, Vol. II, p. 205, No. 22 ; Lüders, No. 73.
156 *E.I.*, Vol. II, p. 205, No. 23 ; Lüdcrs, No. 74.
157 *Vienna Oriental Journal*, Vol. I, pp. 177ff., No. 8. See also *I.A.*, Vol. 33, p. 108, No. 23 ; and Lüders, No. 76.
158 *E.I.*, Vol. II, p. 205, No. 24, Lüders, No. 77.
159 See *Vienna Oriental Journal*, Vol. 10, pp. 171f ; see also *I.A.*, Vol. 37, pp. 33f ; Lüders, No. 78.
160 *J.U.P.H.S.*, 1950, Vol. 10, p. 38.
161 *J.A.S.B.*, Vol. 39, pt. I, p. 129, No. 16 ; Lüders, No. 79.
162 *E.I.*, Vol. II, p. 206, No. 25 ; Lüders, No. 80.
163 *E.I.*, Vol. I, p. 389, No. 14 ; Lüders, No. 121.
164 *E.I.*, Vol. II, pp. 209f ; No. 37 ; Lüders, No. 122.
165 *E.I.*, Vol. II, p. 207, No. 29 ; Lüders, No. 110.
166 *E.I.*, Vol. II, p. 207.
167 See his *List* No. 110.
168 *E.I.*, Vol. I, p. 392, No. 23; Lüders No. 113.
169 *E.I.*, Vol. II, p. 208, No. 34 ; Lüders, 119.
170 *E.I.*, Vol. X, p. 120. No. 16 ; Lüders, No. 107d.
171 See *J.R.A.S.*, 1912, pp. 106 ff.
172 See *J.U.P.H.S.*, 1950, Vol. 23, pp. 36-71.

173 See McCrindle's *Ancient India as described by Ptolemy* (ed. S. N. Majumdar), p. 124.

174 *E.I.*, Vol. II, No. XIV (39).

175 P. 1766.

176 P. 62 (Jacobi's translation).

177 See *Prakrit sāhitya kā itihąsa*, p. 207.

178 See *Ibid.*, p. 219.

179 See *Nandīcūrnī*, p. 8; see also Haribhadra's Com. on *Nandi*, pp. 17f.

180 See 2.1.

182 We will afterwards see that this *gaṇa* survived upto the end of the 18th century.

CHAPTER VI

Jainism in Orissa

Mahāvīra who originally hailed from Northern Bihar visited, as we have noticed in a previous chapter, a few areas of Western Bengal during his missionary career. According to the *Kalpasūtra*[1] the Master had spent a year of his missionary career in Paṇiyabhūmi which was actually included in Lāḍha or West Bengal. The *Ācārāṅga*,[2] which is certainly a very old text, informs us that Mahāvīra had visited areas of both Western and Southern Bengal. Therefore, it is likely that Mahāvīra visited places which were not far from the borders of Orissa. A somewhat late text viz. the *Āvaśyakaniryukti*[3] records that Mahāvīra more than once had visited Tosalī a prominent city of Orissa. The same text informs us that the king of that place had tied Mahāvīra with chords seven times. But this particular text was probably composed after 300 A.D., and its evidence therefore has little value. But it is likely that within a few years of Mahāvīra's demise some of his followers, hailing probably from Southern Bengal carried the message of the Nirgrantha religion to Orissa and succeeded in converting some people of that country. In both the canonical texts of the Jains[4] and Buddhists[5] we come across a certain king Karaṇḍu (also called Karakaṇḍa, Karakaṇḍaka) of Dantapura[6] (which was situated in the Kaliṅga country) who was a very pious man. According to both the Buddhists and Jains this king afterwards became a Pacceka Buddha. The Jains[7] also have nothing but deference for this ancient royal sage of Orissa. Since this king is mentioned in both the Buddhist and Jain texts he was probably a historical figure. According to the Jain commentaries[8] Karakaṇḍu was a son of king Dadhivāhana of Campā. This Dadhivāhana, acording to the same commentaries,[9] was a contemporary of Śatānīka, the father of the celebrated Udayana. It therefore follows that king Karaṇḍu-Karakaṇḍu was an exact contemporary of the Buddha and Mahāvīra and was universally admired for his pious nature. It is exceedingly significent that this particular king of Orissa, who flourished in the 6th century B.C., is called a Pacceka Buddha (Ardha Māgadhī *Patteyabuddha*) in the texts of both Buddhists and Jains. It is probable that Khāravela was inspired by the deeds of this great monarch of Orissa and tried to follow in his footsteps.

We have already observed that Jainism was probably introduced in Orissa by some zealous monks of Bengal during the closing years of the 5th century B.C. According to the Jain commentaries[10] the king Kākavarṇa of Pāṭaliputra was arrested in the Isitalāga lake of Tosalī by the king of that place. But the son of Kākavarṇa avenged the humiliation of his father by occupying Tosalī and releasing his father. It is therefore a historical fact that hostility between Kaliṅga and Magadha started from about 400 B.C.,[11] the date of Kākavarṇa, who is also known as Kālāśoka. During the days of the Nandas, if we have to believe in the evidence of the famous inscription of Khāravela, there was no love lost between Magadha and Kaliṅga. It is quite likely that Kaliṅga was under the Nanda and early Maurya rulers for a quite long time and probably during the closing years of Bindusāra, the son of Candragupta Maurya, Orissa declared independence. And Aśoka eight years after his accession, successfully crushed the rebellion of Kaliṅga and once more annexed this kingdom. The testimony of Aśoka's 13th Rock Edict shows that only after a bloody and terrible battle, which cost thousands of lives, that Kaliṅga submitted to Aśoka. But there is little doubt that soon after Aśoka's death, Orissa declared independence.

The Meghavāhana dynasty, to which the great Khāravela belonged, according to the first line of the Hāthigumphā inscription, was a branch of the great Cedi family. In this connexion we should remember that according to the *Mahābhārata*[12] the five sons of the great Cedi monarch Uparicara Vasu became kings of five different countries. The name of one of the sons was Maṇivāhana which may be mistake for *Meghavāhana*. We have already noticed that one Dadhivāhana was the father of Karakaṇḍu, the celebrated king of Orissa, who reigned in the 6th century B.C. That kings belonging to the Cedi family reigned in the eastern parts of India is also proved by a *śloka* of the *Mahābhārata*,[13] according to which Pauṇḍra Vāsudeva, the well known rival of Vāsudeva Kṛṣṇa and the king of Vaṅga, Puṇḍra and Kirāta beyonged to that celebrated family. It is therefore not at all surprising to find a branch of that great family ruling in another state of eastern India.

The Hāthigumhā Inscription[14] opens with an adoration to the Arahats and Siddhas just like any Jain canonical text. According to this inscription Khāravela was the third king of the Mahāmeghavāhana dynasty (*tatiye Kaliṅgarājavase*). Unfortunately, we do not know the names of the first two kings of this dynasty. We are first told that upto his 15th year Khāra-yela played various games apparently under the loving care of his parents. Afterwards, for nine years as a *yuvarāja* he received extensive training in the following branches of learn'ng—*lekha, rūpa, gaṇanā, vavahāra* and *vidhi*. He become *mahārāja* at the age of 24. In the first year of his reign Khāravela was engaged in repairing the buildings and defensive walls of his capital, which were damaged by storm (*vātavihita*) and made arrangements for the erection of the embankments of a *śītala taḍāga* (lake) which was probably the principal source of water-supply to the city of Kaliṅga-nagara. He also restored all the gardens of the city. We are further told that Khāravela made a total expenditure of 35 hundred thousands (apparently *kārṣāpaṇa*) for the entertainment of his subjects In the 2nd year of his reign, without taking any heed of Śātakarṇi (*acitayaṭā Śātakaṁniṁ*), he sent a huge army to the western direction consisting of *haya, gaja, nara* and *ratha* (apparently a *caturaṅga* army) which reached the bank of the river Kaṇhaveṇṇā (i.e. Kṛṣṇā) and plundered the city of Asika-nagara, which was apparently situated on the river Kṛṣṇā. The Śātakarṇi of this inscription has been satisfactorily identified with Śātakarṇi I of the Śātavāhana dynasty. There is, however, no reason to believe that there was an all-out war between the two monarchs. It is probable that Asika-nagara was not included in the empire of Śātakarṇi I but was a town belonging to one of his vassal kingdoms. The relevant words also suggest that Khāravela did not himself lead his army in its march towards the western direction. And we are also not in a position to know whether he was able to annex any new territory to his empire. In the 3rd year the king engaged himself in cultural activities. We are told that he gladdened his subjects by holding popular festivals (*samājas* and *utsavas*). It should be noted here that Khāravela, although a Jain, was shrewd enough to understand the real feeling of his subjects and did nothing to dempen their enthusiasm regarding festivals. It is apparent from the relevant words of the inscription (in the 5th line) that the king himself was a great lover of music and was probably acquainted with the literature on *Kāmaśāstra* which specifically speaks of the Arts mentioned in the 5th line of this inscription. It should here be noted that unlike Aśoka, he had no affected attitude towards *Samājas*.[15] Jainism, like the religion of the Buddha, did not approve of the holding of the *Samājas*,[16] but this king never wanted to impose his faith forcibly on his people.

In the 4th year, once more, Khāravela was engaged in martial activities; but the actual significance of the first few words of the fifth line is not clear as majority of those words are practically lost; but it is apparent from the concluding words of this line that Khāravela forced the Raṭhikas and Bhojakas to pay him some sort of tribute.[17] The Raṭhikas and Bhojas are mentioned in 5th and 13th Rock edicts of Aśoka respectively. According to the *Mahābhārata*[18] Bhojakaṭa was the capital of Vidarbha. This city derived its name from the Bhoja tribe who are even mentioned in the Vedic texts.[19] The kingdom of Bhojakaṭa is mentioned in a Vākāṭaka inscription[20] of the 5th century A.D. The inscription of Khāravela does not suggest that the Bhojakas and Raṭhikas submitted to him after any particular military engagement. It is more likely that Khāravala's military stature was enough to extract from such tribes some sort of allegiance. The early Śātavāhana inscriptions[21] suggest that Raṭhikas had some friendly relation with the Andhra monarchs. In connexion with the achievements of Khāravela's 4th year we get the expression *vijādharādhivāsaṁ* and Sircar believes[22] that Vijādhara or Vidyādhara may be the name of a local ruler. But any one who is familiar with the early Jain literature knows that the term 'Vidyādhara' is generally used to mean *rākṣasas* or non-Aryans. In the *Paumacariyaṁ* of Vimala, a work of the 1st century A.D., the *rākṣasas* of Laṅkā are constantly called Vidyādharas.[23] Therefore, it is more probable that Khāravela in his 4th year carried out some successful raids against a few non-Aryan tribes living in the hilly regions of Orissa. In the 5th year, once more, the king was engaged in constructive activities. We are told that he brought into the capital the canal (*paṇāḍi*) excavated three hundred years ago by a Nanda king. The reading *Naṁdarāja* is absolutely clear and there is little doubt that the Kaliṅga country was under the Nandas in the 4th century B.C. This is also suggested by the Purāṇic evidence according to which Mahāpadma Nanda became a *Samrāj* after his conquest of the entire sub-continent. We have already observed that attempts were made by the Magadhan rulers to conquer Orissa even before the rule of the Nandas. This passage of this inscription further proves that this Cedi king of Orissa was not only a great conqueror but also a magnanimous and able monarch who did everything for the uplift of the economic condition of his empire. We have already noticed that in the first year of his reign he made arrangements for the adequate supply of drinking water to his capital. In the 6th year also this king did not undertake any fresh military expedition. But we are told that he performed the Rājasūya[24] sacrifice and spent a lot of money on this particular occasion. D. C. Sircar[25] believes that as a Jain, Khāravela could not have performed this sacrifice and therefore he suggests a slightly different reading for that word. But we should not forget that the demarcation line between the Hindu and Jain religions was rather thin in those days, and as suggested by a passage of the *Bhagavatī*[26] even Mahāvīra did not hesitate to accept non-vegetarian food. The king Khāravela, as we will see elsewhere, is described as having repaired *deva* temples. So there is nothing surprising to find an able military conqueror like him performing the Rājasūya sacrifice.[27] Regarding his achievements in the 7th year it is not possible to say anything in view of a quite a few missing or damaged words. But it seems from the available words that he did not undertake any military expedition in that year. But in the 8th year the Orissan monarch resolved to carry out some ambitious military expeditions into the heart of Northern and Eastern India. Even here also a few words are missing; but fortunately for us quite a few proper names are preserved. They are Goradhagiri (probably Barabar hills), Rājagaha, Mathurā and Yavana (king). It has rightly been conjectured that with a large army (*mahatā senā*) Khāravela himself first attacked Magadha and plundered Rajgir and Barabar hills. Afterwards, emboldened by his success, he proceeded towards Mathurā which was under an Indo-Greek ruler at that time and succeeded in chastising him The name of this particular Indo-Greek king has been read as *Dimita* by Jayaswal, but who cannot be the king, Demetrios, who ruled in the first half of the 2nd century B.C., at least one hundred years before Khāravela. The passage of this inscription, however, strongly suggests that in the middle of the 1st century B.C., Mathurā was under a later Indo-Greek ruler. The Jain commentaries,[28] tell us about a certain Yavana king of Mathurā who assassinated the Jain monk Daṇḍa in the Jauṇāvaṁka park of this city. It is tempting to suggest that Khāravela wanted to punish this particular Greek king of Mathurā for his persecution of Jain monks of this city. In any case, the expedition of the 8th year was a complete success and evidently enhanced the prestige of this valiant Orissan monarch. We are further told that after this expedition he satisfied the Brāhmaṇas by showering on them lavish presents. In the 9th year this victorious monarch celebrated his military success by building a *pāsāda* (palace) called Mahāvijaya which involved an expenditure of 38 hundred thousand *kārṣāpaṇas*. The significance of the expression *mahāvijayapāsāda* has been missed by scholars who have written on this inscription. The word *mahāvijaya* is used in the *Ācārańga*[29] and *Kalpasūtra*[30] in connexion with Mahārīra's descent on the earth. It signifies divine abode in those texts.[31] We are told that Mahāvīra descended on earth from the Mahāvijaya mansion of the heaven. We have little doubt that Khāravela, who was a Jain, was acquainted with the story regarding Mahāvīra's birth as told in the *Ācārańga* and *Kalpasūtra*. The expression *mahāvijaya* occurs twice in Khāravela's inscription, the first time as we have noticed as the name of the place built by him at a great cost, and the second time in the concluding line of this inscription as an epithet of this king, which has been translated as 'great conqueror' by Jayaswal and Banerji[32] but which Sircar takes as Khāravela's *viruda*.[33] It was considered a sacred word by ths early Jains since it was connected with the story of Mahāvīra's birth.

In the 10th year also the king undertook some military expeditions towards the North and it in this connexion the word *Bharadhavasa* (i.e. Bhāratavarṣa) is used. But due to the damaged nature of a few other words here, we cannot have a correct idea about his actual military achievements of this year. In the 11th year the king was also in a war-like wood. The proper name *Pīthuṁḍa* is used in this connexion which according to Barua[34] stands for the famous *tīrtha* of Pṛthūdaka near Kurukṣetra and which according to Rājaśekhara was the northernmost boundary of Madhyadeśa. Bnt Jayaswal and Banerji[35] believe it to be the Pihunda of Ptolemy. We are further told in connexion with Khāravela's military exploits of the 11th year that he came in clash with the Tamil states but the reading even in this case is not perfectly clear. In the 12th year the monarch was engaged in wars against a few North and East Indian kings. The two words *Uttarāpadharājāno* prove that kings of North India came into open conflict with Khāravela. We are also told that king Bahasatimita was forced to acknowledge Khāravela's military superiority. Formerly, scholars used to identify Bahasatimita with Puśyamitra Śuṅga ; but there is little doubt that the king should be idenified with the monarch of the same name mentioned in the Pabhosa cave inscription of the time of Udāka.[36] King Khāravela also, we are told, set up in his capital the Jina of Kaliṅga (*Kāliṅga Jina*) which was taken away from Kaliṅga by king Nanda. The importance of this line of the inscription can hardly be overemphasised. It not only shows that the worship of Jain images we prectised in the 4th century B.C., but also demonstrates the weakness of the Nanda kings for this religion. In our last chapter we discussed a particular verse of the *Paumacariyaṁ* which indirectly proves the popularity of the Jain religion during the Nanda rule. We are not in a position to know the exact name of the Nanda king who carried away the Jina of Kaliṅga; but it is just possible that the celebrated Mahāpadma Nanda himself was the culprit. After defeating the contemporary Magadhan king, who was in all probability, Bahasatimita, our king Khāravela returned in triumph to his capital along with the Kaliṅga-Jina. It has been conjectured by Jayaswal, and Banerji[37] that this particular Jina was Śītalanātha. But in the absence of any evidence we cannot accept it. We are further told that Khāravela brought treasures from the Paṁḍarāja (i.e. the Pandyan king). Some other constructive activities were also carried out in the same year.

After this, it seems, Khāravela did not undertake any more military expedition. He directed his energy to religious affairs and as a lay devotee (*Uvāsaga*) he tried to serve the Jain monks. The inscription in its concluding portion gives a magnificent tribute to this wonderful royal personality, who, we are told, was not only o devoted Jain, but also the worshipper of other religious seets (*sava-pāsaṁdapūjaka*) and who also endeavoured his best to rebuild dilapidated *deva* temples. The writer of this inscription knows that as a Cedi king, Khāravela is a descendant of the great Uparicara Vasu,[38] who in the inscription is called *rājasi* (*rājarṣi*). In the *Mahābhārata*[39] also Uparicara Vasu is called a *rājarṣi*. There is reason to believe that the writer of the Hāthigumphā inscription was acquainted with the story of Uparicara Vasu as told in the *Mahābhārata* and the character Khāravela, described here, is strikingly similar to that of Uparicara described in the *Mahābhārata*. We should further note that elsewhere in the *Mahābhārata*[40] Uparicara is called a Vaiṣṇava and a devoted worshipper of Nārāyaṇa. And it is significant that in this inscription[41] Khāravela gets the epithet *Cakadhara* (i.e. Cakradhara) which is a typical Vaiṣṇava expression. The Jains, from the earliest times, had great deference for Kṛṣṇa and Nārāyaṇa; one of their Tīrthaṅkaras viz. Ariṣṭanemi is represented as a kinsman of Vāsudeva. It is significant that Khāravela openly encouraged the holding of *Utsavas* and *Samājas*; in the *Mahābhārata*[42] Vasu Uparicara is described as the king who founded the *utsava* of the god Indra. Probably the *utsava* referred to in the Hāthigumphā inscription was the well-known Indrotsava first started by Khāravela's celebrated predecessor.

The inscription of Khāravela is the first complete historical record of the achievements of a king of ancient India. We do not get much idea about Aśoka's real career (beyond his missionary activities) from his inscriptions. Other pre-Christian inscriptions are either too brief or too much concerned with some particular religious purpose. But this inscription gives us a very lucid and accurate account of this exceedingly interesting monarch. The most significant thing about this king is that in spite of being a Jain and apparently a believer in the doctrine of Ahiṁsā, he was a very successful military conqueror. But there is no reference to the killing of any opponent. Most of his adversaries were only forced to submit (cf. the words *pādau vandāpayati*). We may recall here Aśoka's killing of thousands of soldiers of Kaliṅga in the battlefield; the war between Magadha and Kaliṅga was resumed in Khāravela's time; this time, however the other side was victorious; but apparently the *bhikṣu-rājā* Khāravela did not indulge in any senseless killing. He could have paid Magadha back in her own coin; but as a *dharmarājā* and a worthy descendant of Rājarṣi Vasu, he treated his opponents with tolerance and justice.

It is a matter of great regret that so far we have not been able to come across any reference to this celebrated Jain king in any literary text of the Jains. But not all the Jain manuscripts, preserved in the Bhāṇḍārs have been published. With the discovery of more texts, probably some new light will be thrown on this problem. Another reason why Khāravela was forgotten afterwards is that Jainism steadily lost popularity in Orissa in the post-Christian period.

A few other inscriptions in the Udayagiri and Khaṇḍagiri caves disclose the names of a few Jain devotees[43]. No. 1346 of Lüders' list belonging to the Mañcapurīgumpha records the establishment of a cave (*leṇa*) in honour of Arahaṁta by Khāravela's chief queen (*agamahisī*) who was a daughter of Rājan Lālaka, the great grandson (*popota*)[44] of Hathisiha. There is little doubt that Lālaka, although the father-in-law of Khāravela, was a subordinate ally of his son-in-law. It is not clear why instead of mentioning either the father or grandfather of Lālaka, the inscription refers only to his great-grandfather. It is probable that Hastisiṁha, who probably flourished in the middle of the 2nd century B.C., was a petty chieftain of Orissa. He has not been given any royal title in this inscription. But this inscription goes far to prove that Khāravela's chief queen like her husband was a devoted worshipper of Tīrthaṅkaras. The reference to the Jain monks also prove the developed stage of the Jain church in Kaliṅga. Another inscription discloses[45] the name of either a predecessor or successor of Khāravela viz. Vakadeva and like the former he is called the king of Kaliṅga and is represented as belonging to the Meghavāhana family. The inscription shows that he too, was a Jain.

A few other inscriptions (Lüders list Nos. 1348-53) disclose the existence of a few Jain devotees. No. 1348 yields the name of a prince called Vadhuka who too, was a Jain votary. Nos. 1349 and 1350 probably represent the gifts of common people. But No. 1351, according to Lüders is the gift of the town-judge. Nos. 1352 and 1353 are also probably the gifts of important persons. Another inscription[46] records the donation of a servant (*pādamūlika*) called Kusuma.

These inscriptions abundantly prove the immense popularity of Jainism in Orissa. The Mathurā inscriptions do not disclose the names of any royal devotee of this religion. But in Orissa the kings themselves probably inspired their subjects to befriend Nirgrantha monks. It is also interesting to note that although the Mahāmeghavāhana kings of Orissa claim descent from the celebrated Cedi family, they bear names which are typically non-Sanskritic.[47]

We have already observed that the message of the Nirgrantha religion was probably carried to Orissa by the Jain monks of Southern Bengal. Probably these monks belonged either to Tāmraliptikā or Kotivarṣiyā *śākhās* mentioned in the *Therāvalī*. But the popularity of Jainism in Kaliṅga during the days of the Nandas shows that even before the birth of the *Śākhās* and *gaṇas* the Jain religion made some converts in Orissa. And during the rule of the Mahāmeghavāhana kings Jainism became the principal religion of Orissa.

Some later sculptures of Udayagiri and Khaṇḍagiri caves and few inscriptions[48] of the 10th or 11th century prove that even long after Khāravela the Kumārīparvata (i.e. Udayagiri and Khaṇḍagiri hills) remained a favourite place of pilgrimage for the Jain monks. In a later chapter we will discuss the sculptures of the caves of Udagiri and Khaṇḍagiri hills.

NOTES

1 P. 264.
2 P. 85.
3 Vss. 501f.
4 See *Uttarādhyayana* (S. B. E, Vol. 45), pp. 85f.
5. See *Kumbhakāra Jātaka.*
6 *Loc. cit.*
7 See *Uttarādhyayana*, pp. 85f.
8 *Āvacū*, II, pp. 204-7; *Uttaracū*, p. 178.
9 *Āvacū*, I, p. 318; *Āva N*, 521.
10 *Bṛhatkalpabhāṣya*, Vss. 3149-50.
11 See *PHAI*, pp. 221f.
12 I, 63. 29ff.
13 II. 14. 18.
14 See *EI*, Vol. 20, pp. 71ff.
15 See 1st Rock Edict, line 4.
16 See our work entitled *Ancient Indian Literary and Cultural Tradition*, p. 166.
17 For these two tribes see *EI*, 20, p. 84.
18 II. 31. 11.12.
19 See *Aitareya Br.* VIII. 12 VIII. 14; VIII. 17.
20 See *Sel. Ins.*, p. 445.
21 *Ibid.*, pp. 191, 193.
22 *Sel. Ins.*, p. 215, fn 4.
23 See our paper entitled 'Vimalasūri's *Paumacariyaṁ* in *JAIH* (Vol. 6), pp. 105 ff.
24 See *EI*, 20, p. 84
25 See *Sel. Ins.*, p. 215 fn 8.
26 See p. 2468.
27 The reading *rājasūya* in the original inscription is perfectly clear.
28 *Āva cū, II*, p. 155.
29 P. 174 (Sailana).
30 P. 4 (Cal. Univ.).

31 See *Pāiasaddamahaṇṇavo* (Prakrit text series) p. 680.
32 *EI.*, 20, p. 89.
33 *Sel. Ins.*, p. 221 fn 2.
34 See *IHQ.*, pp. 261 ff ; see also *Sel. Ins.*, p. 217 fn 1.
35 See *EI.*, 20, p. 72 ff.
36 *Sel. Ins.*, p. 96.
37 *EI*, 20, p. 85.
38 The spelling here is *Vasū*.
39 I. 63. 32, 38.
40 XII, Chs. 335 ff.
41 See line 17.
42 1. 63. 17ff.
43 See Lüders' *List*. Nos. 1342-1353.
44 See for a different interpretation *A.S.I.A.R.*, 1922-23, pp. 129-30.
45 No. 1347 of Lüders' *List* ; p. 222 of *Sel. Ins.*
46. No. 1344 of Lüders' *List*.
47 For etymological explanation of the name *Khāravela*, see *Sel. Ins.*, p. 214 foot note.
48 See *A.S.I.A.R.*, 1922-23, p. 130.

CHAPTER VII

Jainism in North India

(200 B.C. to 600 A.D.)

It is difficult to give a correct account regarding the state of Jain religion in different parts of North India after the Maurya period. Epigraphic references are few and far between, and we have to depend mainly on the evidence supplied by literary texts, both Jain and non-Jain. Archaeology also helps us a great deal and the discoveries of early Jain images enable us to have some idea about the popularity of this religion in particular localities.

We have already seen that long before the Kuṣāṇa period, Jainism became popular in Mathurā and Orissa. We have also indicated the route taken by the Jain monks of earlier days. As we have already said, the Jain monks of Bengal were mainly responsible for the early popularity of Jainism in Orissa. But beyond a few references to *kulas* and *śākhās,* we do not know practically anything regarding Jainism in Bengal after the demise of Mahāvīra. We will have to refer afterwards to the Chinese evidence regarding the popularity of Jainism in Bengal. But regarding a few other ancient places of North India, we are slightly more fortunate Archaeological and epigraphic sources give us some idea about the state of Jainism in places like Kauśāmbī, Śrāvastī, Rājagṛha, Ahicchatra, Takṣaśilā, Siṁhapura and a few places of Western India. Thanks to the iconoclastic zeal of the Muslim invaders, very few among the pre-Gupta or even post-Gupta Hindu temples have survived and the early Jain temples have fared no better. The Jain literary evidences suggest the existence of Jain temples in almost all principal cities of North India; but all of them have simply vanished in the thin air 'leaving no rack behind'.

Kauśāmbī like Śāketa was one of the early centres of

Jainism. We have already referred, on the basis of the evidence supplied by the *Paumacariyaṁ*, to the temple of Suvratasvāmin at Śāketa. That Śāketa was connected with Muni Suvrata is also proved by the evidence of the *Vividhatīrthakalpa*[1] of Jinaprabha. We have also opined that the temple of Suvrata at Śāketa was, in all probability, built before 300 B.C. It is quite natural that the Jains should be eager to build shrines in famous cities connected with Brāhmaṇical culture and religion. We have already said that Jainism itself originated by 800 B.C. at Vārāṇasī, one of the greatest cities of ancient India, and during the time of Mahāvīra, became popular at Vaiśālī, Rājagṛha, Śrāvastī, Kauśāmbī and a few other towns.

An inscription[2] assignable on the palaeographic grounds to the first century B.C., found at Pabhosa near Kauśāmbī, proves that the Jain monks, living at that famous town, enjoyed royal patronage. The two short inscriptions found at Pabhosa, refer to the cave (*lena*) excavated by Āṣāḍhasena, the king of Adhicchatra (Ahicchatra), who was the maternal uncle of Bahasatimitra or Bṛhaspatimitra. This Āṣāḍhasena[3] seems to be a local ruler of North Pañcāla region and is generally placed in the first century B.C. According to Führer[4] the inscriptions refer to the Kāśyapīya monks, which may mean monks belonging to the school of Vardhamāna Mahāvīra, who was a Kāśyapa Kṣatriya. But D. C. Sircar[5] rejects this reading and opines that the inscriptions refer to the monks of Ahicchatra. That Pabhosa cave was sacred to the Jains from the pre-Christian times, is proved by the discovery of Jain images and carvings from there[6]. Three standing Jain images, cut in rocks, are also to be found there[7]. The Pabhosa cave was visited by Yuan Chwang in the seventh century A.D.[8] There is little doubt that a number of Jain monks lived in this cave in pre-Christian period and naturally most of them were residents of Kauśāmbi, which is only two miles from that place. This city has yielded a number of Jain antiquities of the Kuṣāṇa period[9]. Kauśāmbī, is still looked upon as a holy place by the devout Jains. It was the birth-place of Padmaprabha, the sixth Tīrthaṅkara. Major R. D. Basu in 1908 had discovered an inscription[10] of the year 12 of king Śivamitra which mentions three monks Baladāsa,

Śivamitra and Śivapālita. R. D. Banerji believes that this inscription is dated in the Kaniṣka era of 78 A.D., and therefore its date corresponds to 90 A.D. As late as 1834, a small Digambara temple was built at Kosam[11].

We have already seen that Lord Mahāvīra himself was probably responsible for the introduction of the new Nirgrantha religion at Kauśāmbī during the rule of the celebrated king Udayana, probably in the beginning of the 5th century B.C. The reference to the Kauśāmbikā *śākhā,* which originated in the first half of the third century B.C., in the *Therāvalī* also directly proves the early popularity of Jainism in that region.

Like Kauśāmbī, the great city of Śrāvastī was associated with Jainism from pretty early times. It was believed to be the birth-place of the third Tīrthaṅkara viz. Sambhavanātha. This city was very intimately associated with the life and activities of both Mahāvīra and Buddha. It was at this town that the first Ninhava Jamāli declared himself a *Jina*. This city was also a great centre of the Ājīvika religion. The *Bhagavatī*[12] gives us the information that it was at this town that Gośāla declared himself a *kevalin*. The death of that famous Ājīvika philosopher took place at this town sixteen years before the demise of Mahāvīra. Lord Buddha spent the major part of his ascetic-life here at the Jetavana-Vihāra which was built by prince Jeta for the Buddhist community at a very high cost. Śrāvastī was the capital of Pasenadi (Prasenajit) of Kosala, a prominent figure in the Pāli texts. The Jains, however, almost completely ignore this royal personality.

The *Therāvalī* refers to the Śrāvastikā *śākhā* which originated in the third century B.C., and this particular Śvetāmbara branch was obviously associated with the city of Śrāvastī. We have already seen that this city was looked upon as the birth-place of Sambhava. It is interesting to note that one of the mounds of the ruined city is still known as the mound of Sobhnath, which is a vernacular corruption of the original Sambhavanātha. A detailed description of the ruined temple has been given by Vogel in his Report[13]. The description leaves little room to doubt that the original temple of Sambhavanātha was built a few centuries before the birth of Christ. We have to remember that Śrāvastī was in utter ruins when Fa-hien visited this city in about 400 A.D. The original temple of Sambhavanātha was probably still there when the Chinese pilgrims came to India. The ruined temple has yielded a good number of Jain images including those of Ṛṣabhanātha and Mahāvīra[14]. The icons belong to the Śvetāmbara sect and have stylish affiliation with those found from Mathurā[15]. The temple of Sambhava at Śrāvastī was rebuilt several times and finally it was destroyed during the reign of Ala-Ud-din as we learn from Jinaprabha[15]. That Śrāvastī afterwards became a famous centre of Digambara religion is evident from the *Bṛhatkathākośa*[17] of Hariṣeṇa, a text composed in 931 A.D.

Adicchatra or Ahicchatra, the ancient capital of North Pañcāla, was certainly an important seat of early Jain religion. The site, represented by modern Ramnagar in Bareilly district, U.P., was excavated first by Führer, who unearthed a number of Jain images and other antiquities. According to the Śvetāmbara Jain tradition, Ahicchatra was sacred to Pārśvanātha and there was actually a shine dedicated to this Tīrthaṅkara at this town. Śīlāṅka, who flourished in the second half of the ninth century A.D., in his *Ācārāṅgavṛtti*[18] distinctly refers to this shrine. Jinaprabha in his *Vividhatīrthakalpa*[19] gives a graphic and beautiful description of the shrine, dedicated to Pārśva. Śīlāṅka informs us that Pārśva was worshipped here as Dharaṇīnda. But according to Jinaprabha[20] the shrine of Dharaṇīnda was near the original shrine (*mūlaceiya*) of Pārśva. Epigraphic evidence at our disposal, fully supports the Jain tradition regarding the existence of a shrine, dedicated to Pārśva, at Ahicchatra. A Kuṣāṇa inscription[21], found engraved at the perestal of an image of Neminātha, bearing the date 50 (i.e. 128 A.D.), refers to the shrine of 'divine Pārśvanātha'. Cunningham also discovered an inscribed pillar of the Gupta period which mentions Ācārya Indranandin and also refers to the temple of Pārśva. A number of Jain inscriptions of the Kuṣāṇa period have also been discovered from this place and at least one of them refers to the city of Ahicchatra[22]. The Kuṣāṇa inscriptions from this city contain the following dates—9, 18, 31, 4 4 and 74. Most of the Jain and Buddhist sculptures from Ahicchatra belong to the Mathurā school of Art. The names of *gaṇa, kula* and *śākhā* are usually like those of Mathurā, the most common *gaṇa* being Koḷiya. The images discovered here, are generally nude and this led Führer to suppose that they belonged to the Digambara temple of Ahicchatra. But it must have to be remembered that even before the emergence of he Digambara sect, some of the Jinas were shown as naked. Even on the pedestals of nude Jina figures we have the names of well known Śvetāmbara *śākhās* and *kulas*[23] which proves that they were fashioned before the formal separation of the Digambaras from the original Nirgrantha religion. Several nude Mathurā images of Jina refer to some well-known *śākhās* and *kulas* mentioned in the Śvetāmbara *Theṛāvalī*. For reasons, best known to him, Lüders doubts the discovery of Jain images from Ahicchatra[24]. But the faithful account of Führer regarding the discovery[25] leaves no room to doubt the authenticity of the 'Reports'. Further, from the list of drawings in the same report made by draftsmen Ghulam Rasul Beg and Sohan Lal, we learn that among the discoveries made, were a four-faced lion pillar from the Jain temple, an *āyāgapaṭa*, a fragment of frieze, illustrating the transfer of embryo and some railing pillars[26].

The Jain Kuṣāṇa inscriptions from Ahicchatra disclose the names of the following lay devotees—Gahapalā, the wife of Ekraḍala, the daughter-in-law of Śivaśiri and the daughter of Grahamitra ; all these persons are mentioned in the inscription of the year 9, corresponding to 87 A.D. ;[27] in the inscription of the year 12 we have Jinadāsī, Rudradeva, Dāttāgālā, Rudra, Grahamitra, Kumāraśirī, Vamadasi, Hastisenā, Grahaśiri, Rudradatā, Jayadāsī and Mitraśirī, all of whom were carpenters by caste[28] ; in the inscription of the year 74 we have[29] Dharavalā and Āryadāsī. The names of the following Jain monks also occur in the inscriptions discovered of Ahicchatra viz. Tarika[30] in the inscription of the year 9, who belonged to the Koḷiya *gaṇa*, Sthāniya *kula* and Vairā *śākhā* ; Puśila[31] (Koḷiya, Bambhadāsiya and Ucenagarī) and another unnamed monk[32] belonging to the Vāraṇa *gaṇa* and Vajanagaī *śākhā*. The most definite proof of the existence of Jain monks at Ahicchatra is supplied by a Lucknow museum Jain Image inscription[33] that refers to a monk (whose name cannot be read) belonging to Petivāmika *kula* and Vajanagarī *śākhā*, who is called a native of Ahicchatra (*Adhicchatrakā*). All these evidences go far to prove the popularity of Jainism at Ahicchatra in early days.

Another old city viz. Kāmpilya was intimately connected with Jainism in pre-Gupta days.,This town was correctly identified by Cunningham with Kampil in Farrukhabad district, U.P.[34] It was according to the *Mahābhārata*[35], the capital of southern Pañcāla. The city, as we learn from the canonical texts[36], was visited by both Pārśva and Mahāvīra. It was believed to be the birth-place of the thirteenth Tīrthaṅkara Vimala. This place is also mentioned in the *Bhagavatī*[37] and *Aupapātika Sūtra*[38]. The fourth Niṇhava Āsamitta, who flourished 220 years after Mahāvīra's death i.e. in the 3rd century B.C., was associated with this town. The *Uttarādhyayana*[39], a very old Jain canonical text, refers to a certain king Sañjaya, who was a Jain devotee. This place has yielded a few Jain inscriptions[40].

Sāṅkāśya, mentioned prominently in the *Rāmāyaṇa*[41], as the capital of Kuśadhavaja Janaka, Sītā's paternal uncle, was one of the important towns of pre-Buddhist India. It was, according to that epic, situated on the bank of the river Ikṣumatī. It is identified by Cunningham[42] with Sankissa in Farrukhabad district of U.P. This town, it is interesting to take, is mentioned by Pāṇini[43]. Patañjali also refers to it[44]. This city was visited by both Fa-hien and Yuan Chwang. The *Therāvalī* refers to the Saṅkāsiyā *śākhā* under Cāraṇa *gaṇa* i e. Vāraṇa *gaṇa*, established in the third century B.C. This definitely proves Sāṅkāśya's early association with the Nirgrantha religion.

It appears that the religion of Pārśva and Mahāvīra succeeded in penetrating into North-West and western India at a quite early date. We had occasion to refer to the visit of Mahāvīra in Sindhu-Sauvīra, as described in the *Bhagavatī*, in a previous chapter. At present, we have definite evidence to show that even in pre-Christian times, Jainism became quite popular with the people of western India. A recently discovered inscription[45] from Pala, Poona district, Maharashtra, discloses the existence of a cave which was excavated by a monk (*bhadamta*) called Indrarakṣita. This inscription has been assigned, on palaeographical grounds, to the 2nd century B.C. It begins with the typical Jain expression *namo araṁhātānaṁ*. We further learn from the same inscription that Indrarakṣita constructed also a reservoir (*poḍhi*) of water. Let us not forget, that according to the Jains, the twenty-second Tīrthaṅkara Neminātha or Ariṣṭanemi was born in Western India. The earliest source that gives a glimpse of his life is the *Nāyādhammakahāo,* which was not improbably composed by 300 B.C. We have already said that with the exception of Pārśva, no other Tīrthaṅkara before Mahāvīra, can be called historical figures. But the idea of Tīrthaṅkara was developed within a century after the demise of Vardhamāna like the idea of the previous Buddhas[46]. In making Neminātha their twenty-second Tīrthaṅkara, the Jains have very ingeniously used the contemporary Vaiṣṇava tradition current in Western India, regarding the Yādavas and Vāsudeva Kṛṣṇa.

It is extremely significant that the *Therāvalī* refers to a *śākhā* called Saurāṣṭriyā (Prakrit Soraṭṭhiyā) which originated from Ṛṣigupta, a disciple of Suhastin, who flourished in the third century B.C. This definitely proves that Saurāṣṭra had received its first dose of Jainism in the Mauryan period. The inscription from Pala, referred to above, shows that Jainism became popular in other centres of Western India before the second century B.C. It is interesting to note that the inscription, in question, does not give us any idea regarding the *gaṇa, kula* or *śākhā* of Indrarakṣita and in this respect his position is similar to the monk Māgharakṣita of the Mathurā inscription of circa 150 B.C. But unlike the latter, the monk Indrarakṣita himself takes the initiative for constructing a cave. Apparently, he did not receive and financial support from his lay disciples.

Another small inscription[47] from Girnar, Gujarat bearing the date 58 refers to *Pañcānacandamūrti*. The date has been assigned to the Vikrama era of 58. However, we have not been able to examine the palaeography of this inscription, and therefore no conclusion is desirable on the basis of this inscription alone. However, since the *Nāyādhammakahāo* and other canonical texts associate Girnar (Ujjiṁta or Ujjaṁta) with Ariṣṭanemi, we need not be surprised to come across a 1st-century inscription from this hill. The *Kalpasūtra*[48] also associates

Neminātha or Ariṣṭanemi with this hill. These literary references also prove the early association of Gujarat with Jainism.

No early Jain inscription has so far been discovered from North-West India. But we have strong reasons to believe that there were quite a few Jain pockets in that part of India. The ancient city of Kāpiśī, which was visited by Yuan Chwang in the first half of the seventh century A.D., and which has been identified with Opian in Afghanistan by Cunningham[49], had a sizeable Jain population. It is clear therefore that Jainism penetrated in this part of North-West India (the original Indian sub-continent which surely included the whole of Afghanistan) in the early centuries of the Christian era.

Another old city viz. Takṣaśilā was associated with Jainism from early days. Sir John Marshall, who first carried out systematic excavations at Taxila, observes "Taxila must have been adorned by a vast number of Jain edifices, some of which were no doubt, of considerable magnificence".[50] According to Marshall, the shrines in blocks F and G in the excavated area of Sirkap were probably Jain. The Jain literary tradition[51] associates Taxila with Bāhubali, a son of Ṛṣabha, who was believed to be a Jain *Sādhu*. We further learn from the *Āvaśyakaniryukti*[52] and the *Āvaśyakacūrṇī*[53] that Bāhubali had installed a jewelled *dharma-cakra* at Takṣaśilā. The association of Bāhubali with Takṣaśilā is also mentioned in the *Vividhatīrthakalpa*[54] of Jinaprabha. Since Takṣaśilā was one of the greatest cities of ancient India, it is but natural that the Jains should endeavour to extend the sphere of their influence in that city.

Siṁhapura, was another Jain centre from early times. This place has been identified by Stein[55] and Cunningham[56] with modern Ketas in the Salt Range (Punjab, Pakistan). It was visited by Yuan Chwang[57] who saw Śvetāmbara Jains there. That Chinese pilgrim, however, gives a highly distorted account regarding the religious practices of the Śvetāmbaras. Now, according to the canonical texts, Sīhapura (i.e. Siṁhapura) was the birthplace of Śreyāṁsa, the eleventh Tīrthaṅkara. A few Jain scholars identify Sīhapura of the Jain canon with Siṁhapurī near Banaras. But it is more likely that Siṁhapura of Punjab is identical with Sīhapura of the Jain texts. Let us not forget that the

Jains deliberately selected cities af hoary antiquity as the birth-places of those Tīrthaṅkaras who never existed in reality. Siṁhapura was a town of great antiquity as we find it mentioned in connexion with Arjuna's *digvijaya* in the *Mahābhārata*[58] where it appears after the Trigartas, a well-known Punjab tribe. That Jainism reached Punjab by the third century B.C., is also indirectly proved by the fact that the *Therāvalī* refers to the Audambarikā *śākhā* which originated from Rohaṇa in the 3rd century B.C. This *śākhā* was evidently linked with the Audambaras, a well known Punjab tribe. It is therefore permissible to identify Siṁhapura of Yuan Chwang and the *Mahābhārata* with Sīhapura of the Jain texts.

Stein was successful in discovering a great number of Jain antiquities from Siṁhapura. That scholar is of the opinion that the Jain sculptures of Siṁhapura are of better execution than those of Ellora and Ankai. He further informs us that even at the time of his visit, this place was looked upon as sacred by the Jains[59]. The *Varāṅgacarita*[60], a work of the seventh century A.D., refers to Siṁhapura as sacred to Śreyāṁsa.

Let us once more turn our attention to Western India. We have already observed that by the third century B.C., Jainism became more or less popular in Gujarat. A stone inscription[61] of the second century A.D. of one of the grandsons of Jayadāman, the Śaka satrap, is definitely a Jain record for it contains the significant word *Kevalajñāna*. This inscription was discovered at Junagarh and it also refers to the town of Girinagara i.e. Girnar which according to the *Nāyādhammakahāo* and *Kalpa-sūtra* was associated with Neminātha. We have already taken note of the fact that Girnar was looked upon as a sacred hill by the Jains from a much earlier period. It has been suggested[62] that the inscription actually refers to the Samādhimaraṇa of the Digambara Jain saint Dharasena, the original author of the Digambara canon, who according to the tradition resided at Candraguphā of Girnar whence the inscription was discovered. But this is a pure conjecture and can be dismissed outright. In any case, the inscription proves that Jainism was introduced in this area in the early centuries of the Christian era, if not earlier.

The Jain antiquities discovered from Dhank and Bawa Pyara caves in Gujarat prove that these places were under the influence of Jainism in the early centuries of the Christian era[63]. The image of Ṛṣabha, Śānti and Pārśva from Dhank can easily be recognised. The typical Jain symbols from Bawa Pyara caves (Junagarh) are generally assigned to the early centuries of the Christian era[64].

Bhṛgukaccha, one of the oldest ports of India, which is identified with modern Broach in Gujarat, was a popular Jain centre in the early centuries of the christian era. The *Āvasyaka-niryukti*[65], which was not improbably composed around 200 A.D., refers to the defeat inflicted by a Śvetāmbara Jain monk Jinadeva on the two Buddhist monks *Bhadanta* Mitra and Kuṇāla at Bhṛgukaccha. This is also repeated in the *Āvaśyaka-cūrṇī*[66]. It appears that this famous port was a favourite haunt of monks of different schools. At least two Jain Vihāras existed at Bhṛgukaccha viz. Śakunikāvihāra and Mūlavasati about which we will have something more to say afterwards.

Emergence of the Digambara Sect : Although the Digambaras claim a hoary antiquity for their religion, it is a fact that no Digambara record before 300 A.D., has so far been discovered. The earliest Śvetāmbara work that refers to the formal separation of the Digambaras from the original Saṅgha is the *Āvaśyaka-niryukti*[67] (circa 200 A.D.). According to this work a monk called Śivabhūti, who was a disciple of the Śvetāmbara preceptor Kaṇha, founded the Boḍiya (i.e. Digambara) sect at a place called Rahavīrapura 609 years after Mahāvīra's Nirvāṇa. The *Uttarādhyayananiryukti* also refers to this schism. According to these texts Śivabhūti was the last *Niṇhava*. It is interesting to note that in the original Śvetāmbara canon[68] only seven *Niṇhavas* are mentioned, the last one being Goṣṭhamāhila, who founded his doctrine called Avaddhiya at the town of Daśapura 584 years offer Mahāvīra's death. The *Sthānāṅga* which refers to the seven rebels has no knowledge of the Digambaras and only in the Niryukti texts do we find references to them. We are not aware of any Digambara sacred work that could have been composed before the date suggested in the Niryukti texts regarding the formal separation of the two sects. The town of

Rahavīrapura, where Śivabhūti lived, cannot be properly identified, although it has been suggested that it was near Mathurā[69]. The evidence of the Śvetāmbara canon therefore suggests that the Digambaras formally separated only in the second century A.D. It appears that the Digambaras also indirectly support the tradition recorded in the Śvetāmbara commentaries[70]. According to them the original canon was forgotten after Lohācārya, who according to them died 565 years after Mahāvīra. It is interesting to note that Vimala's *Paumacariyaṁ* shows no acquaintance with the Digambaras; and this work was written according to its own testimony 530 years after Mahāvīra's Nirvāṇa.

However, the detailed and biased account regarding Śivabhūti given in the Śvetāmbara Cūrṇī texts can be dismissed offhand.

Now, the name Śivabhūti is not absent in early Digambara works. The *Bhāvapāhuḍa*[71], ascribed to Kundakunda, a work probably written around 300 A.D., refers to the monk Śivabhūti who is probably no other than the Śivabhūti of the Śvetāmbara commentaries. He is also mentioned in Devasena's *Ārādhanāsāra*[72], written in the tenth century A.D.

There is a Digambara tradition according to which Āryamaṅkhu was one of the original authors of the Digambara canon. This gentlemen is placed 683 years after Mahāvīra's death. We have already said that Maṅguhasti is mentioned in the Mathurā inscription of the year 52 corresponding to 130 A.D. We have further observed that this Maṅguhasti is to be identified with Maṅgu of the *Nandīsūtra*. The Śvetambara commentaries[73], it is very significant to note, gives an unfavourable picture of this saint. We are told that be was born as Yakkha after his death at Mathurā. The date given in the inscription, mentioned above, and the date given to Āryamaṅkhu in the Digambara tradition, support each other. Therefore it is permissible to believe that the second century Jain saint Maṅgu was one of the founders of the Digambara sect. This also indirectly confirms the Śvetāmbara evidence regarding the actual time when the Digambara formally separated. Therefore, the birth of the Digambara sect is to be placed around 150 A.D.

It has to be remembered that Pārśva allowed an under and an upper garment, while Mahāvīra forbade clothing altogether. This information we get in such an early text as the *Uttarādhyayana*[74] which was not improbably composed in the 4th century B.C. It seeems that from early times the Jain monks, according to their individual whims, indulged in both kinds of practices viz. wearing cloth or going about naked. These two modes of conduct were known as *Jinakalpa* and *Sthavirakalpa* respectively. Mahāvīra himself, as we have already noticed, discarded clothing altogether 13 months after he became an ascetic. But Pārśvanātha, whom we consider to be the real founder of Jainism, never went about naked. The *Bṛhatkalpabhāṣya*[75] further informs us that the doctrine of the first and last Tīrthaṅkaras was based on nudity (*ācelakka*), while that of intervening 22 Tīrthaṅkaras, allowed both nudity and wearing garments. Most of Mahāvīra's close followers naturally went about naked; but it seems that Mahāvīra himself never insisted on the strict observance of nudity. The *Āvaśyakacūrṇī*[76] refers to one Municanda who practised *Jinakalpa* and was considered a rebel by Mahāvīra. Regarding nudity the *Ācāraṅga*[77] says if a naked monk thought that he could bear the pricking of grass, cold and heat, stinging of flies and mosquitoes or any other painful things, he could leave his private parts uncovered; but when the number of articles in a monk's equipment increased and when the monks began staying more and more among the people, then he could cover his private parts with *kaṭibandha*. Afterwards the *kaṭibandha* was replaced by *colapaṭṭa*.[78]

The evidence of some Mathurā sculptures suggests that even the Śvetāmbaras sometimes represented their Tīrthaṅkaras as nude. So we need not be unduly perturbed it we come across nude Jina figures of pre-christian days. As a matter of fact, one of the early celebrated Jain teachers, viz. Mahāgiri, according to the *Āvaśyakacūrṇī* was an exponent of *Jinakalpa*, i.e. the doctrine of nudity. Suhastin, another great Śvetāmbara monk practised *Sthavirakalpa*. The evidence of that work further suggests that *Jinakalpa* continued upto Āryarakṣita.[79] It also appears that the Digambaras, who insisted on absolute nudity, continued the tradition of *Jinakalpa* monks and probably a rebel group under Śivabhūti finally raised the standard of rebellion and formed a new sect in the middle of the 2nd century A.D. However, we must confess that the mystery surrounding the birth of the Digambara sect has yet to be solved. We will have something more to see on this point in connexion with the discussion of the canonical literature of the Jains. We have also no comment to offer on the suggestion that Rathavīrapura (Rahavīrapura) was near Mathurā.

(B)

Jainism in the Gupta Period: All the available sources indicate that by the beginning of the 4th century A.D., Jainism became an all-India religion. Generally, however, in North India the Śvetāmbaras were predominant and in the south the Digambaras. We will, in this section, endeavour to give readers an idea of the condition of the Jain religion in North India in the Gupta period, and in doing so we will have to take the help of available epigraphic and literary sources.

Probably the earliest Jain inscriptions of this period come from the celebrated city of Vidiśā. We have two Jain image inscriptions both of which are now preserved in the local museum at Vidiśā.[80] These inscriptions are not only important for the history of Jainism but also for the political history of the Gupta period. Both these inscriptions refer to *Mahārājādhirāja Rāmagupta*. As the title indicates, this Rāmagupta was a paramount sovereign and not merely a local ruler. Coins of Rāmagupta are already known.[81] In the official Gupta records the name of Rāmagupta is understandably absent. The play *Devīcandragupta*[81a] of Viśākhadatta, which is preserved only in fragments, delineates Rāmagupta as the successor of Samudragupta and a weak monarch who did not hesitate to offer his wife to the Śaka king of Ujjayinī. His younger brother Candragupta, by a clever stratagem, succeeded in killing the Śaka king.[82] Afterwards, we are told, he also killed his brother and married his wife Dhruvadevī. The discovery of the Jain inscriptions prove that Rāmagupta is not a product of imagination but the actual successor of Samudragupta. We have already referred to his coins ; and now these inscriptions engraved on the pedestals of Puṣpadanta and Candraprabha show that he was responsible for the construction of those images of the Jain Tīrthaṅkaras. This he did on the advice of Celukṣamaṇa, the son of Golakyāntā and pupil of Ācārya Sarppasena Kṣamaṇa, the grand-pupil of Candra Kṣamācārya-kṣamaṇa-Śramaṇa, who was a *pāṇipātrika* i.e. one who used the hollows of his palms as alms and drinking-bowl. The celebrated Śivārya, the author of the *Bhagavatī-Ārādhanā*, as we will see afterwards, calls himself *pāṇidalabhoi*, which probably indicates that like him Candra was a Digambara monk.[82a] This inscription, therefore, proves that Rāmagupta had some genuine respect for the Jains. Characters of the inscriptions agree closely with that of Allahabad *Praśasti* and we are not aware of the existence of any other *Mahārājādhirāja* Rāmagupta of the 4th century A.D.

Another inscription[83] found from Udaygiri near Vidiśā and dated in the year 106 of the Gupta era corresponding to 426 A.D. of the reign of Kumāragupta refers to the erection of an image of Pārśva by Śaṅkara, a disciple of Gośarman, who was a disciple of Bhadrācārya of Āryakula. The inscriptions of the time of Rāmagupta, Kumāragupta's uncle, as we have already seen, proves the popularity of Jainism in the Vidiśā region. Śaṅkara, we further learn from the same inscription, was formerly a warrior but afterwards accepted the Jain religion. These inscriptions go far to prove that Vidiśā was a stronghold of Jainism and received royal patronage.

Literary evidences also prove the popularity of Jainism in the western part of modern Madhya Pradesh. The *Vasudeva-hiṇḍī*[84] a Jain text, based on the missing *Bṛhatkathā,* and probably composed in the 5th century A.D., distinctly refers to the temple of Jīyantasvāmin Mahāvīra at Ujjayinī. Discovery of a good number of Jain sculptures, belonging to the Gupta period, from different places of Madhya Pradesh also show that Jainism enjoyed some popularity in those places. They also indirectly prove the existence of Jain temples in the Gupta period in Madhya Pradesh. We have icons from Sira Pahari (near Nachna, Panna district), and also from Panna proper.[84A] We will discuss these icons in greater details, in a separate chapter of the next volume. A temple of Jīvaṁtasvāmin is also referred to in the Jain Commentaries.[85] In another Jain text of the 7th century we have a reference to an image of Jīyantasvāmin at Vidiśā. Daśapura (modern Mandsor, M.P.) also was a stronghold of Jainism. This is proved by the fact that Niṇhava Goṣṭhāmahila[86] established at this town an independent doctrine known as Abaddhiya 584 years after Mahāvīra's death i.e. in the 1st century A.D. Quite a good number of Śvetāmbara monks of the early 1st century A.D., we are told, were connected with Daśapura.[87] Tosaliputta who is mentioned in the *Āvaśyakaniryukti,* we are told, stayed at a park called Ucchughara at Daśapura. He had the knowledge of Diṭṭhivāya, the 12th Aṅga text. Rakkhiya, his famous disciple, spent his entire life at Daśapura. His younger brother Phaggurakkhiya, was also converted by him. Both Mahāgiri and Suhatthi visited Vidiśā in the early third century B.C. in order to pay homage to the image of Jīvantasvāmin there.[88] This shows that from early times different places of Madhya Pradesh were connected with Jainism. It appears that the Śvetāmbara monks belonging to Kauśāmbika *śākhā* were responsible for the propagation of Jainism in Madhya Pradesh. Afterwards we will see that in the post-Gupta period also Jainism was quite popular in that state.

An inscription[89] from Mathurā dated in the Gupta year 113 corresponding to 433 A.D. of the reign of *Paramabhaṭṭāraka, Mahārājādhirāja* Kumāragupta refers to an apparently prominent Jain monk called Datilācārya, who belonged to the Vidyādharī *śākhā* and Koḷiya *gaṇa.* A disciple of this monk named Sāmāḍhya built an image (*pratimā*) under the command of the said *guru.* The Vidyādharī *śākhā,* referred to here, is mentioned in the *Therāvalī* as Vijjāharī, which was apparently founded in the 3rd century B.C. This is the only epigraphic reference to this *śākhā* known to us.

Another inscription[90] from Mathurā and dated in the year 299 of an unknown era refers to the erection of an image of Mahāvīra and a temple (*devakula*) by Okhā, Sarika and Śivadinā. The inscription is in Sanskrit and if it is dated in the Kaniṣka era, it corresponds to 377 A.D. ; and this was the view of Bühler. But the peculiar Kuṣāṇa title *rājātirāja* given to the reigning king, whose name is missing, probably indicates that it should be referred to some earlier era.

We should take here a brief notice of the two Join councils held in the fourth century A.D., at Mathurā and Valabhī. The council at Mathurā was held under the presidentship of Khaṁḍila (Skandila) 827 years (or according to some 840 years) after Mahāvīra's Nirvāṇa. The earliest work that refers to this council is the *Nandīcurṇī*[91] composed in the 7th century A.D. Another council was held almost simultaneously at Valabhī under the presidentship of Nāgārjuna. According to commentators the canon compiled in the council of Mathurā was somewhat different from that compiled at Valabhī. The earliest Jain council, held at Pāṭaliputra in the last quarter of the 4th century B.C., will be discussed later in this book.

The next important Jain inscription belongs to the reign of Skandagupta. This inscription[92] has been found from Kahaum in Gorakhpur district, U.P. It is dated in the year 141 of the Gupta era corresponding to 461 A.D. of the tranquil (*śānte*) reign of Skandagupta. From this inscription we learn that this place was formerly called Kakubha (line 5). We are told of the setting up of 5 images (*pañcendra*) of Tīrthaṅkaras (probably Ādinātha, Śānti, Nemi, Pārśva and Mahāvīra) by a person called Madra, who traced his descent from one Somila, and who had equal respect for *dvija, guru* and *yati*. This inscription appears to be a Digambara record. There are traces of Jain shrines near the pillar bearing the inscription[93].

A copper plate inscription[94] of the Gupta year 159 from Paharpur, Bangladesh is one of the most interesting Jain records of the Gupta period. The inscription is incidently the earliest Jain record from Bengal. It records an endowment for the worship of Arhats to a *Vihāra* in Vaṭagohālī[95] near Paharpur, presided over by the disciples descended from the Nirgrantha *Ācārya* Guhanandin of Kāśī. This Guhanandin is further described as belonging to Pañcastūpanikāya. The persons who were responsible for the endowment were a Brahmin named Nāthaśarman and his wife Rāmī. The language of the inscription proves that this Brāhmaṇa pair were zealous devotees of

Guhanandin. It is apparent also from the same inscription that this Guhanandin flourished at least a century before the date of this inscription. We learn that it was originally founded by *śiṣyas* and *praśiṣyas* of Guhanandin. Probably this *vihāra* was built some 50 years before the date of this copper-plate. Guhanandin himself probably lived in the last quarter of the 4th century A.D. at Kāśī. In no Jain inscription before this date do we come across a Brāhmaṇa Jain devotee, although the canonical texts, as we have already noticed, mention quite a few Brahmin converts. The Jain Vihāra referred to above, according to the inscription, was situated in the Nāgiraṭṭa *maṇḍala* of Puṇḍravardhana *bhukti*.

The expression *Pañcastūpanikāya* is to be found in the non-canonical literature of the Digambaras. The great Vīrasena, the famous author of the *Dhavalā* and Jinasena, the author of the *Ādipurāṇa* belonged to the Pañcastūpanikāya sect[95a]. In Hariṣena's *Bṛhatkathākośa*[96] we have an account of the founding of five *stūpas* (*pañcastūpa*) at Mathurā. It is probable that the Digambara monks belonging to the Pañcastūpa sect of Mathurā afterwards sent a few of the members of their sect to different parts of India. It is also not unlikely that Vārāṇasī was the earliest seat of this particular sect. In any case, we have to regard Pañcastūpanikāya sect as one of the earliest branches of the Digambara school. In South Indian inscriptions also we come across Pañcastūpanikāya monks. The Paharpur inscription, therefore proves the early popularity of the Digambara religion in Bengal. We have already taken note of the fact that Bengal accepted Jainism long before any other state of India, and it appears that in the Gupta period the Digambaras succeeded in extending their sphere of influence in Bengal at the expense of the Śvetāmbaras.

An inscription[97] of early Gupta character near Śon Bhāṇḍār cave at the ancient town of Rājagṛha refers to a Jain Muni called Vairadeva who is given the epithet *ācāryaratna*. The lower half of a small naked Jina image still can be seen cut out of the rock close to the inscription. It has been suggested[98] that this Vairadeva is the same as Ārya Vajra of the *Āvaśyakaniryukti*[99]. Sten Konow suggested[100] that the cave referred to in the inscription was constructed in the 2nd-3rd century A.D. The expressions *ācārya* and *muni* probably show that it is a Digambara record and in that case, the suggested identification of Vairadeva with Vajra cannot be accepted. Further, the Digambara invariably preferred Sanskrit to Prakrit in all their early records, and this is the case with both Paharpur and Rajgir inscriptions.

Another small mutilated inscription[101] on a Neminātha figure in early Gupta script has been found from Rajgir. The image is fixed on a small ruined Jain temple at Vaibhāra hill and refers to *Mahārājādhirāja* Candra, who may be either Candragupta I or Candragupta II. This image of Neminātha in black basalt is one of the earliest Jina images of the Gupta period.

We have already referred to the Gupta inscription[102], noticed by Cunningham, in the ruins of Ahicchatra which mentions *Ācārya* Indranandin. This place, as we have already seen, was sacred to the Jains from a much earlier period.

The evidence[103] of the *Kuvalayamālā*, composed by Udyotanasūri in 700 Śaka (778 A.D.) shows that king Toramāna who ruled at the town of Pavvaiyā situated on the bank of the Candrabhāgā (Chenab) in the Uttarāpaṭha was a disciple of Harigupta Ācārya, born in the Gupta family. We are further told that the city could boast of a great number of scholars, apparently Jain *Sādhus*. This city cannot be properly identified, but it was certainly in Punjab. Harigupta, it is interesting to note, is described as a scion of the Gupta family. Toramāṇa is known from inscriptions[104] and coins and definitely ruled around 500 A.D. His *guru* Harigupta should be placed therefore in the 2nd half of the 5th century A.D. This Harigupta is further described as the *guru* of *Mahākavi* Devagupta who is apparently mentioned also in the *Mahāniśītha*[105]. It is interesting to note that quite a few Śvetāmbara *Ācāryas* had Gupta-ending names. The *Mahāniśītha*[106] refers to one Ravigupta, who should be placed in the 5th century. The *guru* of Agastyasimha, the author of the *Daśavaikālikacūrṇī* was Ṛṣigupta[107] who belonged to the Koliya *gaṇa* and Verasāmi *śākhā* and who could not have flourished later than 400 A.D.[108]

The evidence of the *Kuvalayamālā* therefore proves that a stern military conqueror like Toramāṇa had a soft corner for

Jainism and probably like Khāravela he embraced this religion during his old age. We have already seen that there were a few Jain pockets in Punjab from early times. The capital of Toramāṇa, Pavvaiya, which was situated on the Candrabhāgā was surely a Jain centre in the Gupta period like Siṁhapura. The inscription of Toramāṇa[169] from Kurā, Salt Range (Punjab, Pakistan) shows that Punjab was within the empire of Toramāṇa.

Jainism, as we have already noticed, was firmly established in Gujarat even before the Christian era. In the Gupta period, Gujarat undoubtedly was the chief centre of Jainism in India. This is indirectly proved by the fact that the Śvetāmbara canon was finally edited at Valabhī 980 or 993 years after Mahāvīra's Nirvāṇa. Two commentaries[110] of the *Kalpasūtra* refer to the council at Valabhī and the Digambara work the *Bṛhatkathākośa*[111] (931 A.D.) also allude to the Valabhī council. The council was held, according to the Jain commentators[112], during the rule of Dhruvasena of Ānandanagara which has been identified with Vadanagara in Northern Gujarat. We have already seen that an earlier council under Nāgārjuna was held at Valabhī in the 4th century A.D, which coincided with the Mathurā council.

Now Dhruvasena of the Jain commentators should be identified with the first king of that name who according to the inscriptions[113] ruled from at least the year 206 of the Gupta era to 226 of the same era. The Jain commentators further inform us that the *Kalpasūtra* was recited in the court of this king, on the sad occasion of the demise of his son. The Jain account is confirmed by inscriptions according to which the Maitraka-Valabhī ruler Dhruvasena I, like his elder brothers, was succeeded by his younger brother Dharapaṭṭa. This was evidently due to the fact that Dhruvasena had no son to succeed him after his death. The date given by the Jain commentators prove that this Dhruvasena (526 A.D. to 546 A.D) should be placed either 980 or 993 years after Mahāvīra's death which also directly shows that Lord Mahāvīra died only in the 2nd quarter of the 5th century B.C., and not earlier, as supposed by many Jain writers. But this we would like to discuss in a separate Appendix.

There is, however nothing to show that Dhruvasena himself

was inclined towards Jainism. Inscriptions[114] prove that he was a devout Vaiṣṇava and not a single king of this illustrious family is known to have befriended the Jains. A few royal members of this family are known to have patronised the Buddhists[115], the bitter rivals of the Śvetāmbara Jains. But Jainism continued to prosper in Gujarat in spite of the absence of royal patronage. An old manuscript of the *Viśeṣāvaśyakabhāṣya*[116] of Jinabhadragaṇi discovered in the Jaisalmer bhāṇḍār informs us that this work was composed at Valabhī in Śaka 531 (i.e. 609 A.D.) during the reign of Śilāditya. Now, the inscriptions of this king range between G.E. 286 and 290 (606 A.D. to 610 A.D.) and, therefore, there is no doubt that the date given in the manuscript is absolutely genuine. It further shows that Valabhī at that time was a stronghold of Jainism and probably the home-town of this famous Jain scholar. King Śilāditya is mentioned by Yuan Chwang[117] as having ruled 60 years before his time. Now, the latest known date of Śilāditya's father and predecessor Dharasena II is G.E. 270 (=590 A.D.) which shows that Yuan Chwang's '60' should be corrected as '50'.

There are other evidences to show that Jainism was in a flourishing condition during the rule of the Maitraka-Valabhī kings. The *Kuvalayamālā*[118] (Śaka 700=778 A.D.) distinctly refers to the fact that the grand-disciple of Devagupta viz. Yajñadatta who evidently flourished around 600 A.D., "adorned the Gurjara-deśa with Jain temples". The language of the colophon of this text directly shows the tremendous popularity of Jainism in both Gujarat and Rajasthan in the 6th and 7th centuries A.D. Quite a few Śvetāmbara images[119] have recently been discovered from the ruins of Valabhī which have been assigned to the 6th century A.D. It has also been suggested[120] that Jinabhadra Vācanācārya mentioned in a 6th-century image-inscription from Akota (Gujarat) is to be identified with Jinabhadragaṇi, the famous Jain scholar, who was probably a native of Valabhī. The *Vividhatīrthakalpa*[121] refers to the fact that there was a shrine dedicated to Candraprabha at Valabhī before its destruction by the Muslims in V. S. 845 (787 A.D.).[122]

The Digambara text, the Jain *Harivaṁśa,* which was completed in 783 A.D. at Vardhamāna (Vaḍavan, Gujarat) gives us the highly interesting information[123] that the work was commenced in the temple of Pārśva which was built by king Nanna. There is no doubt that this Nanna is identical with the king of the same name mentioned as *kaṭaccuri-kulaveśma-pradīpa* in 'the Mankani Inscription,[124] who definitely ruled in the last quarter of the 6th century A.D. in this part of Gujarat. The Kaṭaccuris and the Kalacuris were mainly Śaivas but the evidence of Digambara Jinasena shows, that at least one of its earlier members, had a catholic outlook, so far as religion is concerned. It is probable that the temple of Pārśva, built by Nanna was a Digambara shrine and in that case it should be looked upon as the earliest known Digambara temple of Gujarat. It should, however be remembered, that according to the Digambara tradition, the earliest canonical authors of this sect were connected with Girinagara.[125] It should further be pointed out that Digambara Divākara of Karṇāṭa country, according to the Śvetāmbaras,[126] was defeated and converted by Vṛddhavādī at Bhṛgukaccha.

Jinasena also refers to another Digambara temple, dedicated to Śāntinātha, at Doṣtaṭikā (near Girnar) where he completed his text in the Śaka year 705. This temple, too, was probably built a century or two before this date.

Rajasthan, as we have already noticed, was connected with Jainism from a much earlier period. However we have practically no Jain inscription or any other evidence to prove the connexion of this state with the Jain religion in the Gupta period. However, the evidence of the *Kuvalayamālā*[127] shows that Bhinnamāla (Bhinmal) was looked upon as a Jain place of pilgrimage in the 6th century A.D. It refers to the five temples of Agāsavaṇā which was also in Rajasthan. The Jain monks of Mathurā, who used to visit Gujarat in the early centuries of the Christian era, had to pass through Rajasthan. In the post-Gupta period, however, as we will see later, Rajasthan was very intimately connected with the Jain religion.

Discovery of Jain images[128] of the Gupta period from a few pockets of U.P. and Bihar prove its popularity in those places. We will discuss these sculptures in a separate chapter of the next volume of this work. However, we must refer to the beautiful Jain metal images of the Gupta period, discovered from Chausa,[129] Bhojpur district, Bihar. They are now preserved in the Patna museum.[130]

Quite a few places of modern Maharashtra state were connected with Jainism from early times. Literary[131] and archaeological [132] evidences show that Tagara, mentioned in the *Periplus*[133] was a popular Jain centre in the early centuries of the Christian era. That ancient city is now represented by Ter. A few scholars identify Tagara with Terāpura, mentioned in the *Bṛhatkathākośa*,[134] and assert that even in pre-Christian times the place was connected with Jainism. The *Vyavahārabhāsya*,[135] a text of the eighth century, informs us that *Vyavahāra* Dharma was established at Tagara by eight monks.

Discovery of Jain images from Ellora, Patur[136] of the Gupta period prove that Jainism was slowly emerging as an important religious sect in Maharashtra in the Gupta period. Śūrpāraka,[137] according to the Jain literary tradition, was connected with Jainism. Monks like Vajrasena, Samudra and Maṅgu visited Śūrpāraka.

We should refer, in this connexion, to the unique bronze Pārśvanātha,[138] assigned to the 1st century B.C. and now preserved in the Prince of Wales Museum, Bombay. This image reminds us of the celebrated Maurya image of Lohanipur (Bihar)[139] which has been accepted as the earliest Jina image of India. According to U.P. Shah this image of Bombay Museum bears close affinity in style with a terracotta figurine from Mohenjodaro.[140] The findspot of this image is not known; but it was surely found from some place of western India, where Jainism was introduced around 300 B.C.

In a number of pre-Christian and post-Christian non-Jain texts there are frequent references to the Jains. Bhāsa,[141] Subandhu[142] and Bāṇa[143] frequently refer to the Jains. It appears from Subandhu's *Vāsavadattā*[144] that the Digambara Jains were looked upon as the bitterest rivals of Hindu philosophers. This work was in existence in the early Gupta period and is mentioned by Bāṇa. The poet Bāṇa, had some regards for the Jains as one Jain Vīradeva was a childhood friend of this great writer.[145] Therefore, we can assign Vīradeva to the last quarter of the 6th century A.D. In the *Kādambarī*[146] Bāṇa openly praises the Jains for their magnanimity. References to the Jains in the *Bhāgavata,*[147] *Brahmāṇḍa*[148] etc. also indirectly show its popularity in the early Christian period.

Varāhamihira (early 6th century) refers to the mode of fashioning of Jina image in his *Bṛhatsaṁhitā.*[149] The later Pāli works of Ceylon also refer to the Jains.

Quite a good of number of Jain writers flourished in this period. Pādalipta, the author of the missing *Taraṅgavatī,* a Prakrit poem, probably composed in the Śātavāthana period,[150] was one of the earliest Jain poets. We have already referred to Vimala, who also flourished in the 1st century A.D. The *Vasudevahiṇḍī*[151] is surely a product of these Gupta period. Among Jain philosophers of North India of this period we may mention Vṛddhavādī, Mallavādi, Jinabhadragaṇi and others. We will have something more to say on them in a separate chapter of the present volume.

It should here be pointed out, that unlike Buddhism, the Jain religion did not receive any largescale princely patronage in its early career. The only exception was Khāravela, who also patronised Brāhmaṇical Hinduism. The Buddhists, on the other hand, did everything to befriend princes and potentates. However, Jainism appealed directly to the masses and gradually became popular in almost every part of India by the beginning of the Christian period.

NOTES

1 Edited, Jinavijaya, p. 86.
2 *EI,* Vol. II, pp. 242f. ; Sircar, *Select Inscriptions* etc., pp. 95ff.
3 See Raychaudhuri, PHAI, pp. 393f.
4 *EI,* Vol. II, pp. 242f.
5 *Sel. Ins.* etc., p. 96fn. 6.
6 See *Allahabad Gazetteer* (ed. H. R. Nevill), p. 263 ; see also *JRAS,* 1898, pp. 516ff.
7 See Cunningham *ASI,* Vol. 21, pp. 1-3.
8 See Watters, *On Yuan Chwang's Travels in India,* Vol. I, pp. 371f.
9 *ASIAR,* 1913-14. pp. 262ff ; also plates LXX, a, d, e.
10 *Loc. cit.*
11 See Nevill, *Allahabad Gazetteer,* p. 153.

12 Sailana edition, Vol. 5, p. 2402.

13 *ASIAR,* 1907-8, pp. 113ff.

14 See *JRAS,* 1908, p. 1102 and plate V.

15 See Vogel in *ASIAR,* 1907-8, pp. 115-16 ; and also Sir John Marshall in *JRAS,* 1908, pp. 1085-1120 ; see in this connexion *Annual Progress Report of the Superintendent of Archaeological Survey* (*N. Circle*) *for the year ending 1908,* p. 34.

16 P. 70.

17 (Ed. A. N. Upadhye), pp. 8 ; 348f.

18 P. 418 (Āgamodaya Samiti).

19 P. 14.

20 *Loc. cit.*

21 See Führer, *Prog. Rep. of the Epigraphical and Archaeological Branch N.W.P. and Oudh for 1891-92,* p. 3.

22 See R. D. Banerji, *EI,* Vol. X, p. 120 ; see also Lüders, *List,* No. 107d.

23 See *EI,* Vol. X, pp. 109f.

24 See *JRAS,* 1912, pp. 153 ff.

25 See 1891-2 report, pp. 3, 5 etc.

26 *Ibid.,* pp. 13-14 ; see also Smith in *JRAS,* 1903, pp. 7-11.

27 *EI,* Vol. X, p. 110.

28 *Ibid.,* p. 111.

29 *Ibid.,* pp. 115f.

30 *Ibid.,* p. 110.

31 *Ibid.,* p. 111.

32 *Ibid.,* p. 116.

33 See Lüders, *List,* No. 107d.

34 *AGI,* p. 413.

35 I. 137. 73.

36 *Nāyā,* 157 ; *Upā,* 35.

37 P. 2348.

38 (Sailana ed.), pp. 278ff.

39 (*SBE*), p. 80.

40 *Annual Report of the Superintendent of Hindu and Buddhist Monuments* (N. Circle), 1918-19, p. 4 ; see also *Jaina Siddhānta Bhāskara,* Vol. 5, pp. 84ff.

41 I. 70. 3.

42 *AGI,* pp. 424ff.

43 IV. 2. 80.

44 Com. on I. 3. 11.

45 See *Jaina Śilālehha Saṁgraha* (*Bhāratīya Jñānapīṭha*), Vol. V, p. 3.

46 Quite a few of the previous Buddhas are mentioned in the earlier part of the original Pāli canon; they were also known during the days of Aśoka.

47 See *ASI*, Vol. 16, p. 357.

48 P. 164.

49 *AGI*, pp. 21 ff; see also S. N. Majumdar's note in p. 671 of the same work.

50 *ASIAR*, 1914-15, p. 2.

51 See Sukthankar's note in *ASIAR*, 1914-15, pp. 39 ff.

52 Vs. 322.

53 Vol. I, p. 180.

54 P. 27.

55 See *Vienna Oriental Journal*, 1890, Vol. IV, pp. 80 ff., and 260 f.

56 *AGI*, pp. 142 fl.; for the criticism of Watters, see *Y.C.*, Vol. I, pp. 249 ff.

57 *Y.C.*, Vol. I, pp. 248 ff.

58 II. 27. 20.

59 *Vienna Oriental Journal*, pp. 80 ff.

60 Ed. A. N. Upadhye, 27, 82.

61 *EI*, Vol. 16, p. 241; Lüders, *List*, No. 966.

62 See Jain, J. P., *The Jaina sources of the History of Ancient India*, pp. 112-13.

63 See Sankalia, *Archaeology of Gujarat*, p. 53; pp. 166ff; also *JRAS*, 1938, pp. 427f; and plates III and IV; see also *NIA*, 1939, p. 563

64 Sankalia, *op. cit.*, pp. 166ff.

65 VS. 1299.

66 Vol. II, p. 201.

67 VS. 782.

68 *Sthānāṅga*, 587.

69 See Muni Kalyāṇavijaya, *Śramaṇa Bhagawan Mahāvīra*, (Hindi), pp. 292ff.

70 See *Bṛhatkathākośa*, 131. 69; see also Devasena, *Darśanasāra*.

71 VS. 53.

72 VS. 49.

73 See *Niś Cū*, Vol. II, pp. 125-26; *Āva Cū*, Vol. II, p. 80; also *Niś Bhā*, 3200.

74 (Sailana ed.) 23.13.

75 (Ed. Puṇyavijaya) VI. 6369 (p. 1681).

76 Vol. I, pp. 285-286, 291.

77 See *SBE*, Vol. 22, pp. 69-73.

78 See *Bṛhatkalpabhāṣya*, Vol. III, VS. 6964.

79 Pp. 406ff.

80 See *JOI*, Vol. XVIII, 1969, pp. 247-51 ; also *EI*, Vol. 38, pp. 46-49.

81 See *PHAI*, p. 553 ; also *The Classical Age*, pp. 17f.

82 See also *Harṣacarita* (Chowkhamba), pp. 354-55.

82A See *Jaina Art and Architecture* (ed. A. Ghosh), 1974, Vol. I, pp. 127f.

83 See *IA*, Vol. XI, p. 310 ; Kielhorn, *List*, No. 441.

83A Ghosh, A, *op cit.*, pp. 129f. ; see also *Anekānta* (Hindi), Vol. 15, pp. 222-3.

84 Part I, p, 61.

85 See *Āva Cū*, Vol. II, pp. 156-7.

86 *Sthā*, 587.

87 See *Prakrit Proper Names*, Vol. I, pp. 361-62.

88 *Ibid.*, Vol. II, p. 660.

89 See *EI*, Vol. II, No. XIV (39).

90 Lüders, No. 78 ; also *JRAS*, 1896, pp. 578f.

91 P. 8.

92 *CII*, Vol. III, p. 67 ; *Sel. Ins.*, pp. 316f. ; Bhandarkar, *List*, No. 1278.

93 See in this connexion *IHQ*, Vol. 28, pp. 298-300.

94 *EI*, Vol. 20 pp. 61ff ; Sel. *Ins.*, pp. 359ff. ; Bhandarkar, *List*, No. 2037.

95 See N. Premi, *Jaina Sāhitya aur itihāsa* (Hindi), pp. 127ff.

96 12. 132ff.

97 See Guérinot, *List*, No. 87 ; and also *ASIAR*, 1905-6, p. 98, fn. 1. See in this connexion T. Bloch, *A.R.* of *ASI* (Bengal circle), 1902, p. 16.

98 *JBORS*, Vol. 39 (1953), pp. 410-412.

99 VS. 769.

100 *ASIAR*, 1905-6, p. 166.

101 *Ibid.*, 1925-26, pp. 125f.

102 *ASI*, Vol. I, pp. 263ff.

103 See colophon of that text edited by A. N. Upadhye.

104 See *Sel. Ins.*, pp. 420ff. ; see also *EI*, Vol. I, pp. 239f.

105 See Jain, J. C, *Prakrit Sāhitya kā itihāsa*, p. 147.

106 *Loc. cit.*

107 Colophon, VS. 2.

108 See Punyavijaya's *Introd.* Vol. 6 of the *Bṛhatkalpasūtra.*

109 *Sel. Ins.*, pp. 422-ff.

110 Vinayavijaya, *Kalpasūtravṛtti*, p. 206; also the V*ṛtti* on the same text by Dharmasāgara, pp. 129-130.

111 131. 69.

112 See Vinayavijaya, *op. cit.*, pp. 1, 9, 201 and Dharmasāgara, *op. cit.*, 9, 130.

113 See Bhandarkar, *List,* Nos. 1293 and1308.

114 See Bhandarkar, *List,* No. 1293.

115 The lady Duddā, who was the sister's daughter of Dhruvasena I, was the foundress of a Buddhist convent at Valabhī (see Kielhorn, *List of Inscriptions of Northern India,* No. 460). She is mentioned in a large number of Valabhī inscriptions.

116 See *Jaina Sāhitya kā Bṛhad itihāsa,* (Varanasi), Vol. III, pp. 130ff. ; see also *Purātana Jaina vākya sūcī,* Introd., p. 145.

117, Watters, *op. cit.,* Vol. II, p. 242.

118 Colophon, VSS. 7-10.

119 See *Bulletin of the Prince of Wales Museum,* No. 1, p. 36 ; see also Shah, U.P., *Studies in Jaina Art, pl.,* XII. See in this connexion *Jaina Art and Architecture,* Vol. I, p. 135.

120 See *Lalit Kala* Nos. 1-2, p. 59 ; see also *Jaina Art and Architecture,* Vol. I, p. 138.

121 P. 29.

122 This is probably the exact date of the destruction of Valabhī by the Muslims. The last known date of Ṣilāditya VII, in whose reign the city was destroyed, is the Gupta year 447 (see Bhandarkar, *List,* No. 1375), corresponding to 767 A.D. Probably he reigned for a few years more and finally was overthrown by the Muslims. See also *Al-Bīrūnī's India,* Vol. I, p. 192. The story told by Al-bīrūnī is similar to that given by Jinabhadra. For some other views, see *The Classical Age,* pp. 150f.

123 66. 53.

124 *Imp. ins. Bar.* St. I, pp. 4ff. ; see also *The Classical Age,* p. 197.

125 See *Jaina sāhitya kā bṛhad itihāsa,* Vol. IV, p. 28 ; see also Introd. to *Saṭkhaṇḍāgama,* Vol. I by H. L. Jain.

126 *Vividhatīrthakalpa,* p. 88.

127 Colophon, VS. 6.

128 See *Jaina Art and Architecture,* Vol. I, pp. 131f ; see also p. 121.

129 *Ibid.,* pp. 124ff.

130 See *Patna Museum Catalogue of Antiquities,* ed. P. L. Gupta, pp. 116-17.

131 See *Prakrit Proper Names,* Vol. I, p. 332.

132 *ASIAR,* 1902-3, pp. 188, 195, 199, 204.

133 Edited Schoff, para 51.

134 Story No. 56. Terāpura, here, is however described as situated in the Ābhīra country, see VS. No. 52.

135 P. 3. 350.

136 *Prog. Rep. of ASI.* (W. India), 1901-2, p. 3 ; 1902-3, pp. 4-5.

137 See *Prakrit Proper Names,* Vol. II, pp. 863-63.

138 *Jaina Art and Architecture*, Vol. I, pp. 87f.
139 *Ibid.*, p. 71.
140 See *Bulletin of the Prince of Wales Museum*, Vol. 3, pp. 63-65.
141 See *Avimārakam*, 5th Act.
142 See *Vāsavadattā* (L. H. Gray), pp. 157, 174 etc.
143 *Kādambarī* (Chowkhamba), p. 160.
144 Pp. 157, 174 etc.
145 See *Harṣacarita* (Chowkhamba), p. 75.
146 P. 160.
147 V, chs. 4ff.
148 (Motilal Banarasidass, Delhi, 1973) p. 87 ; see also *Bhaviṣya*, I. 43.36.
149 57. 45.
150 See Jain, *Parkrit sāhitya kā itihāsa*, p. 377.
151 *Ibid.*, p. 381.

CHAPTER VIII

Jainism in South India

(Early Phase)

Before discussing the state of the Jain religion in different parts of South India we must, at the very outset, refer to an interesting passage[1] in the Buddhist *Mahāvaṁśa,* according to which the king Pāṇḍukābhaya constructed houses and temples for the Nigaṇṭha ascetics at Anurādhapura. We are told that this king built, at first, a house for Nigaṇṭha Jotiya, which was to the east of the cemetery. In that house there lived another Jain ascetic whose name is given as Giri. We are furher told that the same king built a temple for another Nigaṇṭha *Sādhu* called Kumbhaṇḍa. From the same chapter[2] of the *Mahāvaṁśa* we learn that Pāṇḍukābhaya also built dwellings for the Ājīvikas and other sects.

Now, Pāṇḍukābhaya is generally placed in the fourth century B.C. by competent authorities including Geiger,[3] and the evidence of this Pāli text proves the presence of Jain ascetics in Ceylon as early as the fourth century B.C. The *Mahāvaṁśa* is a work of the fifth century A.D.,[4] and its evidence cannot be easily brushed aside. We should also note that in the *Dīpavaṁśa,* which was composed a century earlier,[5] and which Buddhaghoṣa frequently quotes in his commentary on the *Kathāvatthu,* there is a reference to the same Nigaṇṭha Giri.[6] Thus the combined evidence of these two Pāli texts prove the presence of the Jains in Ceylon in the pre-Mauryan times. It is natural, therefore, to suppose that these Jains migrated to Ceylon from Tamil-speaking areas of South India. And once we accept this, we have to take it for granted that Jainism was more or less firmly established in the southernmost corners of the peninsula by the 4th century B.C.

In a previous chapter we endeavoured to show that Jainism

spread to Orissa within a few years of Mahāvīra's death. It appears that wandering Nirgrantha monks carried the message of Mahāvīra to Southern India, especially to the lands adjoining Bay of Bengal within a few decades of the demise of Lord Mahāvīra. Let us not forget than an ordinary Nirgrantha monk, who seldom cared for personal comfort, and who practically wandered about penniless, was not expected to be daunted by the hazards of a foreign land. The evidence of the Pāli texts, referred to above, indirectly shows that Jainism reached the land of the Tamils before the end of the fourth century B.C. In the earliest extant literature of the Tamils we have enough indications to prove that Jainism was popular in quite early times in the regions south of the Kāverī. It should here be emphasised that the Jain monks of Bengal and Orissa were responsible for the early propagation of Jainism in Tamil Nādu and not those of Karṇāṭaka, as is usually believed. The evidence of the Ceylonese texts and that of the Tamil Sangam poetry indicate that Jainism surely reached the Southern Dravidian areas in the pre-Mauryan period and certainly before its introduction in the modern Karṇāṭaka state. We have already observed that there is nothing to prove that the first Maurya emperor became a Jain *Sādhu* before his death and consequently the tradition regarding the migration of the Jains under Bhadrabāhu and Candragupta, recorded in the Digambara works, connot be accepted in the present state of our knowledge. And even if we accept the veracity of the Digambara tradition, we cannot say that the first group of the Jain *Sādhus* of Tamil Nadu and Kerala came from Karṇāṭaka. It appears exceedingly probable, and as will be shown later, that the Digambara Jains of the 2nd century A.D. from North India popularised Jainism in Karṇāṭaka. The Jain religion, that we find portrayed in the Sangam poetry, was the undivided Nirgrantha religion, propounded by Pārśva and Mahāvīra.

Regarding the chronology of the works of the Sangam period there is a great deal of controversy. According to a few scholars[7] these texts were composed after 400 A.D. But it should be remembered that the original Sangam texts do not apparently show any acquaintance with the Pallavas, who dominated the political scene of Southern India from the 3rd century A.D. The absence of the word *dīnāra* in the original Sangam texts is also significant. The historical geography, as gleaned from these texts, show that they refer to a period when Southern India had brisk and lively commercial intercourse with the outside world, particularly Rome and Alexandria. Lastly, we should refer to the well-known Gajabāhu (Tamil Kayavāgu) synchronism. In the *Śilappadikāram*[8], the Sangam epic, we are told, that king of Laṅkā Gajabāhu was a contemporary of its author, who was Ceral Ilango, the younger brother of the Cera king Senguṭṭuvan. Now, in the Ceylonese chronicles we have two Gajabāhus, the first of whom reigned in the 2nd century A.D.[9] The second Gajabāhu ruled only in the 12th century. And there is absolutely no doubt that the Tamil epic refers to the first Gajabāhu as a contemporary of the author of the *Śilappadikāram*. Further we are told, that the Pattani worship was introduced in Ceylon from Tamil country during that king's time. And we have traces of its worship even now in Ceylon. It follows therefore, that the two epics *Śilappadikāram* and *Maṇimekalai* written by two friends who were contemporaries of Gajabāhu I of Ceylon, are the products of the 2nd half of the 2nd century A.D. And, therefore, the information contained regarding Jainism in these two works, are referable to that time.

But before we discuss the evidence supplied regarding Jainism in these two epics, we must discuss the information contained in the two earlier Sangam texts, viz. the *Tolkāppiyam* and *Kural*.

The *Tolkāppivam*[10], a grammatical work of 1612 Sūtras, according to the Jains, was written by some Nirgrantha ascetic during the 2nd Sangam. Quite a few scholars have upheld the Jain contention that it was written by a member of that sect in the pre-Christian period[11]. It has been pointed out that in the prefatory verse of the text the author calls himself *padimayion* i.e. one who observes, according to the commentator, the Jain vow known as *padimai*[12]. In the section called *Marabiyal*, the *Tolkāppiyam* speaks of *Jīvas* with one sense, such as grass and trees, *Jīvas* with two senses, such as snails, *Jīvas* with three senses, such as ants, with four senses, such as crab, with five senses, such as higher animals and with six, such as human beings. This classification of *Jīvas* abundantly proves[13], that the author was perfectly at home with the traditional Jain classification of *Jīvas*. Such classification of *Jīvas* is also to be found in other Tamil Jain works like the *Nīlakeśi* and *Merumandiram*[14]. This grammatical text was written before the epics and should be placed between 100 B.C. and 50 A.D.[15] And if we accept this date, we have to assume that Jainism was not only in vogue in the Tamil-speaking areas of South India in the 1st century B.C., but it was firmly rooted in that country. We have already observed, on the evidence supplied by the *Dīpavaṁśa* and *Mahāvaṁśa* that Jainism reached the Southern Dravidian states and Ceylon by the 4th century B.C. We should also refer in this connexion, to another piece of information, supplied by the *Mahāvaṁśa*[16], according to which, during the reign of the Ceylonese king Vaṭṭagāmaṇi (29-17 B.C.), the Nirgrantha monastery of Anurādhapura was destroyed completely. It shows that Jainism, which was introduced in Ceylon, in the pre-Mauryan times, continued its existence there for roughly 300 years before yielding its ground to Buddhism.

The celebrated *Kural*[17], another Sangam work, is strongly claimed by the Jains, as a collection of the verses, composed by ancient Jain sages of the Tamil country. That this work was in existence before the Tamil epics is evident from the fact that the *Maṇimekalai*, a poem written just before the *Śilappadikāram*, quotes a verse from it. This work is mainly based on the concept of Ahiṁsā[18]. We have to remember that the Jain commentator of the *Nīlakeśi*, freely quotes from the *Kural*, and whenever he quotes, he introduces his quotation with the words 'as is mentioned in our scripture'. From this, it is clear, that the commentator considered this work as an important Jain scripture in Tamil[19]. Further, we have the evidence of the Tamil *Prabodhacandrodaya* where the Jain ascetic recites a verse from the *Kural* which praises Ahiṁsā[20]. This proves that even to the non-Jain author of the Tamil *Prabodhacandrodaya* the *Kural* was a Jain poem. Competent scholars like Kanakasabhai[21] and Chakravarti[22] also believe this poem to be a product of the Jain imagination. However, it should be remembered that the teaching of the *Kural* appealed to all sects, as it was based on some fundamental ethical principles. Since the *Maṇimekalai* quotes a verse from it, we can tentatively place the *Kural* in the 1st century A.D., if not earlier.

The most important Sangam work from the Jain point of view is undoubtedly the *Śilappadikāram*, one of the twin Tamil epics. This work, according to its internal testimony[23], was composed by Ceral Ilango, the younger brother of the king Śenguttuvan, who as we have already noticed, was a contemporary of the Ceylonese Gajabāhu, who flourished in the 2nd half of the 2nd century A.D.

From the poet's preface (*padikam*) of that text we learn that this work was composed at Vañji,[24] the capital of the Cera king. We are further told that the poet was then residing in the hermitage of Kaṇavāyil, which the commentator[25] explains as a Jain temple (*paḷḷi*). From the same work we learn[26] that an astrologer had predicted that Ilango would succeed his father in the Cera throne. Naturally, this prediction was not liked by his his elder brother Śenguṭṭuvan and the younger prince, in order to destroy the suspicion of his elder brother, went to the temple of Kuṇavāyil, which was situated near the eastern gate of Vañji and "standing before eminent saints (*pāṭiyor*) he renounced all thoughts of the burden of the earth in order to secure the kingship of the vast realms a far off and eternal bliss, incapable of approach by even the faculty of reason". It appears, therefore, that the author embraced Jainism in his advanced youth and was residing in a Jain temple near Vañji, when he wrote this epic. We further learn that he decided to write a poem, based on the life of Kovalan, the father of the heroine of the *Maṇimekalai*, the Buddhist epic, which was composed by his friend Sittalai Sāttanār.

Dikshitar, the English translator of the *Śilappadikāram*, refuses to believe[27] that Ilango was a Jain. It is true that the poem refers to a number of gods and goddesses like Śiva, Viṣṇu, Murugan, Durgā etc.[28] But quite a number of crucial passages of the text harp on the doctrine of Ahimsā; and there are lines of the text, which could only be written by devout Jains and none else. The concluding passage of the text abundantly proves that the poet was a dedicated Nirgrantha Muni and a believer in the doctrine of Karman.

The *Śilappadikāram* gives a very beautiful and useful account of the state of Jainism in the three Dravidian states of Cola, Pāṇḍya and Cera. Since this account was written by a poet of the 2nd century A.D., its evidence has tremendous value for the students of Tamil Jainism. We learn from this work that there were Jain shrines in the capitals of all these three kingdoms. At Kāveripattinam, which was the ancient capital of the Coḷas[29], there was a temple of the Nigrantha[30] (*niggantakoṭṭam*). It is most likely that this Kāveripattinam is the same as Khaberis Emporium mentioned by Ptolemy[31]. Apparently the same temple of the Nirgranthas is referred to elsewhere in this work[32] as built of stone. We are further told that the lay discriples of the city (*Śrāvakas*) were responsible for the construction of this temple, which was apparently built at a very high cost. The high-shining *śilātala* made of *candrakānta* (moonstone) of this temple has also been mentioned in this text[33]. In this connexion the poet tells us that a class of Jain asceics, who were known by the name of the Cāraṇārs used to visit this temple on certain occasions, which included the car-festival[34]. Now, we learn from other Jain texts that the car-festival was exceedingly popular among the devout Jains of North India. The earliest non-canonical North Indian Jain text that refers to this festival is Vimala's *Paumacariyaṁ*[34a], which describes the *Jina-ratha* festival. Decorated Jina images were placed on the chariots, which the devotees used to take out on certain occasions. The car-festival was popular among the Buddhists[35] and the Hindus.[36] Among the Jains the car-festival was associated with the observance of the elaborate Aṣṭāhnikā festival which was celebrated thrice a year (Āṣāḍha, Kārttika and Phālguna).[37] The reference to the car-festival in the *Śilappadikāram* shows the general popularity of Jainism among the masses. It further proves that, by the 2nd century A.D., Jainism became quite deep-rooted in the Cola country.

Regarding the Cāraṇārs, who used to visit the Nirgrantha temple of Kāveripattinam, we have to make here a few observations. So far, it appears, none has been able to explain clearly who were the Cāraṇārs referred to in this Tamil epic. According to the Aṅga text the *Sthānāṅga*[38] the Cāraṇas were one of the nine *gaṇas* directly under Mahāvīra. The *Vyavahāra-sūtra*[39] refers to them as monks with fifteen years' standing. The Prakrit Dictionary,[40] compiled by Pandit Hargovind Das explains *cāraṇa* as a group of Jain monks. It is tempting to connect these Cāraṇas with the Cāraṇa *gaṇa,* mentioned in the *Therāvalī,* which originated in the 3rd century B.C. But it has been shown that, *cāraṇa* there, is a mistake for *vāraṇa,* mentioned in the Mathurā inscriptions. The *Sthānāṅga* reference shows that the Cāraṇa monks were in existence even during Mahāvīra's time. It would not be a mistake to suppose that the Cāraṇas were the Jain counterparts of the Brāhmaṇical Parivrājakas. They used to wander all over the country, carrying with them the message of Pārśva and Mahāvīra. The *Vyavahārasūtra*[41] refers to a particular power possessed by such monks, which it calls by the name of *Cāraṇa-labdhi.* It further appears from another Jain text[42] that there was a work called *Cāraṇa-bhāvanā,* which was probably the sacred book of these monks. The work is now lost. Elsewhere in the Jain Āgamic literature the Cāraṇas are also mentioned.

The *Śilappadikāram*[43] delineates the Cāraṇārs as monks possessing the highest knowledge. They had the knowledge of the past, present and future. They had put aside attachment and anger. There is little doubt that these monks were responsible for the popularity of Jainism in South India, and it was because of their activities that even non-Jains became great admirers of the Jain religion.

Our epic also describes the temple of the Nirgranthas at Uraiyur called by the name Kandarapaḷḷi.[44] The temple was situated in an extensive grove adjoining Arangam (Śrīrangam) and the image of Arivan (probably Ādinātha), described as the first god, under the three umbrellas. The connexion of Aśoka tree with the Jain temple of this place is also significant. This tree was sacred to the Jain Tīrthaṅkara Mallinātha and there is a beautiful description of an Aśokan grove in the *Aupapātikasūtra.*[45]

We should also refer to the residence (*paḷḷi*) of the Jain nun Kavundi, which was not far from Kāveripattinam[46] on the northern bank of the Kāverī. This lady, we are told, was anxious to visit Madura in order to worship "Arivan by listening to Dharma, preached by the sinless saints, who have by their purity got rid of all their Adharma". This temple of Madura was also built of stone.[47] Another Sangam text of great antiquity viz. the *Maduraikkanchi*[48] gives a beautiful and graphic description of the big Nirgrantha temple of Madura. It runs thus "Nirgranthas crowd the cloisters of the monks of their saints, the walls of which are exceedingly high, and painted red, and are surrounded by pretty, little flower-gardens". This shows that this particular Jain temple of the great city of Madura was built at a very high cost and was obviously a remarkable shrine of that ancient city.

We have already referred to the Nirgrantha shrine of Vañji, which was near the eastern gate of that city and which was the residence of the author of this text. This shows that Jainism was not only popular in the Cola and Pāṇḍya kingdoms, but also Kerala. Vañji has been identified with a place not far from the present Cochin and it was like Madura and Kāveri-pattinam a very ancient city.

The *Śilappadikāram* also throws welcome light on the Jain nuns of South India of those days. Among the equipments of Kavundi, [49] mention is made of begging bowl and peacock-feathers, which are still used by the Jain nuns everywhere. This shows that the life led by the nuns was not much different from that of the present day. Kavundi's hunger for knowledge and respect for the Cāraṇārs mark her as a remarkably august personality. Her affection for the heroine (Kannaki) makes her a character of flesh and blood.

This epic refers to the five types of Jain monks[50] viz. Arhat, Siddha, Ācārya, Upādhyāya and Sādhu. Arivan is described as the 'bestower of Aṅga'[51] which implies that the Jain literature was perfectly well-known at that time in South India.

We have tried to give readers some idea regarding the condition of the Jain religion in S. India as revealed in this celebrated Tamil epic. However, it should not be supposed that the poet, being a Jain, has given only a picture of his religion in this work. He has equal respect for all religious sects and his descriptions of gods and goddesses including Viṣṇu,[52] Durgā[53] are equally attractive. His acquaintance with the theistic Hinduism[54] and Vedic Brāhmaṇism are also deep and intimate. Let us not forget that the author, being a prince, was taught almost every branch of learning in his youth, before he became a Nirgrantha ascetic. This is the reason why he has been able to display such amazing knowledge regarding other sects in this immensely readable epic. He also knows the Ājīvikas.[55] But, again and again, he returns to his favourite theme viz. the glorification of the philisophy of *karman*[56] and non- injury.[57] The hero Kovalan,[58] it appears, led the life of a pious Jain *śrāvaka*, avoiding meat-eating and taking food in the day-time.

From the Buddhist epic *Maṇimekalai*[59] written by Sattanar in the 2nd century A.D., we also get some information about the Jains in South India. Since it is a poem, written by an oponent of Jainism, it is but natural that the Jains will be unfavourably painted here. In the 1st canto we find a drunkard ridiculing a Nirgrantha ascetic with these words—"welcome, thou reverend sir, I worship thy feet. Pray listen to me. The soul which dwells in thy unclean body pines like a prisoner confined in a close cell. Drink, therefore, of this toddy, which is drawn by the spathe of the cocoanut palm, and which will give pleasure both in this world and see if my words are true".[60] We will afterwards see that in the *Mattavilāsaprahasana* also the Jains are ridiculed for their uncleanliness. However, elsewhere in the *Maṇimekalai,*[61] it appears, the poet has tried to give a correct account of the Jain philosophy. Since the passage is extremely interesting, we are quoting it in full "He (Nigeṇṭa) said that his god is worshipped by Indras : and that the Book revealed by him describes the following : the wheel of Law, the axle of Law, Time, Ether, Eternal atom, good deeds, bad deeds, the bonds created by these deeds and the way to obtain release from these bonds. Things by their own nature or by the nature of other objects to which are they are attached are temporary or everlasting. Within the short period of *kṣaṇa* (second) they may pass through the three unavoidable stages, appearance, existence and dissolution. That a margosa tree sprouts and grows is eternal: that it does not posseses that property is temporary. Green gram when made into a sweetmeat with other ingredients does not lose its nature, but loses its form. The wheel of Law (*Dharma*) pervades everywhere and moves all things in order and for ever. In the same way the axle of law retains everything (and prevents dissolution). Time may be divided into seconds or extend to Eons. Ether expands and gives room for everything. The soul entering a body will through the five senses, taste, smell, touch, hear and see. An atom may become a body or assume other forms. To stop the origin of good or evil deeds, and to enjoy the effect of past deeds, and to cut off all bonds of release (is salvation)".

The above summary of the Jain philosophy given in this 2nd-century Buddhist Tamil poem reminds us of the similar account given in the *Dīgha Nikāya.*[62] A similar account is given about the philosophy of the Ājīvikas.[63] However a far more intimate and affectionate picture of the Arhat or Tīrthaṅkara is given in the *Śilappadikāram,*[64] which is reproduced here in full: "The All-knowing, the incarnation of Dharma. He who has transcended all limit of understanding, All-Merciful, victor among victors, the accomplisher, the adorable one, the origin of dharma, the overlord, absolute righteousness, the essence, the holy one, the ancient one, the all-wise, the vanquisher of wrath, the master, the Śiva-gati, supreme leader, the exalted one, the possessor of all virtues, the transcendental light, the great truth, the all-god, the supernatural sage (*Cāraṇar*), the root cause of all, the master of mysterious powers (*siddan*), the paramount one, the infinitely radiant illumination, the dweller in everything, the *guru,* the embodiment of nature, our great god, the abode of never-diminishing eminence, the emperor of virtues, the Śaṅkaran, the Caturmukha, the Īśan, the Svayambhū, the bestower of Aṅgas, the Arhat, the ascetic of grace, the one-god, the master of eight attributes, the indivisible eternal substance, the dweller in the heaven, the foremost of the Vedas, and the shining light that dispels ignorance. None can escape the prison of this body unless he obtains the illumination of the revealed Veda, proclaimed by him, who has the various above-mentioned names".

We have already pointed out that the poet of the *Śilappa-dikāram* was a man of wide vision end extensive learning. This is the reason why in the above description of the Tīrthaṅkara he has used epithets which are found in the description of Brahman or Śiva in the Hindu mythology.

Let us turn our attention to some of the places of Tamil Nadu and Kerala connected with Jainism from the earliest times. The above discussion has abundantly shown the popularity of the Jain religon in the three southern kingdoms of Cola, Pāṇḍya and Cera. A very good number of places associated with the Jain religion and culture from different parts of these states have been discovered. Although the inscriptions discovered from these Jain holy places are of somewhat later date (mostly after the 7th century A.D.), there is little doubt that most of these places were associated with Jainism from a much earlier period. We have early Brāhmī inscriptions datable from 3rd century B.C. and 1st century A.D., which have been discovered from the hills connected with Jainism in Tamil Nadu and Kerala. These Brāhmī inscriptions have not yet been properly read and therefore their contents continue to baffle researchers. Quite a few of them possibly contain the earliest specimens of the Tamil language, but most of them are a curious mixture of regional Prakrit and Tamil. Further, all these epigraphs contain only a few words, which is the reason why we have not been able to do full justice to them.

Let us first turn our attention to the Jain sites of Tamil Nadu. The present Madura district, it appears, was the most important stronghold of the Jain religion in this state. We have already seen that according to the Sangam literatury texts Madura was noted for its Jain temples and large number of lay devotees. We must not forget that as a result of religious persecution, almost all the Jain shrines of Madura city, disappeared in course of time. The exceedingly high red walls of Jain monasteries, referred to in the *Maduraikkanchi,* are now things of the past. But in other places of the district, an unusally large number of sites (particularly in the hills) are known to contain Jain relics. Among these sites the following may be mentioned here in alphabetical order—Aivarmalai, Alagarmalai,

Anaimalai, Karungālakkudi, Kilolavu, Kongar—Puliyangulam, Muttupatti, Poygaimalai, Seṭṭipoḍanu and Utamapalai. This list of Jain sites in Madura district, is by no means, exhaustive. We should also note that majority of these sites are situated on hills.

Aivarmalai is nine miles from Palni and is 1402 feet above the sea-level.[65] The hill here, according to the tradition, was associated with the Pāṇḍavas. Such traditions are common everywhere in India. On the north-east side of a natural shelter of the hill, which is 160 feet long and 13 feet high, we have 16 images of Tīrthaṅkaras. A number of inscriptions have been discovered from this place and they will be discussed in the Xth chapter of this work.

The range of hills known as Alagarmalai[66] is some 12 miles North-west of Madura. Brāhmī inscriptions, assignable to the 2nd century B.C., have been discovered from the Pillow side of the stone-beds in a cavern of the hill, which were obviously used by the ascetics who lived there. Since the later inscriptions, found in the same cavern, associate the place with Jainism, it is permissible to conjecture that the Nirgrantha *sādhus* used the stone-beds in pre-Christian times and the Brāhmī inscriptions were caused to be inscribed by them. It has further been surmised[67] that the natural caves formed by the overhanging rocks with plain walls and vaulted roofs were provided with wooden facades in pre-Christian period. We have already observed that the Jain ascetics of pre-Christian times led a very simple, almost a hard life and usually avoided populous towns and villages. It is also reasonable to conjecture that the Cāraṇas, referred to in the Sangam texts, were the monks who inhabited such caverns.

Anaimalai or the elephant hill, which is six miles east of Madura, is "the most striking mass of perfectly naked solid rock".[68] It is about two miles long, a quarter of a mile wide and 250 feet high. It bears a fair resemblance to an elephant lying down. On a big boulder of this hill we have a series of sculptures representing the Tīrthaṅkaras. The overhanging portions of the boulder form a sort of natural cave which was probably used by the Jain monks. There are signs of rude walls. In front of the cave there is a rock-platform, which commands the most beautiful view across the green fields. The Jain ascetics, it appears, had an eye for the picturesque[69]. It is reasonable to surmise that the lay devotees of the city of Madura, used to supply necessary articles for living to the venerable monks living there. This cavern is still known as Śamanar Kovil or temple of the Jain *munis*. We will in a later chapter discuss the inscriptions of this cavern.

Karungālakkuḍi, another Pañcapāṇḍava hill is known for its ancient cavern and Brāhmī inscriptions[70]. In later period also this hill was inhabited by the Jain ascetics. Kilalavu[71] is also a hill-site situtated in the Melur tāluk of Madura district. This hill contains a very large number of stony beds, carefully sheltered, indicating a big settlement of ascetics in the earlier period. Other details regarding this site will be discussed afterwards.

Kongar-Puḷiyanguḷam[72] is another hill site with rock-cut beds in the Tirumangalam Taluk of Madura. There is an interesting image here of the great Jain saint Ajjanandi about whom we will have something more to say afterwards.

Muttupatti[73] is the name of a village in the Nilakkottai taluk where we have a huge overhanging boulder that has a few ancient stone-beds and Brāhmī inscriptions. A number of later inscriptions, found from this site, will be discussed elsewhere.

Poygaimalai[74] is eleven miles to the west of Tirumangalam in Madura district. In a natural cave of this hill are carved in relief a series of Jina sculptures. The hill is popularly known as Samanar Kovil or the Jain temple.

Seṭṭipoḍavu[75] (meaning 'the hollow of the eminent merchant') is an extremely interesting cavern near Kilakkudi, a village in Madura taluk. It was surely a very popular Jain resort from early times. A good number of interesting inscriptions have been found from this place. These inscriptions supply us with important information regarding the Jain religion of later times; all these things will be discussed in a later chapter. Uttamapalai[76] is a Jain site in Periyakulan taluk and has several interesting inscriptions.

In the district of Tinnevelly there was an extremely important stronghold of the Jain faith in a place now called Kalugamalai.[77] This hill has treasured natural caverns with beds and inscriptions in Brāhmī characters. A very good number of later Jain inscriptions and sculptures have also been found from this hill.

Among other celebrated Jain sites of Tamil Nadu the following may be mentioned—Pāṭalipura[78] (South Arcot), Colavāṇḍipuram[79] (South Arcot), Pañcapāṇḍavamalai[80] (N. Arcot). In the former Pudukkottai state, now included in Tamil Nadu, we have the following interesting Jain sites—Śittannavaśal[81], Nārttāmalai[82], Āluruttimalai[83], Bommamalai[84], Melamalai[85], Tenimalai[86], Cheṭṭipaṭṭi[87] etc.

A number of sites in modern Kerala connected with Jainism have been discovered. We have already taken note of the fact that according to the *Śilappadikāram* there was a well known Jain monastery near the Cera capital Vañji. Tiruccānttumalai[88] also known as the hill of the Cāraṇas near Chitaral in this state was a famous Jain centre of pilgrimage in ancient times. The temple is now known as the shrine of Bhagavatī, but the icons here abundantly prove that it was a Jain centre. In the natural cave on the top of the hill have beautiful Jain sculptures and inscriptions from 8th to 10th century A.D., which will be discussed afterwards. Jain sculptures and inscriptions have also been discovered from Nagarkoyil[89].

Let us turn our attention to the state of Jainism during the days of the Pallavas. The Pallavas, as is well known, were Brāhmaṇical Hindus. But there are indications that during the reign of the Pallavas, Jainism remained one of the dominant religious systems and more than one royal member of the dynasty favoured the monks belonging to this sect.

The first notable event in the history of Jainism in the post-Sangam period was the establishment of Drāviḍa Saṅgha by Vajranandin at Dakṣiṇa-Mathurā, 526 years after king Vikrama. This information is supplied by Digambara Devasena in his *Darśanasāra*[90] composed in 990 V.S. or 933 A.D. Therefore according to Devasena Drāviḍa Saṅgha was founded in 464 A.D. at Madura, which as we have already seen, was intimately connected with the Jain religion. A few years before this date, of the town of Pāṭalikā in Pāṇarāṣṭra[91] in Śaka 380 i.e. 458 A.D., the Digambara *Lokavibhāga* was composed by Sarvanandin in the 22nd year of Siṁhavarman, the king of Kāñcī. We have already referred to the place called Pāṭalipura in South Arcot which is generally identified with Pāṭalikā of Sarvanandin. These two important evidences directly prove that Jainism was in flourishing condition in the 5th century during the Pallava rule in South India. It should here be mentioned that the chronological evidence regarding the beginning of Siṁhavarman's rule, supplied by the *Lokavibhāga*, has greatly helped scholars to reconstruct early Pallava history.

Turning now to inscriptions before 600 A.D., we find there are at least two where a royal member of the dynasty of the Pallavas is associated with the Jain religion. The first inscription[92] dated in 6th year of Siṁhavarman II, father of Siṁhaviṣṇu and grandfather of Mahendravarman, was discovered a few years ago. The great importance of this inscription can hardly be overemphasised. It records the grant of a village to the Jain sage Vajranandin of Nandi Saṅgha at Vardhamāneśvara Tīrtha for conducting the worship of Lord Jina. Since this Siṁhavarman was the grand-father of Mahendravarman, this inscription should be placed around circa 550 A.D.[93] It also refers to his son Siṁhaviṣṇu, who is described as the conqueror of the Cola country and at whose request the grant was made. The grant is partly in Sanskrit and partly in Tamil. Incidentally, this record contains one of the earliest specimens of epigraphic Tamil.[94] From the Tamil portion we learn that the land regarding the grant was at a place called Paruttikkanru which is a locality near Kanchi. Narabhaya, the minister figures as the *ājñāpati* of the grant. The same Siṁhaviṣṇu, who is here depicted as a patron of Jainism, appears elsewhere[95] as a devotee of Viṣṇu.

The reference to Vardhamāneśvara Tīrtha is of great significance. It proves the existence of a sacred Jain place near Kanchi, named after the last Jain Tīrthaṅkara. It is tempting to identify this Tīrtha with the celebrated Jina-Kāñcī. But this remains only a suggestion for the time being.

Another member of the early Pallava royal family appears in a Western Gaṅga inscription of the 12th year of the reign of

Avinīta[96], discovered from Hoskote (Bangalore district, Karnatak) as a patroness of the Jain religion. We are told in this inscription that a *devāyatana*, dedicated to Arhats, was constructed by the mother (*jananī*) of the Pallava overlord (*adhirāja*) Siṁhaviṣṇu at the village of Pulligere in Korikunda division (*bhāge*). We further learn that this temple was meant for the use of the monks of Yāvanīka Saṅgha (i.e. Yāpanīya Saṅgha). But the most crucial passage of the inscription is that which refers to the fact that the lady (viz. the mother of Siṁhaviṣṇu) constructed the Jina temple with a view to enhance the glory of her husband's family (*bhartṛkulakīrtijananyārtham*) viz. the Pallavas. Her husband was evidently Siṁhavarman II of the Pallava inscription, referred to above. It further shows that, not only the royal lady herself (cf. *ātmanaśca dharmapravardhanārtham*), but also the members of husband's family had soft corner for the Jain religion. This inscription is to be placed in circa 560 A.D. according to our calculation.

The above discussion shows that the Pallavas, in spite of their weakness for traditional Hinduism, had great deference for the Jains. Let us not forget that, long before the emergence of the Pallavas as a political power, the Jains had carved for themselves a permanent place in the religious life of South India.

Jainism in Karṇāṭaka and Andhra :

Let us now turn our attention to Karṇāṭaka which from pretty early period produced some of the remarkable Jain saints. We have already opined that the tradition regarding the migration of the Jains under Bhadrabāhu and Candragupta cannot be accepted at the present state of our knowledge. Further, the earliest author that refers to Candragupta's conversion to Jainism is Yativṛṣabha, the author of the *Tiloyapaṇṇati* (early 7th century), who lived nearly 1000 years after Candragupta Maurya. Śravaṇa Belgola, which according to the tradition, was the place of Candragupta's death, has not produced any inscription which can be dated before 600 A.D.

The Western Gaṅgas, who ruled in Southern Karṇāṭaka

from the middle of the 4th century A.D., were great patrons of the Jain religion and culture from the very beginning of their history. The earlier speculations [97] regarding the beginning of the Western Gaṅga rule have now been proved wrong. The Penukonda plates[98] of Mādhava II (sometimes called Mādhava III), which were accepted as genuine even by Fleet, and which had been assigned to circa 475 A.D. by him, refers to a number of his predecessors. The founder Koṅkaṇivarman (Mādhava I) should be placed in the middle of the 4th century A.D. This is also confirmed by the fact that the third king Āryavarman or Harivarman was installed in his throne by his Pallava overlord Siṁhavarman I, who according to the *Lokavibhāga* ascended the throne in 436 A.D.

According to later records the earliest king Koṅkaṇivarman Mādhāva, who came from the North was helped by a great Jain saint called Siṁhanandi Ācārya in his attempt to carve out an independent kingdom in the South. The earliest record that refers to the help rendered by a Jain to Koṅkaṇivarman is a damaged copper plate of the reign of Śivamāra I (670-713 A.D.) which clearly states that at a suggestion of a Jain teacher Koṅkaṇivarman had cut down a stone pillar.[99] However, in the earlier copper plates of the dynasty no Jain teacher is connected with this valiant feat of the founder of the dynasty. Another inscription viz. the Udayendiran grant of Hastimalla dated circa 920 A.D. tells us that the Gaṅga family prospered because of Siṁhanandi's help.[100] A third inscription dated Śaka 884 of the reign of Mārasiṁha[101] also refers to this fact and the valiant feat of cutting asunder a great stone pillar gy Koṅkaṇivarman. A fourth inscription[102] of the eleventh century (dated A.D. 1077) gives the same information regarding Siṁhanandi's act and his contribution to the establishment of the Gaṅga empire. However the most beautiful and detailed account regarding Siṁhnandi's achievement is given in a long lithic record[103] found from Shimoga district of Karṇāṭaka, dated Śaka 1043 (1121 A.D.). From this account we learn that the two sons of one king Padmanābha called Daḍiga and Mādhava, who came from North in search of fortune, found a beautiful spot in an extensive place (now located in Cuddapah district, Andhra Pradesh) and there they saw a Jain temple (*caityālaya*) and in that shrine they met Siṁhanandi Ācārya, the sun of the Krāṇura *gaṇa,* who is directly called in the inscription 'the promoter of the Gaṅga kingdom' (*Gaṅga-rājya-samuddharaṇam*), who accepted them as his disciples. We are further told that the Jain saint gave the brothers a sword (*khaḍga*) and a whole kingdom. Mādhava, one of the brothers, being so honoured, cut down a stone-pillar[104] with his sword, which promted Siṁhanandi to make a crown from the petals of the *karṇikāra* blossom and place it on the heads of the brothers. He further gave them his peacock fan as their banner and in due course provided them with an army. This inscription also records the advice which that *munipati* gave to those two brothers "If you fail in what you promise, *if you dissent from the Jain śāsana,*[105] if you take the wives of others, if you are addicted to spirits or flesh (*madhumāṁsa*), if you associate with the base, if you give not to the needy, if you flee in battle, your race will go to ruin".

Thus with Nandagiri as their fort (*koṭa*), Kuvalāla (Kolar) as their city and Gaṅgavāḍi as their kingdom and *Jinamata* as their faith, the two brothers Daḍiga and Mādhava ruled their kingdom.

The account contained in the above-mentioned stone is more or less legendary. But as we have already noted, the connexion of Jain Siṁhanandi with the foundation of the Gaṅga kingdom is known from other sources. Its account regarding the earlier history of the Gaṅga dynasty can be dismissed off-hand. Its attempt to make Padmanābha, the father of the two brothers (Daḍiga and Mādhava) is, to say the least, ridiculous. We know from the early and genuine Gaṅga copper plates including Penukonda that Padmanābha is the deity addressed in the first line of those records. Padmanābha, is a popular name of Viṣṇu, although according to the Jains,[106] Padmanābha is the first Arhat of the future age. It is, however, most likely that by the word '*Padmanābha*' lord Viṣṇu is meant in the Gaṅga inscriptions.

Siṁhanandi's connexion with the founder of the Gaṅga dynasty is also confirmed by an old commentary of the *Gommaṭasāra.*[107] It thus appears to be a historical fact that

Mādhava I Koṅkaṇivarman, who founded the Western Gaṅga kingdom in the middle of the 4th century A.D., owes his success to the activities of a Jain saint. But there is no direct evidence to prove that Mādhava I himself became a Jain convert. Further, an overwhelming majority of early Western Gaṅga inscriptions are grants made to Brāhmaṇas and other non-Jains. It appears, however, that the Western Gaṅga monarchs beginning from the founder of the dynasty, had special love for Jainism, although no Jain record, belonging to the reign of first few Gaṅga kings, has been yet discovered.

The first king of this dynasty of whose reign we have definite Jain records is Mādhava III (sometimes called Mādhava II). One inscription[108] of his reign has been discovered from Nonamangala (Kolar district). This inscription is dated in the 13th year of his reign. As is well known, his undated Penukonda plate inscription[109] is assigned to circa 475 A.D. by Fleet. That inscription further informs us that he was installed in the throne by his Pallava overlord Skandavarman, the son of Siṁhavarman I. So we have to assign Mādhava III to the last quarter of the 5th century A D. This inscription discloses the name of Ācārya Vīradeva and refers to a Jain temple erected by the monks of the Mūlasaṅgha at Pebbolala *grāma* of Mudukottūra *viṣaya*. The temple was apparently situated in the Kolar district of Karṇāṭaka. The king Mādhava, we are told, granted to this temple the village of Kumārapura along with some other lands which were apparently situated near the village. It is apparent that the temple, mentioned here, was built before the 5th century A.D., the date of this inscription; but how long before, we cannot guess. The epithets bestowed on the Jain *guru* Vīradeva prove that he was held in highest esteem by Mādhava III. If is also interesting to note that the grant was made in the bright fortnight of Phālguna, which is the time for the great Aṣṭāhnikā festival. Mādhava III, however, in spite of his fondness for the Jain religion, was a tolerant king, as is evident from his grants made to other religious sects including the Buddhists.[110]

The next king Avinīta Koṅkaṇivarman had a long rule and may be assigned to the 1st half of the 6th century A.D. Three inscriptions of his reign are Jain grants, although the genuineness of one has been doubted. The earliest is a Nonamangala (Kolar district) grant,[111] dated in the first year of his reign. We are told that the king, on the advice of his preceptor *parama arhat* Vijayakīrti 'whose fame had pervaded all regions' granted land to the Uranur Arhat temple which was established by Candranandin and others. The same inscription refers to another Jain temple called Perur Evāṇi Adigal Arhat temple. Both these temples were apparently situated in the Kolar district. It is interesting to note that the Jain saint Vijayakīrti in this inscription is represented as the preceptor (*upādhyāya*) of the king. Ācārya Candranandin of Mūlasaṅgha apparently flourished before Ācārya Vijayakīrti.

The second Jain grant of king Avinīta is dated in the 12th year of his reign.[112] This inscription was discovered from Hoskote (Bangalore district, Karṇāṭaka). It records the grant of land to a Jain temple at Pulli-ura village of Korikunda-bhāga. We have already noticed this inscription in connexion with Pallava Siṁhaviṣṇu. The reference to the well-known Yāpanīya Saṅgha is quite interesting. This inscription and the inscription, noticed above, show Avinīta's close and intimate relationship with the Digambara Jains of various groups. This inscription, as we have already noticed, proves the contemporaneity of Pallava Simhaviṣṇu and Gaṅga Avinīta and is therefore of great historical importance. However, there are reasons to believe, and as will be shown elsewhere, Avinīta was a senior contemporary of Siṁhaviṣṇu.

The third Jain inscription[113] of the reign of Avinīta is now the property of the Lutheral Museum, Basel (Switzerland). It refers to Koṅguṇimahādhirāja Avinīta and also gives the date Śaka 388. It was found in the Mercara treasury (Coorg district, Karṇāṭaka). But the inscription is clearly a later forgery as is evident from the details given regarding the date and *nakṣatra* and also the script which is clearly of 8th or 9th century A.D. But the details regarding Avinīta's predecessors, given in this inscription, are the same as that found in genuine Gaṅga records. It appears therefore that the inscription was forged at a later date by some intelligent Jain monks, who had access to official Gaṅga records. Even they have cleverly given some of the names of witnesses found in genuine, early records.

This forged grant further refers to a minister of 'Akālavarṣa Pṛthivī-vallabha' who was probably a Rāṣṭrakūṭa king. But what a minister of a Rāṣṭrakūṭa king had to with a grant of a Gaṅga ruler is not clear. Probably the forgery was made during the days of the Rāṣṭrakūṭas. Further, the reference to the *anvaya* (lineage) of Kundakunda looks highly suspect.

This forged inscription gives the following list of the Jain Ācāryas of the *anvaya* of Kundakunda—

Guṇacandra-bhaṭāra
|
Abhayanandi-bhaṭāra
|
Śīlabhadra-bhaṭāra
|
Jayanandi-bhaṭāra
|
Guṇanandi-bhaṭāra
|
Candranandi-bhaṭāra

Since this inscription is a forged document of 8th or 9th century, we cannot rely on the evidence of this record and accept the list of monks as persons belonging to the days of early Gaṅga rulers. Other details given in this grant should also be ignored.

Avinīta's son and successor Durvinīta ruled, in all probability, in the 2nd half of the 6th century A.D. Like his father he too, had a long reign.[114] We must remember that the great-grandson of Durvinīta viz. Bhūvikrama started ruling from 625 A.D.[115] So Durvinīta must be placed before 600 A.D. This is confirmed partly by the discovery of a mutilated manuscript of the *Avantīsundarīkathā*[116] which makes Durvinīta a contemporary of Siṁhaviṣṇu. We have already seen that Durvinīta's father Avinīta was a contemporary of Siṁhaviṣṇu. Therefore it appears that Avinīta's son was a junior contemporary of that Pallava monarch.[117]

No Jain inscription of the reign of Durvinīta has yet been discovered. But a later record, dated Śaka 977 (1055 A.D.) of the time of Someśvara I, the Kālyaṇa-Cālukya monarch, refers to a temple dedicated to Pārśva, which according to it, was built by Durvinīta.[118] This definitely proves that Durvinīta, like many of his predecessors, patronised the Jains.

A few scholars are firmly of the opinion that Durvinīta was a disciple of the great Jain savant Pūjyapāda The basis of their surmise is one of his records, dated in his 40th regnal year.[119] According to this inscription he composed a work called the *Śabdavatāra*.[120] Prof. Saletore argues[121] that Durvinīta merely put into Kannada the original *Śabdavatāra,* a grammatical treatise written by Pūjyapāda. But this is a mere conjecture. We must remember that according to Devasena (933 A.D.), Vajranandi, the founder of Drāvida Saṅgha, who flourished about 468 A.D, at Madura was a disciple of Pūjyapāda. But we have already seem that Durvinīta could not have flourished before the 2nd half of the 6th century A.D ; and Pūjyapāda must have died at least 50 years before Durvinīta's probable date of birth. Therefore there is no basis for the view that Durvinīta was a disciple of Pūjyapāda. However, it is just possible that sometime after Pūjyapāda's death, Durvinīta, on his own initiative, translated the grammatical treatise of that Jain savant.

In a later chapter we will continue this discussion on the state of Jainism during the rule of the later Western Gaṅga rulers. Let us now turn our attention to the condition of the Jain religion in the Kadamba kingdom from the earliest times.

The Kadambas like the Western Gaṅgas came into the limelight from the middle of the 4th century A.D. Like the latter they too were great patrons of the Jain religion and culture. The earliest inscription[122] of the dynasty of the founder Mayūraśarman is assigned to the middle of the 4th century A.D. The first king of this dynasty, who definitely showed special favour for the Jains, was Kākusthavarman whose Halsi grant (Belgaum district, Karṇāṭaka) is dated in the 80th year of the *paṭṭabandha* of his ancestor Mayūraśarman.[123] It has been suggested[124] that the year 80 may also be referred to the Gupta era ; in that case the inscription should be assigned to circa 400 A.D., which is also supported by the palaeography of the record.

The inscription begins with an adoration of the holy Jinendra who is represented almost as a theistic deity. Some of the grants of Mṛgeśvarman and Ravivarman begin with the same verse. It was issued from Palāśikā (Halsi, Belgaum district) by Kākusthavarman, who is represented as the '*yuvarāja* of the Kadambas'. By this grant a field in the village called Kheṭagrāma, which belonged to the holy Arhats, was given to the general Śrutakīrti as a reward for saving the prince. It is said that the confiscators of the field, belonging to the king's own family or any other family, would me guilty of *pañcamahāpātaka*. According to the Jains the five sins are destruction of life, lying, unchastity and immoderate desire. The inscription ends with the words *Ṛṣabhāya namaḥ*.

It is apparent from the inscription that the Jinendra temple of the ancient city of Palāśikā was built before the date of this inscription and probably some time in the 4th century A.D.

Several grants of Mṛgeśvavarman, the grandson of Kākusthavarman, who ruled in the last quarter of the 5th century A.D.,[125] are connected with the Jain religion. The first inscription[126] found at Banavāsi is dated in the 3rd regnal year. It records a grant of black-soil land (*kṛṣṇabhūmikṣetra*) in the village called Bṛhat-Paralūra to the divine, supreme Arhat 'whese feet are rubbed by the tiara of the lord of gods' for the purpose of the glory of sweeping out the temple, anointing the idol with ghee, performing worship and repairing anything that may be broken. Another piece of land was also granted for decorating the idol with flowers. The term *devakula* is also used in this connexion. The *paṭṭikā* is said to have been written by Dāmakīrti Bhojaka. We have another Banavāsi grant[127] dated in the 4th year of Mṛgeśa's reign which was issued on the 8th of the bright fortnight of *varṣā* when the king was residing at Vaijayantī. The dating of the inscription was surely due to the Jain influence[128], as it was the time of the Navdīśvara or Aṣṭāhnikā festival. By this grant the *dharmamahārāja* Śri Vijayaśiva Mṛgeśvavarman made a gift of a village of the name of Kālavaṅga. It was divided in three equal portions; the first was meant for the temple of

Jinendra which was situated at a place called Paramapuṣkala. The second portion was meant for the Saṅgha of the Śvetapaṭa-mahāśramaṇa who followed scrupulously the original teaching of the Arhat and the third for the use of the Nirgrantha-mahā śramaṇas.

The reference to the Śvetapaṭa *sādhus* is of great significance. It clearly proves that the Śvetāmbaras were equally popular in Karṇāṭaka in the 5th century A.D. The statement that they followed the good teaching of the Arhat implies that they were held in special esteem in those days. It is also evident from the inscription that the Jinendra temple mentioned here, was the joint propery of the monks of both the sects. Needless to say, these monks belonging to the main branches, of Jainism, lived in perfect harmony in the 5th century A D. The seal of the grant, according to Fleet, bears the device of a Jinendra.

The third inscription of Mṛgeśavarman, bearing on Jainism, is the Halsi grant[129] dated in the 8th year of that king. It begins like the inscription of Kākusthavarman with an adoration to Jinendra in exactly the same words. The king Mṛgeśa is further described as *Tuṅga-Gaṅgakulotsādī* and *Pallavapralayānala* which suggest his success over the Western Gaṅgas and Pallavas. Then we are told that, while residing at Vaijayantī, through devotion of his father (Śāntivarman), he caused to be built a *jinālaya* at the town of Palāśikā (Halsi) and gave to the holy Arhats thirty three *nivartanas* of land between the river Mātṛsarit and Iṅgiṇī-saṅgama for the Yāpanīyas, Nirgranthas and Kūrcakas. The executor of the grant was *bhojaka* Dāmakīrti. Flect takes the *bhojakas* as the official priests in Jain temples. But who were the Kūrcakas mentioned in this inscription? It appears that they were bearded ascetics[130] and were distinguished from other Nirgrantha monks, who did not keep any beard. Some other grants of Mṛgeśvarman are meant for the Brahmins and other non-Jains which show that he was not a converted Jain[131].

The next king Ravivarman was not only a very able ruler and a great conqueror but also a sincere patron of the Jain religion. We must at first refer to his Halsi grant[132] dated in the eleventh year of his reign which refers to his brother Bhānuvarman, who was probably the governor of Palāśikā[133] under Ravivarman. We are told that Bhānuvarman and one Paṇḍara Bhojaka granted land to the Jina at Palāśikā which was situated in a village called Kardamapaṭī. We are further told that the land was given for the purpose of worshipping the Lord Jina on every full-moon day. We must then refer to two undated Halsi grants of the time of Ravivarman both of which are of great importance.

The first undated Halsi grant[134] of Ravivarman records the interesting history of a family that received favour from the days of king Kākusthavarman. According to it, in former days a Bhoja named Śrutakīrti, who acquired great favour of Kākusthavarman, enjoyed the village of Kheṭa. We have already taken note of the fact that king Kākusthavarman granted a field in that village to *senāpati* Śrutakīrti for serving him. After Śrutakīrti's death, at the time of Śāntivarman, his eldest son Mṛgeśa, after taking his father's permission, granted the village to the mother of Dāmakīrti. It appears that Dāmakīrti was the son of Śrutakīrti. The eldest son of Dāmakīrti was *pratīhāra* Jayakīrti, whose family is said have been established in the world by an *ācārya* named Bandhuṣeṇa. In order to increase his fortune, fame, and for the sake of religious merit, Jayakīrti, through the favour of king Ravi gave the village of Parukheṭaka (probably larger Kheṭa) to the mother of his father. This interesting grant further refers to the 8-day festival of Lord Jina at Palāśikā in which king Ravivarman himself participated. We are further told that the expenses for this Aṣṭahnikā festival in the month of Kārttika should be met from the revenue of the village. The grant further refers to the Yāpanīya monks and their chief Kumāradatta. The last few lines of the inscription conclusively show that king Ravivarman did everything to promote the worship of Jina at Palāśikā. It further appears that Sūri Kumāradatta, mentioned in this inscription, was a celebrated Jain savant, belonging to the Yāpanīya sect and was universally admired for his learning and holiness. We must note carefully the following lines of this inscription "wheresoever the worship of Jinendra is kept up, there is increase for the country, and the lords of these countries acquire strength (*orjas*).

The second undated Halsi grant of Ravivarman[135] is historically more important since it refers to the killing of Viṣṇuvarman, his Kadamba kinsman, and his triumph over Caṇḍadaṇḍa, the lord of Kāñcī. The actual donor was Śrīkīrti, the younger brother of Dāmakīrti and the object was to increase the merit of their mother. A copper plate inscription,[135A] dated in the 34th year of this king, found from Chitradurga district (Karṇāṭaka) records a grant of land to a Jaina temple.

It should here be remembered that Ravivarman did not favour the Jains alone; other religions sects also received good treatment from him. This is proved by his inscriptions found from dicerent places[136] Ravivarman ruled in the closing years of the 5th and the first quarter of the 6th century A.D.[137]

The Jains also enjoyed patronage during the rule of Harivarman, who unlike his father Ravivarman, was not a very strong king. We have two dated Halsi grants of his reign. The first is dated in the 4th year of his reign.[138] It records that at Uccaśṛṅgī, the king at the advice of his uncle (*pitṛvya*) named Śivaratha, gave the grant of a village to an Arhat temple of Palāśikā, which was built by one Mṛgeśa, the son of *senāpati* Siṁha. On behalf of the temple, the grant was received by Candrakṣānta, who is described as the head of a Kūrcaka Saṅgha named after Vāriṣeṇācārya. It thus appears that a particular member of Kūrcaka sect called Vāriṣeṇācārya established, before this date, a particular Saṅgha, which was named after him. We have already taken note of these Kūrcakas, who are mentioned in an inscription of the time of Mṛgeśavarman. The village Vasuntavāṭaka which was given as grant was situated at Kandura-viṣaya. The inscription ends with a verse addressed to Vardhamāna.

The second Halsi grant[139] of Harivarman's reign is dated in his 5th regnal year. It is interesting that Palāśika is described here as the capital (*adhiṣṭhāna*) of this king. We are told that the king, being requested by Sendraka chief Bhānuśakti gave the grant of a village called Marade for a Jain *caityālaya* of Palāśikā, which was the property of Śramaṇa-saṅgha called Ahariṣṭi and who were under Ācārya Dharmanandin. The Sendrakas were obviously the feudatories of the Kadambas. The Harivarman, however, before the end of his reign, became a Śaiva.[140]

Another branch of the kadamba dynasty, who ruled in the southern part of the original Kadamba dominion, also patronised the Jains. We have a grant[141], of the time of Kṛṣṇavarman I (circa 475-485 A.D.), the brother of Śāntivarman, issued from Triparvata (probably Halebiḍ). By this grant a piece of land at a place called Siddhakedāra, which was in Triparvata division, was granted to Yāpanīya Saṅgha by Yuvarāja Devavarman for the maintenance, worship and repair of a *caityālaya,* which was probably near Siddhakedāra.

The above discussion shows the flourishing condition of Jainism in different parts of the Kadamba dominion. It appears that there were a number of Jain temples at Palāśikā, which was a flourishing town in those days. These inscriptions, as noted above, have disclosed the names of a great number of Jain savants, some of whom were even respected by the reigning monarchs. The references to different Jain sects like the Nirgranthas, Śvetapaṭas and Kūrcakas prove that all these schools had their followers in the Kadamba dominion. The lay followers used to celebrate, with great pomp, the various Jain festivals and, needless to say, such festivals made the Jain religion extremely popular among the masses. The Kadamba kings, it appears, in spite of their religious catholicity, had special love for the Jain religion. It was mainly because of their patronage that Jainism became a dominant religious force in Karṇāṭaka.

Turning to the Western Cālukyas, some of whom ruled before 600 A.D., we find at least one king directly patronising the Jains. But we must at first refer to a spurious grant of the time of Pulakeśin I, known as Altem grant[142]. This inscription gives the date Śaka 411 (i.e. 489 A.D.) for Pulakeśin I, which is an impossible date for that king. We have now a genuine date viz. Śaka 465 for that king[143], supplied by an inscription inscribed on the Badami fort. As pointed out by Fleet, the script of Altem grant belongs to a much later age.

It is, therefore, desirable that we should discuss the contents of the inscription in a later chapter.

An undated stone inscription[144] of the time of Kīrtivarman I, who ruled in the 2nd half of the 6th century A.D., from Ādūr (Dharwar district, Karṇāṭaka) is an important Jain record. Now, we know that Kīrtivarman I's rule[145] terminated in 597 A.D.; therefore this inscription should be placed between 543 A.D. (Śaka 465) and 597 A.D. It begins with an adoration to Vardhamāna. Then it records the grant of a field for the *dānaśālā* of the Jinālaya which had been built by one of the Gāmuṇḍas or village headman. The inscription refers to Vaijayantī, but due to its damaged nature nothing definite can be known about its connexion either with Kīrtivarman or Jainism. We are then told that, while Kīrtivarman was reigning as supreme sovereign, and while a certain Sinda king was governing the city of Pāṇḍīpura (the ancient name of Ādūr[146]), a number of Gāmuṇḍas gave to the temple of Jinendra some rice-land to the west of the village of Karmagālur. The inscription refers to a line of Jain monks, the earliest of whom was Vinayanandin, who is here compared with Indrabhūti (the great disciple of Mahāvīra). He obviously flourished around the last quarter of the 5th century A.D. The disciple of this Vinayanandin was Vāsudeva, whose disciple's disciple was Śrīpāla, who was responsible for the setting up of the stone tablet. The grant was received on behalf of the Jina temple (which was at Ādūr) by Prabhācandra. It is interesting to note that this stone inscription has been discovered from a region which was formerly under the Kadambas. It further shows that Jainism received equal patronage even during the days of the Cālukyas and in a later chapter we will see how sincerely the Cālukyas favoured the Jains.

Regarding the condition of Jainism in Andhra Pradesh[147] before 600 A.D., nothing practically is known. However from a somewhat later Eastern Cālukya inscription,[148] which will be discussed elsewhere, we learn that a number of Jain saints flourished in the Vezwada region between 450 A.D. and 600 A.D. The names are as follows—Candraprabhācārya, his pupil's pupil Ravicandrācārya and his disciple's disciple Ravinandin. These

Jain teachers, who are mentioned in the Musinikonda grant of Viṣṇuvardhana III, were the spiritual predecessors of Kālibhadrācārya, who was a contemporary of Ayyaṇa Mahādevī, the wife of Kubja Viṣṇuvardhana (early 7th century).

In a grant of Pallava Siṁhavarman found from Nellore district of Andhra Pradesh (5th century) there is a reference to the Ājīvikas.[149] So far as Jainism is concerned, due to various reasons, the early monuments, connected with it, have simply disappeared from Andhra Pradesh.

Quite a good number of Jain teachers of South India like Kundakunda, Samantabhadra, Divākara, Pūjyapāda etc., certainly flourished before 600 A.D. We will discuss in a separate chapter the details of their life and activities.

NOTES

1 (Geiger), p. 75.

2 X. 102.

3 See Geiger, *Introd,* p. XXXVI.

4 See Winternitz, *Hist. of Indian Literature,* Vol. II, p. 211 ; see also *The Classical Age,* p. 407.

5 See Winternitz, *op. cit.,* p. 210 ; *The Classical Age,* pp. 406-07.

6 (Ed. H. Oldenberg) 19. 14.

7 See the entry on the *Tamil Literature* in *Encyclopaedia Britannica* ; see also Vaiyapuri, *Tamil Language and Lit.,* p. 151.

8 See Dikshitar (translation), p. 343.

9 *The Age of Imperial Unity,* pp. 239-40.

10 For a list of different Tamil editions of this text see Chakravarti, *Jain Literature in Tamil,* p. 19 fn. 2.

11 See for different views on its date, Chakravarti, *op. cit.,* p. 24 foot note.

12 Chakravarti, *op. cit.,* p. 21.

13 See Vaiyapuri, *op. cit.,* pp. 65 f. ; Chakravarti, p. 22.

14 Chakravarti, *op. cit.,* p. 22.

15 See T. P. Meenakshisundaram, *A Hist. of Tamil Literature* (1965), p. 17.

16 33. 78.

17 Translation by G. U. Pope (London, 1886). For the list of Tamil editions of *Kural* see Chakravarti, *op. cit.,* p. 28 foot-note.

18 See Chakravarti, *op. cit.,* pp. 33 ff.

19 *Loc. cit.*

20 Chakravarti, *op. cit.,* p. 38.

21 *The Tamils Eighteen Hundred Years Ago,* p. 139.
22 Pp. 33 ff.
23 See Dikshitar (translation), pp. 343-4.
24 See Padikam, p. 77.
25 See Dikshitar, p. 77 fn 2.
26 *Ibid.,* pp 343-4.
27 *Ibid.,* pp. 68 f.
28 *Ibid.,* pp. 181 ff. ; 231 ff. etc.
29 The name of this town was known to the Jātaka writers.
30 See Dikshitar, p. 152.
31 See McCrindle, *Ancient India* etc., p. 63.
32 Dikshitar, *op. cit.,* p. 216,
33 *Ibid.,* p. 157.
34 See the present writer's *Ancient Indian Literary and Cultural Tradition,* p. 188.
35 See Legge, *Record of the Buddhistic Kingdoms,* pp. 18 f. ; see also *Bṛhatkathākośa,* 12. 116.
36 Even now the Hindus observe the car-festival.
37 See Chatterjee, A. K. *op. cit.,* p. 188.
38 Para 680.
39 10. 29.
40 P. 322.
41 10. 29.
42 See Mehta and Chandra, *Prakrit Proper Names,* Part I, p. 258.
43 See Dikshitar, *op. cit.,* p. 163.
44 *Ibid.,* p. 171.
45 Sailana edition, pp. 22 ff.
46 Dikshitar, p. 158.
47 *Ibid.,* p. 216.
48 Lines 453 ff. ; quoted in Kanakasabhai's. *The Tamils Eighteen Hundred years ago,* p. 136.
49 Dikshitar, *op. cit.,* p. 158.
50 *Ibid.,* p. 157.
51 *Ibid.,* p. 164.
52 *Ibid.,* pp. 231 ff.
53 *Ibid.,* pp. 181 f.
54 *Ibid.,* pp. 231 ff.
55 *Ibid.,* p. 308.
56 See Chakravarti, *op. cit.,* p. 52 ; also Dikshitar, *op. cit.,* p. 227.
57 See Dikshitar, p. 220 ; see also p. 344.
58 Ibid., p. 220.
59 For its summary see Kanakasabhai, *op. cit.,* pp. 162-189 ; also Vaiyapuri, *op. cit.,* pp. 169-190.
60 See Kanakasabhai, *op. cit.,* p. 165.
61 *Ibid.,* p. 215.

62 See *Sāmaññaphala Sutta.*

63 Kanakasabhai, *ibid.*, p. 214.

64 Dikshitar, *op. cit.*, p. 164.

65 See *Madura District Gazetteer.* (ed. W. Francis) pp. 300-01 ; see also Desai, P. B., *Jainism in South India* etc., pp. 60-61.

66 See Desai, *op. cit.*, p. 57 ; see also *ARE,* 1910, p. 69.

67 See *JOR,* Vol. XIII, p. 3.

68 *Madura District Gazetteer,* p. 254.

69 *Ibid.*, p. 256.

70 See Desai, *op. cit.*, p. 60 ; see also *ARE,* 1912, p. 50.

71 See Desai, *op. cit.*, p. 60 ; see also *ARE,* 1910, pp. 68-69.

72 See Desai, *op. cit.*, p. 58 ; see also *ARE,* 1910, p. 66.

73 Desai, *op. cit.*, p. 57 ; *ARE,* 1910, p. 67.

74 Desai, *op. cit.*, p. 60 ; *ARE,* 1909, p. 70.

75 See Desai, *op. cit.*, p. 58.

76 *Madura District Gazetteer,* pp. 321 f., see also Desai, *op. cit.*, p. 57.

77 Desai, *op. cit.*, p. 64 ; *ARE,* 1907, p. 47.

78 Desai, *op. cit.*, pp. 48-49 ; see also *EI,* Vol. XIV, p. 334. According to the *Periya Purānam* this place was a seat of a large Jain monastery in the 7th century A.D. See also Chakravarti, *op. cit.*, p. 9.

79 See Desai, *op. cit.*, pp. 49-50.

80 *Ibid.*, pp. 39-41.

81 *Ibid.*, pp. 51 ff.; see also *Manual of Pudukkottai State,* 1944, Vol. II, p. 1092.

82 *Desai, op. cit.*, p. 53 ; *Manual of Pudukkottai State,* p. 1968.

83 Desai, *op. cit.*, p. 53.

84 *Ibid.*, pp. 53 f.

85 *Ibid.*, p. 54.

86 *Loc. cit.*

87 Desai, *op. cit.*, p. 55.

88 *Ibid.*, pp. 68 f. ; see also *Travancore Archaeological Series,* Vol. I, p. 194.

89 See *Travancore Archaeological Series,* Vol. II, pp. 127-129.

90 P. 24 (quoted in J. P. Jain's *The Jaina Sources* etc., p 160 fn. 1.).

91 See *EI,* Vol. 14, p. 334.

92 See *A.R.E.* 1958-59, A 10, also pp. 3-4 ; for the text see *Transaction of the Archaeological Society of South India,* 1958-59, pp. 41 ff.

93 See *A.R.E.*, 1958-59, pp. 3 f.

94 See Kamil Zvelebil, *Tamil in 550 A.D.*, Prague, 1964.

95 See *S.I.I.*, Vol. II, pp. 391 ff.

96 See *M.A.R.*, 1938, pp. 80 ff. ; see also *Jaina Śilālekha Saṅgraha,* Vol. IV, No. 20.

97 For a summary of various such speculations, see Saletore, *Mediaeval Jainism,* pp. 7 ff.

98 See *EI,* Vol. 14, pp. 334 f.

99. *M.A.R.,* 1925, p. 91.

100 *S.I.I.,* Vol. II, p. 387.

101 *M.A.R.,* 1921, p. 19.

102 *E.C.,* Vol. VII, Nr. 46, p. 139.

103 See *Jain Śilālekha Saṁgraha,* Vol. II, No. 277.

104 It has been suggested that Mādhava I Koṅkaṇivarman probably destroyed an Aśokan pillar with his sword; see Rice, *Mysore Inscriptions, Introd,* p. xlii; see also Saletore, *op. cit.,* pp. 15 f.

105 Italics ours.

106 See *Pāia-Sadda-Mahaṇṇavo,* p. 496.

107 See *M.A.R.,* 1921, p. 26.

108 *E.C.* Vol. X, Malur, No. 73.

109 *EI,* Vol. 14, pp. 334 ff.

110 See *Mysore Gazetteer,* Vol. II, Part II, (1930), p. 621.

111 *E.C.,* Vol. X, Malur, No. 72.

112 *M.A.R.,* 1938, pp. 80 ff.

113 *E.C.,* Vol. I (Reprint), No. 1.

114 See *M.A.R.,* 1912, Para 67. The Gummareddipura plates show that he ruled at least for 40 years.

115 *M.A.R.,* 1925, No. 105.

116 See *Mysore Gazetteer,* Vol. II, Part II, (1930), pp. 626 f.; see also *M.A.R.,* 1938, pp. 87 ff.

117 It appears that Viṣṇuvardhana mentioned in the *Avantisundarīkathā,* as a contemporary of Durvinīta and Siṁhaviṣṇu, is a different king and not to be identified with Kubja Viṣṇuvardhana, the founder of the Veṅgī house.

118 See *Jain Śilālekha Saṁgraha,* Vol. IV, No. 141; see also *I.A.,* Vol. 55, p. 74; and Saletore, *op. cit.,* pp. 53 f.

119 See Saletore, *op. cit.,* pp. 19 ff.

120 *M.A.R.,* 1912, pp. 31-32.

121 *Mediaeval Jainism,* pp. 21 ff.

122 *M.A.R.,* 1929, p. 50; also Sircar, *Select Inscriptions* etc., pp. 473 f.

123 See Sircar, *Successors of the Śātavāhanas* etc., p. 255; see also *IA,* Vol. VI, p. 23.

124 *Ibid.,* p. 234 fn.

125 See *The Classical Age,* p. 272.

126 *I.A.,* Vol. VII, pp. 35-36.

127 *Ibid.,* pp. 37-8.

128 See Sircar, *op. cit.,* p. 262.

129 *I.A.,* Vol. VI, pp. 24-25.

130 See M.M-Williams, *S.E.D.,* p. 300.

131 See *E.C.,* Vol. IV, p. 130; Vol. VIII, p. 12.

132 *I.A.,* Vol. VI, p. 28.

133 Sircar, *op. cit.,* p. 269.

134 *I.A.*, Vol. VI, pp. 25-26.
135 *Ibid.*, pp. 29-30.
135A *M.A.R.*, 1933, pp. 109 ff.
136 See *EI*, Vol. 16, p. 264 ; *EI*, Vol. VIII, pp. 146 ff. etc.
137 See *The Classical Age*, p. 273.
138 *I.A.*, Vol. VI, pp. 30-31.
139 *Ibid.*, pp. 31-32.
140 See *E.I.*, Vol. 14, p. 165.
141 *I.A.*, Vol. VII, p. 33.
142 See A. V. Naik, *A List of Inscriptions of the Deccan*, No. 3.
143 *Ibid.*, No. 1.
144 *I.A.*, Vol. XI, pp. 68-71.
145 *The Classical Age*, p. 233.
146 *I.A.*, Vol. XI, p. 69.
147 See in this connexion *Journal of Andhra Research Society*, Vol. XIII, pp. 185-196.
148 See *Report on South Indian Epigraphy* 1916-17, No. A-9.
149 *E.I.*, Vol. 24, pp. 296 ff.

CHAPTER IX

Jainism in North India

(600 A.D. to 1000 A.D.)

Despite the paucity of Jain records in North India in the post-Gupta period, it is possible to write a more or less faithful account of the state of the Jain religion, not only with the help of inscriptions, but also literary works. We have already noticed that the religion of the Tīrthaṅkaras was firmly established in almost every part of India by 600 A.D. We should remember in this connexion that a large number of Jain commentaries came to be written in the post-Gupta period, which also indirectly proves the popularity of this religion. However, Gujarat, Rajasthan, Bengal and parts of Madhya Pradesh and Uttar Pradesh were especially connected with this religion. In other parts of Northern India, this religion merely continued its existence in the post-Gupta period. We will endeavour in this chapter to give a historical account of the Jain religion in different parts of Northern India.

We should, at the very outset, refer to the extremely valuable account given by the Chinese pilgrim Yuan Chwang, who came to India in the 2nd quarter of the 7th century A.D. It is apparent from his account that Jainism was quite popular in different places of India during the time of his visit. He especially refers to the Jains who lived in his time at Kāpiśī[1], Siṁhapura[2], Rājagṛha[3], Puṇḍravardhana[4] and Samataṭa[5]. It, however, appears from the account of that Chinese pilgrim that the Digambara Jains were more popular in India in his days than the Śvetāmbaras. The only reference to the Śvetāmbaras that we get in his narrative is in connexion with the description of Siṁhapura. We have already referred to the discoveries made by Stein from this place. From Murti (ancient Siṁhapura) in Salt Range an old Jain temple has been discovered[6]. It appears that during the time of Yuan Chwang's visit there was a large Jain temple-complex at Siṁhapura.

Rājagṛha, which was intimately associated with the activities of Mahāvīra, was a flourishing Jain centre during Yuan Chwang's visit. We are told that he saw many Digambaras on the Vipula mountain practising austerities incessantly. "They turn round with the Sun, watching it from its rising to its setting"[7]. We have already referred to the fact that in the Gupta period also Jainism was quite popular at Rājagṛha.

The undivided Bengal was one of the greatest centres of Jainism from practically the days of Lord Mahāvīra. But unfortunately, beyond a few references to various *Śākhās* connected with Bengal, nothing tangible is known regarding the state of Jainism here in the pre-Gupta days. The Paharpur inscription, which has already been discussed, surely proves the popularity of the Digambara religion in North Bengal in the Gupta period. The account of Yuan Chwang conclusively shows the tremendous popularity of Jainism in Puṇḍravardhana and Samataṭa, the two provinces of ancient Bengal. In both these states the pilgrim noticed 'numerous Digambaras'. In spite of such popularity, neither the literary texts, nor the available inscriptions throw any light on Jainism in Bengal in the post-Gupta period. Archaeology also has not given us any help so far. However, the discovery of a large number of Jain temples and icons, particularly from Bankura[8] and Purulia[9] proves the popularity of Jainism in West Bengal during the Pāla period. It further appears that a few Jina images of Bankura and Purulia, which are generally assigned to the Pāla period, are actually the products of an earlier age. A detailed and systematic study is necessary to ascertain the actual position in this respect.

There are only a few known Jain inscriptions of Northern India belonging to the 7th century A.D. Form Pindwara (Sirohi district, Rajasthan) was discovered a brass image of Ṛṣabhanātha with an inscription of Saṁvat 744 corresponding to 687 A.D.[10] The image was first noticed by D. R. Bhandarkar.[11] It was discovered from the fort of Vasantgaḍh and is now preserved in the Mahāvīra temple there. Vasantagaḍh was formerly known as Vasantapura, but its oldest name was Vaṭapura.[12] The present Jain temple is, however, not old. We gather from this damaged inscription that one Droṇoraka Yaśodeva had the Jina image built by the architect Śivanāga. There is little doubt that the temple, where this icon was installed, existed in the 7th century A.D. We have some other evidences to show that Jainism was quite popular in Rajasthan in the post-Gupta period. Udyotanasūri, who wrote his *Kuvalayamālā* in Śaka 700 during the time of Pratīhāra Vatsarāja, refers[13] to the fact that Śivacandragaṇi, the disciple of *Mahākavi* Devagupta and disciple's disciple of Harigupta, the *ācārya* of Hūṇa Toramāṇa, visited Bhinnamāla on pilgrimage. This surely shows that Bhinnamāla or Bhīnmāl (Jalor district) was a great Jain centre from the 7th century, if not earlier. Jinaprabha[14] refers to this place as sacred to Mahāvira. It was the capital of the Cāpa king Vyāghramukha in the year 628 A.D., as we learn from Brahma-gupta.[15] From a later inscription we learn that Mahāvīra himself came to this city.[16] The kings of the Cāpa dynasty, as we will note afterwards, were great patrons of Jainism. It further appears from the *Kuvalayamālā* that some of the spiritual predecessors of Udyotanasūri were specially connected with Rajasthan. We should further remember that Jāvālipura (modern Jalor) was a very well known Jain centre and the native town of Udyotanasūri. That author further informs us that his work was completed in the Ṛṣabhadeva temple of that city which was also adorned with a large number of Jain shrines. The temple of Ṛṣabha, according to Udyotanasūri,[17] was built by one Ravibhadra. A number of Jain saints, according to the author of the *Kuvalayamālā,* lived in this town. Another place, called Agāsavaṇā, which was probably situated not far from Jalor, was also adorned with a large number of Jain temples. This place was connected, according to the author, with the activities of Vedasāra, who lived in the 2nd half of the 7th century A.D.

That Jainism was in a flourishing condition in Rajasthan during the days of Vatsarāja is further proved by an inscription,[18] discovered from Osia (Jodhpur district) and is dated V.S. 1013 (956 A.D.). We learn from this inscription that there was a temple dedicated to Mahāvīra in the extensive city of Ukeśa, which existed during the days of Vatsarāja. The temple afterwards had fallen in disrepair and was renovated by a merchant called Jindaka in the year 1013 (956 A.D.). It is clear from the inscription that the Mahāvīra temple here existed even before the days of Vatsarāja and probably built a century or two before his time. It is interesting to note that Jinaprabha, the famous author of the *Vividhatīrthakalpa* mentions Upakeśa (Ukeśa of this inscription) as a place sacred to Lord Mahāvīra.[19] The well known Upakeśa *gaccha* apparently derived its name from this place.[20]

It was during the days of Vatsarāja in the year Śaka 705 that another Jain poet produced a work of considerable merit. We are referring to Jinasena II, the author of the *Harivaṁśa-purāṇa*.[21] However, there is nothing to show that Vatsarāja himself took active part in the promotion of Jainism. He, however, appears to be a person of religious catholicity. His personal religion was Śaivism, as we learn from one of the records of his great-grandson Bhoja I.[22]

Chronologically the next important Jain record from Rajasthan is the Ghaṭiyālā inscription[23] of Kakkuka, which supplies the date V.S. 918 or 861 A.D. Ghaṭiyālā is some 20 miles north of Jodhpur city. We learn from this record that the chief Kakkuka, who is described as belonging to the Pratīhāra family, founded a Jain temple in 861 A.D., and handed it over to a Jain community of *gaccha* Dhaneśvara. The same chief also erected two pillars at the village of Rohiṇīkūpa (probably situated not far from the find-spot of the inscription). The *gaccha*, mentioned here, is otherwise unknown. This inscription and the inscription of Osia prove the immense popularity of Jainism in the Jodhpur area from the days of Vatsarāja, if not earlier.

Then we must refer to an extremely important inscription,[24] now preserved in the Ajmer Museum. It was discovered by Captain Burt and according to local report it was fixed in the wall of a solitary temple, situated two miles from the village of Bijapur in the present Pali district, Rajasthan. There are altogether three dates viz. 973, 996 and 1053 corresponding to 915, 938 and 997 A.D. respectively.

We learn from this inscription that king Vidagdha, who is described as the *Rāṣṭrakūṭa-kulakānanakalpavṛkṣa,* and who was the son of Harivarman, being induced by his spiritual preceptor (*ācārya*) Vāsudeva, built a temple for the god Jina (Ṛṣabha) at the town of Hastikuṇḍī (modern Hathundi close to the village of Bijapur, 10 miles south of Bali) in the year 973 corresponding to 915 A.D. The king then weighed himself against gold, of which two thirds were allotted to the god and the remainder to the Jain preceptor (viz. Vāsudeva). This inscription further mentions the disciple of Vāsudeva called Sūri Śāntibhadra. We are then told that the *goṣṭhī* of Hastikuṇḍī renovated the temple (of Ṛṣabhanātha), originally built by Vidagdha and after its restoration the image was installed by Śāntibhadra in the Vikrama year 1053 corresponding to 997 A.D. We further learn that the original grant of Vidagdha, which was made in V.S. 973 was renewed in the year 996 i.e. 938 A.D. by Maṁmaṭa, the son of Vidagdha. This Maṁmaṭa, as we learn from this inscription, played a very prominent part in the political affairs of Northern India in his time. The son of Maṁmaṭa viz. Dhavala is also mentioned in the inscription as having given the gift of a well called Pippala to the temple. The *Praśasti* of the first part of the inscription, which was actually inscribed afterwards in 997 A.D., according to the epigraph, was composed by the Jain saint Sūryācārya. We further learn from the first part that the original image, before restoration, had been set up by certain members of the *goṣṭhī,* whose names are enumerated.

The second part of this inscription, which is an independent record, was incised earlier. Here one Balabhadra appears as the *guru* of Vidagdha. It records that Vidagdha had erected a *caityagṛha* for his *guru* Balabhadra and gave certain endowments in the year 973. Some interesting details regarding the nature of the grant by Vidagdha are given in this part of the record. These details are extremely important for the students of economic history.[25] Two thirds of these proceeds were to go to the Jina (Arhat) and a third to Balabhadra as *vidyādhana* i.e. fees for imparting knowledge. The closing verse of the second half expresses the wish that these endowments may be enjoyed by the spiritual progeny of Keśavasūri.

The inscription, discussed above,[26] not only discloses the names of a number of Jain saints, who lived in the tenth century A.D. in Western Rajasthan, but also a number of royal personages of this Rāṣṭrakūṭa branch who actively helped the Jain religion. The Jain poet-saint Sūryācārya, the author of the first part of the inscription, was certainly a very accomplished man of letters, as is evident from the language of this inscription. These Rāṣṭrakūṭa kings were not only sincere patrons of Jainism but also successful military generals. It is also evident from the inscription that the king Vidagdha, who flourished in the first quarter of the tenth century, had two Jain preceptors viz. Balabhadra and Vāsudeva in honour of whom he built two Jain temples. His son and successor Maṁmaṭa also patronised the Jains, a policy followed by the next king Dhavala, who probably became a Jain *Sādhu* before his death. The first and the last verse of the first part of the inscription, composed by Sūryācārya, are in praise of the Jina.

Several other Jain inscriptions from Rajasthan, belonging to the tenth century A.D., have been discovered. We should particularly mention the recently discovered[27] epigraph from Rajorgarh (Alwar district) which gives the date V.S. 979 or 923 A.D. It discloses the existence of a temple, dedicated to Śāntinātha, which was built by the Jain architect Sarvadeva, son of Dedullaka and grandson of Arbhata of the Dharkaṭa family hailing from Pūrṇatallaka. The ancient name of Rajorgarh, according to this inscription, was Rājyapura.[28] Another recently discovered inscription[29] comes from Bharatpur district. It gives the date Vikrama 1051 corresponding to 994 A.D. This inscription refers to a *guru* called Śrī Śūrasena of Vāgaṭa Saṅgha. It is incised on the pedestal of a Jina image.[30] Mahāsena, the author of the *Pradyumnacaritakāvya*[31] belonged to this Saṅgha.

A few more Jain inscriptions of Rajasthan before 1000 A.D. are also known. G. H. Ojha in his monumental work on the history of Rajputana[32] has referred to a damaged, fragmentary inscription of the time of Guhila king Allaṭa, who reigned in the middle of the tenth century A.D. This Jain inscription was discovered from Ahar near Udaipur, a place still known for its Jain shrines. For the reign of Śaktikumāra, another Guhila prince, who reigned in the last quarter of the tenth century, we have two undated Jain inscriptions[33] also from Ahar.

Ojha also refers to a number of other Jain inscriptions found from different old Jain temples of Rajasthan.[34] The flourishing state of Jainism in Rajasthan is also evident from an intimate study of the *Vividhatīrthakalpa* of Jinaprabha who refers to a number of Jain centres of pilgrimage, quite a few of which were situated in Rajasthan. We should particularly mention Satyapura, which according to Jinaprabha, was first attacked by the Muslims under Mahmūd of Ghaznī in the Vikrama year 1081 corresponding to 1024 A.D. The temple according to Jinaprabha was built even before the destruction of Valabhī in V.S. 845. Satyapura, which Jinaprabha places in Marumaṇḍala is the modern Sanchor in Jalor district and is near the Gujarat border. The temple of Satyapura was dedicated to Mahāvīra and is also mentioned in a later inscription found from Sanchor.[35]

The famous Chitor or Citraflūṭa, which was the native town of the celebrated Jain savant Haribhadra, who probably flourished a few years before Udyotanasūri,[36] in the middle of the 8th century A.D., was another well known Jain centre of pilgrimage. Even now Chitor has remains of old Jain temples. He belonged to the Vidyādhara *kūla* and was the disciple of Jinadatta.[37] His literary activiites will be discussed in a later chapter. Another Jain savant Elācārya was also probably a native of Citrakūṭa and was a contemporary of Haribhadra.[38] A few years ago a fragmentary Digambara Jain inscription was discovered from Chitor.[39]

Let us now turn our attention to the condition of he Jain religion from 600 A.D. to 1000 A.D. in Gujarat. We have already seen that Gujarat was connected with the activities of Jain monks from the Mauryan period. By 600 A.D. it was firmly entrenched in Gujarat and numerous cities and villages of this state could boast of splendid Jain temples. Quite a good number of Jain writers have fortunately mentioned the shrines religion from 600 A.D to 1000 A D. in Gujarat. We have already taken note of the fact that Jinasena II, the author of the *Hari-vaṁśapurāṇa,* has referred two Jain temples of Vardhamāna and Dostaṭikā, both situated in Gujarat. The temple of

Vardhamāna (Vadavān) was dedicated to Pārśvanātha and that of Dostaṭikā to Śāntinātha. Both these temples were Digambara shrines and were built probably around 600 A.D. It was at Vardhamāna that another Digambara poet viz. Hariṣeṇa composed his *Bṛhatkathākośa* in 931 A.D.[40] In the Vikrama Saṁvat 1361 corresponding to 1302 A.D., Merutuṅga completed his *Prabandhacintāmaṇi* at this town.[41] This town therefore was well known to both the Digambaras and Śvetāmbaras.

The great city of Valabhī, which was an important centre of Jainism in the Gupta period, continued its existence till the last quarter of the eighth century A D. The city was well known for its celebrated shrine of Candraprabha. There was also a famous temple at this great town, dedicated to Mahāvīra. We are told in several Jain texts that the famous Jain icons of Valabhī were taken to various other towns before its destruction by the Muslims in 845 V.S. or 787 A.D. Jinaprabha[42] tells us that icon of Candraprabha at Valabhī, which was established by Gautamasvāmin, the great disciple of Mahāvīra was transferred to Prabhāsa also known as Devapattana or Śivapattana before 845 V.S. The confirmation of this account is found in another Jain historical text viz. the *Purātanaprabandhasaṅgraha.*[43] There is little doubt that the shrine of Candraprabha was established in all probability centuries before it was transferred to Prabhāsa. We further learn from the *Vividhatīrthakalpa*[44] and *Purātanaprabandhasaṅgraha*[45] that the icon of Vīra or Mahāvīra was transferred before the destruction of Valabhī to Śrīmāla or Bhīnmāl. Some other icons of this town were taken various other Jain holy places including Śatruñjaya.

The great Jain saint Mallavādi, according to the Jain tradition was a resident of Valabhī and it was because of his influence that Jainism became popular in Gujarat at the cost of the Buddhists.[46] Another town of Gujarat, which was associated with Jainism from early days was Bhṛgukaccha The great Śakunikāvihāra of this town was one of the greatest and most celebrated Jain shrines of Western India. Several Jain texts[47] refer to this *vihāra* which was apparently built in the Gupta period A number of Jain works were afterwards written to sing the glory of this *vihāra.*[48] Afterwards some of the greatest

Jains of Western India including Hemacandra visited this vihāra and did everythiing to beautify it. The 8th century Jain commentary viz. the *Vyavahārabhāṣya*[49] describes Bhṛgukaccha as a place sacred to the Jains. A recently discovered[50] bronze image inscription from this place refers to the Mūlavasati of Bhṛgukaccha. The inscription which is incised on the pedestal of an image of Pārśva has the date Śaka 908 corresponding to 986 A.D. It refers to a work called Pārśvilla, the disciple of Śīlabhadragaṇi, who belonged to the *anvaya* of Lakṣmaṇasūri of Nāgendrakula. It is apparent from the inscription that the temple called Mūlavasati existed at Bhṛgukaccha in the early mediaeval period.

We should then refer to the great Jain centre of Girnar also called Urjayanta. We have already taken note of the fact that this hill was associated with the Jain religion from a very early period. In the 10th century a great Jain lay devotee called Ratna, hailing from Kashmir[51] donated a golden image of Neminātha to the Jain Saṅgha here. From a very early period it was considered to be a sacred duty for every pious Jain to undertake a trip to this holy hill, believed to the place of Nirvāṇa of Neminātha. Like Girnar, the hill at Palitana in Gujarat, which is known as Śatruñjaya, was considered sacred from a pretty early period. However this hill sprang into prominence only after the 10th century A.D.

The Cāpas of Gujarat, who started their polical career even before the downfall of the Valabhī kingdom, were sincere patrons of the Jain religion. Nothing is known regarding the religious leaning of the earliest Cāpa king Vyāghramukha, whose name is disclosed by Brahmagupta and who ruled in 550 Śaka. According to the Jain writers Vanarāja of Pañcāsara, who later founded the city of Aṇahillapura, was the earliest prince of this dynasty. But as we have already noted, one Vyāghramukha was a prince of this dynasty and ruled around 628 A.D. at Bhinnamāla.

Several Jain writers have claimed that Vanarāja like Mādhava of the Gaṅga dynasty was helped by a Jain saint in his attempt to carve out an independent kingdom. The *Prabandhacintāmaṇi*[52] distinctly states that Vanarāja was helped in his childhood by a Jain monk named Śīlaguṇasūri. That Jain saint was convinced from the very beginning that the boy Vanarāja would become in future a *Jinaśāsanaprabhāvaka* i.e. 'a propagator of the Jain faith'. We are further told by the learned author of the *Prabandhacintāmaṇi* that the boy Vanarāja was brought up by *Gaṇinī* (head nun) Vīramatī. The Jain monk Śīlaguṇasūri foresaw from the horoscope of the boy that he was to become a great king. Afterwards Vanarāja founded according to Merutuṅga, in Vikrama Saṁvat 802 corresponding to 744 A.D. the city of Aṇahillapura. At first he offered his *guru* Śīlaguṇasūri his entire kingdom which the latter naturally declined to accept. Then at the instance of his Jain preceptor, Vanarāja built in the capital a temple dedicated to Pārśvanātha.[53] According to an earlier Jain text called *Nemināthacariyu*[54] written in 1160 A.D. in the capital of Vanarāja a Jain merchant of the name of Ninnaya built a temple, dedicated to the first Tīrthaṅkara Ādinātha or Ṛṣabha. Therefore the combined evidence of the two above-mentioned texts show that Vanarāja was definitely a patron of the Jains and a number of Jain shrines were founded during his reign in his kingdom. The account regarding Śīlaguṇasūri's connexion with Vanarāja is confirmed by the *Purātanaprabandhasaṅgraha*[55]. It is interesting to note that a Jain inscription[56] of Vanarāja gives the data Saṁ 802 which is found in the *Prabhandhacintāmaṇi* of Merutuṅga. This proves that the Jain tradition regarding Vanarāja is based on historical facts. The temple of Pañcāsara Pārśvanātha is still to be seen at Pattana although it is embellished with later additions. The *Prabhāvakacarita* also refers to the concessions given to the *caityavāsi* monks by Vanarāja[57]. Nothing practically is known regarding the Jain connexion of Vanarāja's successors. However a verse, quoted in the *Prabandhacintāmaṇi*, proves that the Cāpas were patrons of Jainism. The translation of the verse runs thus "This kingdom of Gurjaras, even from the time of king Vanarāja, was established with the Jain *mantras* (counsels), its enemies indeed has no cause to rejoice"[58]

Before we start our discussion on the condition of the Jain religion during the successors of the Cāpas in Gujarat, we must turn our attention to the available epigraphic records, discovered from Gujarat, throwing light on the Jain religion. The earliest of such records are the well known Surat plates of Karkarāja Suvarṇavarṣa dated Śaka 743 corresponding to 821 A.D. This inscription is an exceedingly important Jain record. It not only discloses the names of Jain saints who lived in the 8th century A.D. in Gujarat but also throws welcome light on the exact condition of the Jain religion at that time.

The record opens with a homage to the gospel of Jinendra. It runs thus "Victorious is the gracious gospel, propounded by the best of the Jinas, which is perpetual abode of prosperity, which is clear in its entirety, which is based on *Syādvāda* and which brings about beatitude to one with a controlled mind". This inscription records the grant of a piece of land to a Jaint savant of the name of Aparājita, who is described as the disciple of Sumati, and a grand-disciple of Mallavādi[59], belonging to the Sena Saṅgha branch of the Mūla Saṅgha. According to the Digambara *Paṭṭāvalis* Mūlasaṅgha branched off into three subsections known as Deva Saṅgha, Nandi Saṅgha and Sena Saṅgha.[60] This inscription therefore confirms the veracity of the testimony of the *Paṭṭāvalis*. We have already noticed in connexion with our discussion of South Indian Jainism that Nandi Saṅgha was in existence in the Far South even in the 6th century A.D. It appears that within a few years of the emergence of the Digambara sect it was sub-divided into a number of smaller schools, both in the North and the South.

The field which was granted to Aparājita in the year Śaka 743 is described in the inscription as situated near Nāgasārikā (modern Nausari, 20 miles South of Surat) which was one of the greatest cities of ancient Gujarat. The grant was made for the purpose of daily worship, cooked rice offerings and repairs and renovation of the monastery (*vasatikā*) which is described as an ornament of Sambapura and was attached to the temple of Arhat situated within the boundaries of Śrī Nāgasārikā. There is no doubt that the temple of Arhat at Nāgasārikā, mentioned in his inscription, was built before the 8th century A.D. The last two verses of the inscription are in praise of the Jina and the religion preached by him. The donor Karkarāja Suvarṇavarṣa was a cousin of the Rāṣṭrakūṭa emperor Amoghavarṣa I and was a feudatory under him in the Gujarat region.

It appears that this branch of the Rāṣṭrakūṭa family like the main branch actively patronised the Jains. But at present there is no trace of any Digambara temple at Nausari. There is however a Śvetāmbara shrine which was built in the 13th century.[61]

Jain inscriptions before 1000 A.D. are extremely rare in Gujarat. We have just now discussed the Surat plates of Karkarāja. A few epigraphs of Girnar were probably inscribed before 1000 A.D. The only other significant Jain inscription is that known as Varuṇāśarmaka[62] grant dated in the Vikrama Saṁvat 1033 corresponding to 975 A.D. It was issued during the reign of Mūlarāja I by his son *Yuvarāja* Cāmuṇḍarāja. We are told that the latter granted a field for the benefit of a Jain temple at Varuṇāśarmaka which is identified with Vadasama in Mehsana district of eastern Gujarat. The inscription significantly refers to *Jinabhavana,* and *Jinabimba.* This shows that the early kings of the Caulukya dynasty of Gujarat were not against Jainism. However, we cannot say that all of them were sincere patrons of Jainism. However, at least one of the officers of Mūlarāja was a Jain.[63] But there is no doubt that Jainism was very popular in Gujarat during the reign of the early Caulukya kings. In the next volume of this work we will discuss in greater details the position of the Jain religion in Gujarat after 1000 A.D.

Let us now turn our attention to Madhya Pradesh, which as we have already noticed, had several influential Jain centres from early times. However, it should be remembered that the ruling dynasties of this state did openly favour orthodox Hinduism or Brāhmaṇical religion. The Jain religion, however, was held in esteem by individual kings of different dynasties ruling in this state in our period i.e. between 600 A.D. and 1000 A.D. Let us first take note of the available Jain inscriptions.

From the well known Jain temple-complex at Sonagiri (Datia district, M.P.) has been discovered an epigraph of the seventh century[64] which directly proves the great antiquity of tha Jain centre. It refers to a Jain devotee called Vadāka, who was the son of Siṅghadeva. A very good number of Jain temples of quite early period have been discovered from different places of Madhya Pradesh. But not many inscriptions of this period are known. Among the few Jain inscriptions from Madhya Pradesh, belonging to our period, the most important is, however, the Khajuraho inscription[65] of the reign of Candella Dhaṅga dated in the Vikrama Saṁvat 1011 corresponding to 955 A.D. It is a carved on the left door-jamb of the temple of Jinanātha at Khajuraho. The inscription records a number of gifts in favour of the temple by one Pāhilla, and who is described as held in honour by king Dhaṅga. He is further described in the earlier part of the inscription as endowed with the qualities of tranquillity and self-control and as possessing compassion for all beings. A number of gardens are mentioned as gifts to the temple of Jinanātha. The inscription further refers to Śrī Vāsavacandra, who is described as the *guru* (preceptor) of Mahārāja, who is no other than Dhaṅga. This inscription, which is the earliest dated Candella record, conclusively proves the tremendous popularity of Jainism in the Candella dominion. This is also directly proved by the beautiful Jain temples of the Candella territory including Khajuraho.

A few other Jain inscriptions of our period from Madhya Pradesh are also known. An inscription[66] near Mandasor refers to Ācāryas Śubhakīrti and Vimalakīrti. The script of this inscription is datable to the tenth century A.D. An earlier Jain inscription[67] from Madhya Pradesh, giving the date 875 A.D., has also been discovered.

From the literary sources we get more meaningful and extensive information regarding the state of Jainism in Madhya Pradesh before 1000 A.D. The existence of a temple, dedicated to Pārśvanātha at Dhārā, the famous capital of the Paramāras, is disclosed by the *Darśanasāra*[68] of Devasena, which was composed in that shrine in Vikrama Saṁvat 990 corresponding to 933 A.D. It may be suggested that the ruler of Dhārā at that time was Vairisiṁha, the father of Harṣa Sīyaka of Harsola grant.[69] The temple of Pārśva, mentioned by Devasena, was surely a Digambara shrine and probably proves that soon after the foundation of this city, the Digambaras were permitted to build their temples there. Remnants of ruined Jain temples have been noticed at Dhar,[70] the ancient Dhārā. The Muslims destroyed both the Hindu and Jain temples there.[71]

During the rule of Harṣa Sīyaka the Jains enjoyed great popularity in the Paramāra kingdom. A number of Jain writers flourished during his rule and during the reign of his successor Muñja. During the closing period of the rule of Harṣa Sīyaka the famous Jain writer Dhanapāla composed his *Pāiyalacchī* in the Vikrama Saṁvat 1029 corresponding to 1072 A.D.[72] We are told by the poet that he composed this text for his sister Sundarī at Dhārā. From the later works like the *Prabhāvaka-carita* and *Prabandhacintāmaṇi* we learn that his grandfather Devarṣi was originally a Brahmin of Sāṅkāśya and afterwards migrated to Ujjayinī.[73] Dhanapāla, we are told, became a Jain under the influence of his younger brother Śobhana. The year in which Dhanapāla prepared his *Pāiyalacchī,* the Rāṣṭrakūṭa capital Mānyakheṭa was ransacked by the army of the Mālava king, From the *Tilakamañjarī,* which was composed during the rule of Bhoja, we learn that he was honoured by king Muñja who conferred upon him the title of Sarasvatī.[74] It thus appears that Dhamapāla was an honourable member of the Paramāra royal court during the reign of the three kings viz. Harṣa Sīyaka, Vākpati Muñja and Bhoja.

Another poet who flourished in the 2nd half of the 10th century during the reign of the Paramāra kings was Mahāsenasūri, belonging to Lāṭavargaṭa Saṅgha. His *guru* was Guṇākarasena, who was a disciple of Jayasena. From a short *Praśasti* discovered from Kārañjā Jain bhāṇḍār, we learn that the poet, who was the author of the *Pradyumnacaritakāvya,*[75] was honoured by no less a person than Muñja. Afterwards a high official of Muñja's brother viz. Sindhurāja became his devotee. The name of this high official (*mahattama*) is given as Parpaṭa. This proves that not only the Paramāra kings themselves, but also their officials were patrons of Jainism. Sindhurāja, it appears ruled for a short time in the closing years of the 10th century.[76]

Another Jain who flourished during the time of Muñja was Ācārya Amitagati who wrote his *Subhāṣitaratnasandoha* in the Vikrama Saṁvat 1050 when Muñja was 'ruling the earth'.[77]

Afterwards the same Ācārya composed his celebrated *Dharmaparīkṣā* during the reign of Bhoja in the Vikrama Saṁvat 1070. He belonged to the Kāṣṭhā Saṅgha. The names of his spiritual predecessors are as follows—Vīrasena, Devasena, Amitagati I, Nemiṣeṇa and Mādhavasena.[78] The earliest *guru* Vīrasena therefore flourished in the 9th century A.D. Incidentally the date supplied by Amitagati regarding Muñja is the last known date of that celebrated king.[79]

Let us turn our attention to the state of Jainism in Maharashtra after 600 A.D. We have already seen that Jainism was introduced in this state by the Mauryan period. Not many Jain inscriptions of this period from Maharashtra are, however, known. But we definitely know that during the rule of the Western Cālukyas and the Rāṣṭrakūṭas Jainism was tremendously popular, not only in the Lower Deccan, but also in the modern Maharashtra state. According to Jinaprabha[80] Tīrthaṅkara Candraprabha was worshipped from very early times as Jīvitasvāmin at Nāsika. At Pratiṣṭhāna, another old city of Maharashtra, which is identified with Paithan, there was a famous shrine, dedicated to Muni Suvrata.[81] Recently an important Jain inscription of the early 10th century A.D.[82] was discovered from Nasik district of Maharashtra. The inscription is incised on three plates which were found from a place called Vajirkheda, four miles east of Malegaon in Nasik district. The inscription tells us that at the time of his *paṭṭbandha* ceremony Rāṣṭrakūṭa Nityavarṣadeva (Indra III) who meditated on the feet of his grandfather Kṛṣṇa II (Akālavarṣa), in Śaka 836 (915 A.D.) granted two villages to a Jain monastery called Amoghavasati and the site of the monastary itself to the preceptor Vardhamāna, who was the disciple of Lokabhadra of Draviḍa Saṅgha. The *gaṇa* and *anvaya* of Vardhamāna were Vīra and Vīrṇṇāya respectively. We are further told that Amoghavasati was situated at Candanāpurī, which is the present Candanpuri situated two miles south of Malegaon. It has been suggested[83] that Amoghavasati, referred to in the inscription, was built by the Rāṣṭrakūṭa Amoghavarṣa, who was a great Jain patron, as we will notice in the next chapter. It is also quite likely that the emperor Amoghavarṣa I himself gave grants to this Jain temple of Candanāpuri. The undated Kalvan plates[84] of the time of Paramāra Bhoja (early eleventh century) show that the Śvetāmbara Jains had their monastery at Muktāpalī in the same Nasik district. It is apparent from that inscription that the temple of Suvratasvāmin of that place was built centuries before the time of Bhoja I. The record under discussion further shows that the monks, belonging to Draviḍa Saṅgha had migrated to Nasik district afterwards. Such migrations of Jain monks were quite common in those days, as we will see afterwards.

The second part of the same grant registers a gift of six villages to the Jain monastery of Uriamma at the town of Vaḍanera and the residential monastery itself to the same preceptor Vardhamāna. Uriamma is a Kannaḍa name for Jvālāmālinī, the *yakṣiṇī* of Candraprabha. The villages which were given away as gift are in the Nasik district, and Vaḍanera is modern Vadner, 15 miles North-west of Malegaon. Both the parts of the grant, we are told, were written by the poet Rājaśekhara, who is probably to be identified with the celebrated poet of that name. The editor of this inscription thinks that probably Rājaśekhara, after Mahendrapāla's demise, in 910 A.D., went to the royal court of Indra III. It has further been pointed out that the verse No. 2 of the first part of the record is a *maṅgalaśloka* in the *Pramāṇasaṅgraha* of Akalaṅka.[85]

The inscription, discussed above, not only discloses the existence of two Jain shrines in Nasik district of Maharashtra in the early mediaeval period, but also bears testimony to the fact that this religion enjoyed great royal patronage during the days of the Rāṣṭrakūṭas. In the next chapter we will have something more to say on this point. It further appears that the well known poet Rājaśekhara became a Jain during the later part of his life. However, in the absence of further evidence, we cannot be dogmatic on this point.

The popularity of Jainism in Maharashtra in our period is further proved by the beautiful Jain caves of Ellora, most of which were excavated by 800 A.D.[86] We will discuss their artistic value in the next volume of this work. In the last chapter we had occasion to refer to the spurious Altem copper plates discovered from Kolhapur district of Maharashtra. The inscription proves the existence of a great Jain temple in Kolhapur district in the ancient period. The other details, given in this inscription, cannot be accepted, unless otherwise verified. However, there is no reason to disbelieve that a feudatory of the Western Cālukyas did not build a Jain temple at Alaktakanagara (Altem) sometime about 600 A.D.[87]

Several places of modern Uttar Pradesh were directly connected with the Jain religion in our period. We should first refer to the celebrated group of Deogarh temples[88] in Jhansi district, situated on the river Betwa (Vatravatī). Probably some of the temples here, were built in the Gupta period but majority of them came into existence only in our period. The most important inscription of Deogarh is that of the time of Pratīhāra Bhoja[89] which gives the date both in the Vikrama and Śaka eras. The date given in the Vikrama era is 919 and in the Śaka 784, corresponding to 862 A.D. The inscription has been found in the temple of Śāntinātha. The inscription proves that the shrine of Śāntinātha existed before 826 A.D. We further learn that Deoghar was known formerly as Luacchāgira. It further mentions Mahāsāmanta Viṣṇurāma who had the title *pañcamahāśabda* given to him by *paramabhaṭṭāraka, mahārājādhirāja, parameśvara* Śrī Bhojadeva. The inscription which is incised on a pillar (*stambha*) of the temple further refers to one Śrīdeva who was the disciple of *ācārya* Kamaladeva. Anoher inscription[90], which is dated V.S. 1016. mentions Tribhuvanakīrti, a disciple of Devendrakīrti, who was a disciple of Ratnakīrti of the Sarasvatī *gaccha* of Śrī Mūlasaṅgha. Ratnakīrti, therefore, flourished around 850 A.D., if not earlier. A third inscription[91] of the 9th century A.D. from this place refers to a Jain *muni* called Nāgasenācārya. Another inscription[92] has the date V.S. 1051 corresponding to 994 A.D. A very good number of inscriptions from Deogarh belong to the period after 1000 A.D., and they will be discussed in the next volume of this work.

It should be remembered that Deogarh continues to be a sacred place for the Jains even at the present day. The celebrated Viṣṇu temple, belonging to the Gupta period, of this place is undoubtedly the oldest shrine of Deogarh. However, it appears that this place was not known to Jinaprabha, the author of the celebrated *Vividhatīrthakalpa.*

Let us now turn our attention to Mathurā, which as we have already seen, had been a great Jain centre from the 2nd century B.C., if not earlier. In the literary texts, composed in our period, Mathurā is repeatedly mentioned as a celebrated Jain centre. The *Bṛhatkalpabhāṣya,*[93] composed in the 8th century, refers to the Jain shrines in residential areas of Mathurā. The *Bṛhatkathākośa*[94] of Hariṣeṇa describes Mathurā as *Jināyatanamaṇḍitā* i.e. 'abounding in Jain temples'. This text was composed in 931 A.D. Jinaprabha[95] informs us that in the Vikrama year 826 corresponding to 768 A.D, the great Śvetāmbara savant Bappabhaṭṭi established an image of Mahāvīra (*Vīrabiṁba*) at Mathurā. This is also confirmed by the evidence of the *Prabandhakośa.*[96] According to Devasena in the Vikrama Saṁvat 953 corresponding to 895 A.D., Rāmasena established Māthura Saṅgha at Mathurā[97]. This shows that Mathurā continued as a favourite resort for both the Śvetāmbaras and Digambaras.

A few Jain inscriptions of our period[98] have been discovered from Mathurā which also prove that Mathurā retained its popularity as a Jain centre between 600 A.D. and 1000 A.D. However, it should be remembered that the popularity of Jainism at Mathurā gradually diminished in course of time, with the migration of the Jain monks, towards Rajasthan, Gujarat and Karṇāṭaka. The ruling dynasties of Northern India did not patronise Jainism like the ruling dynasties of the three abovementioned states. This point we will discuss afterwards. For the present, let us turn our attention to some other places of Uttar Pradesh.

Several old cities of Uttar Pradesh like Ahicchatra, Kāmpilya, Kāśī, Sāṅkāśya, Śrāvastī, Kausāmbī etc. had Jain centres, and Jina images from these cities of our period have been discovered and they will be discussed in the next volume. A few small Jain inscriptions and images of our period have also been found from different places of Uttar Pradesh[99]. In this connexion we should take note of the statement of the author of the *Prabodhacandrodaya*[100], a play written in the 11th century, that as a result of persecution by the Brahmins, the Digambara Jains and Buddhists fled to Pañcāla, Mālava, Ābhīra and Ānarta. We should remember that the play was staged in the court of Candella Kīrtivarman and therefore its evidence has real value[101]. There is very great reason to believe that by 1000 A.D., Jainism was almost completely eclipsed from majority of places in Uttar Pradesh, Bihar, Bengal and Orissa.

In the Śvetāmbara Jain works, we are told about the achievements of a great Jain saint of the name of Bappabhaṭṭi, who is described as a contemporary of king Āma of Kanauj, Dharmapāla of Bengal and Vākpati, the author of the celebrated Prakrit poem *Gauḍavaho*.[102] This great Jain saint, was responsible, according to the Śvetāmbara works, for the promotion of Jainism in different places of Northern India in the 8th century A.D. However, his chief patron king Āma is not known from epigraphic sources. It has been conjectured[102A] that he should either be identified with Nāgabhaṭa II or Indrāyudha-Indrarāja. Bappabhaṭṭi set up in his lifetime Jain shrimes at Mathurā, Gopagiri (Gwalior), Aṇahillapura and other places[103]. Elsewhere, we are told, that it was due to him that the Śvetāmbaras could regain control over the famous Raivataka hill.[104]

Turning now to the extreme Northern part of India we find only a few evidences regarding the existence of Jainism in Punjab, Himachal Pradesh and Haryana. We have an important inscription[105] from Kangra, Himachal Pradesh, which discloses the names of two Jain saints, belonging to Rājakula *gaccha*, which is probably the same as Rāja *gaccha*. A certain Siddharāja is described as a disciple of Sūri Amalacandra, a pupil of Sūri Abhayacandra. Siddharāja's son was Dhaṅga and Dhaṅga's son Caṣṭaka. The wife of Caṣṭaka was Ralhā and the two sons were born of her and both of them were devoted to the law of Jina (*Jainadharmaparāyaṇau*). The elder was called Kuṇḍalaka and the younger Kumara. We are told that they were responsible for the construction of the image (of Pārśvanātha). The date given is Saṁvat 30 which according to Bühler is equivalent to 854 A.D.[106] The earliest Sūri Abhayacandra should be placed around 700 A.D.

We have already taken note of the fact that one *śrāvaka*

Ratna (Rayaṇa) from Kashmir founded a *maṇibimba* of Neminātha[107] in the year V.S. 990 corresponding to 932 A.D. on the sacred hill of Raivataka. This shows that there were a few Jains in Kashmir in the 10th century A.D. Kalhaṇa, however, in his *Rājataraṅgiṇī* has not mentioned the Jains even once. However, archaeological evidences[108] at our disposal, prove that Jainism was not entirely unknown in some places of Kashmir. However, this religion was looked upon only as one of the minor religious sects in Kashmir, Himachal Pradesh, Punjab and Haryana.

Recently a few Śvetāmbara and Digambara Jain images, belonging to the 8th and 9th centuries A.D., have been discovered from Punjab[109]. We have later Jain inscriptions from the Himalayan areas which show that Jainism somehow lingered in those areas till a very late period.

In eastern India Jainism maintained its existence till the end of the 10th century A.D. However, no important Jain inscription has been found from either West Bengal or Bangladesh which can be assigned between 600 and 1000 A.D. The only Jain record[110] of the Pāla period has been discovered from Bargaon, near Nālandā (Bihar). The inscription belongs to the 24th year of Rājyapāla, who ruled in the first half of the tenth century A.D.[111] The record is incised on a pillar near a ruined Jain temple and refers to one Vaidyanātha, son of Manoratha of Vaṇikakula. However, there is no dearth of Jain images, belonging to the Pāla period, either in Bengal or Bihar. Some of these Jain icons will be discussed in the next volume of this work.

From Orissa a number of Jain inscriptions, belonging to the post-Gupta period, have been found. The earliest of such inscriptions is a Śailodbhava grant, belonging to the 7th century A.D. This inscription[112] mentions one Jain *muni* called Prabuddhacandra and his teacher Arhadācārya Nāsicandra. This proves the prevalance of Jainism in Orissa in the 7th century A.D. We have another 7th century inscription[113] found from Ratnagiri hills (Cuttack district) which is a Jain record of four lines in east Indian character of the 7th century A.D. It refers to the installation of Jain images and points to the existence of an early Jain esablishment on these hills, which are famous for their Buddhistic ruins.

Two Digambara Jain inscriptions have been discovered from Udaygiri-Khaṇḍagiri caves. They belong to the tenth century A.D., and were inscribed during the reign of Udyotakeśarī of the Keśarī dynasty of Orissa. The first inscription[114] discovered in the cave called Lalitendu Keśarī's cave was incised in the 5th year of the reign of Udyotakeśarī and refers to the repair of the old Jain temples. It also preserves the name of a Digambara saint called Yaśanandi. It is interesting to note that the inscription refers to the Udaygiri-Khaṇḍagiri hills as Kumāraparvata, which reminds us of the Kumārīparvata of Khāravela's record. The present writer has been able locate the only literary reference to this hill. In the *Bṛhatkathākośa*[115] of Hariṣeṇa, composed in 931 A.D., there is mention of Kumāragiri of Oḍraviṣaya. It is no doubt the same as Kumāragiri or Kumārīgiri.

The second inscription[116] was inscribed in the 18th year of Udyotakeśarī's reign and mentions Śubhacandra, the disciple of Kulacandra, belonging to the Deśī *gaṇa* and Āryasaṅghagraha *kula*. The Deśī *gaṇa* is also known from inscriptions found from different places of Karṇāṭaka and Madhya Pradesh[117]. However the *kula* mentioned here is not otherwise known. Another inscription found from the same hill refers to the above-mentioned Jain *munis*.[118]

These inscriptions prove that Jainism continued to flourish in Orissa as late as the 10th century A.D. After 1000 A.D. Jainism gradually became less popular and with the rise of new theistic sects this religion almost completely disappeared from Orissa.

The present writer is strongly of the opinion that the famous Somadeva, the author of the *Yaśastilakacampū*, who is also mentioned in an inscription[119] dated Śaka 888, and who is described there as belonging to the Gauḍa Saṅgha was originally a Jain saint from Bengal. There is no need to suppose the existence of Saṅgha of this name in Uttar Pradesh.[120] We must remember that Jainism was very popular in Bengal. Since Bengal was connected with Jainism from early times it is natural to suppose that the Jain monks, belonging to this state, were held in esteem by monks, belonging to other states of India. With the decline of Jainism in Bengal in the 10th century A.D., the monks of this state naturally sought asylum in other parts of the country. It is also interesting to note that Somadeva in his *Yaśastilakacampū*[121] refers to a Jain shrine of Tāmralipta, the ancient port of Southern Bengal.

To sum up, we must repeat that with the exception of Gujarat and Rajasthan and a few select pockets elsewhere, Jainism was fighting a losing battle in Northern India. In Rajasthan and Gujarat it was because of the enthusiasm of traders that this religion managed to retain its hold. In other parts of India Śaivism and Vaiṣṇavism became the dominant religions systems. In eastern India the Pālas mainly patronised the Buddhists. In central India the kings belonging to Kalacuri, Candella, Cāhamāna, Guhila and other dynasties did practically nothing to promote the cause of this religion. In northernmost parts of India, the ruling dynasties did never care for Jainism. Kashmir was a citadel of the Śaivas and Punjab of both the Śaivas and Vaiṣṇavas. But in South India, especially in Karnatak the picture was different, and we will now turn our attention once more to the South.

NOTES

1 Watters, *On Yuan Chwang's Travels in India,* Vol. I, p. 123.

2 *Ibid.*, Vol. I, p. 251.

3 *Ibid.*, Vol. II, p. 154.

4 *Ibid.*, Vol. II, p. 184.

5 *Ibid.*, Vol. II, p. 187.

6 See *Annual Progress Report of the Superintendent, Hindu and Buddhist Monuments, Northern Circle,* 1918-19, p. 12.

7 Watters, *op. cit.,* Vol. II, p. 154.

8 See *J.A.S.B.*, 1958 (Vol. 24) No. 2, 'Some Jain Antiquities from Bankura, by Sm. D. Mitra.

9 See *Jain Journal,* 1969, Vol.-IV, No. 4; see also R. D, Banerji, *Eastern Indian School of Mediaeval Sculpture,* p. 145; see also *Jain Journal,* Vol. V, No. 1.

10 *A.S.I.A.R.* (Western Circle), 1905-6, p. 52; see also *A.S.I.A.R.,* 1936-37, p. 122.

11 *A.S.I.A.R.* (W. Circle), 1905-6, pp. 48 ff.
12 *Ibid.*, p. 50.
13 (S.J.G.M.) No. 45 (ed. A. N. Upadhye), colophon, VS. 6.
14 *Vividhatīrthakalpa,* p. 86.
15 Quoted in p. 200 fn. 1 of *P.H.N.I.* by G. C. Chowdhary.
16 *A.S.I.A.R.* (W. Circle), 1906-7, p. 39.
17 Verses 18-20.
18 Bhandarkar, *List* No. 72; See also P. C. Nahar, *Jaina Lekha Saṅgraha,* Vol. I, pp. 192 ff; also *A.S.I.A.R.,* 1908-09, p. 108.
19 P. 86.
20 See *I.A.*, Vol. 19, pp. 233 ff.
21 See Chatterjee, A. K. *Ancient Indian Literary ond Cultural Tradition,* pp. 89 ff.
22 Bhandarkar, *List,* No. 25.
23 *E.I.*, Vol. IX, pp. 280 f.
24 See *J.A.S.B.*, Vol. LXII, Pt. I, pp. 309 ff.; See also *E.I.*, Vol. 10,
25 *E.I.*, Vol. 10, p. 19; this portion of the inscription also contains some interestisg coin-names.
26 See also Ray, H. C. *D., H. N. I.*, Vol. I, pp. 560 ff.
27 See *Jaina Śilālekha Saṅgraha,* Vol. V, No. 16; also *Indian Epigraphy* (*Annual Report*), 1961-62, B 128.
28 See *Indian Archaeology,* 1961-62, p. 85.
29 See *J.A.S.B.*, (Letters), 1953, Vol. 19, pp. 109-110.
30 *Loc. cit*
31 See *Jaina Sāhitya kā Bṛhad Itihāsa,* Vol. 6, p. 476.
32 Vol. II, p. 428.
33 *Ibid.*, pp. 434-37.
34 See Vol. IV, Pt. I, p. 58; Vol. V, Part I, p. 63, etc.
35 See *A.S.I.A.R.*, (W. Circle), 1906-7, p. 36.
36 In the colophon of his work the *Kuvalayamālā* Udyotanasūri (VSS. 14-15) refers to Haribhadra as one his teachers.
37 See the colophon of the *Āvaśyakavṛtti* quoted in *The Jaina Sources of the Hist. of Ancient India* by K. P. Jain, p. 190 fn. 5.
38 See Jain, *op. cit.*, p. 188 fn. 4.
39 See *Indian Archaeology,* 1955-56, p. 31.
40 Ed. A. N. Upadhye, *praśasti,* VS. 4.
41 Ed. Jinavijaya, *praśasti,* the concluding line.
42 See *Vividhatīrthakalpa,* p. 29.
43 Ed. Jinavijaya, p. 83.
44 P. 29.
45 P. 83.
46 See *Prabandhacintāmaṇi,* p. 107; *Purātanaprabandhasaṅgraha,* p. 130; *Prabandhakośa,* pp. 21 ff.
47 See *Jain sāhitya kā bṛhad itihāsa,* Vol. VI, pp. 131, 363, 438.

48 See especially the *Sudaṁsaṇācariya* by Devendrasūri who composed the text in the 12th century. See for further details Jain, J. C. *Prakrit sāhitya kā itihāsa*, pp. 561 ff. According to Muni Punyavijaya this text is based on an earlier work; see Jain, *op. cit.*, p. 561 fn. 1. A detailed account regarding it will be found in the *Vividhatīrthakalpa*, pp. 20 ff.

49 See Jain, J.C., *op. cit.*. p. 219.

50 See *Lalit Kala* (Nos. 1-2), 1955-56, plate XII, fig. 10A.

51 See *Purātanaprabandhasaṅgraha*, p. 97.

52 P. 12.

53 *Ibid.*, p 13.

54 Ed. Jacobi, p. 152.

55 P. 12.

56 Guérinot, *List*, No. 116; see also Burgess and Cousens, *Antiquities of Northern Gujarat* (*ASI*, Vol. 32), p. 45.

57 P. 136.

58 P. 13.

59 *E.I.*, Vol. 21, pp. 133 ff.

60 See *E. R. E.*, Vol. 7, p. 474 and also *E.I.*, Vol. 21, pp. 133 ff.

61 See *E.I.*, Vol. 21, pp. 133 ff.

62 *Bhāratīya Vidyā*, Vol. I, p. 73; also *H.I.G.*, Vol. III, No. 136A.

63 See Majumdar, A. K., *Caulukyas of Gujarat*, 1956, p, 32; also *A.I.O.C.*, Vol. 7, p. 1157.

64 *Jain Lekha Saṅgraha* (*M.D.J.M.*), Vol. V, No. 5 also *Indian Epigraphy* (*Annual Report*), 1962-63, B. 381.

65 See *E.I.*, Vol. I, pp. 135-36.

66 See *Jain Lekha Saṅgraha*, Vol. IV, No. 114; also *Indian Epigraphy* (*Annual Report*), 1954-55, p. 45.

67 See *Jain Lekha Saṅgraha*, Vol. II, No. 129; also Cunningham, *A.S.I.*, Vol. 10, p. 74.

68 VSS. 49-50; quoted in N. Premi's *Jain Sāhitya aur itihāsa*, p. 175, fn. 1.

69 *E.I.*, Vol. 19, pp. 236 ff.

70 See *Prog. Report of A.S.I., N. W. Provinces* and *Oudh Circle*, 1892-93, pp. 21-28.

71 *Loc. cit*

72 See VS No. 276.

73 See Premi, *op. cit.*, p. 409; see also *Prabandhacintāmaṇi*, pp. 36 ff.

74 See G. C. Choudhary, *P.H.N.I.*, p. 88.

75 See Premi, *op. cit.*, p. 411 fn. 2.

76 See *D.H.N.I.*, Vol. 2, pp. 858 ff.

77 See Premi, *op. cit.*, p. 283

78 *Ibid.*, p. 278.

79 See Bühler in *E.I.*, Vol. I, p. 228.

80 See Pp. 53f ; also p. 85.

81 *Vividhatīrthakalpa,* pp. 59f.

82 See *E.I.*, Vol. 38, pp. 5-22.

83 *Ibid.*, p 11.

84 *E.I.*, Vol. 19, pp. 71 ff.

85 *E.I.*, Vol. 38, p 8 ; also *N.I.A.*, Vol. 2, pp. 111 ff.

86 See *The Classical Age,* p. 499.

87 For the text of the inscription see *Jaina Ṣilālekha Saṅgraha,* Vol. 2, pp. 85 ff.

88 See *Jain Siddhānta Bhāskara,* Vol. 8, pp. 67-73. See also *Bhārat ke Digambara Jain Tīrtha* (Bhāratīya Jñānapīṭha), Bombay, 1974, Vol. I, pp. 179-195.

89 *E.I.*, Vol. 4, pp. 309-10.

90 Ins. 148 (App. to Jain Inscriptions from Deogarh).

91 See *Jaina Ṣilālekha Saṅgraha,* Vol 5, No. 26.

92 *Ibid.*, No. 20.

93 See J. C. Jain, *Prakrit Sāhitya kā itihāsa,* p. 223.

94 2.1 ; see story No. 12 where we have an account of the founding of 5 *stūpas* at Mathurā.

95 *Vividhatīrthakalpa,* p. 19.

96 P. 41.

97 See Jain, J. C., *op. cit.*, p. 321.

98 See *Antiquities of Mathurā,* p. 53 ; see also *Jaina Ṣilālekha Saṅgraha,* Vol. 2, No. 161 ; Vol. 4, No. 112.

99 See *Jaina Ṣilālekha Saṅgraha,* Vol. 4, No. 116 ; Vol. 5, No. 19.

100 See Cunningham, *A.S.I.*, Vol. 20, p. 104.

101 See *D.H.N.I.*, Vol. II, p. 695.

102 See *Prabandhakoṣa,* pp. 26-46.

102A *P.H N.I.*, pp. 24 ff.

103 *Prabandhakośa,* p. 41.

104 See *Prabandhacintāmaṇi,* p. 123 ; *Purātanaprabandhasaṅgraha,* pp. 98 f.

105 See *E.I.*, Vol. 1, p. 120.

106 *Loc. cit.*

107 See *Purātanaprabandhasaṅgraha,* p. 97 ; see *Vividhatīrthakalpa,* p. 9.

108. See *Annual Progress Report of the Archaeological Deptt. Jammu and Kashmir,* 1917-18, p. 7 ; 1918-19, p. 3.

109 All India Radio News Bulletin, 30.6.1975.

110 *I.A.*, Vol. 47, p. 111 ; see also *J. R. A. S. B.*, 1949, Vol. 15, p. 7 f. and plate I.

111 See Majumdar, R. C., *Hist. of Ancient Bengal,* p. 124.

112 See *E.I.*, Vol. 29, pp. 38 ff.

113 See *Indian Archaeology, A Review,* 1954-55, p. 29.

114 See *E.I.*, Vol. 13, pp. 165 f.

115 61.67 (edited A. N. Upadhye).

116 See *E.I.*, Vol. 13, pp. 165 f. ; see also *Jaina Ṣilālekha Saṅgraha*, Vol. 4, No. 94.

117 See *Jaina Ṣilālekha Saṅgraha,* Vol. 4, *prastāvanā*, pp. 7 ff.

118 *Ibid.*, Vol. 4, No. 95.

119 For the text of this inscription which was originally discovered from Parbhani, Maharashtra see Premi, *op. cit.*, pp. 193 ff. ; see also N. Venkataramanayya, *The Cālukyas of Vemulavāḍa*, pp. 92 ff. The other details regarding this inscription will be discussed in the next chapter.

120 See Premi, *op. cit.*, p. 184.

121 See in this connexion Handiqui, K. K., *Yaśastilaka and Indian Culture*, p. 414.

CHAPTER X

Jainism in South India

(600 A.D. to 1000 A.D.)

We have already seen that Jainism was more popular in the Southern states than in those of the north. Except in parts of Gujarat and Rajasthan this religion was steadily losing ground in other areas of Northern India. The picture was somewhat different at least in one South Indian state viz. Karṇāṭaka, where the ruling dynasties actively befriended it. We propose to discuss at first the condition of this religion under the Western Cālukyas, who were the masters of large parts of Southern and Western India for quite a long time.

We have already seen that a few of the earlier kings of this dynasty, who ruled before 600 A.D., were friendly towards this religion. Kīrtivarman I who ruled upto 597 A.D., was succeeded by his brother Maṅgaleśa. Recently, a new inscription of his reign has been discovered, which proves the popularity of the Jain religion during his time. The inscription[1] is in Telegu-Kannaḍa characters and the language is Sanskrit. There are altogether three plates which were found from Hūli, district Belgaum of Karṇāṭaka. The inscription is undated but refers to Maṅgalarāja, who is no other than Mangaleśa of the Badami house and it should therefore be assigned to circa 600 A.D. It records a grant of land to a Jain monastery by the Sendraka chief Raviśakti, son of Kannaśakti. Hūli continued as a Jain centre for a long time and we have another Jain inscription from this place dated A.D. 1043[2]. This is the second copper plate record of Maṅgaleśa, the other being the Nerur grant[3].

The Jain religion received a new impetus during the reign of Maṅgaleśa's illustrious successor Pulakeśin II, the son of Kīrtivarman I. The well known Aihole stone inscription[4] which is dated in the Śaka era 556 and composed by the poet Ravikīrti is undoubtedly the most important historical Western Cālukya record. The inscription was discovered from an old temple at Aihole in Hungund *taluk* of Bijapur district. It was composed, according to the poet Ravikīrti, 3735 years after the Bhārata war. The record opens with the following words, "Victorious is the holy Jinendra, he who is exempt from old age, death and birth--in the sea of whose knowledge, the whole world is comprised like an island". After describing the exploits of Pulakeśin II and his predecessors, the poet Ravikīrti informs us in verse No 35 that "this stone mansion of Jinenedra, a mansion of every kind of greatness, has been caused to be built by the wise Ravikīrti, who has obtained the highest favour of that Satyāśraya, whose rule is bounded by the three oceans". This Satyāśraya is no other than Pulakeśin II, the conqueror of Harṣa. The concluding verse is also very interesting. It runs thus, "May that Ravikīrti, be victorious, who full of discernment, has used, the abode of the Jina, built of stone, for a new treatment of his theme, and who thus by his poetic power, has attained the fame of Kālidāsa and Bhāravi". There is little doubt that the poet Ravikīrti was not only a sincere and dedicated Jain, but also one of the celebrated men of letters of his time. It is evident from the inscription that he was in the good books of the emperor Pulakeśin II, which indirectly proves that the Cālukyan monarch himself had deference and love for the religion of the Jinas. It has been suggested[5] that the poet Ravikīrti was a monk of the Yāpanīya Saṅgha; but there is really no evidence to prove this point. But he was surely a Digambara Jain.

A long stone tablet, discovered from Lakshmeśvara in Dharwar district has several inscriptions of different dynasties[6]. The second part[7] of this record mentions king Satyāśraya and Cālukya Raṇaparākramāṅka and his son Ereya. A contemporary of this Satyāśraya was Durgaśakti. These kings, who were evidently the feudatories of Satyāśraya, are described as Sendra kings, belonging to the line of Bhujagendras i.e. Nāga family. It records grant of land to the *caitya* of the god called Śaṅkha Jinendra at Puligere (modern Lakshmeśvara). According to Fleet[8] the inscription is of early date, repeated here for the sake of confirmation and preservation. He further believes that "Raṇaparākramāṅka is perhaps intended for Raṇarāga, the father of Pulakeśin I and son of Jayasiṁha I". In that case, this inscription is referable to early 6th century A.D. So far as the Sendra kings are concerned, we have already noted that, they were from the very beginning, patrons of the Jain religion. However, the identity of Satyāśraya of this inscription is yet to be solved. If this Satyāśraya is Pulakeśin I, then the inscription should be taken as a record of the middle of the 6th century A.D. And we actually know that Pulakeśin I had the titles *Satyāśraya* and *Raṇavikrama.*[9] That Pulakeśin I himself was a Jain patron is known from the spurious Altem record, which has already been discussed. We should further remember that the record, under discussion, was inscribed in the 10th century A.D., and possibly represents a later copy of an original copper plate.[10] We have already seen that in a genuine copper plate of about 600 A.D., a few Sendra kings are mentioned and they bear Śakti-ending names. And this inscription also refers to two Sendra kings who bear similar names. This probably shows that the contents of the present record cannot be questioned.

Another long stone tablet from the same site viz. Lakshmeśvara has several interesting inscriptions.[11] All the records are later copies of original copper plate or stone inscriptions. The earliest inscription[12] refers to the reign of Vinayāditya's 5th or 7th regnal year corresponding to 608 Śaka i.e. 686 A.D. It records a grant to an *ācārya* of Mūlasaṅgha *anvaya* and Devagaṇa sect. The king was at that time stationed at Raktapura. Then we must refer to another part of the same stone tablet which is dated in the 34th year of Vijayāditya[13] corresponding to Śaka 651 when he was encamped at Raktapura. The village which was given away as grant was situated near the town of Pulikara. The donee was his father's priest Udayadevapaṇḍita also called Niravadyapaṇḍita, who was the home-pupil of Śrī Pūjyapāda and belonged to the Devagaṇa sect of Mūlasaṅgha. We are further told that the grant was made for the benefit of the temple of Saṅkha Jinendra at the city of Pulikara, the present Lakshmeśvara. We have already said that the inscriptions of Lakshmeśvara are later copies of earlier records. This is the reason why they are looked upon as spurious.[14] But there no reason why we should disbelieve their contents. The Jain priest Udayadevapaṇḍita was surely looked upon with respect by the Cālukyan king Vijayāditya. It is apparent from the inscription that Udayadevapaṇḍita was not the immediate pupil of Pūjyapāda but definitely belonged to his *anvaya*. It is quite likely that this Pūjyapāda was the well known Jain savant of the same name who flourished a few centuries before the time of Vijayāditya.

Then we must mention yet another inscription from the same place.[15] It belongs to the time of Vikramāditya II and gives the date Śaka 656 corresponding to 734 A.D. We are told that in the second year of king Vikramāditya Śaṅkhatīrtha-vasati of the city of Pulikara (Puligere of other inscriptions) and the temple called White Jinālaya were embellished and repaired and that certain land was given for maintaining the worship of Jina. It was issued from Raktapura. The donee was Vijayadevapaṇḍita who was the disciple of Jayadeva-paṇḍita and the latter of Rāmadeva Ācārya belonging to Mūla-saṅgha and Devagaṇa. There were thus two prominent Jain shrines at this place, one called Śaṅkhatīrtha and the other of the name of Dhavala-Jinālaya. It further appears that this Dhavala Jinālaya was then in a dilapidated condition and was badly in need of repair. It is interesting to note that in the *Vividhatīrthakalpa*[16] Śaṅkha-Jinālaya is mentioned as one of the holy places, connected with the Jain religion. This inscription of Vikramāditya II, as Fleet observes,[17] was copied from a previous stone tablet or copper plate for the sake of confirmation and preservation.

Three other inscriptions, belonging to the time of Western Cālukyas, have to be mentioned now. The first comes from Dharwar district[18] and it belongs to the 11th year of Vijayāditya and Śaka 630. This copper plate refers to a Jina temple of Puligere, built by queen Kuṁkumadevī. The second,[19] which is more important, also comes from Dharwar district and belongs to the 6th year Kīrtivarman II. It therefore corresponds to 751 A.D. The inscription was discovered from a place called Annigeri situated in Navalgund Tāluk of Dharwar district. The object of the inscription is to record the construction of a *cediya* (Jain temple) by Kaliyamma, who was holding the office of the headman of Jebuḷageri and the erection in front of it of a sculpture by a certain Koṇḍiśularakuppa, whose other name was Kīrtivarma-Gosāsi. The latter is clearly the name of his master (*prabhu*) as stated in the last line. The writer was one Dīśapāla. Anoher inscription[20] of the time of Kīrtivaman II comes from Adur situated in the Hangal Tāluk of Dharwar district. It records some land grants to the temple of Jinendra.

Quite a few short label inscriptions have been found from Aihole.[21] They have been assigned to the 7th century A.D. They are engraved on the pillar in the Jain temple close to the Meguti temple at Aihole (the site of Ravikīrti's inscription). A few such names are also preserved at Badami and they also are assigned to the 7th century A.D.[22]

Hariṣeṇa in his *Bṛhatkathākośa*[23] refers to one king Vijayāditya of Dakṣiṇāpatha who may be identical with the Cālukyan king of the same name. Elsewhere also he refers to the glorious condition of the Jain religion in South India. As we have already noted, another South Indian Jain poet Raviṣeṇa, who flourished in the 7th century A.D., has repeatedly mentioned the prosperity of the Jains in South India.

It should not, however, be supposed that the Cālukyans themselves were Jains. Majority of their inscriptions prove that they were devout Hindus, strongly believing in traditional form of Brāhmaṇical religion. However, like their predecessors, the Kadambas, they from the very beginning, extended their hand of cooperation to the Jain religion. And it should further be remembered that all the Jain inscriptions of the Western Cālukyas of Badami have been found from the state of Karṇāṭaka, which which was so strongly associated with the Jain religion from the early centuries of the Christian era.

Let us now once more turn our attention to the state of the Jain religion in the Gaṅga territory. We have already seen that the Western Gaṅga rulers actively associated themselves with the progress of the Jain religion from the days of their founder. We will now briefly examine the Jain inscriptions of this dynasty which were written after 600 A.D.

Durvinīta was succeeded by his son Muṣkara or Mokkara[24] probably before the end of the 6th century A.D. A Jain temple was erected in his name at Lakshmeśvara and it was called Mokkara-vasati[25] The erection of this temple proves the extension of the Gaṅga kingdom in that direction.[26] Muṣkara was succeeded by Śrīvikrama, and it appears that both of them had very short reign-periods. This is evident from the fact that we have a genuine, dated inscription[27] of Śrīvikrama's son Bhūvikrama which proves that the latter ascended the throne in Śaka 531 corresponding to 609 A.D. No Jain inscription of either Śrīvikrama or Bhūvikrama is known. But we have evidence to show that during the reign of Śivamāra I (670-713 A.D.), the son of Bhūvikrama, the Jains enjoyed royal patronage. An inscription[28] from Kulagāṇa in Cāmarājanagar Tāluk of Mysore district belongs to his reign. The second line of this inscription refers to Mādhava I's indebtedness to a Śramaṇācārya. The king Śivamāra I is here called *Avanimahendra* (line 16) and the lord of whole Pāṇāṭa and Puṇṇāṭa. According to this inscription several persons granted lands and home-sites with the approval of the king, who is also called Koṅgaṇi Muttarasa. The king himself also made a grant to the Jain Candrasenācārya, the *kartārar* (manager) of the temple. The fact that so many persons contributed for the temple shows that it was an important shrine in this part of Karṇāṭaka. The inscription is undated, but there cannot be any doubt regarding its genuineness. Śivamāra I, it appears, like many of his predecessors, befriended the Jains openly.[29]

The successor of Śivamāra I was Śrīpuruṣa, who was his grandson. He had a very long reign extending from 725 A.D. to the last quarter of the 8th century A.D.[30] This ruler was a great patron of the Jain religion. The well known Devarhalli plates,[31] found from Mysore district, is dated in Śaka 698 (776 A.D.) and the 50th year of the king's reign. The village of Devarhalli is situated in the Nāgamaṅgala Tāluk of Mysore district. The inscription refers to a line of Jain *gurus* belonging to Nandisaṅgha of Mūlagaṇa. The name of the *gaccha* is given as Pulikal, which is probably connected with Puligere or Pulikara, the ancient name of Lakshmeśvara, famous for its Jain temples. The earliest Muni, was Candranandin, who was succeeded by his disciple Kumāranandin, who in his turn was succeeded by Kīrtinandi Ācārya and the latter by Ācārya Vimalacandra. The earliest *guru* Candranandin therefore flourished in the middle of the 7th century A.D. We are then introduced to a line of feudatory kings and the names of two members of this line are given viz. Nirgunda *alias* Paramagūḷa. The wife of the latter viz. Kundācci was the daughter of Maruvarman and her mother was a daughter of the Pallava overlord (*adhirāja*). This lady Kundācci had built a Jain temple called Lokatilaka on the Northern side of Śrīpura (near Gūdalūr which is to the west of Nilgiris). This inscription refers to the grant of the village of Ponnaḷḷi for the repair, maintenance etc. of this temple. There is a long list of other grants made by several persons. The inscription was written by Viśvakarmācārya and the epithet *ācārya* shows that he too was a Jain ascetic. According to the last two lines of the grant this gentleman also received some land.

There is little doubt that the Jain temple by Kundācci, who had Pallava blood in her veins, was a celebrated shrine of Śrīpura. It is quite likely and as the inscription proves, that Śrīpuruṣa himself took personal interest in the welfare of this Jain temple. A stone inscription of 801 A.D., belonging to his reign,[32] also indirectly shows his love for the Jain religion. The destruction of *basadis* is regarded in that inscription as equivalent to the destruction of Vārāṇasī. Another genuine copper plate inscription of Śrīpuruṣa[33] refers to a grant made to a Jain *caityālaya*. This inscription also refers to his successor Śivamāra II. This particular record was discovered from Narasiṁharājapura in Belur tāluk of Chikmagalur district. It is incised on five copper plates. The inner side of the first plate, the two sides of the second plate and the inner side of the third contains the inscription of Śrīpuruṣa. It opens with an invocation of Jina "Victorious is the sole sun of the world, who has witnessed all the worlds and who by the rays of the *Syādvāda* has illuminated the veil of darkness of the other creeds". This inscription, it is interesting to note, also refers to the feat of cutting down a stone pillar on the part of Mādhava I, by order of a Nirgrantha ascetic. The inscription surprisingly refers to Śrīpuruṣa as the son of Śrīvikrama. Then the record goes on to say that the chief of his friends Nāgavarma of the Pasiṇḍi Gaṅga family (a new Gaṅga family), who was anointed as Gaṅga-rāja, and his sister's brother, a sun in the Kadamba family, named Tulu-ādi, united in making a grant, with pouring of water of the village of Mallavalli, situated in the Tagare country, to the *caityālaya* in the Toḷḷa village, situated in the same country. A few gifts are also recorded. The first part of the record ends with an obeisance to the Jina. This record of Śrīpuruṣa is undated; the editor assigns it to 780 A.D.[34] The Tagare country is also referred to in an inscription of Kadamaba Bhogivarman[35].

The outer side of the third plate[36] of the inscription from Narasiṁharājapura contains a Jain record of Śivamāra II. According to it when the illustrious Śivamārar was ruling the earth, Viṭṭarasa, a Kadamba chief under him was the governor of Sindanāḍu 8000 and Tagarenāḍu 70. This Kadamba chief granted a village called Karimani to the *cediya* of Toḷḷar, apparently the same village, mentioned in the inscription of Śrīpuruṣa. The last two plates contain yet another undated inscription[37] of Śivamāra II. It states that while the illustrious Śivamārar was ruling, his maternal uncle Vijayaśakti-arasa granted to the *cediya* of Muḷivalli some land, and parts of two villages. The same record, contains an account of few other gifts. It is interesting to note that a few of the witnesses mentioned in this inscription, are also mentioned in the record of Śrīpuruṣa contained in the first three plates. This proves that this inscription of Śivamāra II cannot be far removed from that of his father. It is also evident from the second inscription of Śivamāra II that there was another Jain shrine in the same locality.

That Śivamāra II was a staunch and sincere patron of the Jains is further proved by two other inscriptions. The first comes from Belgaum district,[38] which tells us that he had erected a *basadi* in Kummadavāḍa (modern Kalbhāvi). It is a stone inscription. The second is also a stone inscription[39]. The epigraph was found on a boulder near Candranāthasvāmin *basadi* at Śravaṇa Belgoḷa and contains only two words—*Śivamārana basadi* in Kannaḍa. It has been suggested that the Candranāthasvāmin temple was the *basadi* meant in this inscription[40].

There is an important Jain inscription[41] of Yuvarāja Mārasiṁha, the son of Śivamāra II dated Śaka 719, corresponding to 797 A.D., which was found from Manne in Bangalore district. His father was still alive at that time, but a prisoner in the Rāṣṭrakūṭa court. Yuvarāja Mārasiṁha is here described as ruling the entire Gaṅga-maṇḍala. "The plates must have been engraved after the father was at liberty and in power for 15 years or so after the grant was made, and probably at that time Mārasiṁha, the son, was dead".[42] This grant refers to a *senādhipati* (commander) called Śrīvijaya, who is described as holding 'Arhat as supreme' and who built a Jina temple at Mānyanagara (Manne). By this grant a village called Kiruvekkura was given as gift by prince Mārasiṁha. It then refers to a line of Jain teachers beginning from Toraṇācārya of Koṇḍakundānvaya. His original home was the village called Śālmalī. His disciple was Puṣpanandin and the latter's disciple Prabhācandra. The earliest *guru* Toraṇācārya therefore flourished around 700 A.D. The *śāsana* was written by Viśvakarmācārya, who too was probably a Jain ascetic. Another set of copper plates from Manne[43] gives the date Śaka 724 corresponding to 802 A.D., but this record refers to Prabhutavarṣa Govindarājadeva (Govinda III), the Rāṣṭrakūṭa sovereign, as the overlord. This inscription, although a Jain record, opens with an adoration to Viṣṇu. It further refers to Govinda III's elder brother Raṇāvaloka, who had accepted the command of the younger brother Govinda III, and who was at that time the supreme governor of the Gaṅga territory. We are told that on the application of the son of Bappayya, who was a disciple of Prabhācandra (mentioned in the earlier record dated Śaka 719) of Udāragaṇa, living in the Śālmalī village, famous in the Taidat Viṣaya, the king Prabhutavarṣa made a grant for the Jina temple of Mānyapura, built by the victorious ruler Śrīvijayarāja. It appears that this feudatory of the Gaṅgas, after 719 Śaka, had transferred his allegiance to the Rāṣṭrakūṭas and apparently was a favourite of the Rāṣṭrakūṭa provincial governor. The grant was made to "provide for dances, performed by dancing girls, singing, drums, sandal and worship of the god". A full village and a part of another were given as gift. This inscription therefore proves that the Rāṣṭrakūṭas continued the religious policy of the Gaṅgas in the conquered provinces.

Śivamāra II was succeeded in the main line by his nephew Rājamalla I (817-853 A.D.).[44] His own son Mārasiṁha, mentioned in the Manne grant of Śaka 719, founded another Gaṅga line and probably died before his father[45]. The younger brother of this Mārasiṁha was known as Pṛthivīpati and was a staunch Jain. This is proved by an inscription from Śravaṇa Belgola. We are told that along with his queen, he witnessed the *nirvāṇa* of the Jain *ācārya* Ariṣṭanemi on the Katvapra hill at Śravaṇa Belgola[46]. The king of the main line Rājamalla I was a Jain patron. He was the founder of a cave, dedicated to the Jains at Vallimalai in North Arcot district. This is proved by a short inscription in Grantha characters found there[47]. Rājamalla I was succeeded by his son Nītimārga I (853-870 A.D.), who is described in the well known Kudlur plates of Śaka 884 of Mārasiṁha III[48] as a "bee at the lotus feet of adorable Arhat Bhaṭṭāraka". This shows that this king was not only a Jain patron, but a converted Jain himself. His another well known name was Eregaṅgadeva.

We should now refer to an earlier Gaṅga inscription of prince Duggamāra[49], the younger brother of king Śivamāra II, discovered from Hebbalaguppe from Heggadaḍe Vankote Tāluk of Mysore district. According to it Śrī Narasingere Appor Duggamāra gave lands to the sowing capacity to the Jain temple (*koyilvasadi*) constructed by the great architect Nārāyaṇa. The local inhabitants also donated lands for the temple. The approximate date of this inscription, according to the editor, is 825 A.D.[50].

The next king, in the main line, was Rājamalla II, who ascended the throne, according to the Biliur stone inscription[51] in 870 A.D., the Śaka 809 being his 18th regnal year. Two Jain inscriptions of his reign are known. The first is the above stone inscription from Biliyur, Virajapet Tāluk of Coorg district. It is a royal grant of 12 villages, the Biliyur 12, to the Jain monk

Sarvanandideva, disciple of Śivanandi-siddhānta Bhaṭāra for the maintenance of the temple called Satyavākya Jinālaya at Peṇṇegaḍaṅga. Since Rājamalla II bore the title of Satyavākya, the temple appears to have been named after him. However, we should remember that a few of his predecessors also bore that title, and the Jain temple, referred to in this inscription, could have been built by any one of them

The second Jain inscription of his reign is the Narasapura inscription[52] dated Śaka 824, corresponding to 903 A.D., discovered from Kolar Tāluk of Kolar district. One of the plates is missing. The inscription was issned on the bright fortnight of Phālguna, an auspicious day for the Jains. According to this inscription the king gave a grant for the Jain *basadi* at Koṇṇamaṅgala, erected by Megante-Nandāka Gādeya. It also mentions a female disciple called Kamuṅgare Kanti of Uttanandi-puri Maṇḍalabhaṭāra. Another Jain *basadi*, built by one Śrīvarmayya is also mentioned in this inscription and for which some land was donated by the king.

The younger brother of Rājamalla II viz. Būtuga I was also a devout Jain. This is proved by the Kudlur inscription, which has already been referred to. Here Būtuga, who married a daughter of the illustrious Amoghavarṣa I, is described as a 'devout Jain'. This is also confirmed by the Gaṭṭivādipura plates dated 904 A.D.[53]

The next king in the main line was Nītimārga II (907-935 A.D.). In the Kudlur plates he is called a Jain[54]. An inscription of his reign[55] refers to the setting up a tombstone for a Jain teacher named Elācārya, who it is said, lived on water only for one month and expired after a fast of another eight days.

After Nītimārga II his two sons Narasiṁha and Rājamalla III ruled successively for very short period. The youngest son Būtuga II also known as Nanniya Gaṅga ascended the throne around 937 A.D. In the Kudlur plates he is described as a Jain devotee and we have Jain inscriptions of his reign. In the Sudi plates dated Śaka 860, found from Ron Tāluk of Dharwar district,[56] we are told, that the king while he was staying at Purikara during the Nandīśvara festival gratified six female mendicants with gifts and having washed the feet of Nāgadevapaṇḍita of the holy Vadiyūr *gaṇa* at Suṇḍī gave sixty *nivartanas* of land to the Jain *caityālaya,* built by his wife Divalāmbikā. She is described here as the symbol of manifest goodness through the purity of her accurate perception. The Sudi inscription, however, has been declared spurious by Fleet; but Narasiṁhachar regards it is genuine[57].

A fragmentary stone inscription[58] of Nanniya Gaṅga i.e. Būtuga II from Ichāvādi (Shimoga Tāluk, Shimoga district) is a very important Jain record. The record is undated. The inscription records the the grant of wet fields by the king and his queen to a Jain temple. It then refers to a long line of Jain teachers, belonging to Krāṇura *gaṇa,* beginning from Nandibhaṭṭāraka. The other names in chronological order are as follows—Bālacandrabhaṭṭāraka, Meghacandra, Guṇanandi (described as expert in logic and literature), Śabdabrahma, Akalaṅka (who defeated the Buddhists and Sāṅkhyas), Meghanandi, Prabhācandra, Śāntakirti, then a few names are erased and then Municandrasiddhāntadeva and then his disciple, whose name is erased. It appears that during the time of this unnamed Jain saint the king Nanniya Gaṅga built the Jain temple. The inscription shows that not only Nanniya Gaṅga himself, but other kings of his dynasty openly favoured the Jains. We propose to identify Akalaṅka of this inscription with the celebrated Jain philosopher of the name; this point will however, be discussed in a later chapter. From the Kudlur grant also it appears that Nanniya Gaṅga was a Jain scholar and defeated the Buddhists in debate[59].

The elder son of Būtuga II viz. Maruladeva probably died before his father. This prince also was a devout Jain[60]. He married the daughter of Rāṣṭrakūṭa Kṛṣṇa III. His younger brother Mārsiṁha III probably was a direct successor of Būtuga II.

Mārasiṁha III (960-974 A.D.) was undoubtedly one of the greatest Jains of the 10th century. Several important Jain inscriptions of his reign conclusively prove that he was not only a great Jain himself, but did everything to promote Jainism in Karṇāṭaka. We must at first refer to the two inscriptions found from Kadlur (Mandya Taluk, Mysore district), both of which are dated in Śaka 884. The earlier one was issued in December, 962 A.D.[61] A line of Jain teachers, beginning from Prabhācandra of Mūlasaṅgha and Sūrasta *gaṇa*, has been introduced in this inscription, which consists of three plates. His disciple was Kalaneledeva and this saint was the *guru* of Ravicandra. Ravicandra had as his disciple one Elācārya, the donee of this grant. Verse 45 and the lengthy passage in prose refer to the gift of the village Kadalur in Kongal-deśa made to Elācārya by Mārasiṁha III for providing the worship and offering to the *jinālaya,* constructed by the mother of Mārasiṁha called Kallabbā, who was the daughter of Siṁhavarman Cālukya. It is apparent from this inscription that Mārasiṁha was a loyal feudatory of the Rāṣṭrakūṭas. He was crowned by Kṛṣṇa III.[62] We are further told in this inscription that another purpose of the grant was the worshipping of *sudhācitra* (stucco painting) and *citra* (painting) as well as for the four kinds of *dānas* to the Jain deities and ascetics. The king Mārasiṁha was at that time stationed at Melpāṭi, a place mentioned in an earlier grant of Rāṣṭrakūṭa Kṛṣṇa III[63]. The second Jain inscription[64] from Kadlur is dated March, 963 A.D., and is one of the most important Jain records of the tenth century. This inscription not only shows Mārasiṁha III as a sincere and devout Jain but also gives additional information about a few of his predecessors, which have already been noticed. Mārasiṁha here is described as one "who washed out all taints with the water of the daily bath of Jina and one who was devoted to the worship *gurus*". We are than told a brief life-history of the Jain saint Vādighanghala, who was originally a Brāhmaṇa of Parāśara *gotra.* His first name was Muñjārya. His ancestors lived in the Varāṭadeśa of the North. This gentleman, it appears from the inscription, was a Jain teacher of vast learning and was well versed in Lokāyata, Sāṅkhya, Vedānta, Bauddha and above all in Jain philosophy. Like a sun he destroyed the mass of darkness, represented by the misleading teachings of other schools, we are told. "His eloquence in the exposition of literature made king Gaṅga Gāṅgeya Satyavākya, a cuckoo in the grove of delighters of all learning, his pupil". Gaṅga

Gāṅgeya was a title of Būtuga II. We are further told that he was held in the highest esteem by the Rāṣṭrakūṭa sovereign Kṛṣṇa III. This great Jain saint is further described as worshipping the "lotus feet of Jineśvara". To this celebrated Brāhmaṇa Jain saint king Mārasiṁha III in March 963 A.D., gave as *śrutaguru's* fee (religious teacher's fee) a village called Bagiyur included in Baḍagara 300 of the Punāṭu 6000 in Gaṅgapāṭi. The income of this village was 20 *gadyānas*.[65]

A stone pillar inscription[66] of extraordinary importance, regarding the achievements of Mārasiṁha III, has been discovered from Śravaṇa Belgola. It refers to several military feats of this great Gaṅga king. However, we are not concerned at present with those achievements of Mārasiṁha. A crucial passage from our point of view is that which says that "he maintained the doctrine of Jina and erected Jain temples (*Vasati*) and *Mānastambhas* at various places". This passage is enough to show his tremendous zeal for the Jain religion. The record closes with the statement that he relinquished the sovereignty and keeping the vow of *sallekhanā* for 3 days in the presence of Ajitasenabhaṭṭāraka, died at Baṅkāpura in Śaka 896 corresponding to 974 A.D.[67] We cannot resist the temptation of reproducing the last few lines of this inscription "O Cola king, calm your failing heart by gentle rubbing; O Pāṇḍya, you have escaped slaughter, stay on. O Pallava, run not away in fear from your territory; do not retreat, but remain; the Gaṅga chieftain Nolambāntaka has gone to the abode of gods".

We should now take a brief notice of a very interesting rock inscription[68] found from Gopinātha Guṭṭa in Chik-ballapur Tāluk of Kolar district. This is a low hill at the north-eastern base of Nandidroog. The inscription according to Rice resembles the early inscriptions of the Gaṅgas and should be assigned to the 8th century A.D.[69] It opens with a homage to Ṛṣabha. It refers to the Jain shrine of this hill, which according to it, was formerly built by Rāma in Dvāpara and afterwards rebuilt by Kuntī. This Jinendra *caitya* had caves for *Ṛṣis*. This description, according to Rice, applies to Nandidroog. At present the shrine in the spot, where the inscription has been discovered, is dedicated to Gopālasvāmin. But the description of the inscription shows that this place had a very important Jain temple-complex from a much earlier period. It can be said with conviction that the Jain temple of this place was one of the earliest shrines of Karṇāṭaka.

Let us once more return to the Gaṅgas. The successor of Mārasiṁha III was Rājamalla IV, who had an able minister in the person of Cāmuṇḍa Rāya, one of the greatest Jains, Karṇāṭaka has ever produced. He is the author of the celebrated Kannaḍa work the *Cāmuṇḍa Rāya Purāṇa,* written in 978 A.D. In this text we have an account of the twenty-four Jain Tīrthaṅkaras. But the greatest achievement of this Gaṅga minister was the erection of the colossal image of Gommaṭeśvara at Śravaṇa Belgola. The date of the execution of this object was about 982 A.D.[70] We will have something more to say on Cāmuṇḍa Rāya in connexion with our discussion of the inscriptions of Śravaṇa Belgola. An earlier Gaṅga Jain minister had ended his life in *Sallekhanā* fashion at this town. We are referring to Narasinga who died about 950 A.D., and was a minister of Eregaṅga or Nītimāra II.[71] A few other persons, connected with the Gaṅgas, are also mentioned in some Jain inscriptions from Śravaṇa Belgola. For the reign of Rājamalla IV we have a Jain inscription[72] dated Śaka 899 found from Coorg district.

The above discussion regarding the state of Jainism during the rule of the Gaṅgas proves that in almost every part of the territory, ruled by the Western Gaṅga kings, there were Jain shrines. Most of these temples gave shelter to eminent Jain saints who were respected by even non-Jains for their pure character and godliness. It further appears that some other kings, belonging to contemporary dynasties, were influenced by the religious outlook of the Western Gaṅga kings.

Before discussing the state of the Jain religion during the rule of the Rāṣṭrakūṭas, we must briefly discuss its condition during the rule under a particular line of feudatory kings viz. the Raṭṭas of Saundatti (Belgaum district, Karṇāṭaka). The ancient name of Saundatti was Sugandhavarti. This place apparently sprang into prominence in the 9th century A.D. The earliest inscription[73] from this place is dated in the Śaka year 797 corresponding to 875 A.D. It refers to the Rāṣṭrakūṭa

Kṛṣṇa as the overlord and it appears that this Kṛṣṇa is no other than Kṛṣṇa II[74]. This stone epigraph is found in the present Aṅkeśvara temple at Saundatti. The founder of the house was one Mecaḍa, who had a son named Pṛthvīrāma; this gentleman is described as a *mahāsāmanta* under Kṛṣṇa II. We are further told that he was a lay disciple of Indrakīrti. This Indrakīrti was a disciple of Guṇakīrti and the latter of Mūlabhaṭṭāraka of Kāreya *gaṇa* hailing from Mailāpatīrtha. It is evident that the earliest preceptor of this line was a resident of Mailāpa Tīrtha. In the year 797 Śaka the feudatory king Pṛthvīrāma granted some land for a Jinendrabhavana (temple dedicated to Jinendra), which was constructed by him at Sugandhavarti. It further appears that at his time Pṛthvīrāma was a very insignificant chieftain as his *adhiṣṭhāna* (capital) is described only as a village (*grāma*) in this epigraph. From some other inscriptions we further learn that the Kāreya *gaṇa*, to which Indrakīrti and others belonged, was a branch of the well known Yāpanīya Saṅgha[75]. The language of this epigraph definitely proves that Raṭṭa Pṛthvīrāma was a converted Jain. His successors too, as we will see now, were also Jains.

Chronologically the next inscription of the Raṭṭas is dated in the Śaka year 902, corresponding to 980 A.D. This is another stone epigraph[76] from the same temple; it discloses the name of Mahāsāmanta Śāntivarman, who was a grandson of Pṛthvīrāma. At this time, according to this epigraph, Cālukya Tailapadeva i.e. Taila II was the overlord of this chieftain. It appears that the Raṭṭas quietly transferred their allegiance, after the fall of the Rāṣṭrakūṭas, to the Cālukyas. The Jain temple-complex of this place, it appears, was a family shrine of the Raṭṭas. This is the reason why we get the expression *Raṭṭara-paṭṭa Jinālaya* in the introductory part of this epigraph. The mother of Śāntivarman also made donations to the Jain temple of this place. The gift was received by the prceptor Bāhubali Bhaṭṭāraka. It appears from the epigraph that the earliest preceptor of Bāhubali's line was Ravicandra, who was succeeded by the following—Arhanandin, Śubhacandra, Maunideva and Prabhācandra. The earliest *sādhu* Ravicandra therefore flourished in the first half of the 9th century A.D. There preceptors belonged to the

Kaṇḍūra *gaṇa,* which also was a branch of the Yāpanīya Saṅgha[77].

A few later inscriptions[78] from Saundatti also prove that even after 1000 A.D., Jainism continued to flourish in this area. The kings of Raṭṭa family throughout their history maintained close relationship with this religion.

From Belgaum district we have another very interesting Jain inscription, which on palaeographic grounds, can be assigned to the 7th century A.D. This inscription is known as Gokak plates[79] and it discloses the name of a king called Dejja Mahārāja, who is described as belonging to the *anvaya* of the Rāṣṭrakūṭas (line 5). The inscription records a gift of 50 *Nivartanas* of land in Jalāragrāma of Kasmāṇḍī *viṣaya* for the continuous worship of the divine Arhat and for the maintenance of learned Jain ascetics, devoted to the teaching of this religion. Ācārya Āryanandin, belonging to Jambūkhaṇḍagaṇa, a savant of exceptional learning, received the gift from king Indrananda, son of Vijayānanda Madhyamarāja of the Sendraka family. He is described as a feudatory of Dejja Mahārāja, whose relationship with any known branch of the Rāṣṭrakūṭas is not yet known. Another intriguing feature of this inscription is its date. It is dated in the year 845 of the Āguptāyika kings, the significance of which still remains a mystery. If it is equivalent to the era of 58 B.C., then the inscription will have to be assigned to the last quarter of the 8th century A.D. But it is just possible that some era, established earlier,[80] is referred to in this inscription.

The Nolamba Pallavas,[81] who ruled after 800 A.D., were good patrons of the Jain religion. We have two inscriptions before 1000 A.D., which prove that the kings of this dynasty extended patronage to the Jains. An inscription of Mahendra Nolamba dated Śaka 800 corresponding to 878 A.D., records a grant to a Jain temple in Dharmapuri district in present Tamil Nadu.[82] The inscription is written in Kanarese language. From the compound of the famous Mallikārjuna temple of Dharmapuri has been discovered another Jain inscription[83] of the reign of the same king. It is dated in the Śaka year 815, corresponding to 893 A.D. This epigraph records a grant to a Jain *vasadi* by two persons called Nidhiyaṇṇa and Caṇḍiyaṇṇa. The former received from the king the village of Mūlapaḷḷi, which he made over to Kanakasena Siddhānta Bhaṭāra, the pupil of Vinayasena Siddhānta Bhaṭāra. These monks belonged to the Senānvaya of Mūlasaṅgha. The particular *gaṇa,* to which they belonged, is given as Pogarīya. The revenue of the village was to be utilised for the repair of the temple.

Before turning our attention to the State of Andhra we must refer to two famous places now included in Karṇāṭaka, which were associated with Jainism from early times. The first place is Śravaṇa Belgola is Hassan district, which was associated with Jainism from at least 600 A.D. The earliest inscription, discovered from this celebrated centre of Jainism, is dated in 600 A.D.[84] This inscription mentions ancient Jain saints like Gautama Gaṇadhara, Lohārya, Jambu, Viṣṇudeva, Aparājita, Govardhana, Bhadrabāhu, Viśākha, Proṣṭhila, Kṛttikārya, Jayanāman, Siddhārtha, Dhṛtiṣeṇa, Buddhila and other teachers. It then mentions the fact that Prabhācandra, an eminent Jain divine, attained Samādhi or Nirvāṇa at Kaṭavapra or Candragiri hill of Belgola. After him 700 more saints likewise attained Nirvāṇa on the same hill. It has been suggested that the writing was put on the stone long after Prabhācandra's death. The palaeography of the inscription suggests that it was inscribed in circa 600 A.D.

Quite a few inscriptions, discovered from the same hill, belong to the period between 650 A.D. and 800 A.D. They record[85] the Sāmadhi of a few prominent Jain saints including one female ascetic.[86] No. 11 records the Samādhi of one Ācārya Ariṣṭanemi (c. 650 A.D.) and mentions one king Diṇḍika as witness. This king, however, cannot be correctly identified. No. 21 mentions a monk called Akṣayakīrti, who is described as a resident of Southern Madhurā (Madura), which shows that this old city continued as a leading Jain centre even after 600 A.D. We have already discussed a few historical inscriptions of Śravaṇa Belgola in connexion with the discussion of the state of Jainism during the rule of the Western Gaṅgas. A few more will be discussed in connexion with the Rāṣṭrakūṭas.

The second Jain holy place of Karṇāṭaka was Kopaṇa or Kopbal in modern Raichur district. This place has yielded a number of Jain inscriptions which show that from 7th century onward, this place was known as a celebrated Jain Tīrtha. It has been suggested that Kopaṇa should be identified with Kung-kan-na-pu-lo of Yuan Chwang,[87] which according to that pilgrim, was situated some 2000 li north of Draviḍa country. The earliest epigraphic reference to this town is found in an inscription[88] of the time of the Bādāmi Cālukya king Vijayāditya, who reigned from 696 A.D. to 733 A.D. However, there is nothing in that epigraph to show that it was then considered a Jain sacred place. The earliest Jain inscription[89] from this place is dated in the Śaka year 803, corresponding to 881 A.D. It states that the Jain teacher Sarvanandin Bhaṭāra, a disciple of Ekācaṭṭugada Bhaṭāra of the Kuṇḍakunda lineage, having stayed here and graciously imparted the teachings of the holy doctrine to the residents of the town and after practising austerities for a considerable time, attained final emancipation by the vow *Saṁnyasana* or *Sallekhanā*.

Among other important inscriptions from this place, which were inscribed before 1000 A.D., we should refer to the short epigraph,[90] found near Kopbal, mentioning Jaṭāsiṁhanandin. It has been suggested that this saint should be identified with the Jain poet of the same name and the author of the *Varāṅgacarita*.[91] This sacred place is also mentioned in inscriptions, discovered from other places. In an inscription of about 800 A.D., of Gaṅga king Mārasiṁha Ereyappa there is a reference to a witness named Mādhava of Kuppāl.[92] The earliest reference to this Jain Tīrtha in Śravaṇa Belgola inscriptions is to be assigned to 1000 A.D.[93] A few other inscriptions of that place also contain references to the Jain pilgrims hailing from Kopbal.[94]

We must now turn our attention to the condition of the Jain religion in Andhra Pradesh during the days of the Veṅgī Cālukyas. We have already briefly referred to the Musinikonda grant, which was renewed during the reign of Viṣṇuvardhana III[95] in the Śaka year 684 corresponding to 762 A.D. According to this inscription Ayyaṇa Mahādevī, the wife of Kubja Viṣṇuvardhana (624-641 A.D.), gave a grant of the village of Musinikuṇḍa in Toṅka Natavāḍi *viṣaya* to the Jain saint called Kālibhadrācārya for the benefit of the Jain temple called Nadumbi-vasati at Vezwada, which was probably built by that queen herself. This grant was to be utilised for the purpose of performing uninterrupted *pūjā* of the venerable Arhats. The saint Kālibhadrācārya is spoken of as having made the entire circle of kings, obedient to him, by the power of his spiritual knowledge, Aṣṭāṅgadivyajñāna. There is little doubt that this great Jain saint of Andhra was held in special veneration by he queen of Kubja Viṣṇuvardhana, the founder of the Veṅgī Cālukya line. We have already commented on his spiritual predecessors, who flourished before 600 A.D. They belonged to the Kavarūri or Surasta *gaṇa* and Saṅgha *anvaya*.

Chronologically the next Jain record of the Eastern Cālukyas belongs to the reign of Jayasiṁha II (696-709 A.D.). This was found on a broken slab near Macherla in Palnad Tāluk of Guntur district.[96] It refers to Sarvalokāśraya Jayasiṁhavallabha and registers a grant of land by Kalyanavasantulu to "Arahanta Bhaṭṭāra". The gift was to be maintained by the family of Raṭṭagudis of Koṁthuru This inscription therefore proves the existence of a Jain temple in this part of Guntur district in Andhra Pradesh in the 7th century A.D.

A Jain record[97] dated in the 37th year of Viṣṇuvardhana III found from Sattenapalle Tāluk of Guntur district refers to a temple of Jain at Munugoḍu. There is also a reference to a Muni called Suvratatīrtha. It further mentions that a certain person called Boyugaṭṭa, a servant of king Goṅka effected some repairs to this temple, which was built by one Aggoti. Another short epigraph in the same stone slab mentions Mahāmaṇḍaleśvara Goṁkaya, evidently the person of the same name of the earlier epigraph. It registers a gift of land to the Siṭa Jineśvarālaya at Munugoḍu. Another inscription of the same slab refers to the gift of land to the *vasadi* called Pṛthivītilaka, evidently a Jain temple, built by an earlier Eastern Cālukya king. It also mentions a certain Billama Nāyaka.

No Eastern Cālukya Jain inscription, belonging to the 9th century A.D., is known. We have, however, three Jain inscriptions of the time of Amma II Vijayāditya who ruled in the middle of the 10th century A.D.[98] The first is known as Maliyapundi grant and the other two Kuluchumbarru and Masulipatnam grants. The Maliyapundi grant[99] was originally discovered from Madanur, 10 miles from Ongole, which is now the headquarter of the district of the same name in Andhra Pradesh. The inscription opens with a beautiful verse addressed to Jinendra. The donee was a Jinālaya called Kaṭakābharaṇa, founded by Durgarāja, an officer of Amma II. This temple, according to this inscription was situated to the south of Dharmavuramu (Dharmapurī) in Nellore district. Durgarāja had the designation Kaṭakarāja which suggests that he was a superintendent of the royal camp. At the request of this officer king Vijayāditya i.e. Amma II made a gift of the village of Maliyapūṇḍi for the benefit of the temple in the year Śaka 867 i.e. 945 A.D. which was the 12th year of his reign. This Jain temple was in charge of Śrī Māndiradeva, the disciple of Divākara, and grand-disciple of Jinanandin belonging to the Yāpanīya Saṅgha, Nandigaccha and Koṭimaḍuvagaṇa. The language of the inscription proves that king Amma II himself had great respect both for the Jain temple of this place and Māndiradeva, who was the manager of the temple. The preceptor and grand-preceptor of Māndiradeva, who belonged to the famous Yāpanīya Saṅgha, were evidently very learned Jain ascetics and flourished in the 9th century A.D.

The second Jain inscription during the reign of Amma II is an undated copper plate record. Its findspot is not known. The plates are now in the British Museum. It registers the grant of a village named Kuluchuṁbarru[100] in he Attilināṇḍu *viṣaya* to a Jain teacher called Arhanandin, belonging to the Valahāri *gaṇa* and Aḍḍakali *gaccha*, for the purpose of providing for repairs to the charitable dining hall of a Jain temple called Sarvalokāśraya Jinabhavana. The very name of the temple suggests that it was built by one of Amma II's predecessors, many of whom bore the title *sarvalokāśraya*. The grant was evidently made by Amma II, but it was caused to be given by a certain lady called Cāmekāmbā, who belonged to the Paṭṭavardhika lineage and was a pupil af Arhanandin. The later portion of the grant is in Telegu and it records a present made by Arhanandin himself to the writer of the record, whose name was Bhaṭṭadeva. Fleet successfully locates the village Kulu-chumbarru near the town of Attili in the present West Godavari district of Andhra Pradesh. The lady Cāmekāmbā belonged to the Cālukya lineage and was a favourite mistress of the king.[101] She is a described as a lay pupil of Arhanandin, who was a disciple of Ayyapoṭi and the latter of Sakalacandrasiddhānta, who is described as well — versed in the Siddhānta writings. This particular inscription definitely shows that both Amma II and his favourite mistress had some soft corner for the Jain religion.

The third Jain inscription of the time of Amma II is the undated Masulipatnam grant[102] consisting of five plates, first found from the district court of Masulipatnam or Machilipatnam in Krishna district of Andhra Pradesh. The record, it is interesting to note, begins with an invocation to Viṣṇu. The king Amma II, however, was a *parama-māheśvara*[103]. The inscription refers to a Jain pontiff (*ācārya*), the preceptor of two nobles Bhīma and Naravāhana II. He was the renowned Jayasena, who bore the surname Nāthasena and was the disciple of the illustrious Candrasena, who is described as well versed in the Siddhānta and who attained proficiency in *parasamaya*, which signifies that his soul became absorbed in the non-self for the liberation of mankind from bondage. He was honoured, according to this inscription, by the Śrāvakas, Kṣapaṇakas (Jain ascetics), Kṣullakas (Śrāvakas of high order) and Ajjakas probably meaning educated laymen. For the benefit of this celebrated Jain savant Bhīma and Naravāhana II constructed two Jain temples (*Jinabhavana*) at Vijayavāṭikā (Bezwada or Vijaywada) and for that purpose the king Ammarāja himself granted the village of Pedda-Gālidiparru, having converted it into a *devabhoga* and exempted it from all kinds of burden and taxation. The village was situated in the Velaṇāṇḍu *viṣaya* in modern Guntur district. The engraver Jayantācārya too, was probably a Jain. The present sites of two Jain temples, mentioned in this inscription, cannot be properly identified. The two chieftains Bhīma and Naravāhana II, according to the editor of the inscription, were Śūdra chiefs; they are further described as devoted to Jinadharma (*Jinadharmaniratacaritrau*).

The above discussion of the Jain inscriptions of the Eastern Cālukya kings abundantly prove that Jainism was in more or less flourishing condition in the eastern districts of modern Andhra Pradesh from 600 A.D. to 1000 A.D. Let us now turn our attention to other parts of Andhra Pradesh. We should first refer to the Cālukyas of Vemulavāḍa, who were great Jain patrons and who ruled in the modern Karimnagar district of Andhra Pradesh, roughly corresponding to ancient Sapādalakṣa country. The earliest Jain inscription of the rulers of this feudatory Cālukya dynasty is the Karkyala stone inscription of the time of Arikeśarī II (930—958 A.D.). The importance of this inscription[104], which is inscribed on a hillock called Bommalaguṭṭa at Kurkyala, 13 miles west of Karimnagar, can hardly be overemphasised. It refers to a Jain devotee called Jinavallabha, who is described as the brother of the great Jain poet Pampa, the celebrated author of the *Vikramājunavijaya* also called *Pampabhārata* and the *Ādipurāṇa*. In this inscription the two brothers are described as Brāhmaṇas of Vatsa *gotra*. This is supported by the evidence of the *Pampabhārata*..[105]

Jinavallabha himself, according to this inscription, constructed a *vasadi* called Tribhuvanatilaka, a tank called Kavitāguṇārṇava and a garden called Madanavilāsa. The inscription further records the installation by Jinavallabha of the images of the first and the last Tīrthaṅkara i.e. Ṛṣabha and Vardhamāna at the *vasadi* constructed by him. A *caityālaya*, dedicated to the first Tīrthaṅkara, is also mentioned in this connexion Jinavallabha, we are told, used to celebrate the festival of the bathing of Jina at Vṛṣabhādri, the exact location of which has not yet been determined but which is near Dharamvaram. He is further described as the disciple of Jayamgoṇḍa Siddhānta Bhaṭāra of the Deśiya *gaṇa* and Koṇḍakunda *anvaya*.

The same inscription tells us that Jinavallabha's *caityālaya* at Vṛṣabhādri became as famous as the fame of Pampa. He used to offer food to the Jain ascetics and during the festivals entertained the pilgrims, visiting this shrine. King Arikeśarī II of Vemulavāḍa, we are told, in this inscription, gave Pampa as a mark of his appreciation of the *Vikramārjunavijaya,* the village Dharmavura,, described as an abode of the Brāhmaṇas, resembling the famous Kalāpagrāma, as *agrahāra*. We are then told "the incredulous who would ask stupidly again and again whether a copper plate inscription has been written, whether the famous Arikeśarī had actually granted Dharmavura as *agrahāra* and whether the celebrated Pampa had accepted it, should repair to the Vṛṣabhādri which proclaims the fame of Pampa as well as the greatness of *Jinadharma* and see the letters of the inscription carved thereon and satisfy themselves".

The details given in this epigraph regarding Pampa, tally generally with that given by that poet in his works.[106] In this inscription Jinavallabha is described as a devotee of Ādyanta Tīrthaṅkaras i.e. Ṛṣabha and Mahāvīra and also of Cakreśvarī. In his *Ādipurāṇa*, his brother too calls himself a devotee of Vardhamāna, Ṛṣabha and Cakreśvarī. The gift of village granted to Pampa by Arikeśarī is also mentioned in the *Vikramārjunavijaya.*[107] We should also remember that Pampa composed his *Ādipurāṇa* in Śaka 863 corresponding to 941 A.D., and his *Vikramārjunavijaya* was composed afterwards as it mentions the *Ādipurāṇa*. Therefore the inscription should be placed around 945 A.D.

Another inscription[108] of the time of Arikeśarī II dated Śaka 869, it is interesting to note, contains five verses from the *Vikramārjunavijaya* or *Pampabhārata*. It has further been pointed out that the site of Pampa's *Samādhi* has actually been referred to in a Sanskrit inscription from Bodhan.[109] But this cannot be confirmed at the present state of our knowledge.

We have several Jain inscriptions of the Vemulavāḍa kings, bearing the date Śaka 888 corresponding to 966 A.D. A stone inscription[110] of that date from Repaka (Karimnagar district) introduces a chief named Vujaya, who bears a string of titles and records his gift of land to a *Jinālaya,* built by him. The latter half of this inscription refers to the genealogy of a family of disciples of Jain faith, who were holding a fief comprising

Atukuru 70 and Pammi 12. Some of the members of this family were Kāma, Rāma, Tukkya, Revaṇa, Puṇyarāma, Kommaya and others. Names of a line of Jain ascetics are also given. In the end we are told that the *Jinālaya* was built by king Arikeśarī, who was probably Arikeśarī II. A short stone inscription[111] from Vemulavāḍa states that Baddega, the king of Sapādalakṣa, constructed a *Jinālaya* for Somadeva, the chief of Gauḍa Saṅgha. This Somadeva, as we have already observed, was probably a Jain monk from Bengal, who migrated to the Sapādalakṣa country in the third quarter of the 10th century A.D. From Parbhani plates[112] dated Śaka 888 of the time of Arikeśarī III we learn that a village of the name of Vanikaṭupula was given to Somadeva Sūri, the disciple of Nemideva and grand-disciple of Yaśodeva, belonging to Gauḍa Saṅgha. It also refers to the fact that a Jain temple of the name of Śubhadhāma Jinālaya, built by Arikeśarī's father Baddega was under the supervision of this Jain savant, who is further described as the author of the *Yaśodharacarita* i.e. *Yaśastilakacampū* and *Syādvādopaniṣad*. High praise has been bestowed on him for his encyclopaedic knowledge. We also learn from this inscription that Arikeśarī was a feudatory of Kṛṣṇarājadeva, son of Akālavarṣa, Pṛthvīvallabha, Mahārājādhirāja, Amoghavarṣa. This Kṛṣṇarāja is evidently the Rāṣṭrakūṭa overlord Kṛṣṇa III, the celebrated son and successor of Amoghavarṣa III. We should remember that Somadeva had completed his *Yaśastilkacampū*[113] during the reign of the same Rāṣṭrakūṭa emperor Kṛṣṇa III on the 13th day of Caitra, Śaka 881 when Kṛṣṇa III was encamping at Melapāṭī after conquering the kings of Pāṇḍya, Siṁhala, Cola and Cera countries. He further states in this work that he was at this time a resident of Gaṅgadhārā, the capital of Baddiga, the son of Arikeśarī II. That Somadeva was a disciple of Nemideva is also known from that poet's *Nītivākyāmṛta*[114]. In the *Yaśastilakacampū*[115] Somadeva is described as belonging to the Devasaṅgha, which is probably another name of the Gauḍasaṅgha.

The two inscriptions, mentioned above, certainly show that the kings belonging to this feudatory Cālukya line, were genuine patrons of Jainism. Two great Jain poets of the 10th century viz. Pampa and Somadeva lived in their kingdom and were favoured by them. In a later chapter of the present work we will have something more to say on the achievements of these two literary giants.

We should now turn our attention to the condition of the Jain religion during the days of the Rāṣṭrakūṭa kings. We have already referred to a few Jain epigraphs where some Rāṣṭrakūṭa monarchs have been mentioned. That the kings of this great dynasty were good patrons of this religion will not only be evident from some inscriptions but also a very good number of Jain literary works, which were completed during the Rāṣṭrakūṭa period.

No Jain inscription, belonging to the earlier members of the Rāṣṭrakūṭa family, is yet known. But it has been suggested on the basis of a Śravaṇa Belgola inscription dated 1129 A.D. that Akalaṅka, the great Jain philosopher, was patronised by Dantidurga.[116] The earliest Rāṣṭrakūṭa Jain inscription comes from Śravaṇa Belgola.[117] It refers to the reign of Raṇāvaloka Kambayya, son of Dhruva and elder brother of Govinda III. This prince was the eldest son of Dhruva and was the governor of Gaṅgavāḍi under his illustrious father. Dhruva was apparently alive at the time, when this inscription was written. He is described here as the son of *Śrīvallabha Mahārājādhirāja Parameśvara Mahārāja*. The inscription records a grant and proves Kambayya's (Stambha) affection for the Jain religion. Though the inscription is undated, we can assign it to the last quarter of the 8th century A.D. We have already discussed the contents of the Manne plates[118] dated Śaka 724 which also shows that this prince had a soft corner for the Jain religion.

Govinda III, the younger brother of Stambha and the successor of Dhruva, who is mentioned as the overlord in Manne plates of his elder brother, was probably an admirer of the Jain religion. The Kadaba plates[119] dated Śaka 735 corresponding to 814 A.D., and found from Tumkur district of Karṇāṭaka, refers to the reign of Prabhūtavarṣa, who is no other than Govinda III. This inscription discloses the existence of a line of Jain monks of the Nandī Saṅgha of the Yāpanīyas. The name of the *gaṇa* is given as Punnāgavṛkṣamūla. The earliest *ācārya* was Śrīkīrti, his disciple was Kuli-Ācārya, then comes Vijayakīrti and the latter's disciple was Arkakīrti. The last-named saint, we are told, was successful in removing an evil influence of Saturn on Vimalāditya, who was the sister's son of Cākirāja, the ruler of the entire province of the Gaṅgas. It is clear from the inscription that Vimalāditya was a Cālukya chief under Cākirāja, the supreme Rāṣṭrakūṭa governor of Gaṅgavāḍi. The grateful Vimalāditya and his uncle Cākirāja were pleased to give an entire village called Jālamaṅgala for a Jain temple at Śilāgrāma, which was on the western side of Mānyapura. This Mānyapura was probably identical with the town of the same name mentioned in the Gaṅga inscriptions. Vimalāditya was the son of Yaśovarman and grandson of Balavarman. There is absolutely no valid reason to doubt the authenticity of this record. Recently another Jain inscription[119A] of the time of Govinda III from Dharwar district has been discovered.

The successor of Govinda III viz. Amoghavarṣa I, who ascended the throne in 814 A.D., was one of the greatest patrons of the Jain religion in the 9th century. We have already seen that there existed a Jain shrine in Nasik district, which was named after him. We will at first discuss the available Jain inscriptions of his reign and then we will turn our attention to the evidence supplied by the Jain literary texts.

From a broken slab found from Ranebennur in Dharwar district has been discovered an important Jain inscription[120] which yields the date Śaka 781. Although the epigraph does not disclose the name of the reigning monarch, it was evidently written during Amoghavarṣa's reign and within his empire. The date corresponds to 859 A.D. The inscription refers to a Jain shrine constructed by one Nāgalūra Pollabe and therefore it was known as Nāgula *vasadi*. Lines 12 to the end record the gift of land made as a life-time document (*jīva-śāsana*) for this temple by several villagers. The gift, we are told, was received on behalf of the temple, by Nāganandin Ācārya of the Siṅghavura *gaṇa*.

Much more important than the above-mentioned record is the Konnur stone inscription[121] dated Śaka 782 of the reign of the same king. The inscription was discovered from a place called Konnur, which is situated on the south bank of the river Malaprabhā in Nawalgund Tāluk of Dharwar district. At present the stone containing the inscription is built into a wall of the local Paramesvara temple. Above the writing there are a few sculptures of Tīrthaṅkaras. The Śaka date corresponds to 860 A.D. The epigraph has altogether 72 lines, of which, lines 1-59 represent the inscription of the time of Amoghavarṣa I. According to this inscription, emperor Amoghavarṣa, while residing at Mānyakheṭa, at the request of his subordinate Baṅkeśa (Baṅkeya) in recognition of the important services, rendered by him, granted the village of Taleyura (line 38) and some land of other villages for the benefit of a Jaina sanctuary, founded by Baṅkeya at Kolanura to the sage Devendra, who was a disciple of Trikālayogīśa, belonging to the Pustaka *gaccha*, Deśīya *gaṇa* and Mūla *Saṅgha*. It is interesting to note that the opening verse of the inscription invokes the blessing of both Viṣṇu and Jinendra. There is a magnificent tribute in verse No. 44 to the doctrine of the Jinas, "Ever victorious, like a royal edict be this doctrine of the Jinas, which destroys the false doctrines of peoples, who are filled with an excessive pride, arising from ignorance; which brings about the true happiness of all, who act in obedience to the commands of the wise; which is the place of glory of the excellent Syādvāda by which things appear under manifold forms, and grants the quintessence of good conduct". The date, according to Kielhorn,[122] is absolutely correct. But it is a later copy of an original copper plate, according to the inscription itself.[123] There is no reason why we should disbelieve this clear statement of the inscription. The later porion of the inscription after line 59 refers to the Jain monks who flourished in the 12th century.

A number of literary works very clearly prove that Amoghavarṣa I was a converted Jain. Guṇabhadra, the author of the *Uttarapurāṇa* and a contemporary of Amoghavarṣa I asserts that his preceptor Jinasena was a *guru* of that celebrated Rāṣṭrakūṭa monarch.[124] Altekar refers to the fact that Jinasena in his *Pārśvabhyudaya* claims himself to be the chief preceptor (*paramaguru*) of Amoghavarṣa I[124A]. But this is impossible, because that poem was written before 783 A.D., as it is mentioned in Jinasena II's *Harivaṁśa* composed in Śaka 705. And Amoghavarṣa ascended the throne only in 814 A.D., and at that time he was a very young lad. However, another later writer[125] asserts that the *Pārśvabhyudaya* was composed in the court of Amoghavarṣa. That Amoghavarṣa was a believer in the doctrine of Syādvāda is also repeated in the *Gaṇitasārasaṅgraha*[126] of Mahāvīrācārya, who was an exact contemporary of that monarch. Amoghavarṣa himself in his *Praśnottararatnamālā*[127] pays homage to Vardhamāna. Now, it is definitely known that this work was written by that king.[128] However, it should not be supposed that because of his Jain leanings, he was indifferent to Hindu deities. That he was a devotee of Mahālakṣmī is known from one of the inscriptions[129]

A few contemporary Jain writers have clearly shown their bias for this great Rāṣṭrakūṭa king. Śākaṭāyana, a contemporary Jain grammarian, wrote a commentary on his own grammatical work and named it as *Amoghavṛtti*. This shows his respect for that Rāṣṭrakūṭa monarch. In that *Vṛtti* there is a reference to Amoghavarṣa's burning down his enemies (*adahadamoghavarṣo-rātīn*).[130] Jinasena himself is full of praise for this great Rāṣṭrakūṭa monarch.[131] Yet another contemporary Jain writer viz. Ugrāditya, the author of the medical treatise *Kalyāṇakā-raka*,[132] which was composed on Mount Rāmagiri, situated in the level plains of Veṅgī in the country of Trikaliṅga, refers to the fact that he delivered a discourse on the uselessness of meat diet in the court of Śrī *Nṛpatuṅga Vallabha Mahārājādhirāja*, who is no other than Amoghavarṣa I. We should also mention the fact that a few verses of the *Kavirājamārga* are in praise of Jina[133]. However, in the very beginning of this work, Amogha-varṣa has paid glowing tribute to Viṣṇu, which suggests his equal deference for the Brāhmaṇical deities. It should also be pointed out in this connexion that the two famous Digambara com-mentaries viz. *Dhavalā* and *Jayadhavalā* were named after Amoghavarṣa I, who was also known as Dhavala and Atiśaya Dhavala.

The successor of Amoghavarṣa I was Kṛṣṇa II for whose reign we have the Saundatti inscription dated 897 A.D., which has already been discussed. Another Jain inscription[134] of his reign is the Mulgund inscription dated Śaka 824, corresponding to 902 A.D. Mulgund was a renowned Jain centre and is situated in the Gadag Tāluk of Dharwar district. We are told in this stone inscription that during the time of Kṛṣṇa II, his governor Cikārya, son of Candrārya, the governor of Dhavaḷa-viṣaya, and belonging to Varavaiśya caste, constructed a lofty temple of Jina at the town of Muḷgunda. His younger son Arasārya (the brother of Nāgārya), who is described as proficient in the new Āgama (*nayāgamakuśalaḥ*) and a man of great liberality, made an endowment for the maintenance of the *jinālaya*, built by his father (*pitṛkāritajinālayāya*). The gift was entrusted into the hands of he preceptor Kanakasena Sūri, who was the disciple of *munipati* Vīrasena and who in turn, was the pupil of *pūjyapāda* Kumārasena Ācārya of Candikavāṭa (Candrikāvāṭa), belonging to Senānvaya. Kumārasena, Vīrasena etc. are also mentioned in the *Cāmuṇḍarāyapurāṇa*[135] and it has been suggested[136] that Kumārasena was the fourth predecessor preceptor from Cāmuṇḍarāya. In that case, Kumārasena should be placed in the middle of the 9th century A.D.

Kṛṣṇa II was probably the patron of Guṇabhadra, the author of the *Uttarapurāṇa*[136A]. This work was completed in Śaka 820 by Guṇabhadra's disciple Lokasena in the reign of Akālavarṣa or Kṛṣṇa II. His patron was Lokāditya, who was a governor of Baṅkāpura in Vanavāsi under that Rāṣṭrakūṭa king. This Lokāditya was a patron of Jainism as we learn from the *praśasti* of the *Uttarāpurāṇa*[137]. Guṇabhadra himself claims that Kṛṣṇa II was his disciple[138]. And there is no reason why we should disbelieve it. An interesting inscription[139] from Śravaṇa Belgoḷa, which has already been referred to, connects a Jain saint called Paravādimalla with one Kṛṣṇa Rājā, who has been identified with this Rāṣṭrakūṭa monarch. There is another Jain inscription[140] which mentions Lokāditya (called Lokateyarasa) and his overlord Kṛṣṇa II. This inscription is dated 902 A.D. and was discovered from Bandalike, ancient Bāndhavanagara in Shikarpur Tāluk of Shimoga district. It appears from that inscription that this place was looked upon as a Jain *tīrtha* (sacred place).

The next king Indra III also had some fascination for the Jain religion. We have a number of Jain inscriptions of his reign. We must at first refer to the well known Dānavulapāḍu pillar inscription, discovered from Jammalmaḍugu Tāluk of Cuddapah[141] district, Andhra Pradesh. The record is not dated and is partly in Sanskrit and partly Kanarese. The first part of the inscription refers to the military prowess of Śrīvijaya, who was a *daṇḍanāyaka* (general) of king Indra III. The second part opens with an invocatory clause which proclaims glory to the prosperous doctrine of the Jina. It appears from the inscription that Śrīvijaya voluntarily resigned this world and became a Jain ascetic in order to attain eternal bliss. This general Śrīvijaya is otherwise unknown. From the same place another Jain inscription[142] of a single Sanskrit verse mentioning Nityavarṣa or Indra III has been discovered. Two other Śrīvijayas are known to Kanarese literature, both of whom flourished long before this Śrīvijaya and both were men of letters[143]. This Śrīvijaya also, it is interesting to note, is described in this epigraph as *anupama-kavi*, meaning an accomplished poet. The *aṣṭavidha karma*, referred to in this inscription, consists of *jñānāvaraṇīya*, *darśanā-varaṇīya, vedanīya, mohanīya, āyuṣya, nāma*, *gotra* and *antarāya*. This Śrīvijaya, it is evident from the inscription, was a very important general of Indra III and was one of the pillars of the Rāṣṭrakūṭa empire.

Another Jain inscription[143A] of the reign of Indra III called Hatti Mattur stone inscription has been discovered from Karajgi Tāluk of Dharwar district, Karṇāṭaka. This is dated in the Śaka year 838, corresponding to 916 A.D. It records the grant of a village called Vutavura by the *Mahāsāmanta* Leṇḍeyarasa. Afterwards the Jain establishment here was converted into a Śaiva temple. This is evident from the second part of the record, which was inscribed a few centuries afterwards.

In the last chapter we had discussed an important Jain inscription of Indra III, found from Nasik district. We should also mention, in this connexion, an inscription from Belgaum district, Karṇāṭaka, which states that a Jain saint called Nemi-nātha, the preceptor of Maṇicandra, was like a moon in the ocean, which was the dynasty of the Rāṣṭrakūṭas[144]. Evidently this Jain monk was held in highest esteem by the Rāṣṭrakūṭa kings of his time. The inscription has been assigned to circa 900 A.D.

For the reign of Govinda IV we have two Jain inscriptions[145] dated Śaka 847 or 925 A.D. and Śaka 854 or 932 A.D., both of which were discovered from modern Karṇāṭaka state. The first dated Śaka 847, discovered from Gadag Tāluk of Dharwar district, refers to a *jinālaya* built by one Nāgayya[146]. It also refers to another *jinālaya* called Dhora Jinālaya at Bankāpura with the preceptor Candraprabha Bhaṭāra as its head. It is interesting to note that this Jain priest is described as administering a village called Pasuṇḍi (modern Asuṇḍi), which probably shows that the village was an endowment of this Jain temple. The second inscription dated Śaka 854 or 932 A.D., discovered from Adoni Tāluk of Bellary district, refers to a Jain temple[147], built by the queen Chandiyabbe, wife of Kannara, the governor (*mahāsāmanta*) of Sindavādi, 1000. We are told that this queen constructed a Jain temple at Nandavara and made suitable provision for its maintenance. This inscription also refers to a Jain teacher called Padmanandin. It has been suggested that this Kannara is prince Kṛṣṇa III and at this time he was a governor under his cousin Govinda IV[148]. But it is better to regard Kannara of this inscription as a feudatory under Govinda IV.

Kṛṣṇa III was one of the greatest members of the Rāṣṭrakūṭa dynasty. From the holy Kopbal area in Raichur district of Karṇāṭaka we have two inscriptions of his reign. The earlier one[149] has been assigned to circa 940 A.D. and refers to Akālavarṣa Kannardeva and he was no other than Kṛṣṇa III. However excepting a reference to Kopaṇa, there is nothing typically Jain regarding this inscription. The second inscription[150], which is fortunately dated Śaka 887, corresponding to 964 A.D. found near Kopbal from a place called Uppina Beṭgiri is a very important Jain record. It reveals the existence of a feudatory king of the Rāṣṭrakūṭas called Śankaragaṇḍa II who erected a Jain shrine called Jayadhīra Jinālaya which was apparently named after him, *Jayadhīra* being one of his titles. As noted by Desai, this particular feudatory of the Rāṣṭrakūṭas is mentioned in several inscriptions of Northern Karṇāṭaka[151]. That scholar has also drawn our attention to the fact that this chief is mentioned in the *Ajitatīrthakarapurāṇatilakam*[152] of the Kanarese poet Ranna, who wrote this work in 993 A.D. According to that poet Śaṅkaragaṇḍa was a great Jain patron. Therefore, it appears from the combined testimony of these two sources (epigraphic and literary) that this Rāṣṭrakūṭa governor was a great promoter of Jainism in Karṇāṭaka in the 2nd half of the 10th century A.D. It further appears from the title *Rattarameru* given to him in this inscription that Śaṅkaragaṇḍa was of the Rāṣṭrakūṭa extraction. We further learn from this epigraph that another Rāṣṭrakūṭa feudatory namely Rāṭṭayya, who was of Cālukya lineage, donated some land, for the temple erected by Śaṅkaragaṇḍa II, and Nāganandi Paṇḍita Bhaṭāra received the endowment on behalf of the temple, This saint is described here as a disciple of Vinayanandi, who in turn, was a pupil of Śrīnandi of Śūrastha *gaṇa*. From other inscriptions we learn that Śūrastha or Sūrastha *gaṇa* was associated with the Sena *gaṇa* of Mūlasaṅgha.[153]

A few other Jain inscriptions of the reign of Kṛṣṇa III are known. One such inscription[154] has been discovered from Tirumalai hill near Polūr (N. Arcot) in Tamil Nadu, which records the gift of a lamp made to the Yakṣa on the sacred Tirumalaī hill by a servant of the queen of Kṛṣṇa III. This hill was associated with the Jain religion from early times. More than a dozen Jain epigraphs and a number of rockcut Jain figures have been discovered from the same hill. The village near this hill, which bears same name, has still a few Jain families[155]. We should also mention another Jain inscription[156] of the time of Kṛṣṇa III, found from Naregal in the Roṇ Tāluk of Dharwar district. According to this the wife of Gaṅga Būtuga II called Padmabbarasi, constructed a Jain temple at Naregal, and in 950 A.D., the grant of a tank to the charity house, attached to the temple, was made by a subordinate chief called Namayara Mārasiṁghayya. The gift was received by Guṇacandra, the pupil of Vīranandi, who was a pupil of Mahendra Paṇḍita belonging to the Koṇḍakunda *anvaya* of Deśiga *gaṇa*.

The celebrated Jain poet Somadeva wrote his encyclopaedic work *Yaśastilakacampū* during the reign of this great Rāṣṭrakūṭa monarch in the Śaka year 881 when that emperor was stationed at Melapāṭi[157] which has been identified with Melpāḍi in N. Arcot district of Tamil Nadu. The same place is also mentioned in the Karhad plates[158] of Kṛṣṇa III dated Śaka 880 and Karjol inscription[159] dated Śaka 879. We will have something more to say on Somadeva's literary achievements in a later chapter of this volume. Another Jain literary figure namely Indranandi Yogīndra composed his *Jvālāmālinīkalpa*[160] at Malkhed in Śaka 861 during the reign of Kṛṣṇa III.

We have a few Jain inscriptions of the reign of Khoṭṭiga, the brother and successor of Kṛṣṇa III. An inscription from Chitaldrug district dated 968 A.D., mentions the fact that Jakki Sundarī, the wife of Pandayya, a Cālukyan feudatory of Khoṭṭiga built a Jain temple, for which her husband gave a grant.[161] Another inscription, praising the Jain religion, of his reign has been discovered from Dharwar district.[162]

The last representative of the Rāṣṭrakūṭa dynasty was the valiant Indra IV, who unsuccessfully tried to restore the tottering fortune of the empire with the help of his maternal uncle Gaṅga Mārasiṁha. An inscription from Śravaṇa Belgola[163] dated 982 A.D. (Śaka 904) shows that he died like a true Jain. This epigraph describes his wonderful skill in playing polo. It also bestows lavish praise on him and we are told that as as a believer in the doctrine of Mahāvīra, he never uttered a falsehood.

Let us now turn our attention to the state of Tamil Nadu. We have already seen that Jainism was in a flourishing condition in the Southern districts of India from quite early times. In the 7th century also this religion maintained its great popularity in Tamil Nadu. This is directly proved by the testimony of Yuan Chwang. In all the three southern states of India namely Cola, Draviḍa and Mo-lo-ku-ta (Malakuṭa) he noticed numerous Digambaras and their shrines.[164] This testimony from the pen of a person, who was a diehard Buddhist, and who had practically no respect for his religious opponents, is extremely valuable. The same pilgrim laments the alsence of Buddhists and the ruined condition of *Vihāras* particularly in countries of Scuth India. In the *Mattavilāsaprahasana* of Mahendravarman

I, who was a senior contemporary of Yuan Chwang, we have a veiled yet strong criticism of the Jains[165], which indirectly proves that they were present almost everywhere in his kingdom. We have already seen that the Pallavas were not hostile to the Jains. They themselves, however, were Brāhmaṇical Hindus and had special affection for theistic Hindu deities. There is also reason to suspect that during the rule of some of the Pallava kings a few overzealous Śaiva and Vaiṣṇava teachers instigated the nobles and the common people against the Jains and Buddhists. A few later Vaiṣṇava and Śaiva works gleefully narrate the cruel accounts of the persecution of the Jains[166]. There is also reason to believe that Pallava Mahendravarman I himself was a Jain in his early life.[167] Let us not forget that his father Siṁhaviṣṇu was a patron of the Jains. However, it is evident from the *Mattavilāsaprahasana* that Mahendravarman I became a Śaiva later in his life. According to the Śaiva literary tradition, current in South India, Mahendravarman I became a Śaiva under the influence of Appar, the noted South Indian Śaiva philosopher. After his conversion this king became a persecutor of the Jain[168]. The earliest Pallava inscription, connected with Jainism, of our period (600-1000 A.D.) probably belongs to the reign of Parameśvaravarman I (670-695 A.D.). This is the Nalajanampadu stone inscription[169] from Nellore district, Andhra Pradesh. The Parameśvara Pallavāditya of this record is identified with Parameśvara I and he is described here as meditating on the feet on the supreme master, the Lord Arhat. The rest of this Telegu inscription is useless for our purpose.

A few Jain Pallava inscriptions of the region of Nandivarman II Pallavamalla (730-800 A.D.) are known. A rock inscription[170] from Kīl-Sattamaṅgalam dated in the 14th year of that king, in Wandiwash Tāluk of North Arcot district in Tamil Nadu records an endowment of seven *kalañju* of gold by Andai Iḷaiyār Pavaṇandi of the village for feeding ascetics excluding the manager of the monastery. There is an imprecation in the concluding part of the epigraph of incurring sin of distroying Kāmakoṭṭam, probably the famous Śiva temple of Kāñcī.[171] From the same site two more Jain inscriptions of the reign of the same king have been discovered. Both the epigraphs are dated in the 56th year of Nandivarman II. One of them[172] records an endowment of seventeen *kalañju* of gold to a *paḷḷi* called Pavanandivar (evidently named after the ascetic who is mentioned in the epigraph of the 14th year) for the merit of Pūṇḍi Muppavai, daughter of Jinadiyār of Vilukkam, which is identified with the village of the same name in Tindivaram Tāluk in South Arcot district. The Jain saint Pavanandi may be identified with the person of the same name, the author of the *Naṇṇūl,* a Tamil grammatical text[173].

Another Jain shrine is mentioned in an inscription found from Agalur, Gingee Tāluk of South Arcot district. This is dated[174] in the 50th year of Nandivarman II. An undated inscription[175] which has been assigned to this king was discovered from Kāñcī in Chingleput district and records the gift to an Arhat temple. This epigraph, it is interesting to note, mentions an *ācārya* of Ājīvikadarśana, who probably cured Lokamahādevī, the queen of Narasiṁhavarman II. This proves that the Ājīvikas maintained their separate existence in South India as late as the 8th century.

The next Jain Pallava inscription[176] belongs to the reign of Kampavarman, who is identified with Dantivarman,[177] son of Nandivarman II, who ruled in the 1st half of the 9th century A.D. The inscription is dated in the 6th year of Kampavarman's reign and is found in the same site from where three Jain inscriptions of Nandivarman II have been discovered. This is an exceedingly interesting record as it gives us a very clear idea regarding a Jain temple-complex of the Pallava period. The inscription records the renovation of the temple (that is the one established by Pavanandi) and the addition of *mukhamaṇḍapa* to it, the renovation of a *pāḷi*, the construction of a temple of Yakṣī Bhaṭārī (*Iyakkipaḍāri*) and the gift of a big bell to the *paḷḷi* by Mādevī, the wife of Kāḍagadiyariyar[178]. It appears that this entire temple-complex was possibly called *paḷḷi.* It had a main shrine, dedicated to Jina, with a *maṇḍapa* in front, a subsidiary shrine of Yakṣī and the monastery (*pāḷi*) where the Jain monks lived. It is clear from the inscription that in this temple-complex the main shrine and the monastery, which were built some fifty years back, were renovated, while the *mukha-*

maṇḍapa and the shrine for the Yakṣī were added. The entire establishment called *paḷḷi* in this record is again mentioned in an inscription from the same site, belonging to the reign of Rājarāja I, dated in his 13th regnal year, which is equivalent to 997-98 A.D.[179] This *paḷḷi* is there called the temple of Tīrthaṅkara Vimala. This epigraph records the sale of land by one Baladevapidāran, a disciple of Śrī Nandidevar for the maintenance of a perpetual lamp in the temple. At present, however there is no trace of this temple, but there is a temple dedicated to Candranātha in another part of the village.

The Nolamba Pallavas, who came into the limelight during the 9th and 10th centuries A.D., ruled in parts of modern Karnāṭaka and were feudatories of the Western Gaṅgas. Three inscriptions of the time of Nolamba Mahendra are connected with the Jain religion. The earliest epigraph dated Śaka 800, corresponding to 878 A.D., discovered from the fort at Dharmapuri, which is the headquarters of the district of the same name in Tamil Nadu, records a grant[180] to a Jain temple. The second Jain inscription[181] of his reign bears the date Śaka 815 corresponding to 893 A.D. It records that two citizens called Candiyaṇṇa and Nandiyaṇṇa after receiving the gift of the village of Mūllapaḷḷi from the king gave it is as a gift to Kanakasena Siddhānta, the pupil of Vinayasena Siddhānta of the Pogarīya *gaṇa*, Senānvaya and Mūlasaṅgha for the repairs of the *basadi* at Dharmapuri. Even now this place has a few Jain antiquities. Dharmapuri was known in ancient times as Tagadūru[182]. The village Mūllapaḷḷi is now represented by the modern village of Mūlakāḍu, 9 miles west of Dharmapuri.[183] The inscription further informs us that the *basadi* was originally built by two above-mentioned citizens, who are described as sons of the *seṭṭi* of Śrīmaṅgala.

The third Jain inscription of Mahendra's reign has been found from Hemāvati in Anantapur district of Andhra Pradesh. This damaged stone inscription[184] records some donations to a local Jain temple by Mahendra and his son Ayyapa. Another Jain inscription[185] of this Ayyapa has been found from the same site which contains the second inscription of his father Mahendra. It records the fact that Ayyapadeva, presented the village called Budugūru to Lokāyya, who was the younger brother of Dasayya and who is described as the illuminator of the doctrine of the Arhats. And this Lokāyya presented it to the Jain *basadi* built by Nidhiyaṇṇa, apparently the same temple, mentioned in Mahendra's inscription of Śaka 815. This stone epigraphs prove that Mahendra and his son were patrons of Jainism. The undated inscription of Ayyapa is assigned[186] to the early 10th century A.D. It should also be pointed that Mahendra's epigraph of Śaka 815 begins with an invocation to Jinendra.[187] All the above-mentioned inscriptions are in Kanarese.

We should also refer to a Bāṇa epigraph[188] found from Vallimalai (North Arcot) which records the setting up of an image of Devasena, the pupil of Bhavanandin and the spiritual preceptor of the king. The inscription is in Kanarese Grantha characters and may be assigned to the 9th century A.D.

The Imperial Coḷas who started ruling from the last quarter of the 9th century A.D., were Brāhmaṇical Hindus and mainly patronised theistic Hindu deities like Śiva and Viṣṇu. We have, however, quite a good number of inscriptions, connected with Jainism, belonging to the Cola period, which show that the Jains were present almost everywhere in the vast Cola empire. The earliest Jain epigraph of the time of the Imperial Colas belongs to the reign of Āditya I (871-907 A.D.) and was discovered from Veḍal in Arkonam Tāluk of North Arcot district.[189] It is incised on a boulder in front of the natural cave known as Āṇdar-Maḍam. The epigraph records an undertaking given by the lay disciples at Viḍal *alias* Mādevi-Arandaimaṅgalam in Śingapura-nāḍu to protect and feed along with her lady pupils Kanakavīra Kurattiyār, a woman ascetic and disciple of the teacher Guṇakīrtibhaṭṭāraka. This epigraph, which is dated in the 14th regnal year of Āditya (Rājakeśarivarman) further refers to the dispute between 500 male pupils and 400 female ascetics. It was evidently a very big Jain establishment. It further appears tha the female ascetic, mentioned in this epigraph, was the daughter of an influential person. An earlier epigraph from the same site belongs to the reign of Nandivarman II[190], where the Jain temple-complex is called Vidārpaḷḷi. Mādevi Arandaimangalam, mentioned in the epigraph of the time of Āditya I, was another name of Viḍāl. An earlier Jain inscription,[191] dated in the 2nd year of Rājakeśarivarman probably also belongs to the reign of Āditya I. It was found from Tirunagesvaram on the southern bank of the Kāverī. It registers gifts made by merchants of Kumāramārtaṇḍapuram to meet the cost of repairs to the enclosure called Maunakumāramārtaṇḍan and the *gopura* of Milāḍiyarpaḷḷi. From another epigraph it appears[192] that Kumāramārtaṇḍan was a surname of the Pallava king Nandivarman II.

For the reign of Parāntaka I (A.D. 907-955) we have a number of Jain inscriptions. The first epigraph[193] is dated in the third regnal year of Parāntaka I. It was found from Toṇḍur in Gingee Tāluk of South Arcot district. It records the endowment of a village with two gardens and wells as *paḷḷiccandam* to the Jain teacher Vacciraśiṅga Ilamperumānaḍigal at Parambūr and his disciple by the chief Vinnakovaraiyan Vayiri Malaiyaṇ. We have another Jain epigraph[194] of the same year from Tirakkol in Wandiwash Tāluk of North Arcot district. It records a gift of 200 sheeps for the Jain temple called Maisitta Perumbaḷḷi at Śridaṇḍapuram in Ponnur Nāḍu by one Era Nandi *alias* Naratoṅga Pallavariyam of Nelveli, which is probably situated in Tanjore district[195]. The same Jain shrine is also mentioned in another Tamil record of the 10th century[196].

For the 4th year of Parāntaka we have an epigraph[197] from Polur Tāluk of North Arcot district. It is incised on a rock at Tirumalai, a hill known for its Jain antiquities. We have already taken note of an inscription from this hill of the time of Rāṣṭrakūṭa Kṛṣṇa III. The inscription of Parāntaka records a gift to the Jain temple of this place by two persons recruited from Karṇāṭa country. The gift was made for feeding a devotee and for daily offering to Palliyāḷvār i.e. Jain Tīrthaṅkara. The hill was known at that time also as Vaigavūr. A somewhat later Cola inscription[198] (dated in the 12th year of Rājendra I) refers to the fact that in the earlier time a Pallava queen had made provision for the burning of a perpetual lamp in the Jain shrine of this hill.

An inscription[199] of about 945 A.D. of the reign of

Parāntaka I found from Viḷāpakkam in North Arcot district refers to the sinking of a well by one nun called Paṭṭini Kuratti Aḍigal. As the very name signifies, she was an eminent lady teacher. According to the same source she was a disciple of a saint called Ariṣṭanemi Bhaṭārar of the Jain establishment of Tiruppānmalai. We further learn from this inscription that the Jain residents of the place had organised themselves and constituted a representative council of 24 members to look after their interests.

A number of Jain inscriptions belonging to the immediate successors of Parāntaka I are known. The most important of such inscriptions is the copper plate record[200] from Paḷḷankovil situated in Tirutturaipundi Tāluk of Tanjore district. It consists of 6 plates, but unfortunately the plate which contained the name of the reigning king is lost. The inscription discloses the existence of a Jain temple (*paḷḷi*) founded by Śaletti Kuḍiyan. The name of the shrine is given as Sundaraśolapperumbaḷḷi, apparently named after Sundara Cola, the grandson of Parāntaka I. The gift provided for the maintenance of Candranandi Bhaṭāra *alias* Maunidevar of Nandisaṅgha, who most probably presided over the Jain establishment to which male and female ascetics were attached. Since the temple was named after Sundara Cola (956-973 A.D.), it was built in the third quarter of the 10th century A.D. In this connexion we should also refer to the Udayendiram plates of Hastimalla[201] according to which the Digambara Jains had an ancient *paḷḷiccandam* comprising two *paṭṭis* of land which were specially excluded from the gift of the village of Kadaikkottūr made in the reign of Parāntaka I.

At Śirrāmūr in South Arcot district an inscription of the seventeenth year of a Rājakeśari (probably Sundara Cola, 956-973 A.D.) records the provision of a lamp in the *maṇḍapa* of the temple of Pārśvanātha in which the scripture was expounded.[202] So far as the reign of Rājarāja I (985-1014) is concerned, we have already referred to a Jain inscription of his time. We have another Jain inscription[203] of the 8th year of his reign which mentions one Lāṭarāja Vīra Cola, who was a tributary of the Cola king. At the request of his wife he assigned to the god Tiruppānmalai certain income derived from the village Kuraganapāḍi (probably modern Kurambadi, 2 miles east from Pañcapāṇḍavamalai which is 4 miles to the S.W. of Arcot town). This Cola feudatory is described as a worshipper at the holy feet of the god of Tiruppānmalai. The elder sister of Rājarāja I viz. Kundavai had strong affection for the Jain religion. We will discuss this in the next volume of the present work.

Now we should turn our attention to the state of Jainism during the rule of the Pāṇḍyas. The earliest Jain inscription[204] of this dynasty comes from Chitaral in the former Travancore state. The record in Tamil language and Vaṭṭeluttu characters, belongs to the 28th year of the reign of Varaguṇa I (c. 765-815 A.D.)[205] *alias* Neḍuñjaḍayan. The epigraph belonges to the last quarter of the 8th century A.D. It records a gift of golden ornaments to the Bhaṭāriyār of Tiruchchāranattumalai, popularly known as the holy hill of the Cāraṇas, made by the lady teacher Guṇandāngi Kurattigal, disciple of Ariṣṭanemi Bhaṭāra of Perayakkuḍi. Two more inscriptions of the reign of this king are known and both come from Ramanathapuram district. They make mention[206] of Tirukkāṭṭāmpaḷḷi, which seems to have been a Jain temple at Kurandai, an important Jain centre[207] at at Veṇbunāḍu.

We have an important Jain inscription of the reign of Varaguṇa II, which is also important from the historical point of view. This is the Aivarmalai stone inscription[208] found from Palni Tāluk of Madurai district. The epigraph is incised above the natural cave on the Aivarmalai hill, so well known for its Jain relics. Unlike most of the Pāṇḍyan epigraphs, it yields a definite date viz. Śaka 792 corresponding to 870 A.D., which according to the epigraph, was the 8th regnal year of Varaguṇa II. It registers a gift of 500 *kāṇam* of gold by Śāntivīrakkuravar of Kāḷam, the disciple of Guṇavīrakkuravaḍigal for offering to the images of Pārśva Bhaṭāra (i.e. Pārśvanātha) and of the attendant Yakṣīs and for the feeding of one ascetic. The inscription, therefore indirectly proves that the temple-complex of this hill, dedicated to Pārśva, existed before the date of this inscription. A few other short epigraphs of this hill will be discussed below.

Another important Pāṇḍyan Jain inscription is dated in the

20th year of Śaḍayan Māran,[209] who is identified by some with Rājasiṁha II (c. 900-920 A.D.), although Prof. Sastri, it appears, believes that he was a different person[210]. The inscription was discovered from Uttamapaliyam in Periyakulam Tāluk of Madurai district. The epigraph is much damaged but definitely refers to a Jain shrine of this hill, which is known for its Jain antiquities. The Pāṇḍyan king Rājasiṁha II is said to have endowed several Jain temples[211] which proves that he was a Jain patron.

Let us turn our attention to some of the epigraphs of Tamil Nadu, Kerala etc. which are not connected with any ruling dynasty. We have a very early epigraph, which was probably incised even before 600 A.D., and which is also important from the palaeographical point of view. The epigraph was discovered from Tirunātharkunru[212] in Gingee Tāluk of South Arcot. It records the fast unto death (*niśidikā*) in 57 days by Candranandi Āśiriyar. The inscription, according to the editor, marks the transition from Brāhmī to Vaṭṭeluṭṭu and it may be assigned to the 6th century A.D., if not earlier.

We should now discuss the activities of a great Jain saint of South India, who did everything to make his religion popular among the masses. We are referring to Ajjanandi, who was responsible for fashioning a number of images in different parts of the Southern states of India. His name is mentioned in short epigraphs found from Vallimalai in Chitoor district of Andhra Pradesh and from Anaimalai, Aivarmalai, Alagarmalai, Karungālakkuḍi and Uttamapaliyam in Madurai district. His name is also found in the natural cavern at Eruvāḍi in Tinnevelly district and near Chitaral in Kerala. So the three present states of India viz. Andhra Pradesh, Tamil Nāḍu and Kerala were traversed by this great Jain, who left no stone unturned to counteract the hostile propaganda of Śaiva and Vaiṣṇava fanatics, who were bent upon destroying the religion of Pārśva and Mahāvīra in South India. From palaeographical considerations, Ajjanandi should be placed around 800 A.D.

In an epigraph[213] found from Pechcchi Pallam in Madurai Taluk of Maduari district, Ajjanandi's mother Guṇamatiyār is mentioned. One of the epigraphs of Kongar Puliyagulam is actually engraved under the image of that saint,[214] which probably was set up by one of Ajjanandi's disciples, who must have been numerous in the early 9th century. An epigraph found from Vallimalai (Chittoor district) shows that the name of his preceptor was Bālacandra[215]. It further appears that Ajjanandi was a native of the great city of Madura. It has been pointed that this Ajjanandi is to be identified with his namesake, mentioned in the *Jīvakacintāmaṇi,* a Tamil Jain classic.[216] Quite a few other Jain saints are also mentioned in the epigraphs found from different Jain sites of South India. A few like Indusena, Mallisena etc. were probably the contemporaries of Ajjanandi.[217] Needless to say, these saints did everything to popularise the message of the Tīrthaṅkaras in South India.

NOTES

1 See *Indian Archaeology* (1968-69), *A Review,* p. 47 and plate LIIB.

2 *E.I.,* Vol. 18, pp. 172 ff. ; see also Desai, P. B., *Jainism in South India,* pp. 117f.

3 *I.A.,* Vol. 7, pp. 161-62.

4 See *Revised List of Antiquarian Remains, Bombay Presidency,* p. 183 ; see also *I.A.,* Vol. 5, pp. 67 ff., and Vol. 8, pp. 239 ff. This important epigraph was afterwards edited by Kielhorn in *E.I.,* Vol. 6, pp. 1ff. See also Kielhorn's *List,* No. 10.

5 See A. N. Upadhye's paper in *Journal of Bombay University, Arts and Law,* 1933, May, p. 230.

6 See *I.A.,* Vol. 7, pp. 101 ff.

7 *Ibid.,* p. 103.

8 *Loc. cit.*

9 See Raychaudhuri, G. C. *Hist. of the Western Cālukyas* (*JAIH,* Vol. VII), p. 28.

10 *I.A.,* Vol. 7, p. 103.

11 *Ibid.,* pp. 111 ff.

12 *Ibid.,* p. 112.

13 *Loc. cit.* ; see also Kielhorn, *List,* No. 37.

14 See Fleet in *I.A.,* Vol 30, p. 218.

15 *I.A.,* Vol. 7, pp. 106 f.

16 P. 86.

17 See *I.A.*, Vol. 7, p. 104.

18 *Annual Report on Indian Epigraphy*, 1945-46, A-49. See also *Jain Śilālekha Saṅgraha*, Vol. IV, No. 45.

19 *E.I.*, Vol. 21, pp. 204 ff.

20 See Naik, *A List of the Inscriptions of the Deccan*, 1949, No. 73.

21 See *A.R. on Indian Epigraphy*, B. 212-18.

22 *A.R. South Indian Epigraphy*, 1928-29, E 101-31; 1927-28, E 93-238.

23 See 123.2; 146.1.

24 See *Mysore Gazetteer* (New edition), Vol. II (1930), p. 629.

25 *Loc. cit.*

26 *Loc. cit.*

27 *M.A.R.*, 1925, No. 105.

28 *Ibid.*, pp. 90 ff; see also *Jain Śilālekha Saṅgraha*, Vol. 4, No. 24.

29 See Saletore, *Mediaeval Jainism*, pp. 23 f.

30 See *Mysore Gazetteer*, Vol. II, pp. 634 ff.

31 See *E.C.* Vol. IV, Nāgamaṅgala, No. 85, see *Jain Śilālekha Saṅgraha*, Vol. II, No. 121.

32 *M.A.R.*, 1933, pp. 237-8.

33 *Ibid.*, 1920, pp. 27 ff.

34 *Ibid.*, p. 29.

35 See *M.A.R.*, 1918, para 71.

36 Plate XXIA and also p. 29.

37. Pp. 29 f and plate XXI B.

38 See Rice, *Mysore and Coorg* etc., p. 41; see also *Mysore Gazetteer*, p. 642 and *I.A.*, Vol. 18, p. 313.

39 *E.C.*, Vol. II, p. 180 (text); also Intod., p. 43; see *M.A.R.*, 1911, p. 24.

40 See *Mysore Gazetteer* Vol. II, p. 642.

41 See *E.C.*, Vol. IX, No. 60.

42 See *ibid.*, Introd., p. 4.

43 *Ibid.*, No. 61.

44 See *Age of Imperial Kanauj*, p. 160.

45 See *Mysore Gazetteer*, Vol. II, p. 657.

46 *Ibid.*, p. 650, also *M.A.R.*, 1909, para 45.

47 See *E.I.* Vol. IV, p. 140.

48 See *M.A.R.*, 1921, pp. 18 ff.

49 See *ibid.*, 1932, pp. 240-41.

50 *Ibid.*, p. 241.

51 See *E.C.*, Vol. I (Revised edition, 1972), No. 96 and Introd., p. XI.

52 *E.C.*, Vol. X, pp. 25 ff (translation) ; No. 90 (text).

53 *Ibid.*,Vol. XII, p. 135.

54 See *M.A.R.* 1921, p 22.

55 *M.A.R.*, 1914, para 63.

56 See *E. I.*, Vol. 3, pp. pp. 158 ff.

57 *M.A.R.* 1921, para 55.

58 *Ibid.*, 1923, No. 113.

59 See *Mysore Gazetteer,* Vol. II, p. 675 ; see also *The Age of Imperial Unity,* p. 161.

60 *Mysore Gazetteer,* Vol. II, p. 676.

61 *E.I.*, Vol. 36, pp. 97 ff.

62 *Ibid.*, p. 98 ; see also *Mysore Gazetteer,* Vol. II, pp. 678 f.

63 See *E.I.*, Vol. 4, p. 281.

64 *M.A.R.*, 1921, pp. 18 ff. ; see also plates, X. 1-6.

65 For this term see Sircar, *Indian Epigraphical Glossary,* p. 108.

66 See *E.C.*, Vol. II (revised), No. 59 and Plate LXIII. See also Introduction, pp. 44 ff.

67 See also *E.C.*, Vol. X, Mūlbāgal, 84.

68 *Ibid.*, Vol. X, CB, 29.

69 *Ibid.*, Introd., pp. IX f.

70 See *Mysore Gazetteer,* Vol. II, p. 686.

71 See *E.C.*, Vol, II (Revised), No. 150.

72 See *E.C.*, Vol I (1972), No. 98. The date corresponds to 918 A.D. ; it was issued on Phālguna Nandīśvara day. It registers a grant of two villages to Anantavīrya, a disciple of Guṇasena-paṇḍita for the maintenance of a Jain *vasadi* at Peggadūr.

73 See *J.B.B.R.A.S.*, Vol. 10, pp. 194 ff ; see also *Jaina Śilālekha Saṅgraha,* Vol. II, No 130.

74 See Altekar, *The Rāṣṭrakūṭas and their Times,* p. 89 and footnot 52. Desai following Fleet, identifies Kṛṣṇa of this inscription with Kṛṣṇa III, see *Jainism in S. India,* p. 112. But the date of the record, which is given in words, definitely goes against the view of Fleet and Desai. Although, Amoghavarṣa, I, the father of Kṛṣna II was still living, the son was practically the *de facto* king at that time.

75 See Desai, *op. cit.*, p. 113.

76 See *J.B.B.R.A.S.*, Vol. X, pp. 204 ff.

77 Desai, op. *cit.*, p. 113.

78 See *ibid.*, pp. 113 ff.

79 See *E.I.*, Vol. 21, pp. 291 f.

80 For some further details see Desai, *op. cit.*, p. 111.

81 See *Mysore Gazetteer,* Vol. II, pp. 570 ff. ; see also *Age of Imperial Kanauj,*, pp. 162 f.

82 See V. Rangacharya, *A Topographical List of the Inscriptions of Madras Presidency*, 1919, Salem, No. 81.

83 *Ibid.*, No. 74.

84 See *E.C.*, Vol. II (Revised), No. 1; see also *E.I.*, Vol. 4, pp. 24 ff.

85 *E.C.*, II, Nos. 2-9.

86 See No. 7 dated circa 700 A.D.

87 See Watters, *On Yuan Chwang's Travels in India*, Vol. II, p. 237.

88 See Inscription No. 47 in P. B. Desai's *Jainism in South India* etc., pp. 374 f.

89 See *Kannada Inscriptions of A.P.*, No. 57; see also Desai, *op. cit.*, pp. 339 ff.

90 See Desai, *op. cit.*, pp. 343 f; No. 20.

91 *Ibid.*, p. 344; also *Varāṅgacarita*, Introd., p. 22.

92 See *E.C.*, Vol. 4, Sr. 160, p. 143. We should also mention in this connexion, the reference to the death of Sukumārasena *Muni* on the hill of Kopaṇa (Kapaṇādri) mentioned by Cāmuṇḍarāja in his celebrated *Cāmuṇḍrāya Purāṇa*, see Saletore, *op. cit.*, p. 193 and foot note 2.

93 See *E.C.* Vol. II, p. 88.

94 *Ibid.*, Nos., 127, 191, 345 and 384. For some further details on this great *Tirtha* see Saletore, *op. cit.*, pp. 187-197; see also Desai, *op. cit.*, pp. 200 ff.

95 *A.R. on South Indian Epigraphy*, 1916-17, copper plate No. 16; see also *J.A.H.R.S.*, Vol. 13, pp. 185 ff; and *The Classical Age*, p. 253.

96 *A.R. South Indian Epigraphy*, 1941-42, No. 18.

97 *Ibid.*, 1929-30, p. 6, Nos. 17-19.

98 See *The Age of Imperial Kanauj*, pp. 137 f.

99 See *E.I.*, Vol. 9., pp. 47 ff; see also Butterworth and Chetti, *Nellore Inscriptions*, pp. 164 ff.

100 See *E.I.*, Vol. 7, pp. 177 ff.

101 *Ibid.*, p. 182; cf. the case of Vināpoti, the mistress of Badami Cālukya Vijayāditya (Mahākūṭa pillar inscription) and Divalāmbikā (Sudi plates of Būtuga).

102 See *E.I.*, Vol. 24, pp. 268. ff.

103 See *J.A.H.R.S.*, Vol. 13, p. 195 and footnote 1.

104 See *Epigraphia Andhrica*, Vol. II, pp. 21 ff.

105 *Ibid.*, pp. 22 ff.

106 *Loc. cit.*

107 *Loc. cit.*

108 See No. 1 of *Epigraphia Andhrica*, Vol. II.

109 *Ibid.*, pp. 31 ff.

110 See *Inscriptions of Andhra Pradesh* (*Karimnagar district*) ed. P. V. Parabrahma Sastry, No. 5.

111 *Ibid.*, No. 4.

112 See *The Cālukyas of Vemulavāḍa.*, pp. 92 ff; see also N. Premi, *Jaina Sāhitya aur itihāsa*, pp. 190 ff.

113 See Premi, *op. cit.*, p. 179 ard footnote 1.

114 *Ibid.*, pp. 178 f., and p. 179 footnote.

115 *Ibid.*, p. 193.

116 *E.C.*, Vol. II (Revised), No. 67.

117 *Ibid.*, No. 35.

118 *E.C.*, Vol. IX, No. 61.

119 *E.I.*, Vol. 4, pp. 332 ff; also *I.A.*, Vol. 12, pp. 11 ff.

119A See *A.R. of Indian Epigraphy*, 1958-59, B-582.

120 See *Karnatak Inscriptions* (1951), Vol. II, pp. 14-16.

121 See *E.I.*, Vol. 6, pp. 25 ff.

122 *Ibid.*, p. 26.

123 *Ibid.*, p. 25.

124 See Premi, *op. cit.*, p. 150 fn. 4 where the original verses from Guṇabhadra's *praśasti* have been reproduced.

124A See The *Rāṣṭrakūṭas and their Times*, p. 311.

125 See Premi, *op. cit.*, pp. 134 f.

126 *Ibid.*, pp. 151 f. and footnote 6 in p. 151.

127 *Loc cit.*; see also R. G. Bhandarkar, *Early History of the Deccan*, p. 95.

128 See Altekar, *op. cit.*, p. 411; see also *J.B.B.R.A.S.*, Vol. 22, pp. 80 ff.

129 See *E.I.*, Vol. 18, p. 248; also Altekar, *op. cit.*, p. 311.

130 See Premi, *op. cit.*, p. 163.

131 *Ibid.*, p. 153.

132 See Jain, J. P., *The Jain Sources* etc., pp. 204 ff.; see also *praśasti-saṅgraha* (pp. 56-57) of that text published from Sholapur. Premi *op. cit.*, p. 49 (footnote) however, doubts the authenticity of this *praśasti*.

133 See *Mysore Gazetteer*, Vol. II, p. 741 (cf. verses I. 84, 114 and III.5 of that work).

134 See *E.I.*, Vol. 13, pp. 190 ff.; see also *Jaina Śilālekha Saṅgraha*, Vol. II, No. 137.

135 See Desai, *op. cit.*, pp. 134 f.

136 *Loc. cit.*

136A See *J.B.B.R.A.S.*, Vol, 22, p. 85; see also Altekar, *op. cit.*, p. 99.

137 See Saletore, *op. cit.*, p. 89; see also Premi, *op. cit.*, p. 150 fn. 3 where the relevant verse regarding him has been quoted.

138 See *J.B.B.R.A.S.*, Vol. 22, p. 85; and Saletore, *op. cit.*, p. 39.

139 *E.C.*, Vol. II, No. 67.

140 *M.A.R.*, 1911, p. 38; see also Saletore, *op. cit.*, p. 207; see also *Jaina Śilālekha Saṅgraha*, Vol. 4, No. 77.

141 See *E.I.*, Vol. 10, pp. 147 ff.

142 *A.S.I.A.R.*, 1905-6, pp. 121 f. According to this inscription king Indra (Nityavarṣa) caused the pedestal to be made for the bathing ceremony of Śāntinātha. See also V. Rangacharya, *A Topographical List of the Inscriptions of Madras Presidency*, Madras, 1919, pp. 589-90; see also C. L. Jain, *Jain Bibliography*, p. 199.

143 See *E.I.*, Vol. 10, p. 149.

143A See *I.A.*, Vol. 12, pp. 224 f.

144 *A.S.I.A.R.*, 1928-29, p. 125.

145 According to some the earlier inscription dated Śaka 847 belongs to the reign of Indra III, see Desai, *op. cit.*, p. 139. But Indra III, it appears, died in 922 A.D.,; see *The Age of Imperial Kanauj*, p. 13.

146 See *Bombay Karṇāṭaka Inscriptions*, Vol. I, Part I, No. 34.

147 *A.R. of South Indian Epigraphy*, 1916, App. B, No. 540. See also Desai, *op. cit.*, p. 149.

148 Desai, *op. cit.*, p. 149.

149 See *Jain Epigraphs*, Part III, No. 48 in Desai's work *Jainism in South India* etc.

150 *Ibid.*, No. 46.

151 See *ibid.*, pp. 369 f.

152 Āśvāsa XII, verse 9; see also Desai, *op. cit.*, p. 370.

153 Desai, *op. cit.*, p. 372.

154 *A. R. South Indian Epigraphy*, App. B. No. 65

155 Desai, *op. cit.*, p. 42.

156 See *Bombay Karṇāṭaka Inscriptions*, Vol. I, part I, No. 38.

157 For the relevant passage from that text see Premi, *op. cit.*, p. 179 fn. 1.

158 See Naik, *A List of the Inscriptions of the Deccan*, 1949, No. 173.

159 *Ibid.*, No. 172.

160 See Desai, *op. cit.*, p. 48; see also *Jainism and Karṇāṭaka Culture*, p. 34.

161 See *Mysore Gazetteer*, Vol. II, pp. 769-70.

162 See *Jain Śilālekha Saṅgraha*, Vol. 4, No. 87.

163. E.C. II, (Revised ed.), No. 133. It has been suggested that No. 134 from the same place belongs to time of Indra IV (see E. C. II, No. 134).

164 See Watters, *On Yuan Chwang's Travels in India,* Vol. II, pp. 224, 226, 228.

165 (Chowkhamba ed.) p. 9. P. B. Desai, therefore, is not correct when he says that this play does not refer to the Jains (see *op. cit.,* p. 35).

166 See in this connexion *I.A.,* Vol. 40, p. 215; Vol. 42, p. 307. See also Desai, *op. cit.,* pp. 33 f. See also *S.I.I.,* Vol. I, p. 29.

167 See Desai, *op. cit.,* p. 34.

168 The *Periyapurāṇam* refers to the destruction of several structural monuments of the Jains at Cuddalore by Mahendravarman I, see *I.A.,* Vol. 40, p. 215. See also *The Classical Age,* p. 260.

169 See *E.I.,* Vol. 27, pp. 203 ff.; also *Nellore Inscriptions,* p. 676.

170 *A.R. on Indian Epigraphy,* 1968-69, p. 60 and No. B 219.

171 *Loc. cit.*

172 *Loc. cit.;* see also B 220.

173 See *ibid.,* p. 6.

174 *Ibid.,* B 268.

175 *A.R. on Indian Epigraphy,* 1954-55, B. 360.

176 *Ibid.,* 1968-69, B. 221.

177 See *The Age of Imperial Kanauj,* pp. 165 ff.

178 See *Seminar on Inscriptions,* Madras, p. 159.

179 *A.R. on Indian Epigraphy,* 1968-69, B. 223.

180 See Rangacharya, *op. cit.,* Salem, 81.

181 See *E.I.,* Vol. 10 pp. 54 ff.

182 *Ibid.,* p. 64.

183 *Loc. cit.*

184 *S.I.I.,* Vol. IX, pt. I, No. 19.

185 See *E.I.,* Vol. 10, p. 70.

186 *Ibid.,* p. 65.

187 *Ibid.,* p. 68.

188 See *E.I.,* Vol. IV, pp. 141 f.

189 See *S.I.I.,* Vol. 3, Part 3, No. 92; see also *S.I.I.,* Vol. 13, No. 245.

190. *A.R. South Indian Epigraphy,* 1909, App. B. 82.

191 *S.I.I.,* Vol.. 3, Pt. 3, No. 91.

192 *A.R. South Indian Epigraphy,* 1907, No. 199.

193 See *S.I.I.,* Vol. 19, No. 80.

194 *Ibid.,* No. 51.

195 *Ibid.,* p. 25.

196 See *S.I.I.*, Vol. 13, No. 297.

197 See *S.I.I.*, Vol. 19, No. 89; also *S.I.I.*, Vol. 3, No. 97 and A.R. of 1907, No. 66.

198 See *S.I.I.*, Vol I, No. 68.

199 *A.R. on S. Indian Epigraphy,* 1900, App. B. 53.

217 *S.I.I.*, Vol. 14, Nos. 197-119.

200 *A.R. on Indian Epigraphy,* 1961-62, pp. 4-5; see also *Transactions of the Archaeological Society of South India,* 1958-59, pp. 84 ff.

201 *S.I.I.*, Vol. 2, p. 387 (No. 76).

202 201 of 1902 (*A.R. on Epigraphy,* Madras).

203 *E.I.*, Vol. 4, p. 137.

204 *Travancore Archaeological Series,* Vol. I, pp. 193- ff.; see also Rangacharya, *op. cit.*, Tiruvankur, 2.

205 We have followed the chronology proposed by K. A. N. Sastri in *The Pandyan Kingdom,* pp. 36 ff.

206 *A.R. on Epigraphy* (Madras), 430 and 431 of 1914.

207 See Desai *op. cit.*, p. 62.

208 See *S.I.I.*, Vol. 14, No. 22; see also *E.I.*, Vol. 32, pp. 337 ff.

209 *S.I.I.*, Vol. 14, Nd. 69.

210 Sastri, *op. cit.*, pp. 74 f.

211 *Ibid.*, p. 84.

212 *S.I.I.*, Vol. 17, No. 262; see also the plate facing Introd., p. 1.

213 Rangacharya, *op. cit.*, Madura, No. 101.

214 *Ibid.*, Madura, No. 389.

215 See *E.I.*, Vol. 4, No. 15, D.

216 See *S.I.I.*, Vol. 14, Nos. 107 ff.; see also C. L. Jain, *Jaina Bibliography,* p. 228.

CHAPTER XI

The Śvetāmbara Canonical Literature

According to the tradition, current among the Śvetāmbara Jains, the Jain sacred texts were first collected and edited at Pāṭaliputra more than 160 years after the demise of Lord Mahāvīra. The earliest version of this tradition is to be found in the *Āvaśyakacūrṇī*[1] of Jinadāsagaṇi Mahattara, who flourished in the second half of the 7th century A.D.[2] The great Śvetāmbara writer Haribhadra, who lived in the middle of the 8th century A.D., has also referred to this council[3]. The following story is told regarding this council.

Sthūlabhadra was one of the two sons of Śakaṭāla, the minister of king Mahāpadma. After staying with Kośā, a famous courtesan of the city of Pāṭaliputra for a period of 12 years, he renounced the world under Sambhūtavijaya without suffering any transgression. Now it so happened, that there was a famine at Pāṭaliputra during the time of the 9th Nanda[4] and the monks were forced to leave the city. The famine lasted for 12 years and when the monks returned, they discovered that many portions of the canon were lost. Sthūlabhadra then, on his own initiative, convened a council of learned Jain monks at Pāṭaliputra to collect the entire canon. But the monks discovered that the 12th Aṅga viz. the *Dṛṣṭivāda* could not be recollected and the council decided to send 500 monks including Sthūlabhadra to Bhadrabāhu, who was at that time staying in Nepal and was engaged in *mahāpāṇa-mahāprāṇa* meditation there. He was the only monk, alive at that time, who had the complete knowledge of the *Dṛṣṭivāda*. But within a short time, all but Sthūlabhadra left Nepal, as they could not face the situation there. Bhadrabāhu, we are told, taught Sthūlabhadra the fourteen *Pūrvas* (an important part of the *Dṛṣṭivāda*) withholding the meaning of the last four texts for some reason and he was not allowed to teach the last four texts to any one else. Later on, with the death of Sthūlabhadra (215 years after the demise of Mahāvīra), even the verbal embodiment of these four *Pūrvas* came to an end. Since then the knowledge of the *Pūrvas* went on decreasing and it was completely forgotten by the V.N. 1000[5].

It is clear from the above account that at least the eleven Aṅgas were extant during the council which was held some 160 years after Mahāvīra's Nirvāṇa. However, during the course of our discussion of the Aṅga texts, we will see that portions of those texts were added after the 4th century B.C. It should further be remembered that there were three more Jain councils in which the Āgama texts were subjected to further revision and alteration. A few of the later additions to the Āgamic texts will be discussed in connexion with the scrutiny of the individual texts. Let us now turn our attention to the Aṅga texts, most of which were composed in the pre-Mauryan times. The following eleven Aṅga texts are known—*Ācārāṅga, Sūtrakṛtāṅga, Sthānāṅga, Samavāyāṅga, Bhagavatī* or *Vyākhyāprajñapti, Jñātṛdharmakathā, Upāsakadaśā, Antakṛddaśā, Anuttaropapātikadaśā, Praśnavyākaraṇa* and *Vipākaśruta.*

The *Ācārāṅga*[6] undoubtedly is one of the oldest and most authoritative Jain Āgamic texts. The language and the spirit of this work prove that a major part of it was composed within 50 years of Mahāvīra's demise. A few section, especially those dealing with the birth of Mahāvīra, were added probably a couple of centuries later. The work is divided into two major sections called Śrutaskandha and it appears that the earlier Śrutaskandha was composed long before the second one. This is also vouched for by the evidence of its *Niryukti*[7] which suggests that this portion was composed by the *theras* who were *śrutakevalins*. The style also of the second part is radically different from the first part.

The names of the nine chapters (adhyayana) of the first Śrutaskandha are as follows—Śastraparijñā, Lokavijaya, Sītoṣṇīya, Samvyaktva, Lokasāra, Dhūta, Mahāparijñā, Vimokṣa and Upadhāna. Of these, the 7th one viz. Mahāparijñā is now extinct[8]. The second section contains five *cūlās* (*cūlikā*), of which the 5th called Niśītha is now a separate Āgamic text. The first two *cūlās* contain seven chapters each and the third and the fourth, one each. We have a *Niryukti*[9] on this work by Bhadrabāhu, a *Cūrṇī*[10] by Jinadāsagaṇi (7th century) and also a *Ṭīkā*[11] by Śīlāṅka (c. 850 A.D.). Śīlāṅka in his commentary[12] has referred to an earlier commentator of the *Ācārāṅga* called Gandhahastin.

In the earlier parts of the *Ācārāṅga* there is a distinct emphasis on *Ahiṁsā*. A few sentences from that part are reproduced below—"Some slay (animals) for sacrificial purposes, some kill (animals) for the sake of their skin, some kill (them) for the sake of their blood, thus for the sake of their heart, their bile, the feathers of their tail, their big or small horns, their teeth, their tusks, their sinews, their bones; with a purpose or without a purpose. Some kill animals because they have been wounded by them, or are wounded or will be wounded".

"He who injures these (animals) does not comprehend and renounce the sinful acts; he who does not injure these, comprehends and renounces the sinful acts. Knowing them, a wise man should not act sinfully towards animals, nor cause others to act so, nor allow others to act so. He who knows these causes of sin relating to animals, is called a reward-knowing sage"[13].

Some of the finest teachings of Jainism are incorporated in this Aṅga text. "He who sees by himself, needs no instruction. But the miserable, afflicted fool who delights in pleasures, and whose miseries do not cease, is turned round in the whirl of pains"[14]. The author of this work repeatedly asks the Śramaṇas to be careful regarding women and similar sentiments are expressed almost everywhere in the Indian literature. The truly liberated is one who is not attached to the objects of the senses[15]. However similar teachings are to be found in the Buddhist texts also. We should always remember that both Jainism and Buddhism look upon this world as a place of suffering. And this is the reason why in the religious texts of both the systems we get identical metaphysical speculations.

The *Ācārāṅga Sūtra* gives interesting information regarding religious and social life of pre-Mauryan India. A number of popular festivals in honour of Brāhmaṇical deities like Indra, Skanda, Rudra and Mukunda are mentioned in this text[16]. We should remember that the *Mahābhārata*[17] also refers to the festivals in honour of Paśupati i.e. Rudra and Brahman. References to the festival in honour of Indra are to be found not only in the later Vedic texts, but also in Aśvaghoṣa and other writers including Varāhamihira[18]. The festival of Indra, according to the *Mahābhārata*, was introduced by Vasu Uparicara, the Cedi monarch[19].

The *Ācārāṅga* in the same passage also refers to the festivals of Yakṣas, snakes, tree, hill, river, sea etc. These were simply popular assemblies (*samāja*) which had practically no religious bias. Such *samājas* were not liked by Aśoka as we learn from one of his rock edicts[20]. References to various types of cloth including those made in China, Bengal and Malaya countries are to be found in this text[21]. It is interesting to note that *cīnāṅśuka* is also mentioned in the *Arthaśāstra*[22] of Kauṭilya which probably suggests that the Chinese cloth was known in India even in the pre-Mauryan days. There is no need to suppose that the name 'Cīna' is not older than the third century B.C., as it could have been the name of a particular province of China, from a much earlier period. References to various types of musical instruments including *mṛdaṅga*, *nandīmṛdaṅga*, *jhallarī*, *vīṇā*, *tumbavīṇā*, *paṇava*, *tuṇaya* etc. are also quite interesting[23]. They probably prove that these instruments were used in Jain temples in those days.

The section on Mahāvīra's life has already been discussed in an earlier chapter. There is little doubt that this part of the *Ācārāṅga* was utilised by the author of the *Kalpasūtra*. However, in another part of the *Ācārāṅga*[24] there is a reference to Mahāvīra's wanderings in various parts of Bengal. This part is written in verse and it appears to have been composed a few years after Lord Mahāvīra's demise. We learn from this section that at first the people of Lāḍha were in no mood to listen to the teachings of Mahāvīra. The people there made the dogs bite Mahāvīra and he was subjected to various other humiliations. But it appears that within a few years of Lord Mahāvīra's death, Jainism was firmly established in Bengal, and as we have already suggested, it was from Bengal that the Jain religion spread to Orissa.

The *Sūtrakṛtāṅga*[25], which is the second Aṅga text, is undoubtedly another very old Jain Āgamic text. We have various commentaries on this text including a *Niryukti*[26], a *Cūrṇī*[27] and a *Ṭīkā*[28]. Like the *Ācārāṅga* it has two Śrutaskandhas. In the first there are sixteen Adhyayanas and in the second, seven. The major part of the first Śrutaskandha is in verse and the greater part of the second Book is in prose. Compared to the *Ācārāṅga* it is a more readable work and it contains numerous interesting references. In the earlier sections of this text there is a detailed discussion on the metaphysical doctrines of various schools of thought. For a student of pre-Buddhist Indian philosophy this part of the *Sūtrakṛtāṅga* is an invaluable source-book. This work, it is interesting to note[29], knows the four ages viz. Kṛta, Kali, Tretā and Dvāpara. The author of this text shows his close acquaintance with the Second Book of the *Mahābhārata* by referring to the Śiśupāla episode. We are quoting the relevant passage from Jacobi's translation[30]—"A man believes himself a hero as long as he does not behold the foe, as did Śiśupāla (before he beheld) the valourously-fighting great warrior". It is apparent from the passage that the Jain author had read with enthusiasm and interest the exciting Śiśupāla story so beautifully told in the Sabhāparvan. Elsewhere our author refers[31] to Dvaipāyana and Parāśara, which also indirectly shows his acquaintance with the *Mahābhārata*. The Videhan monarch Nami is also mentioned[32] and he is to be identified with the famous Nimi of Brāhmaṇical and Buddhist texts. Reference to the *Strīveda*[33] shows that works on the science of Erotics existed in India in the 5th century B.C. The earliest systematic work on this subject, as we learn from Vātsyāyana,[34] was written by Bābhravya Pāñcāla, who probably flourished in pre-Buddhist times.

It is extremely interesting to note that the author of the *Sūtrakṛtāṅga* calls Lord Mahāvīra a wise. Brāhmaṇa (*māhaṇa*) at least in two places[35]. The Buddhist canonical authors also make a similar claim on behalf of Gautama Buddha. In the work entitled *Itivuttaka* Buddha directly calls himself a Brāhmaṇa[36]. In the *Aṅguttara Nikāya*[37] Buddha is called Aṅgīras, who was a great ancient Ṛgvedic seer. Both Mahāvīra and Buddha believed that by deeds one becomes a Brāhmaṇa and not by birth. The *Sūtrakṛtāṅga*[38] declares that a Brāhmaṇa is one who has ceased from all sinful actions viz. love, hate, quarrel, calumny, backbiting, reviling of others, aversion to control and love of pleasures, deceit, untruth and the sin of wrong belief. He is never proud and angry and always exerts himself. Similar definition of a Brāhmaṇa will not be hard to come across in the vast *Tripiṭaka* literature. That seeing of a Śramaṇa, was considered a bad omen is indirectly confirmed by this text[39]. In the play *Mṛcchakaṭika*[40] the hero Cārudatta himself expresses a similar sentiment when he saw a Śramaṇa.

In this text peoples living in Gandhāra, Gauḍa, Kaliṅga, Draviḍa are mentioned along with the Śavaras and Caṇḍālas[41]. Probably even in the days of Buddha and Mahāvīra peoples living in the extreme North-west, South and East were looked upon with contempt by the people of Madhya-deśa. But this does not necessarily prove that in the 6th century B.C. eastern or Southern India were culturally more backward in comparison to the centrally located states. This is merely a question of attitude. As a matter of fact, the metropolis of an eastern state viz. Pāṭaliputra became from the 6th century B.C., the cultural capital of Northern India.

Several types of coins like *māṣa, ardha-māṣa, rūpaka* are mentioned in this text[42]. Elsewhere in the Jain canon[43] *kārṣāpaṇa* (including false *kārṣāpaṇa*), *suvarṇa-māṣa, rūppa-māṣa* are referred to. We will afterwards notice that in another Jain text, composed in the early centuries of the Christian era, there is an exhaustive and valuable list of coins current in India in the pre-Gupta times. This work also refers to a number of musical instruments[44]. It is also interesting to note that, unlike the other Jain texts, Brāhmaṇas are mentioned first in a list of four castes given in this canonical work[45]. It appears that the earlier Jain canonical writers had a less affected attitude towards the Brāhmaṇas compared to the later writers.

There is a short description in this text of Nālandā,[46] which as we learn from this work, was a prosperous town, a description confirmed by the account, given in the Buddhist texts[47]. It further refers to a householder called Lepa, who was in possession of a bathing-hall called Śeṣadravyā, which was situated to the north-east of Nālandā. As the name suggests, the hall was built with the materials not used in the building of a house. At this town Gautama Indrabhūti, the famous disciple of Lord Mahāvīra met Udaka Peḍhālaputta of the Medārya *gotra*, who was a follower of Lord Pārśvanātha. The conversation[48] that took place between the two can be compared with the dialogue between a follower of Pārśva and Gautama Indrabhūti, recorded in the 23rd chapter of the *Uttarādhyayana*, which will be discussed afterwards. From this conversation we further learn that some of the followers of Gautama Indrabhūti were also known as Kumāraputras[49], which probably indicate that they belonged to aristocratic families.

The *Sūtrakṛtāṅga* like the *Ācārāṅga* contains beautiful and thought-provoking philosophical expressions and such expressions are in no way inferior to those of the Pāli Buddhist texts. The doctrines of Gośāla and Buddha have been cleverly refuted by Ārdraka, a follower of Mahāvīra in the second half of this text[50]. However, it should be added that the views of other schools have not been properly presented in this text. Such distortions of the philosophical views of other teachers are common in the religious works of almost all schools of thought in India. The Pāli Buddhist texts prove that Buddha had absolutely no deference for other teachers, and all of them have been branded by him as ignorant and unworthy of serious attention[51]. We have already said that, with the exception of a few passages, nowhere in the Jain canon the Buddhists have been attacked directly. However, the poor Ājīvikas have been mercilessly assailed by both Buddha and Mahāvīra.

The *Sthānāṅga Sūtra*[52], which is the third Aṅga text, unlike the first two, does not say anything on the teaching of Mahāvīra. On the other hand, this work contains information on various dogmatic topics, which can be grouped in 1-10 categories. It has a slight resemblance to the *Aṅguttara Nikāya* of the Buddhists, although there are major differences between the two texts. There are ten Adhyayanas and 787 Sūtras and the only reliable commentary[53] on this text is by Abhayandeva Sūri, who wrote it in V.S. 1120, corresponding to 1062 A.D. However, as the commentator himself admits, it was not an easy task for him to write an authentic commentary on such a work[54]. There are, however, interesting references in this Aṅga text. Among the holy places, the name of Prabhāsa[55], is conspicuous by its presence and this shows that even the canonical Jain writers looked upon this Vaiṣṇava holy place as a *Tīrtha*. The name of this place also appears in the *Rājapraśnīya*[56], the second Upāṅga text. This is not surprising if we remember that Kṛṣṇa and Baladeva are included in the list of sixty three holy men (*Śalākāpuruṣa*). The four types of severe austerities, indulged by the Ājīvikas, are also mentioned[57]. The difficult penances, performed by the Ājīvikas, are also referred to in the *Naṅguṭṭha Jātaka* (No. 144)[58]. We are further told that a Jain monk should not cross more than once in a month the following five great rivers—Gaṅgā, Yamunā, Erāvatī (Pāli Acirāvatī), Sarayū and Mahī. These five rivers are mentioned together in several Pāli canonical texts[59] which indirectly prove the contemporaneity of the Pāli and Jain canonical works. In the epics, Mahī and Acirāvatī are not treated as great rivers. It should further be remembered that this Mahī should be distinguished from the Mahī of Western India, which is the "the great river called Mais' of the *Periplus* (Para 42) Mophis of Ptolemy[60]. Sarayū is mentioned as Sarabhū[61] in the Pāli texts which reminds us of the word 'Sarabos' used by Ptolemy[62] for that river. The well-known capital of Kosala in Mahāvīra's time viz. Śrāvastī was situated on the river Erāvatī or Acirāvatī, modern Rapti.

Among the Jain rebels (Ninhavas) the first seven are mentioned and they were Jamāli, Tiṣyagupta, Āṣāḍha, Aśvamitra, Gaṅga, Rohagupta and Goṣṭhamāhila. Since the last one flourished 584 years after the Nirvāṇa of Mahāvīra, this section of the *Sthānāṅga*[63] was composed not before the beginning of the 2nd century A.D. It is, however, quite possible that the list of these seven rebels were added during the Valabhī council, when the Jain canonical texts received their final shape. Nine *gaṇas* under Mahāvīra are mentioned by name[64] and they are—Godāsa, Uttarabalissaha, Uddeha, Cāraṇa, Uḍuvāṭika (Uḍuvāḍiya), Viśvavādika, Kāmardhika (Kāmiḍḍhiya), Māṇava and Koḍiya. Of these Viśvavādika (Vissavāiya), it appears, is an otherwise unknown *gaṇa* and not mentioned in the *Therāvalī*. It should, however, be remembered that these *gaṇas* could not have existed in the 5th century B.C., as according to the *Therāvalī*, they had originated only after Bhadrabāhu.

Ten great cities are mentioned in this text[65] and they are—Campā, Mathurā, Vārāṇasī, Śrāvastī, Sāketa, Hastināpura, Kāmpilya, Mithilā, Kauśāmbī and Rājagṛha. Six of these cities, as we have already noticed, are mentioned in the *Dīgha Nikāya* in the list of six great cities. Regarding Hastināpura, however, we can say, that it disappeared from the map of Northern India long before the sixth century B.C. The Jain canonical author has included the city is his list probably because of its past fame

The 4th Aṅga text the *Samavāyāṅga*[66] is like *Sthānāṅga* a descriptive work There is a commentary[67] on it by Abhayadeva, which was completed at the town of Aṇahilapāṭaka in the Vikrama year 1120, corresponding to 1062 A.D. Almost all the authorities believe it to be one of latest of the canonical texts, for it not only mentions other Aṅga texts, but also the *Nandīsūtra*. The subject matter of the first two third of the work is arranged in numerical groups just like the *Sthānāṅga*, but in this case the numbers do not stop at ten, but go upto a million. Under No. 18, eighteen scripts are enumerated and they include Dāmilī and Polindī scripts[68]. This list can be compared with the list in the *Mahāvastu*[69] and the more exhaustive list given in the *Lalitavistara*[70], both being Buddhist Sanskrit texts. The 72 Arts are also mentioned by name.[71] Reference to gods like Vijaya, Vejayanta, Jayanta and Aparājita remind us of the four gods Aparājita, Apratihata, Jayanta and Vaijayanta mentioned in the *Arthaśāstra*[72] of Kauṭilya.

The author of the *Samāvāyāṅga* shows his thorough acquaintance with the devotional Vaiṣṇava literature. In Sūtra No. 158 there are some typical Vaiṣṇava expressions and the emblems of Baladeva and Kṛṣṇa are described correctly. The *Samavāyāṅga* not only betrays knowledge about Kṛṣṇa's life, but also a thorough acquaintance with the later myths that grew around Vāsudeva Kṛṣṇa.

The 5th Aṅga text viz. the *Vyākhyāprajñapti* or the *Bhagavatī*[73] is undoubtedly the most important canonical work of the Śvetāmbara Jains. Abhayadeva wrote a commentary on this work in the Vikrama year 1128, corresponding to 1070 A.D., at Aṇahilapāṭaka[74]. This voluminous text extends to 41 Śatakas. Since we consider this work as very important, we would like to make a detailed analysis of the contents of this text.

The work opens with an adoration of Jina and also very significantly of the Brāhmī script. In the first Śataka several types of ascetic groups are mentioned including Tāpasas, Ājīvikas and Parivrājakas. Lord Mahāvīra is represented as giving a discourse on various topics to Gautama Indrabhūti in the Guṇaśila shrine which was situated near Rājagṛha. The most important information that we find in the first Śataka is regarding Kālāsavesiyaputta, a follower of Pārśva, who was converted by Mahāvīra. This monk, it appears, had at first misgivings regarding Mahāvīra's religion, based on five restraints. In the second Śataka there is a reference to Kayaṁgalā town, which is the same as Kajaṅgalā of the Pāli canon. However, the canonical writer is not correct when he says that it was not far from Śrāvastī[75]. This Śataka refers to the conversion of Khaṁda of the Kātyāyana *gotra,* who was a disciple of a teacher well versed in the Brāhmaṇical philosophy. We are further told that Mahāvīra for some time lived on the Vipula mountain of Rājagṛha[76]. In this Śataka also Mahāvīra is represented as having converted a few followers of Pārśva[77]. It is interesting to note that the hot-spring of Rājagṛha is mentioned in this Śataka and the name given to it here is Mahātavovatī[78] which reminds us of Tapodā of the Pāli canonical texts[79]. It further appears from this Śataka that even in the 5th century B.C. there were shrines, dedicated to the Jina, for we come across the expression *Jinaghara*[80]. In the 3rd Śataka there are several interesting references. The four Lokapālas[81], the god Śūlapāṇi or Śiva, who is described as *vasahavāhaṇa*[82] i.e. *vṛṣabhavāhana*, and other gods like Indra, Skanda, Vaiśravaṇa etc. are mentioned[83]. It appears from this Śataka that gods like Indra, Skanda, Durgā, Rudra and Vaiśravaṇa were very popular. This will be confirmed by the evidence of other canonical texts, which will be discussed later in this chapter. This Śataka also contains the interesting account of Tāmalī Moriyaputta of Tāmralipta city[84]. We are told that he was at first a big merchant of that famous city-port and afterwards gave up everything to become a recluse. The expression 'Moriyaputta' does not necessarily mean that he was a scion of the Moriya or Maurya family. It further appears from this Śataka[85] that the art of drama was fully developed in the sixth century B.C., an assumption which is supported by the evidence of Pāṇini. A few malignant spirits like Indragraha, Skandagraha, Kumāragraha, Yukṣagraha and Bhūtagraha are also mentioned[86]. Needless to say, these *grahas* were supposed to inflict bodily harm both to children and adults. The 4th Śataka contains nothing interesting. In the 5th Śataka there is a referece to the famous Pūrṇabhadra shrine of Campā[87], which was often visited by Mahāvīra. A beautiful and detailed description of this Yakṣa temple is given in the *Aupapātika Sūtra,* which will be discussed later in this chapter. We have also an exhaustive list of various types of musical instruments in this Śataka[88]. The god Hariṇegamesī, who is generally identified with Kārttikeya, and who was responsible, according to the *Kalpsūtra,* for transferring the embryo of Mahāvīra from the womb of Devānandā to Triśalā, is prominently mentioned in this Śataka[89]. Among other interesting references in the 5th Śataka we have *stūpa, devakula*[90] etc. The *devakulas* or the Brāhmaṇical shrines are also mentioned elsewhere in the *Bhagavatī*[91]. There is little doubt that the shrines, dedicated to Devas, Yakṣas etc., existed in pre-Buddhist days[92]. But as they were built of wood, no trace of them remains to-day. This Śataka also refers to the disciples of Pārśva[93]. In the 6th Śataka there is nothing interesting to note except a reference to various types of measures[94].

The 7th Śataka is important since it contains interesting information on the political history of the 5th century B.C. Here we have an elaborate description of the war between Ajātaśatru and eighteen confederate kings of Kāśī and Kosala[95]. It was surely a bloody war which lasted for a considerable time and came to be known as Rathamusala battle. The ethics of war were scrupulously followed in this battle[96] and this reminds us of the ethics of war which were agreed upon by both the parties before the Bhārata War[97]. A person called Varuṇa, belonging to the Nāga lineage, took part in this war, according to the *Bhagavatī*[98]. However, the account of the war is highly realistic, unlike those given in the two epics, and we are told, that king Ajātaśatru, who was helped by the Vaijis, ultimately emerged victorious. A similar account of war is found in the *Nirayavalikā,* an Upāṅga text, which will be discussed afterwards.

The 8th Śataka contains interesting references to the Ājīvikas and also the lay followers of the Ājīvika religion[99]. There is an elaborate account of various professions[100] and it indirectly proves that the struggle for existence became quite difficult by the 6th century B.C. False weights and measures are also referred to[101]. The 9th Śataka also contains accounts of the conversion of the followers of Pārśva[102] by Mahāvīra, and this once more proves the testimony of the *Ācārāṅga,* according to which Jainism reached North Bihar even before the birth of Mahāvīra. This particular Śataka contains the poignant account[103] of Mahāvīra's meeting with Devānandā, his mother, which we have already discussed in the account of Mahāvīra's life. We are further told that Lord Mahāvīra converted his mother to the Nirgrantha religion and she became a nun under Āryā Candanā[104]. But the most important section of this Śataka is that dealing with Jamāli,[105] which has already been briefly discussed in connexion with the discussion on the life of Mahāvīra. There is nothing here to indicate that he was the son-in-law of Mahāvīra. Like the Master he, too, belonged to the Kṣatriya-Kuṇḍagrāma. In this section[106] some festivals, connected with Indra, Skanda, Mukunda, Nāga etc. are also mentioned. There is a reference to Chinese silk-cloth[107] and to the stick of Indra[108] which was obviously used in the Indra-festival. The 10th Śataka contains nothing of any importance, but the 11th is full of interesting things. Mahāvīra's visit to Hastināpura is recorded here,[109] which, at that time, was probably a mere village. Here also we get references to such terms as *pecchāghara*[110] (i.e. *prekṣāgṛha*) and *raṅgasthāna,*[111] which surely indicate that drama, as a form of entertainment, was very popular in those days. There is also the term *yavanikā*,[112] which also occurs elsewhere in the Jain canon. Let us not forget that even in the *Brahmajāla Sutta* of the *Dīgha Nikāya* the term *prekṣāgṛha* is conspicious by its presence and one of the monks under Buddha was an actor in his earlier life.[113] The town of Ālabhiyā which is mentioned more than once in this Śataka[114] was often visited by Buddha.[115] Lord Mahāvīra too, according to this Śataka visited this town. The account of the conversion of Poggala Parivrājaka is also given here.[116] The 12th Śataka records the account of Mahāvīra's visit to Kauśāmbī during the reign of Udayana. This king, according to the *Bhagavatī*, was the daughter's son (*dauhitra*) of Ceṭaka of Vaiśālī.[117] This statement gets an unexpected confirmation from one of the plays of Bhāsa[118] where Udayana is called the son of Vaidehī and Vaiśālī at that time was included in Videha Janapada. We must also remember that another daughter of Ceṭaka viz. Cellaṇā was the mother of Ajātaśatru and this prince is frequently called Vedehiputta in the Pāli texts.[119] This Śataka further represents Jayantī, a sister of Śatānīka, as a great devotee of Lord Mahāvīra. The 13th Śataka contains the story of Mahāvīra's visit to Vītībhaya,[120] the capital of Sindhu-Sauvīra. We are told that the Master travelled all the way from Campā to Vītībhaya in order to convert the king of Sindhu-Sauvīra. As we have already said, this was surely the longest journey this Nirgrantha prophet undertook, and compared to this 'long march' all the achievements of Buddha pale into insignificance. The 14th Śataka refers to the worship of Pāṭalī tree at Pāṭaliputra[121] and mentions Ambada Parivrājaka of Kāmpilyapura.[122]

The famous 15th Śataka which is entitled *Gośālaka* gives an elaborate and highly authentic account of the career of Gośāla Maṅkhaliputra, the famous Ājīvika philosopher. We have briefly discussed the career of Gośāla in a previous chapter and we propose to make an elaborate study of Gośāla and his religion in a separete Appendix to this volume. According to this account Gośāla died 16 years before Mahāvīra and there is little doubt that his untimely death was welcomed by the followers of both Mahāvīra and Buddha. The Pāli canonical texts also prove that Gautama Buddha regarded the Ājīvikas as the greatest enemies of his religion. This Śataka refers to a few pre-Buddhist shrines including Aṅgamandira of Campā[123] and Kāmamahāvana of Vārāṇasī.[124] It further refers to sixteen Mahājanapadas of those days,[125] a list that differs considerably from that given in the Pāli texts.[126] This Śataka further gives the very revealing information that Lord Mahāvīra ate the flesh of cat (*majjārakaḍa*) and wild cock (*kukkuḍamaṁsa*)[127] when he was down with fever after a debate with Gośāla. The Jains of modern times find this account quite shocking and hasten to offer various explanations for these terms. Such attempts can be compared with those offered by the devout Buddhists for the term *śūkaramaddava* which Buddha ate in Cunda's mango-grove at Pāvā. Needless to say, the prophets of the 6th century B.C., like other people of that time, were addicted to both vegetarian and non-vegetarian food. Eating of fish and flesh did not clash with their ideas of non-violence. There are other evidences to show that the Jains of earlier times were non-vegetarians like others, although by the Gupta period, they became strictly vegetarians. This Śataka further refers to the fact that a king of Puṇḍra country called Devasena afterwards became a devout Ājīvika.[128] This suggests that after the demise of Gośāla, Ājīvikism spread to Northern Bengal. It further appears that this 15th Śataka of the *Bhagavatī* was edited more than once during the councils held afterwards.

In the 16th Śataka we find Indra paying homage to Mahāvīra.[129] As a matter of fact, the religious opponents of Brāhmaṇical Hindus always loved to paint the king of gods as a devotee of their prophet. In almost every non-canonical work of the later Jain writers we have a *praśasti* addressed by Indra to the Jina. The Buddhist canonical writers have gone a step further; even the chief disciples like Moggallāna and Sāriputta are represented as being worshipped by Sakka (Śakra). This section also refers[130] to Vāsudeva and Baladeva. The 17th Śataka has nothing new to tell. The 18th Śataka is quite interesting. There is a reference to Bahuputta shrine of Vaiśālī[131] and this is the only shrine or temple which is referred to in the canonical texts of both the Jains and Buddhists. For a historian the importance of this reference is indeed very great.

It fully justifies our assumption that the *Bhagavatī Sūtra* is a text of great antiquity. This particular temple is mentioned in the *Mahāparinibbāna Suttanta* of the *Dīgha Nikāya,*[132] which is regarded as one of oldest canonical Buddhist texts. Mahāvīra is represented as having stayed in this shrine. We are therefore thrilled to discover that both these great prophets stayed for some time in this famous temple of the celebrated city of Vaiśālī. Let us remember that Lord Mahāvīra himself used to pass nights in the Deva and Yakṣa shrines of those days. This is proved by a passage of this Śataka.[133] This particular Śataka also refers to gold and silver coins (*suvaṇṇamāsā, rūppamāsā*)[134]. The beautiful story of the conversion of Brahmin (*māhaṇa*) Somila is told in this section[135]. The remaining Śatakas of the *Bhagavatī* are largely useless for our purpose.

The above analysis of this celebrated Aṅga text, though brief, amply shows that the *Bhagavatī* is an important source-book of contemporary social and cultural history of Eastern India. It is a matter of regret that we have no early authentic commentary of this text, and the *Vṛtti* of Abhayadeva is almost wholly useless like his other *Vṛttis*. It was simply impossible for a monk of Gujarat, living in the 11th century, to write a faithful commentary on a work, composed in the pre-Mauryan period. This remark of ours holds good for other Jain commentaries as well.

The 6th Aṅga text viz. the *Nāyādhammakahāo* (*Jñātṛdharmakathā*)[136] is another important Jain canonical text. It contains a number of stories which make this text the most readable of all the Jain canonical works. The work is divided into two Śrutaskandhas, of which the first one, which is divided into nineteen chapters (Adhyayana) is important for our purpose. The second Śrutaskandha is almost a repetition of the first.

The first Adhyayana called Utkṣipta records the story of prince Meghakumāra, the son of Bimbisāra, by his wife Dhāriṇī. The name of this prince is, however, absent in the Buddhist texts. This prince, we are told, afterwards embraced the religion of Mahāvīra and became a Jain monk. The second Adhyayana relates the story of merchant Dhaṇṇa (Dhanya) of Rājagṛha. Once he was sentenced to imprisonment for committing a crime.

He and robber Vijaya (majority of thieves and robbers in the Jain literature bear this name), the murderer of his son Devadatta, were fettered together. This pious merchant we are told, shared with that thief in the jail the food-packet (*bhoyaṇa-piḍaga*) sent to him daily by his wife Bhadrā[137]. Later the merchant became a *sādhu* under the Jain ascetic Dharmaghoṣa. The third Adhyayana contains an account of the famous prositute of Campā called Devadattā, who was loved by the sons of the two merchants Jinadatta and Sāgaradatta. This prostitute, once more appears in a later Adhyayana of this canonical text. The fourth Adhyayana relates the story of two turtles and a jackal. The first turtle is killed by the jackal as it exposed itself to the danger, another one, being cautious, remained unhurt in its shell, since it waited until that beast had gone. The 5th Adhyayana is quite interesting as it tells us something about Ariṣṭanemi and other Vṛṣṇis of Dvārakā (Bāravaī). There is also a description of the Surapriya *yakṣāyatana* (shrine) which was situated near the city. It is interesting to note that the five Vṛṣṇi heroes led by Baladeva, mentioned in the *Vāyu Purāṇa*, as *manuṣyaprakṛti* gods, are also referred to in this section of this text[138]. A few other Vṛṣṇi heroes are also mentioned in this section. The mountain Raivataka which is mentioned for the first time, in the *Mahābhārata*[139], is described here as situated near Dvārakā. However, it should be pointed out that this mountain is not near Dvārakā but Girinagara and in the *Mahābhārata* passage Kuśasthalī is described as situated near this mountain (*Kuśasthalīṁ purīṁ ramyāṁ Raivatenopaśobhitām*). It follows therefore that ancient Kuśasthalī is not Dvārakā but Girinagara.[140] The Jain writer of this canonical text, it appears, was not much acquainted with the topography of this area. We have already said that Baladeva, Vāsudeva and others had a place in the Jain mythology and it is therefore not surprising to find a detailed description of them in this canonical text. However, like other Jain texts, Ariṣṭanemi, who was supposed to be a scion of the Vṛṣṇi race, is described as much superior to Kṛṣṇa and Baladeva in this section of the *Nāyādhammakahāo*.

This work also refutes the philosophy of the Sāṅkhya teachers[141]. We are told in the 5th Adhyayana that the Sāṅkhya teacher Śuka (Sua) was converted to Jainism by the Nirgrantha saint Thāvaccāputta. This particular Sāṅkhya teacher, who was well versed in the *Ṣaṣṭitantra*[142], used to move about with a trident. The detailed description of the various implements of this philosopher shows that in spite of his Sāṅkhya leanings, he was a Śaiva. In this connexion we get the words *tridaṇḍa, kuṇḍikā, chatra, karoṭikā, kamaṇḍalu, rudrākṣamālā, mṛttikā-bhājana, trikāṣṭikā, aṅkuśa* etc. Probably the earliest reference to the word *yāpanīya* is to be found in this section of this Aṅga text.

In the 7th Adhyayana we have the story of Rohiṇī which has interesting similarity with the parable of talents in Matthew[143] and Luke.[144] Surprisingly enough, the Jain writer finds a few words of praise for women. The 8th Adhyayana is more interesting as it contains the story of Mallī, the 19th Tīrthaṅkara. In this Adhyayana there is a reference to a Nāga temple near Sāketa[145]. There is a description of a sea voyage and we further learn that the Indian ships used to go to various foreign countries from the river ports of those days including Campā. Here also we have names of those popular Hindu gods and goddesses,[146] who are mentioned in the *Bhagavatī* and other places. The 9th Adhyayana contains an account of ship-wreck and there is an interesting reference to Lavaṇasamudra and Ratnadvīpa. The 10th to 12th Adhyayanas are less interesting. But the 13th Adhyayana gives an interesting account of the philanthropic works done by Nanda, a gem-merchant (maṇiyāra) of Rājagṛha. He built a number of beautiful garden-complexes which included hospitals, painting-houses, kitchens with water-tanks, music-schools etc. The 14th Adhyayana contains the story of the conversion of a lady called Poṭṭilā by a Jain nun called Suvratā. The 15th Adhyayana refers to monks belonging to other sects like Raktapaṭa (Buddhist), Paṇḍaraṅga (Ājīvika), Gautama, Caraka etc.

The most important Book of this Aṅga text is the 16th Adhyayana called Avarakaṁkā which is largely based on the *Mahābhārata* as it gives the story of Draupadī and her five husbands. We are told that in her previous birth Draupadī (Dovaī) was the daughter of a merchant of Campā and her name was Sukumārikā. One day she saw a prostitute named Devadattā enjoying the company of five young men at a Bohemian club of the city called Lalitā[147]. This lady thereupon made a *nidāna* to marry five husbands in her next life and accordingly was born as Draupadī. It is interesting to note that even some of the minor details of the *Mahābhārata* are repeated in this section of the *Nāyādhammakahāo*[148]. However, the Pāṇḍavas are represented as inferior heroes and mere subordinates of Kṛṣṇa. This section further represents Kṛṣṇa as becoming disgusted with the behaviour of the Pāṇḍavas and asking them to leave for the South. Then we are told the story of the foundation of Madura, called in the text Paṁḍamahurā, by the five Pāṇḍavas, a story that has interesting parallels with the story of Pandia or Pandaia, told by Megasthenes, who flourished in the last quarter of the 4th century B.C.[149] The story told regarding the foundation of Madura in this work was later taken up by the Jain narrative writers, who did their best to make the story as absorbing as possible[150]. The Pāṇḍavas died like many other devout Jains on the summit of Śatruñjaya, according to this work. The other 3 Adhyayanas are less interesting. However, the robber Vijaya once more appears in the 18th Adhyayana.

The 7th Aṅga text [151] viz. the *Upāsakadāśā* is also an absorbing and readable work. There is a commentary on this work by Abhayadeva[152], which is practically of no help to us. This work contains stories regarding ten lay disciples of Lord Mahāvīra. The first story is concerning Ānanda, who was a *śramaṇopāsaka* of Vāṇiyagāma near Vaiśālī. There is a reference to Dūipalāsa shrine of that place. This millionaire disciple of Mahāvīra reminds us of Anānthapiṇḍika of the Pāli canon. He is even depicted as superior to Indrabhūti. The second story is told regarding one Kāmadeva of Campā. It is interesting to note that in this story there is a reference to Lambodara (Gaṇeśa)[153], which proves that this god was even worshipped in the pre-Christian period. A newly discovered coin of Hermaeus (1st century A.D.) has the representation of elephant-headed Gaṇeśa. The Ājīvikas are referred in the 6th and the 7th Adhyayanas. The 7th Adhyayana is particularly interesting.

From this section we learn that at the town of Polāsapura there was one Saddālaputta, a famous potter, who had 500 potter shops under him and who was a lay Ājīvika votary. The potters, who worked under him, are described as *bhattaveyaṇā*[154], which suggests that they received regular wages for their work. Pāṇini's Sūtra *vetanādibhyo jīvati* (4.4.12) suggests that even from pre-Buddhist times the system of regular payment in cash to workers and servants was known. The evidence of the *Mahābhārata*[155] also shows that the system of *vetana* was well known from quite early times. This follower of the Ājīvikas, according to the present story, was converted by Mahāvīra. The 8th Adhyayana shows one pious lay worshipper called Mahāśataka, whose chief wife Revatī, we are told, used to consume cow-flesh[156]. The last two Adhyayanas are not much interesting.

The 8th Aṅga text, which is known as the as the *Antagaḍa-dasāo* (*Antakṛtadaśā*)[157], is also not a barren work as it is full of narratives. The accounts of the Vṛṣṇis, led by Vāsudeva, occupy a good portion of this text. However some of the details, given here, are also found in the 6th Aṅga text. There is a list of peoples living in different *janapadas* and this list[158] includes such names as the Arabs, Barbaras, Yavanas, Siṁhala, Pārasika etc. A full list of 72 Arts are also given in this text[159]. There is a highly interesting reference[160] to the Mahākāla *śmaśāna* (cemetery) of Ujjayinī. Like many other Jain texts this work also represents Vāsudeva as inferior to Ariṣṭanemi[161]; that great Indian philosopher and hero is even pictured as a devotee of this Jain Tīrthaṅkara[162]. Two of Kṛṣṇa's wives are distinctly mentioned; they are Rukmiṇī[163] and Jāmbavatī, the mother of Sāmba[164]. In another place we have the complete list of Kṛṣṇa's wives. We have a very interesting story regarding Moggarapāṇi[165] Yakṣa-shrine of Rājagṛha, and it appears from the description of the icon that it was made of wood. The curse of Dvaipāyana, mentioned in the *Ghaṭa Jātaka*[166] and Kauṭilya[167] on the Vṛṣṇis, is also mentioned here[168].

The 9th Aṅga the *Anuttaropapātikadaśā*[169] is practically devoid of any interest. There is a *Vṛtti* by Abhayadeva[170]. There are only two original pieces in this text and they contain legends of persons who were reborn in the uppermost heavens.

The 10th Aṅga text viz. the *Praśnavyākaraṇa*[171] is not the same text[172] described in he *Sthānāṅga* and *Nandīsūtra*. We have a *Vṛtti* by Abhayadeva[173]. There are two Śrutaskandhas called Āsrava and Saṁvara. The work throws considerable light on the social life of those days. There are sections on crimes and punishments[174]. Accurate descriptions of Baladeva and Vāsudeva[175] show that the images of these hero-gods were quite popular. Some of these descriptions were no doubt copied from contemporary Vaiṣṇava literature. There are indirect references to terrible wars described in the two epics, which were fought for women like Sītā and Draupadī[176]. There are many other useful details, whch can only be discussed in a separate volume. It is certainly much more than a mere "loquacious treatise."[177] And there is nothing in this text that can be called interpolations of post-Christian period.

The 11th Aṅga text the *Vipākaśruta*[178] is once more an interesting and readable canonical work. We have a *Vṛtti* on it by Abhayadeva.[179] It has two Śrutaskandhas with ten chapters (Adhyayana) each. The first Śrutaskandha is entitled *Dukhavipāka,* which is much longer, and the second *Sukhavipāka,* which is less interesting.

This work contains some references which are otherwise unknown. The most valuable information is supplied regarding Udayana, whose priest was condemned to death for illcit connexion with the queen Padmāvatī.[180] It is interesting to note that in the 6th century B.C. even a Brāhmaṇa could be executed for serious crimes and it was clearly against the Smṛti laws. However, we have in the story of Cārudatta in the *Mṛcchakaṭika* another such example. A licentious person was condemned to death by embracing a red hot image of woman (*itthipaḍimam*),[181] a punishment approved for such persons in the *Manusmṛti.*[182] There are descriptions of various instruments[183] of torture and we are further told how prisoners were tortured in jail in those days.[184] The great physician Dhanvantari[185] is condemned in the strongest possible language because he prescribed "meat diet". A ludicrous story is told in this connexion regarding the fate of this physician. We learn from this text that the Yakṣas like the Devas were worshipped with flowers, leaves, incense etc.[186] It is possible that the Vardhamānapura, mentioned in this text, is Burdwan of Bengal. We are told that Mahāvīra himself visited this town.[187] Rohiḍa of this text (p. 275) may be identical with Rohītaka of the *Mahābhārata*.[188] These two towns were known for shrines dedicated to Maṇibhadra and Dharaṇa Yakṣas respectively. There is a story in which a daughter-in-law is shown as killing her mother-in-law.[189]

In the *Sukhavipāka*[190] we have a reference to Majjhamiyā, which is identical with Mādhyamikā, which is in Rajasthan. It appears from both the parts of this canonical text that there were Yakṣa shrines almost everywhere in Northern India. In the earlier Śrutaskandha there is a valuable description of a village inhabited by robbers (*corapallī*).[191] Here also the leader of the robbers is a person called Vijaya,[192] who, we are told, had spies (*cārapurisā*) like the king. The king of the country in which this *corapallī* was situated, by applying Machiavellian tactics, succeeded in capturing alive the son of this robber chief. The role played by prostitutes is also described in attractive language.[193]

Let us now turn our attention to the Upāṅga texts which are 12 in number, they are—*Aupapātika, Rājapraśnīya, Jīvajīvābhigama, Prajñāpanā, Sūryaprajñapti, Jambūdvīpaprajñapi, Candraprajñapti, Nirayavalikā, Kalpāvataṁsikā, Puṣpikā, Puṣpacūlikā* and *Vṛṣṇidaśā*. The first Upāṅga text viz. the *Aupapātika* (*Ovavāiya*)[194] is probably the most important among the Upāṅga works. We have in the very beginning[195] of this text, a smart and beautiful description of the celebrated Pūrṇabhadra Yakṣa-shrine of the city of Campā. This description leaves no room to doubt that it was a great temple-complex of the 6th century B.C. It was probably built a few centuries earlier; but nothing of it has survived, simply because the entire complex was built of wood. At the time when Lord Mahāvīra visited the city of Campā, Kūṇika-Ajātaśatru was the king of Aṅga-Magadha with his temporary capital in that city. This text further proves that Kūṇika had great respect for Mahāvīra.[196] The name of his queen is given as Dhāriṇī, which is, however, a stock name for queens in Jain literature. Let us further remember that the Pūrṇabhadra shrine of Campā was a favourite resort of Mahāvīra. The Buddhist texts describe Yakṣa Pūrṇabhadra,[197] but do not show any acquaintance with this shrine of Campā. This text also contains the tragic story of the death of he Brahmin Ambaḍa Parivrājaka with his 7 disciples,[198] when he was going from Kāmpilya to Purimatāla. It is interesting to note, that according to the description of the text, the city of Kāmpilya (Kampillapura) was spread over both the banks of the Ganges.[199] The 72 Arts are enumerated in this text also.[200] This text also refers to several types of Parivrājakas belonging to Brāhmaṇa and Kṣatriya castes.[201] The following 8 types of Brāhmaṇa (*māhaṇa*) Parivrājakas are enumerated—Kṛṣṇa, Karakaṇḍa, Ambaṣṭha, Parāśara, Kṛṣṇa(2), Kṛṣṇa--Dvaipāyana, Devagupta and Nārada. The 8 types of Kṣatriya Parivrājakas are the following—Sīlaī, Sasihāra, Naggai, Bhaggaī, Videha, Rājarāja, Rājā-Rāma and Bala. We are not aware of any other similar list of Parivrājakas elsewhere is the Indian literature. This text also refers to the Ājīvikas[202] and Niṇhavas.[203]

The second Upāṅga work *Rājapraśnīya*[204] is an equally important Āgamic text. There is a commentary on it by Malayagiri, a contemporary of the celebrated Hemacandra,[205] who flourished in the middle of the 12th century A.D. The text is divided into two parts. The first part contains a few interesting references, as for example, *cīnapaṭṭa*,[206] *picchāghara*[207] (*prekṣāgṛha*), *devakula*,[208] *thūva* (*stūpa*)[209] etc. Some of the descriptions remind us of the *Aupapātika Sūtra*. The second part which contains an account of the conversation between king Paesī of Seyaviyā and Kumāraśramaṇa Keśin, a follower of Pārśva is more important and it reminds us of the *Pāyāsi Sutta* of the *Dīgha Nikāya*.[210] The Kumāraśramaṇa monks were known to Pāṇini.[211] There is strong reason to believe that the Buddhist author of the *Pāyāsi Suttanta* was influenced by this Jain text. In the Buddhist poem also the scene of the conversation is said to be Setavyā, which is evidently the same as Seyaviyā. There is no need to connect this king with Prasenajit of Śrāvastī.[212] It is quite interesting to note that a few of the conversations[213] are similar to what we get in the *Milindapañha*. Among the other important references in this part we have horses of Kāmboja,[214] festivals of popular gods,[215] different types of punishments for different castes etc.[216]

The 3rd Upāṅga text *Jīvājīvābhigama*[217] has nine sections and altogether 272 Sūtras. There is a commentary[218] on it by Malayagiri, who has referred to the various readings of the text. According to him it is an Upāṅga belonging to the *Sthānāṅga*. Although it is not a very extensive text, it contains a very good number of useful references, some of which will be noticed below. Almost all the important information are to be found in the 3rd section (*pratipatti*) of this work. Among the various types of wine, menioned here, we have the wine called Kāpiśāyana which is also mentioned by Pāṇini (IV.1.29) and Kauṭilya (II. 25). This wine was produced in the Kāpiśī country (Afghanistan). This section also refers to the cloth produced in Sindhu, Draviḍa, Vaṅga and Kaliṅga countries. Among the ornaments, there is a reference to the necklace made of Dīnāra coins which is also referred to in the *Kalpasūtra*.[219] There are also useful lists of *ratnas,* weapons, metals, *bhavanas*, *naṭas, utsavas, yānas,* diseases, scripts, servants, utensils, etc.

The 4th Upāṅga is called *Prajñāpanā*.[220] Its auhor was Ārya Śyāma, who flourished some 376 years afer Mahāvīra. There are commentaries on it by Haribhadra[221] (8th century) and Malayagiri.[222] It is the largest Upāṅga text and has altogether 349 Sūtras. Like the 3rd Upāṅga it also contains lists of various things. The most significant however is the list of 25½ Janapadas with their capitals.[223] We are reproducing the list with the names of their capitals in bracket—Magadha (Rājagṛha), Aṅga (Campā), Vaṅga (Tāmralipti), Kaliṅga (Kāñcanapura), Kāśī (Vārāṇasī), Kosala (Sāketa), Kuru (Gajapura), Kuśāvarta (Śauripura), Pañcāla (Kāmpilya), Jāṅgala (Ahicchatra,), Saurāṣṭra (Dvārāvatī), Videha (Mithilā), Vatsa (Kauśāmbī), Śāṇḍilya (Nandipura), Malaya (Bhadrilapura), Matsya (Vairāṭa), Varaṇā (Acchā), Daśārṇa (Mṛttikāvatī), Cedi (Śukti), Sindhu-Sauvīra (Vītībhaya), Śūrasena (Mathurā), Bhaṁgi (Pāpā), Vaṭṭā (Māsapurī), Kuṇāla (Śrāvastī), Lāḍha (Koṭivarṣa), Kekaya ½ (Śvetikā). In the same Sūtra a good number of so-called non-Aryan tribes like Śaka, Yavana, Cīna, Hūṇa, Romaka, Andhra, Pārasa etc. are mentioned. A large number of professional classes are also referred to in the same Sūtra. The various scripts, which have already been noticed, are also mentioned in this Sūtra.

The 5th and 6th Upāṅga texts *Sūryaprajñapti*[224] and *Candraprajñapti* throw a flood of light on ancient Indian knowledge of astronomy. The present *Candraprajñapti* is not in any way different from the *Sūryaprajñapti*. The 7th Upāṅga text the *Jambūdvīpaprajñapti*[225] throws some light not only an astronomy but also geography. It has altogether 176 Sūtras. The most significant is the reference to Alasaṁḍa i.e. Alexandria in Śūtra No. 52. The same Sūtra refers to Ārabaka, Romaka, Yavanadvīpa, Siṁhala, Barbara etc. The god Naigameṣī (Kārttikeya) is mentioned, in the Sūtra No. 115.

The last five Upāṅga texts are actually five *vargas* (sections) of one Upāṅga work viz. the *Nirayavalikā*.[226] As we have already said, this particular work throws some welcome light on the contemporary history. We have already referred to the fight between Ceṭaka and Ajātaśatru described in this Upāṅga text. This Upāṅga text has a *Vṛtti*[227] by Candrasūri, who flourished in the early 12th century A.D. We are told that one of the sons of Śreṇika called Kāla (his mother was one Kālī,[228] described as *cullamāuyā* i.e. step-mother of Kūṇika) was killed by Ceṭaka in the *Rathamusala* war. According to the author[229] of the text Kāla went to Naraka because he was killed in a war. Unlike the author of the *Gītā* the Jain writer of the *Nirayavalikā* never balieves that the death in the battlefield enables the hero to attain *svarga*. According to this text Śreṇika-Bimbisāra committed suicide,[230] a statement contradicted by the evidence of the Buddhist canon. We further learn that afterwards the remose-striken Kūṇika-Ajātaśatru transferred his capital to Campā.[231] However he description of the war[232] appears to be exaggerated. Ten other brothers of Ajātaśatru are also named in this text, including Vehalla, son of Cellaṇā.[233] Abhaya is described as the eldest son of Śreṇika by his wife Nandā; but according to the Buddhists his mother was one Padmāvatī a prostitute of Ujjayinī.[234] The Buddhist texts, however, confirm the Jain account that this prince was originally a devotee of Mahāvīra.[235] We are told by the Jain author of this

Upāṅga text that with the help of this prince Śreṇika fulfilled the strage *dohada*-longing[236] of Cellaṇā.

The second *Varga* of this text called *Kalpāvataṁśikā* does not contain much information. But in the 3rd *Varga* called *Puṣpitā* there is a good deal of information. The story of the conversion of Brāhmaṇa Somilla by Pārśva is told in the 3rd chapter of this text. From the 4th Adhyayana of this text we learn that cousin-marriage was not unpopular in those days. Here the goddess Bahuputrikā is described as the goddess looking after the welfare of the children. It therefore appears that the Bahuputta shrine of Vaiśālī, mentioned in the *Bhagavatī* and the Buddhist canon, was dedicated to this goddess. The 4th *Varga* entitled *Puṣpacūlikā* describes the conversion of an old spinster (*buḍḍhakumārī*) called Bhūtā by Pārśva's principal lady-disciple Pupphacūlā. The 5th *Varga* entitled *Vṛṣṇidaśā* as the name indicates, describes the story of the Vṛṣṇis, but adds nothing new. There is also a reference to the Maṇidatta Yakṣa-shrine of Rohītaka.

Let us now turn our attention to the Mulasūtra texts, which are acually three[237] in number. They are— *Uttarādhyayana, Āvaśyaka* and *Daśavaikālika*. There is little doubt that all these three texts are works of hoary antiquity and were probably composed in the pre-Mauryan period. For the historian, however, the most important is the *Uttarādhyayana Sūtra*.[238] The first commentary on this important work is ascribed to Bhadrabāhu and is known as the *Uttarādhyayananiryukti*.[239] It was followed by the *Cūrṇī*, written by Jinadāsagaṇi Mahattara in the 7th century A.D. There are also a number of later commentaries[240] which prove that it was always regarded as one of the most important Āgamic works.

The work is divided into 36 Adhyayanas. The first is entitled *Vinayaśruta*. It deals with the everyday conduct of a Jain ascetic. The very character of this chapter shows, that it incorporates the personal teachings of Mahāvīra and was probably composed in the 5th century B.C. "Better" says Mahāvīra "I should subdue my self by self-control than be subdued by others with fetters and corporal punishment". Some of the finest teachings of Lord Mahāvīra are incorporated in this poem, which does not compare unfavourably with the *Dhammapada* of the Buddhists. A few of the references, contained in this poem, are quite valuable as they throw light on social, cultural and political history of the earlier period. It further appears that the author of this Sūtra was quite at home with the Vaiṣṇava literature and had perhaps some deference for Vāsudeva and Viṣṇu. We are quoting here the passage[241] from the 11th chapter. "As Vāsudeva, the god with conch, discus, who fights with an irresistible strength (has no equal), neither has a very learned monk". This shows that at the time this poem was composed, the worship of Viṣṇu Vāsudeva was quite popular and their images were also known. A well known verse regarding the burning of Mithilā put in the mouth of one of the Janakas of Mithilā, occurs both in the *Dhammapada* and this text[242]. Among the interesting geographical names we have Kāmboja[243], Hastināpura[244], Kāmpilya[245], Daśārṇa[246], Kālañjara,[247] Sauvīra[248] etc. The king Karakaṇḍu of Kalinga,[249] mentioned in this poem was a pious and good-fearing gentleman and is also mentioned in the Buddhist canon[250], which probably proves that he was a historical figure and flourished not later than the 6th century B.C. Kings like Nagnajit[251], Dvimukha[252] etc. are also mentioned in the earlier Indian literature[253]. There are also interesting references to false *kārṣāpaṇa* (*kūḍakahāvaṇa*)[254] and *kākinī*[255] which show that different types of coins were quite well known at the time of its composition. From the mythological point of view we have references to Kāmdhenu[256], Vaiśramaṇa[257] and Nalakūvara[258].

There are at least two chapters of this Sūtra which deserve our special attention. The first is the 23rd chapter recording the conservation beween Keśin, a follower of Pārśva and Gautama Indrabhūti, the famous disciple of Lord Mahāvīra. Both were men of great learning; both had respect for each other. However, the disciple of Mahāvīra, by his superior knowledge, succeeded in destroying the doubts of Keśin and converting him to the faith of the last Tīrthankara. The 25th chapter is another magnificient piece of poetic creation. Here the Brāhmaṇical bloody sacrifice is the subject of criticism. The utter hollowness of such practices is demonstrated by Jayaghoṣa, who was a Jain recluse belonging to the Brāhmaṇa caste. The definition of a Brāhmaṇa is thus given by Jayaghoṣa—"He who is not defiled by pleasures as a lotus growing in the water is not wetted by it, him we call a Brāhmaṇa". Then Jayaghoṣa declares "One does not become a Śramaṇa by the tonsure, nor a Brāhmaṇa by the sacred syllable *Om* nor a Muni by living in the woods, nor a Tāpasa by wearing cloths of *kuśa* grass and bark". According to him one becomes a Śramaṇa by equanimity, a Brāhmaṇa by chastity, a Muni by knowledge, and a Tāpasa by penance. This great Nirgrantha Brāhmaṇa Jayaghoṣa, according to this chapter, afterwards succeeded in converting Vijayaghoṣa, a sacrificing Brāhmaṇa of Vārāṇasī.

The *Āvaśyaka*[259] is also considered an extremely important Jain Āgamic poem. It has six Adhyāyas. There is a *Niryukti*[260] on it by Bhadrabāhu. There is also the magnificent *Viśeṣāvaśyakabhāṣya*[261] by Jinabhadragaṇi written in 531 Śaka and the *Cūrṇī*[262] by Jinadāsagaṇi Mahattara, a work of the 7th century A.D. We have a *Ṭīkā*[263] by Haribhadra (8th century) and also quite a few later commentaries. From the historian's point of view, however, the poem does not seem to possess much importance. However, for a student of Jain monachism this text is of great significance. The *Daśavaikālika*[263A], according to the tradition, was composed by the Brāhmaṇa Nirgrantha ascetic Sayyambhava (Sejjaṁbhava) for his son Manaka. This Sayyambhava was a resident of Rājagṛha[264]. He was a disciple of Prabhava, who in turn, was a pupil of Jambūsvāmin. Śayyambhava, therefore, should be assigned to the early 4th century B.C., and this poem should be regarded as a product of that date. It has an extremely valuable *Niryukti*[265] by Bhadrabāhu, a *Cūrṇī*[266] by Jinadāsagaṇi and a *Ṭīkā*[267] by Haribhadra. There are altogether 12 Adhyayanas including two Cūlikās. Like the *Uttarādhyayana* this poem is full of noble sentiments. There are verses which could only be composed by a supreme poet-philosopher. Most of the verses speak of the monastic life to be led by a Jain monk. However the teachings of Śayyambhava, we feel, are meant for every right-thinking monk or even worldly people. The poem has a universal appeal.

There are altogether six Chedasūtras; they are—*Niśītha*, *Mahāniśītha*, *Vyavahāra*, *Dāśāśrutaskandha*, *Bṛhatkalpa* and *Pañcakalpa*. The Chedasūtras may be compared with the Buddhists Vinaya texts, although they are somewhat later works.

The first Chedasūtra is the *Niśītha*[268], which is the largest text of this group and was originally the 5th section of the 2nd Śrutaskandha of the *Ācārāṅga*. It is also known as the *Ācāraprakalpa*. It has a *Niryukti*[269], a *bhāṣya*[270] by Saṅghadāsagaṇi and *Cūrṇī* by Jinadāsa[271]. The text has altogether twenty chapters. Unlike many other Jain canonical texts, this work throws considerable light on the social, religious and cultural condition of India at the time of its composition. In a very good number of Sūtras the monk is asked not to be tempted by women who are always ready to destroy their chastity. Several festivals are mentioned in the 8th chapter, including those mentioned elsewhere in the Jain canon.

The *Mahāniśītha*[272] is probably a work of somewhat later period and is closely linked with the *Niśītha*. Jinabhadragaṇi Kṣamāśramaṇa, who flourished in the 6th century A.D., is said to have rescued this text from complete destruction[273]. Several Jain savants like Haribhadra, Devagupta, Yaśovardhana, Ravigupta, Nemicandra etc. had honoured this text[274] It has six Adhyayanas and two Cūlikās. There are a few interesting stories which make this text somewhat readable. The *Vyavahāra*[275] is also an interesting canonical text dealing with rules of the Jain church. It is ascribed to Bhadrabāhu and has altogether ten chapters. The *Niryukti* on this text is written by Bhadrabāhu himself; there is a *bhāṣya* on it by an unknown author and a commentary by Malayagiri. This text also throws considerable light on the everyday life of the Jain monks. The 4th Chedasūtra text *Daśāśrutaskandha*[276] is quite well known because its 8th chapter (Adhyayana) is the famous *Kalpasūtra*[277]. The work is ascribed to Bhadrabāhu, who it appears, should be distinguished from Bhadrabāhu, the author of several *Niryuktis*. The earlier sections of the *Daśāśrutaskandha*, like other Chedasūtra texts, deals with the disciplinary rules of the Jain monks. The 8th section i.e. the *Kalpasūtra* gives a very authentic account of

Mahāvīra's life, which we have already discussed. In the 9th chapter of this work Kūṇika is represented as meeting Lord Mahāvīra in the Pūrṇabhadra shrine of Campā. This reminds us of the *Aupapātikasūtra*, where the meeting of the two has been elaborately described. The last section refers to Śreṇika's meeting with Mahāvīra at Rājagṛha.

The 5th Chedasūtra text is the *Kalpa* or the *Bṛhatkalpa*[278]. There is a *Niryukti*, a *bhāṣya* and a *Vivaraṇa* on it. The *Niryukti* and *bhāṣya* verses are, however, indistinguishable. The work is divided into six sections. In an important passage of the first section a monk is asked not go beyond Aṅga-Magadha in the east, Kauśāmbī in the South, Thūṇā (possibly Sthāneśvara) in the West and Kuṇālaviṣaya (N. Kosala) in the North. This possibly proves that the text was composed at a time when Jainism did not reach Gujarat, Kaliṅga or any other distant part of India. There are interesting details in other sections of this text. The *Pañcakalpa*[279] is the same as the present *Pañcakalpa-mahābhāṣya*, which was formerly a part of the *Bṛhatkalpabhāṣya*. The *bhāṣya* is written by Saṅghadāsagaṇi. A few regard *Jīta-kalpasūtra*[280] written by Jinabhadragaṇi as a Chedasūtra text.

We should now turn our attention to the two texts the *Nandīsūtra* and the *Anuyogadvāra*, which are not strictly canonical works, but were regarded as sacred texts from very early times. The *Nandīsūtra*[281] has a *Cūrṇī*[282] by *Jinadāsagaṇi* and a *Ṭīkā*[283] by Haribhadra. Malayagiri also wrote a commentary on it.[284] The original *Nandīsūtra* has 90 *gāthās* and 59 Sūtras. If refers to the teachers who even flourished in the 5th century A.D. like Skandila, Nāgārjuna etc. *Bhārata* (or *Mahābhārata*), *Rāmāyaṇa*, *Arthaśāstra* of Kauṭilya, *Bhāgavatapurāṇa*, *Pātañjala* etc. are mentioned in a passage[285] of the text. The reference to the *Bhāgavata* is interesting since it shows that this particular Purāṇa existed in such an early date. The *Anuyogadvāra*[286] is ascribed to Āryarakṣita. It too, has a *Cūrṇī* by Jinadāsagaṇi and a *Ṭīkā* by Haribhadra. The passage that refers to the *Bhārata*, *Rāmāyaṇa*, *Arthaśāstra*, *Bhāgavata* etc. also occurs with slight variation in this text.[287]

The two works *Piṇḍa*[288] and *Oghaniryuktis*[289] are also sometimes regarded as Āgamic texts. They too contain various rules for the monks and are ascribed to Bhadrabāhu. There is a quotation from Cāṇakya in the *Oghaniryukti*.[290] Both the texts have commentaries.

The *Aṅgavijjā*[291] or the text dealing with the science of prognostication, though not a part of the Jain canon, is one of the most remarkable Jain sacred texts. This science was known to the Buddhists[292] and Brāhmaṇical Hindus[293] from quite early times. The present text of the *Aṅgavijjā* is a product of the early centuries of the Christian era and has altogether sixty chapters. This work has been fittingly described as the treasure-house for the cultural history of India of the early Christian period.[294] Like the *Arthaśāstra* of Kauṭilya it throws light on administration, social and cultural life. We have long lists of professions,[295] ornaments,[296] food-grains,[297] conveyances,[298] textiles,[299] eatables,[300] deities[301] and many other important items. The list of coins[302] given in this text is extremely interesting as well as informative. We have not only well known coin names like *dīnāra, suvaṇa, kāhāpaṇa, purāṇa, nāṇaka, kākanī* etc., but also two new names which are not found elsewhere in the early Indian literature. They are *kṣatrapaka*[303] and *sateraka*.[304] The first type was obviously the coins issued by Kṣatrapa kings of Ujjayinī. This type has been identified by scholars with the *Rudradāmaka*[305] coins mentioned by Buddhaghoṣa. The second type of coin viz. *sateraka* is the Sanskrit or Prakrit equivalent of Greek 'Stater' which was introduced by Indo-Greek kings.

This text also throws welcome light on the different types of boats. Among the more interesting names we have Koṭṭimba, Tappaka and Saṅghāḍa.[306] It is of great interest to note that all these three types of boats are mentioned by the author of the *Periplus*,[307] a text of the 2nd half of the 1st century A.D. Tappaka of this text is evidently identical with Trappaga of the *Periplus* and Koṭṭimba with Cotymba; Sanghāḍa has been identified wihh Sangara of the *Periplus*. All these three types of boats are described as middle-sized (*majjhimakāya*) boats in the *Aṅgavijjā*.

In the list of female deities[308] we have a number of foreign names, which are not found elsewhere in the Indian literature. They are—Apalā, Aṇāditā, Airāṇi, Sālimālinī etc. Apalā is the Greek goddess Pallas Athene, Aṇāditā is the Avestan Anahita, Airāṇi is the Roman goddess Irene and Sālimāliṇī is the Moon-goddess Selene. There are interesting references[309] to women belonging to Lāṭa (Lāḍi), Yavana (Joṇikā), Barbara (Babbarī), Pulinda (Pulindī), Andhra (Andhī), Dravida (Babbrī), etc. We have an exhaustive list of architectural terms[310] in this text; the list of *gotras* are also equally exhaustive.[311] There is also a section[311A] on sexual love. Among the male gods[312] Vaiśravaṇa is pictured as the god of merchants and rich people; Śiva was the lord of cows, buffaloes, and sheep. Senāpati Kārttikeya is associated with the cock and peacock and Viśākha with sheep, ram, boy and sword. Several other gods are mentioned and they are also known from other sources.

The *Aṅgavijjā* is undoubtedly one of the most useful works of the early Christian period. Since it refers to Śaka and Indo-Greek coins it appears that the work was written by 300 A.D., although it incorporates materials of a much earlier period. The language is frankly difficult, but it was undoubtedly composed in Western India. The absence of any commentary creates a great difficulty for modern scholars. The long lists of objects of daily use make it possible for us to understand some of the basic features of early Indian life.

Commentaries: The earliest among the canonical commentaries are the Niryuktis (Nijjuti), which are written in the Āryā metre and are in a mixed Prakrit. They are ascribed to Bhadrabāhu, who should be distinguished from his namesake, the celebrated author of the *Kalpasūtra*. This is definitely proved by the fact that in the *Daśāśrutaskandhaniryukti* there is a verse addressed to Śrutakevalin Bhadrabāhu.[313] Further, quite a few other Jain savants of a much later period are referred to in other Niryukti works, which also show that these Niryuktis could not have been composed before the Gupta period. However, there are reasons to believe that some of the Niryukti verses go back to an earlier period.[314] The Niryuktis on following Āgamic texts are known—*Āvaśyaka, Daśavaikālika, Uttarādhyayana, Ācārāṅga, Sūtrakṛtāṅga, Daśāśrutaskandha, Bṛhatkalpa,*

Vyavahāra, *Sūryaprajñapti* and *Ṛṣibhāṣita*. Of these the last two have not yet been discovered.

The *Āvaśyakaniryukti*[315] is undoubtedly the most important Niryukti text. A number of commentaries on it are known.[316] This work refers to several later Jain monks including Ārya Maṅgu of Mathurā who has been identified by us with his namesake, mentioned in a Mathurā inscription. Since it refers to Śālivāhana or Śātavāhana, we have ta assume that the work was composed after the Śātavāhana period. The war between Nahapāna and Gautamīputra Śātakarṇi was known to the Jain commentators including the author of this Niryukti.[317] The author of this text refers to the *Nandīsūtra* which proves that this particular Niryukti text was written after the composition of that text. This work is referred to in the *Mūlācāra* (6.193), an early Digambara text.

The *Daśavaikālikaniryukti* is a much shorter work consisting of only 371 *gāthās*.[318] It has also a few interesting references.[319] In the *Uttarādhyayananiryukti*[320] there is a reference to Vāsavadattā, the famous quen of Udayana, the king of Kauśāmbī.[321] The *Ācārāṅganiryukti*[322] refers to the Buddhists (Śauddhodani) in one place. This text is otherwise useless for our purpose. The *Sūtrakṛtāṅganiryukti*[322] refers to Nālandā and informs us that it is near Rājagṛha. The *Daśāśrutaskandhaniryukti*[324] begins with an invocation to Bhadrabāhu, who is obviously Bhadrabāhu I. The *Bṛhatkalpaniryukti*[325] and *Vyavahāranir-yukti*[326] do not contain much information.

We do not get much information from the Niryukti texts simply because they are written in a concise and terse style. The Bhāṣya commentaries, like the Niryuktis, are written in verse and follow closely the style of the latter. There are altogether 10 Bhāṣya commentaries on the following texts—*Āvaśyaka*, *Daśavaikālika*, *Uttarādhyayana*, *Bṛhatkalpa*, *Vyavahāra*, *Niśītha*, *Jitakalpa*, *Oghaniryukti* and *Piṇḍaniryukti*. In a few cases, it is difficult to separate the Bhāṣya from the Niryukti. Among the Bhāṣya writers only two names are known, viz. those of Jinabhadra and Saṅghadāsagaṇi. As we have already seen, Jinabhadragaṇi, flourished in Śaka 531 according to a manuscript of the *Viśeṣāvaśyakabhāṣya*. He has further been identified with the monk Jinabhadra Vācanācārya mentioned in an image inscription from Akota (near Baroda). We have further seen that this monk was responsible for the rescuing of the *Mahāniśītha* manuscript, while he was staying at Mathurā. Among his commentaries *Viśeṣāvaśyakabhāṣya* and *Jītakalpabhāsya* are known. We further learn from the above-mentioned inscription that be belonged to the Nivṛti *kula*.

The *Viśeṣāvaśyakabhāsya*[327] is undoubtedly one of the most remrkable creations from the doctrinal point of view. In his other work the *Jītakalpabhāṣya* this great Jain savant has also shown his great erudition.[328] The later writers had great deference for this Jain philosopher.[329]

Saṅghadāsagaṇi is the reputed author of the *Bṛhatkalpabhāṣya, Niśīthabhāṣya* and *Vyavahārabhāṣya*. According to a few, he should be identified with Saṅghadāsagaṇi Vācaka, the author of the first half of the *Vasudevahiṇḍī,* a Prakrit romance.[330] There is no reason[331] why this identification should be rejected. If we accept this identification, we have to place Saṅghadāsa before Jinabhadra, who in his *Viśeṣaṇavatī*[332] has referred to the *Vasudevahiṇḍī*. That author has further shown his intimate acquaintance with the *Vyavahārabhāṣya.*[333]

The *Bṛhatkalpabhāṣya*[334] is a work of considerable length. It has altogether 6490 verses and it is divided into six parts. It refers to preceptor Kālakācārya of Ujjayinī, who according to it,[335] went to Suvarṇabhūmi (Burma). This Kālakācārya was a contemporary of Gardhabhila of Ujjayinī, and seems to have flourished in the 1st century B.C. This text also refers to the glorious condition of Jainism in the Mathurā region. There are also a few romantic verses in this poem, which prove that the Jain monks understood perfectly sentiments connected with heart. This text also throws some light on the coinage of those days. According to it the value of two silver coins of Dakṣiṇāpatha was equivalent to one Nelaka of Kāñcīpura, and that of two silver coins of Kāñcī was equivalent to one silver coin of Pāṭaliputra city.[336] This work also refers to the *devanirmita stūpa* of Mathurā, which has already been noticed in a previous chapter.

The *Niśīthabhāṣya*[337] has a very good number of verses common with the *Vyavahāra* and *Bṛhatkalpabhāṣya*. In the beginning of this commentary we have the story of the four cunning people (*dhūrta*) which was afterwards used by Haribhadra in his *Dhūrtākhyāna*. It also refers to the philosopher Siddhasena and the commentator Govindavācaka, who composed the *Govindaniryukti*.[338] A few poetic and romantic verses are also to be found in this *Bhāṣya*. It also refers to Tālodaka (lake) of Tosalī and the hot-spring of Rājagṛha. The *Vyavahārabhāṣya*[339] is also a work of considerable size. There are many verses against women which remind us of the Smṛti writers. We further learn that people celebrated with great pomp the *stūpamaha* festival at Mathurā. Stories are told regarding Kālaka, Śātavāhana, Muruṇḍa, Cāṇakya and others.[340] The Śakas of Ujjayinī are also mentioned.[341] The other *Bhāṣyas* are not so important and we do not get much information in them.[342]

Let us now turn our attention to the Cūrṇi texts which, unlike the Niryukti and Bhāṣya, are written in prose. The most important Cūrṇī writer was Jinadāsagaṇi Mahattara, for whom we have a definite date. According to his *Nandīcūrṇī*[343] he wrote this work in Śaka 598 corresponding to 676 A.D. The following Cūrṇīs are generally attributed to him—*Niśīthaviśeṣacūrṇī*, *Nandīcūrṇī*, *Anuyogadvāracūrṇī*, *Āvaśyakacūrṇī*, *Daśavaikālikacūrṇī*, *Uttarādhyayanacūrṇī* and *Sūtrakṛtāṅgacūrṇī*.

The *Niśīthaviśeṣacūrṇī*[344] is an important Jain commentary. This work refers to the Maurya emperor Samprati as a great patron of Jainism.[345] This emperor, according to this work, made Jainism popular in Saurāṣṭra, Andhra, Damila, Marahaṭṭa etc. The detailed story of Kālakācārya and Gardabhila is told here and in this connexion we are told that the Jain monk Kālakācārya brought the army of Pārasa (Persia) to Hiṁdugadeśa (Hindusthan) in order to destroy the dynasty of Gardabhila of Ujjayinī (3.59). He refers to the philosopher Siddhasena and to the work called *Kālaṇṇāṇa* written by Pādalipta. The stories of Naravāhanadatta, Taraṅgavatī, Malayavatī, Magadhasenā etc. were known to him. He was also at home with texts like the *Setubandha*, *Vasudevacarita*, *Ceṭakakathā* etc. Among other Cūrṇīs written by Jinadāsa, the *Āvaśyakacūrṇī*[346] has a prominent place. It gives a detailed account of Lord Mahāvīra's wanderings which is obviously based on the accounts of the *Bhagavatī* and *Ācārāṅga*. The account of the Jain monk Vajrasena and his visit to the city Śūrpāraka are told in this commentary. Jinadāsa also was an expert story-teller and some of the stories, told by him, were copied by later writers. He further quotes a verse from Bhāsa's *Pratijñāyaugandharāyaṇa* (3.9). Jinadāsa also refers to a terrible flood that visited Śrāvastī 13 years after Mahāvīra's enlightenment[347]. The *Nandīcūrṇī*[348] mentions the the council held at Mathurā under Skandila. This work, as we have already noticed, was completed in Śaka 598. The *Daśavaikālikacūrṇī*[349] has also a few interesting stories. In one particular story[350] the Buddhists are ridiculed for their unmonklike habits. There is another *Daśavaikālikacūrṇī*[351], which was written by Agastyasiṁha, who belonged to the Verasāmi (Vajrasvāmī) *śākhā* of the Koḍīgaṇa (Koḍiya of the *Therāvalī*). The Verasāmi *śākhā* is the same as Vairī of that text. Agastyasiṁha was the disciple of one Ṛsigupta and it appears that he flourished before Jinadāsa. The *Sūtrakṛtāṅgacūrṇī*[352] refers to the mosquito menace in the Tāmralipta country[353].

Haribhadra, who flourished in the middle of the 8th century A.D., and who was a senior contemporary of Udyotanasūri, has left a number of Sanskrit commentaries called *Vṛttis*. He was a disciple of Jinabhaṭa[354] and belonged to the Vidyādhara *kula*. As we have already noticed he was a native of Citrakūṭa (Chitor) and was one of most learned men of his time. His commentaries on the following Āgamic texts are well known—*Āvaśyaka, Daśavaikālika, Jīvābhigama, Prajñāpanā, Nandīsūtra, Anuyogadvāra* and *Piṇḍaniryukti*. He has expressed his indebtedness to the earlier commentators including Jinadāsa. Śīlāṅka[355], who lived a century later, also wrote several commentaries, of which the *Ācārāṅga*[356] and the *Sūtrakṛtāṅgavivaraṇas*[357] have survived. Another commentator was Śāntisūri who flourished in the early 11th century A.D., and was a contemporary of Paramāra Bhoja, Caulukya Bhīma, and the poet Dhanapāla. We have his *Uttarādhyayanaṭīkā*[358]. In this commentary he has referred to the text, accepted in the council, held under the presidentship of

Nāgārjuna. Śāntisūri belonged to the Koṭikagaṇa and Vairaśākhā[359].

Abhayadeva, who lived in the 11th century A.D., wrote commentaries on all the Aṅga texts, except the first two. He also wrote a commentary on the *Aupapātika*. We have two definite dates for him; they are Vikrama Saṁvat 1120 and 1128, corresponding to 1062 and 1070 A.D.[360]. It is evident from his works that he spent the major part of his life at Aṇahilapāṭaka (Patan, Gujarat). His preceptor was Jineśvara of Candrakula[361]. He further admits his indebtedness to Droṇācārya of Aṇahilapāṭaka who corrected the texts of his commentaries. It should, however, be pointed out that the commentaries of Abhayadeva do not help us much in understanding the Jain Āgamic texts. The Jain commentators of post-Gupta period had practically no idea regarding eastern India where the canonical texts were composed. They also had no understanding of the teachings of the contemporaries of Mahāvīra. Unlike Buddhaghoṣa, they received no help from their predecessors. It is also doubtful whether they understood fully the Ardha-Māgadhī language in which the Jain canon is written.

Lastly we should mention the name of Malayagiri, who was a contemporary of the celebrated Hemacandra. We have at least twenty of his Vṛttis and Ṭīkās[362]; but like the commentaries of Abhayadeva these voluminous texts do not enlighten us much.

NOTES

1 Vol. II, p. 187.

2 We have a definite date for him viz. Śaka 598; see *Nandīsūtracūrṇī* (Prakrit Text Society), p. 83—" *Śakarājño paṁcasu varṣaśteṣu vyatikrāṁteṣu aṣṭanavateṣu Naṁdyadhyayanacūrṇī samāptā iti*".

3 See J. C. Jain, *Prakrit Sāhitya kā itihāsa*, p. 37 fn 1.

4 See *Uttarādhyayanavṛtti* by Kamalsaṁyama p. 23. However, it should be remembered that this statement comes from the pen of a later writer.

5 See *Prakrit Proper Names,* Vol. I, pp. 368 f.

6 Edited by Āgamodaya Samiti, Surat, V.S. 1972-73 (1916 A.D.) ; see also Jacobi's translation in *S.B.E.*. Vol. 22, pp. 1-213. The personal copy of the present writer is the edition published from Thāngaḍh (Saurāṣṭra), Vīra Saṁvat 2489 (1963). For a list of different other editions, see *Jaina Sāhitya kā Bṛhad itihāsa,* Varanasi, 1966, Vol. I, p. 62 fn.

7 See *Prakrit Proper Names,* Vol. I, p. 87.

8 *Loc. cit.*

9 Ed. Dhanpat Singh, Calcutta, V.S. 1936 ; also Āgamodaya Samiti, Surat, V.S. 1972-73.

10 Ratlam, 1928-29 (Ṛṣabhadeva Keśarīmaljī Ṣvetāmbara Saṁsthā).

11 See Jainānanda Pustakālaya, Surat, 1935.

12 See *Jaina Sāhitya kā Bṛhad itihāsa,* Vol. III, p. 384.

13 See *S.B.E.*, Vol. XXII, pp. 12-13.

14 *Ibid.,* p. 20.

15 *Ibid.*, p. 26.

16 *Ibid.*, p. 92.

17 I. 131. 3-4 (Cr. ed.) ; IV. 12. 12-13.

18 See Chatterjee, A. K., *Ancient Indian Literary and Cultural Tradition,* p. 167.

19 I. 63. 18-19.

20 1st Rock Edict (see Sircar. *Select Inscriptions* etc., pp. 15-16).

21 See Jacobi (*S.B.E.*), Vol. 22, p. 158 ; see also for the original Thāngaḍh ed., p. 139 (XIV. 1).

22 II. 11 (the word there is *cīnapaṭṭa*).

23 Jacobi, *op. cit.*, p. 183.

24 *Ibid.,* pp. 84-5 ; (original) IX. 3.

25 Edited (Āgamodaya Samiti, 1917) ; for the English translation see *S.B.E.,* Vol. XLV, pp. 235-451. Hindi translation by Amolaka Ṛṣi, Hyderabad, Vīra Saṁvat, 2446. For various other editions see *Jaina Sāhitya kā Bṛhad itihāsa,* Vol. I, p. 127 fn 1.

26 Ed. P. L. Vaidya, Poona, 1928 ; also included in Āgamodaya edition.

27 Ṛṣabhadeva Keśarīmala Ṣvetāmbara Saṁsthā, Ratlam, 1941.

28 Included in the Āgamodaya edition. This is known as the *Vivaraṇa* of Ṣīlāṅka.

29 *S.B.E.*, Vol. XLV, p. 256.

30 *Ibid.*, p. 261.

31 *Ibid.,* pp. 268-69.

32 *Ibid.,* p. 268.

33 *Ibid.*, p. 274.

34 1.1.10 (Chowkhamba ed.)

35 Jacobi, *op. cit.,* pp. 301, 310.

36 Translated by F. L. Woodward, *Minor Anthologies of the Pālī Canon,* Part II, p. 188.

37 Vol. III (tr. E. M. Hare), p. 175.

38 Jacobi's translation, p. 333.

39 *Ibid.*, p. 370.

40 Chowkhamba edition, p. 371 (Act VII).

41 Jacobi, trans. p. 366.

42 *Ibid.*, p. 374.

43 See *Uttarādhyayana,* XX. 42 (*S.B.E.,* Vol. XLV, p. 105); *Bhagavatī* (Sailana ed.), p. 2662.

44 Jacobi, trans., p. 371.

45 *Ibid.*, p. 418.

46 *Ibid.*, pp. 419-420.

47 See Malalasekera, *D.P.P.N.*, Vol. II, pp. 56-57.

48 Jacobi., *op. cit.*, pp. 420 ff.

49 *Ibid.*, p. 421.

50 *Ibid.*, pp. 409 ff.

51 See especially *Saṁyutta* (Vol. I, trans. Mrs. R. Davids), pp. 89 ff.

52 Ed. by the Āgamodaya Samiti, Bombay, 1918-20. For other editions see *Jaina Sāhitya kā Bṛhad itihāsa,* Vol. I, p. 171 fn. 1.

53 The commentary is included in the Āgamodaya edition.

54 See J. C. Jain, *op. cit.*, p. 57 fn. 1; see also *Jaina Sāhitya kā Bṛhad itihāsa,* Vol. I. pp 172 f.

55 See 3rd Adhyayana; see also Jain, *op. cit.*, p. 57.

56 Ed. Vechardas, p. 243.

57 See Jain, *op. cit.*, p. 58 (4th Adhyayana).

58 See Malalasekera, *Dictionary of Pāli Proper Names,* Vol. II, p. 8.

59 See *Vin.*, II. 237; *Aṅguttara,* IV. 101; V. 22; *Saṁyutta,* II. 135; V. 38.

60 McCrindle, *Ancient India* etc., p. 38.

61 See Malalasekera, *op. cit.*, Vol. II, p. 1073.

62 McCrindle, *op. cit.*, p. 97.

63 Sūtra No. 587.

64 Sūtra No 680.

65 See Jain, *op. cit.*, p. 61 (10th Adhyayana).

66 Āgamodaya edition, Surat, 1929; for other editions, See *Jaina Sāhitya kā Bṛhad itihāsa,* Vol. I, p. 172, fn. 2.

67 The commentary is included in the Āgamodaya edition; see also *Jain Sāhitya kā Bṛhad itihāsa,* Vol. III, pp. 400 ff.

68 Sūtra No. 18.

69 Ed. R. G. Basak, Vol. I, p. 160.

70 P. 125 (ed. P. L. Vaidya).

71 Sūtra No. 72.

72 II. 4. 17.

73 Edited with Abhayadeva's *vṛtti* by the Āgamodaya Samiti, Bombay, 1918-21. For some other editions, see *Jaina Sāhitya kā Bṛhad itihāsa,* Vol. I, p. 187 fn. 1. The personal copy of the present author

is the edition published in seven volumes by the Akhila Bhāratīya Jaina Samskṛti Rakṣak Saṅgha, Sailana, M.P.

74 See *Jaina Sāhitya kā Bṛhad itihāsa,* Vol. III, pp. 402 ff.

75 (Sailana ed.) p. 391.

76 P. 440.

77 Pp. 473 ff.

78 P. 496.

79 See Malalasekera, *op. cit.,* Vol. I, p. 992.

80 P. 509.

81 P. 550; from p. 708 (3rd Śataka) we learn that these four Lokapālas were Soma, Yama, Varuṇa and Vaiśravaṇa.

82 P. 567.

83 P. 578.

84 Pp. 572 ff.

85 See pp. 606, 648.

86 P. 716.

87 P. 752.

88 P. 794.

89 P. 803.

90 P. 887.

91 See pp. 1478, 2759.

92 This is also confirmed by the evidence of the Pāli Buddhist works and Brāhmaṇical Sūtra literature.

93 P. 921.

94 P. 1037.

95 Pp. 1190 ff.

96 See p. 1206.

97 (Gītā Press ed.) VI. 1. 27 ff.

98 P. 1203.

99 Pp. 1385 ff.

100 P. 1387.

101 P. 1523.

102 Pp. 1614 ff.

103 Pp. 1698 ff.

104 P. 1704.

105 Pp. 1705 ff.

106 P. 1707.

107 P. 1695.

108 P. 1715.

109 P. 1888.

110 P. 1948.

111 P. 1912.

112 P. 1933.

113 See Malalasekera, *op. cit.,* Vol. I, pp. 1000 f.

114 Pp. 1960, 1966.

115 Pp. 1966 ff.
117 P. 1986.
118 *Svapnavāsavadattā* (Chowkhamba), 6th Act.
119 See Malalasekera, *op. cit.,* Vol. II, pp. 923 f.
120 Pp. 2231 ff.
121 P. 2346.
122 P. 2348.
123 P. 2425.
124 *Loc. cit.*
125 P. 2443.
126 See Raychaudhuri, *P.H.A.I.* (6th edition), pp. 95 ff.
127 P. 2468.
128 P. 2476.
129 P. 2519.
130 P. 2558.
131 P. 2665.
132 See Malalasekera, *op. cit.,* Vol. II, p. 273.
133 P. 2759.
134 P. 2762.
135 Pp. 2554 ff.
136 Āgamodaya edition with Abhayadeva's *vṛtti,* Bombay, 1916. For other editions see *Jain Sāhitya kā Bṛhad itihāsa,* Vol. I, p. 217 fn. 1.
137 Āgamodaya ed., paras, 33-42.
138 See also trans. N. V. Vaidya, para. 7.
139 (Gītā Press) II. 14. 50.
140 This place is mentioned in the 2nd-century Junagarh inscription of Rudradāman, see Lüders' *List,* No. 965.
141 See Vaidya's trans., para. 60.
142 *Loc. cit.*
143 Section 25.
144 10. 12 ff.
145 Para. 73.
146 Para. 74.
147 Vaidya's trans., para. 118.
148 For further details see my paper in *JAIH,* Vol. VII, pp. 159 ff.
149 See Majumdar, the *Classical Accounts of India,* pp. 223-23 and p. 456.
150 *Harivaṁśa* (of Jinasena), ch. 54 (ed. P. L. Jain).
151 Āgamodaya edition, Bombay, 1920 ; English translation, Hoernle, 1885-1888 (Calcutta). The present author has used the text of the work published from Poona, 1953. It includes a translation by N. A. Gore. For other references see *Jaina Sāhitya kā Bṛhad itihāsa* Vol. I, p. 227 fn. 1.
152 Included in the Āgamodaya edition.
153 (Ed. Gore), text, p. 21.

154 *Ibid.*, p. 40.

155 (Gītā Press ed.) III. 15. 21.

156 Trans. p. 138.

157 Āgamodaya edition, Bombay, 1920; English translation by L. D. Barnett, 1907. For other editions see *Jaina Sāhitya kā bṛhad itihāsa*, Vol. I, p. 233 fn. 1.

158 Trans. (Barnett): p. 29; other references are from Barnett's translation.

159 *Ibid.*, pp. 30-31.

160 *Ibid.*, p. 74.

161 *Ibid.*, pp. 76 ff.

162 *Loc. cit.*

163 See pp. 77 ff.

164 *Loc. cit.*

165 P. 86.

166 Jātaka No. 454.

167 I. 6.

168 P. 80.

169 Āgamodaya edition, Surat, 1920. For other references see *Jaina Sāhitya kā bṛhad itihāsa*, Vol. I fn. 1.

170 Included in the Āgamodaya edition.

171 Āgamodaya edition. Bombay, 1919. The present writer has used the edition from Sailana (M.P.), published in 1975. For other editions see *Jaina Sāhitya kā bṛhad itihāsa*, Vol. I, p. 247 fn. 1.

172 See Schubring, *The Doctrine of the Jainas* (translation by W. Beurlen), Delhi, 1962, pp. 94 f.

173 Included in the Āgamodaya edition.

174 (Sailana ed.), pp. 136 ff; 149 ff. etc.

175 Pp. 212 f.

176 P. 235.

177 Cf. Schubring, *op. cit.*, p. 94.

178 Āgamodaya edition, Bombay, 1920. The present author has used the edition published from Kota in 1935. For other editions see *Jaina Sāhitya kā Bṛhad itihāsa*. Vol. I, p. 255 fn. 1.

179 Included in the Āgamodaya edition.

180 (Kota ed.) p. 200. The condemned priest was Bṛhaspatidatta, the son of Somadatta. He was 64 at the time of his execution, according to our text.

181 P. 185.

182 VIII. 372; see also XI. 104.

183 Pp. 211 ff.

184 Pp. 215 ff.

185 7th Adhyayana.

186 Pp. 244, 248.

187 P. 314.

188 II. 32. 4.
189 P. 308.
190 P. 369.
191 Pp. 118 f.
192 P. 149.
193 Pp. 66, 175.
194 Āgamodaya edition, Bombay, 1916. This edition also contains the *Vṛtti* of Abhayadeva. The personal copy of the present author is the edition published from Sailana (1963).
195 (Sailana ed.) pp 10 ff.
196 *Ibid.*, pp. 56 ff.
197 See *D.P.P.N.*, Vol. II, p. 225.
198 Pp. 278 ff.
199 P. 279—*Gaṁgāe mahānaīe ubhaokūleṇaṁ Kaṁpillapurāo.*
200 P. 302.
201 P. 270.
202 Pp. 212 ff.
203 Pp. 215 ff.
204 Āgamodaya edition, Bombay, 1925. The present writer has consulted the edition of Vechardas, V.S. 1994 (Ahmedabad). This edition has a Gujarati translation. For other editions see *Jaina Sāhitya kā bṛhad itihāsa,* Vol. II, p. 37 fn. 1.
205 See *Jaina Sāhitya kā bṛhad itihāsa,* Vol. III, pp. 415 f.
206 (Ed. Vechardas) p. 88.
207 *Ibid.*, p. 197.
208 P. 63.
209 P. 218.
210 See *D.P.P.N.*, Vol. II, p. 188.
211 II. 1. 70.
212 See Schubring, *op. cit.*, pp. 96 f.
213 For an analysis of these conversations see *Jaina Sāhitya kā bṛhad iithāsa,* Vol. II, pp. 58 ff.
214 P. 301.
215 P. 284.
216 P. 321.
217 Nirṇayasāgara ed. (Bombay) 1919.
218 Included in the Bombay edition.
219 Jacobi, (S.B.E., Vol. XXII), p. 233.
220 Āgamodaya edition, Bombay, 1918-19.
221 Ratlam, 1947 (Ṛṣabhadeva Keśarīmala Saṁsthā).
223 Sūtra No. 37.
224 Āgamodaya edition with the *Vṛtti* of Malayagiri, Bombay, 1929.
225 Edited with tthe *Vṛtti* of Śānticandra, Bombay, 1920.
226 Āgamodaya edition with the *Vṛtti* of Candrasūri, Surat, 1922. The present author has used the edition published from Rajkot, 1960.

227 See *Jaina Sāhitya kā bṛhad itihāsa,* Vol. III, p. 449.
228 Rajkot edition, p. 11.
229 *Ibid.*, p. 22.
230 *Ibid.*, p. 39.
231 *Loc. cit.*
232 Pp. 44 f.
233 P. 40.
234 See *D.P.P.N.*, Vol. I, pp. 127 f.
235 *Loc. cit.*
236 Pp. 30-31.
237 According to some the *Piṇḍaniryukti* and the *Oghaniryukti* are also Mūlasūtra texts. See J. C. Jain's *Prakrit Sāhitya kā itihāsa,* p. 163 and footnote.
238 Edited by J. Charpentier, Uppasala, 1922. For other editions see *Jaina Sāhitya kā bṛhad itihāsa,* Vol. II, p. 144 fn. 2. The standard English translation is by Jacobi in *S.B.E.,* Vol. XLV, p. 1-232.
239 Edited along with Śāntisūri's commentary, Bombay, 1916-17.
240 See Jain, J. C. *op. cit.,* p. 164.
241 Verse No. 21.
242 P. 37 (Jacobi's translation).
243 *Ibid.*, p. 47.
244 *Ibid.*, p. 56.
245 *Ibid.*, p. 57.
246 *Loc. cit.*
247 *Loc. cit.*
248 P. 87.
249 *Loc. cit.*
250 See *D.P.P.N.*, Vol. I, p. 531. The story of the four kings Naggaji, Nimi and Dummukha is told in the *Kumbhakāra Jātaka* (No. 408). It is therefore apparent that both the Jain and Buddhist authors have used the same source.
251 See *Mbh.,* III. 254. 21 (Gītā Press ed.).
252 *Aitareya Brāhmaṇa,* 8. 23 ; the name here is Durmukha Pāñcāla.
253 By earlier Indian literature we mean the Vedic and epic texts.
254 P. 105 (Jacobi's trans.).
255 P. 28.
256 P. 104.
257 P. 117.
258 *Loc. cit.*
259 Āgamodaya edition, Bombay, 1928 and 1932. For other editions see *Jaina Sāhitya kā bṛhad itihāsa,* Vol. II, p. 173 fn. 1.
260 See Āgamodaya Samiti edition, Bombay, 1916-17.
261 Yaśovijaya Jaina Granthamālā, Vīra Saṁvat, 2427-2441.
262 Ratlam, 1928 (Ṛṣabhadevji Keśarimalji Śvetāmbara Saṁsthā).
263 Included in Āgamodaya edition, Bombay, 1916-17.

263A Edited by Leumann in *Z.D.M.G.*, Vol. 46, pp. 581-663. For other editions see *Jaina Sāhitya kā bṛhad itihāsa*, Vol. II, p. 179 fn. 1. The personal copy of the present author is the edition, published at Sailana (M.P.), 3rd Reprint, 1973.

264 See *Prakrit Proper Names*, Vol. II, p. 854.

265 Included in Leumann's edition.

266 Ratlam edition, 1933. There is also the newly discovered *Cūrṇī* by Agastyasiṁha (Kalaśabhavamṛgendra) which has recently been published from Varanasi.

267 Bhīmsī Māṇek, Bombay, 1900.

268 (Sanmati Jñānapiṭha), Agra, 1957-60.

269 Included in the Agra edition of the *Niśītha*.

270 Included in the same edition.

271 See the Agra edition.

272 Ed. W. Schubring, Berlin, 1918.

273 See *Vividhatīrthakalpa*, p. 19.

274 See *Prakrit Sāhitya kā itihāsa*, p. 147 ; also *Jaina Sāhitya kā bṛhad itihāsa*, Vol. II, p. 292.

275 Ed. W. Schubring, Leipzig, 1918. The text edited along with the *Niryukti*, *Bhāṣya* and *Vivaraṇa* of Malayagiri, Ahmedabad, Vikrama Saṁvat 1982-85.

276 Ed. Bhavnagar, Vikrama Saṁvat, 2011 ; this edition contains also the *Niryukti* and the *Cūrṇī*.

277 English translation by Jacobi in *S.B.E.*, Vol. 22, pp. 217-311. For different editions of this valuable text see *Jaina Sāhitya kā bṛhad itihāsa*, Vol. II, p. 217 footnote.

278 Edited by Punyavijaya, Bhavnagar, 1933-1942 ; this edition contains the *Bhāṣya* of Saṅghadāsa and the *Ṭikās* of Malayagiri and Kṣemakīrti.

279 This work has not yet been edited ; see *Jaina Sāhitya kā bṛhad itihāsa*, Vol. III, pp. 276 ff.

280 Ed. Jinavijaya along with *Cūrṇī* and *Ṭikā*, Vikrama Saṁvat, 1983 (Ahmedabad).

281 Edited by Punyavijaya in Prakrit Text Society Series, Varanasi, 1966.

282 Included in Punyavijaya's edition.

283 Edited 1928, Ratlam (Ṛṣabhadevjī Keśarimaljī Śvetāmbara Saṁsthā).

284 Āgamodaya Samiti edition, Bombay, 1924.

285 P.T.S. Ed., p. 49 and footnote.

286 Edited, 1928 (Ratlam).

287 Para. 41 (Āgamodaya Samiti).

288 Devchand Lalbhai Series, Surat, 1918.

289 Āgamodaya edition, Bombay, 1919.

290 P. 152.

291 Prakrit Text Society edition by Punyavijaya, Varanasi, 1957.

292 See *Brahmajāla Sutta* (tr. Rhys Davids, 16-18).

293 *Manusmṛti* VI. 20.

294 See P.T.S. edition, Introd. p. 55.

295 Pp. 159-161.

296 *Ibid.*, pp. 162-163.

297 *Ibid.*, pp. 165-166.

298 *Ibid.*, pp. 164-165.

299 *Ibid.*, pp. 163-164.

300 *Ibid.*, pp. 174-182.

301 *Ibid.*, pp. 204-206 ; see also p. 69.

302 See in this connexion the paper 'Coin Names in the *Aṅgavijjā*' by V. S. Agrawala included in the Introd. pp. 87 ff. of the P.T.S. edition.

303 P. 66.

304 *Loc. cit.*

305 See *Aṅgavijjā,* Introd., p. 90 fn. 1.

306 P. 166.

307 Paras. 44 and 60.

308 P. 69,

309 P. 68.

310 Pp. 136 ff.

311 P. 150.

311A Pp. 182 ff.

312 Pp. 204 f.

313 See *Jaina Sāhitya kā bṛhad itihāsa,* Vol. III. p. 120.

314 *Ibid.*, p. 68 fn. 1 ; see also Muni Punyavijaya in *Muni Śrī Hajarimala Smṛtigrantha,* pp. 718-19.

315 See Āgamodaya edition, Bombay, 1928-32 ; for various other editions, see *Jaina Sāhitya kā bṛhad itihāsa,* Vol. III, p. 71 fn. 1.

316 See *loc. cit.*

317 See *Prakrit Proper Names,* Vol. I, p. 315.

318 Ed. Leumann, *Z.D.M.G.*, Vol. 46, pp. 581-663.

319 See *Jaina Sāhitya kā bṛhad itihāsa,* Vol. III, pp. 97 ff.

320 Ed. (D.L.J.P.), Bombay, 1919-27 ; see also *Jaina Sāhitya kā bṛhad itihāsa,* Vol. III, p. 107.

321 *Gāthā* Nos. 146-148

322 Āgamodaya ed., Surat, Vikrama Saṁvat 1972-73 ; see also Jain, J. C. *op. cit.*, p. 201.

323 Āgamodaya ed., Bombay, 1917 ; see also *Jain Sāhitya kā bṛhad itihāsa,* Vol. III, p. 119.

324 See *J.S.B.I.*, Vol. III, p. 120.

325 *Ibid.*, pp. 123 f.

326 *Ibid.*, p. 125.

327 Ed. Yaśovijaya Jaina Granthamālā, Varanasi, Vīra Saṁvat 2427-2441.

328 For an analysis of this text see *J.S.B.I.*, Vol. III, pp. 130-201.

329 See *Jaina Sāhitya kā bṛhad itihāsa*, Vol. III, pp. 132 f.

330 *Ibid.*, pp. 135 f.

331 J. C. Jain, *op. cit.*, p. 211 rejects this identification, but gives no reason in support of his stand.

332 See *Jaina Sāhitya kā bṛhad itihāsa*, Vol. VI, p. 143 ; also Jain, J. C. *op. cit.*, p. 381.

333 See *Jaina Sāhitya kā bṛhad itihāsa*, Vol. III, p. 137.

334 Ed. Caturavijaya and Puṇyavijaya in six volumes (*Jaina Ātmānanda Sabhā*, Bhavnagar, 1933-42). For an analysis of this text, see *Jaina Sāhitya kā bṛhad itihāsa*, Vol. III, pp. 213-251.

335 See Jain, *op. cit.*, p. 220 ; see also verse No. 229.

336 *Ibid.*, p. 227.

337 Edited (Sanmati Jñānapīṭha), Agra, 1957-1960.

338 See Jain, *op. cit.*, p. 217.

339 Edited K. P. Modi and Ugarchand, Ahmedabad, Vikrama Saṁvat, 1982-85.

340 See Jain, *op cit.*, p. 219.

341 *J.S. B.I.*, Vol. III, p. 271.

342 The *Piṇḍaniryuktibhāṣya* (see Jain, *op. cit.*, p. 231) refers to the famine during the days of Candragupta which is also repeatedly mentioned in the Digambara works.

343 See P.T.S. edition, p. 83.

344 Edited in four volumes by Sanmati Jñānapītha, Agra, 1957-60. For a detailed analysis see *J.S.B.I.*, Vol. III, pp. 321 ff.

345 *Ibid.*, Vol. 4, pp. 128-131.

346 Ratlam edition, 1928-29.

347 P. 601.

348 *P.T.S.* edition, p. 9.

349 Ratlam, 1933.

350 See Jain, *op. cit.*, pp. 257 f.

351 See for detailed description of this text *J.S.B.I.*, Vol. III, pp. 315 ff.

352 Ratlam, 1941.

353 See Jain, *op. cit.*, p. 237.

354 Cf. the concluding words of the *Āvaśyakaṭīkā* quoted in *J.S.B.I.*, Vol. III, p. 377.

355 See *J.S.B.I.*, Vol. III, p. 382.

356 Āgamodaya edition, Vikrama Saṁvat 1972-73.

357 Āgamodaya edition, Mehsana, 1917.

358 Edited, Bombay, 1916-17.

359 See *J.S.B.I.*, Vol. III, p. 393.

360 *Ibid.*, p. 396.

361 *Ibid.*, p. 414.

362 *Ibid.*, p. 417.

CHAPTER XII

The Non-Canonical Śvetāmbara Literature

The earliest Śvetāmbara non-canonical literary text is the missing *Taraṅgavatī*, a Prakrit poem written by Pādaliptasūri, who according to the tradition was a contemporary of the Sātavāhana king Hāla. Some details regarding this poet will be found in the *Prabhāvakacarita*[1] and *Prabandhakośa*[2] according to which he was a resident of Kosala and afterwards visited several places of India. We are further told that he cured king Muruṇḍa of Pāṭaliputra of an incurable disease. His work is referred to in the *Anuyogadvāra* (Sūtra No. 130) and *Viśeṣāvaśyakabhāṣya*[3] of Jinabhadra. This shows that it was recognised as a well known literary text in the early centuries of the Christian era. Later poets and writers like Jinadāsagaṇi Kṣamāśramaṇa, Udyotanasūri, Dhanapāla and others have mentioned Pādalipta with deference and affection.

An abridged version of this work is the *Taraṅgalolā*[4] by Nemicandra written about 1000 years after the original. It has altogether 1642 verses. It appears from this abridged version that the original author was probably influenced by the *Bṛhatkathā* of Guṇāḍhya as it refers to the story of Udayana of Kauśāmbī and his heroine Vāsavadattā.

However the earliest extant non-canonical literary Śvetāmbara work appears to be the *Paumacariyaṁ* of Vimala, the Jain *Rāmāyaṇa*, written according to the testimony of the poet himself, 530 years after the emancipation (*siddhi*) of Lord Mahāvīra. There is absolutely no reason why this date for the composition of this text should not be accepted as genuine[5]. If this date is accepted, then we have to assign this work to the 1st century A.D., and there is nothing in the body of this text that goes against this date[6].

This celebrated poem of Vimala is also known as *Rāghava-caritam.* From a few verses of the second chapter we can understand his attitude towards the Brāhmaṇical Rāma story (obviously that represented by Vālmīki). We are giving below a free translation of those lines—"When I consider the *Padmacarita,* I wonder how the petty and insignificant monkeys could kill the powerful and aristocratic Rākṣasas, who were versed in different sciences and *who had complete faith in the Jinas*[7]. We are further told by the native chronicler (apparently Vālmīki) that all the Rākṣasas including Rāvaṇa used to consume flesh, fat and blood. We further learn that Rāvaṇa's illustrious and valiant brother Kumbhakarṇa used to have an undisturbed sleep for six months. Even if he where hit by big hills, he could not be awakened; he remained asleep even if his ears were filled with jars of oil. Loud sounds of drum, which could even pierce thunder, had no effect on him. And when he used to awake, he felt so hungry that he could serenely swallow elephants, buffaloes and anything that came in his way. After consuming gods, men, elephants, he used to go to sleep once more for six months. We have further heard that Rāvaṇa, after vanquishing Indra in the battlefield brought him in chains to the city of Laṅkā. But who can conquer the mighty Indra, who is capable of uprooting the whole of Jambudvīpa, who has Airāvata as his *vāhana,* and the terrible *vajra* as his weapon? By his very thought he (i.e. Indra) can reduce to ashes any god or man. 'The dear killed the lion, and dog, the elephant' such contradictory sentences are found everywhere in the *Rāmāyaṇa*".

We have deliberately reproduced this long passage in order to show the deep familiarity Vimala had with the original *Rāmāyaṇa,* ascribed to Vālmīki. Not only has he referred to the work of Vālmīki by name, but at the same time, he has mentioned events, described in the original version, using almost the same language. What he has said about Kumbhakarṇa and his undisturbed sleep for six months, are actually found in the *Rāmāyaṇa,* VI. 60. 27-63 and VI. 61. 28. There is absolutely no doubt that Vimala is indebted to the original *Rāmāyaṇa* so far as the above-mentioned passages of his work are concerned. As a devout Jain and a firm believer in the doctrine of Ahiṁsā, he is not prepared to believe that the Rākṣasas of Laṅkā used to consume animal flesh. They are everywhere delineated in his work as Vidyādharas, although sometimes he forgetfully calls them also Rākṣasas (cf. 2.105; 7.92 etc.).

These so-called Vidyādharas, led by Rāvaṇa, are everywhere portrayed as staunch Jains. Although Vimala is committed to writing the story of Padma (i.e. Rāma), his actual hero, at least in the first half af his work, is Rāvaṇa, who like Naravāhanadatta, appears in this poem as perfect knight-errant. As a matter of fact, the ghost of Naravāhanadatta looms large in all the literary works beginning from Vimalasūri down to Hemacandra.

We have already seen that Vimala had a thorough knowledge, not only of the events, narrated in the original *Rāmāyaṇa*, but also with its language. Although he contemptuously bestows on the earlier poets epithets like *kukavi*, *mūḍhāḥ* etc., he actually follows the path trodden by them. Sometimes he does not hesitate to borrow words and phrases of the original *Rāmāyaṇa*. However, while telling the story of Rāma and Rāvaṇa, he also tells something about different Jain Tīrthaṅkaras and other interesting details are also found in his work for which he is indebted to none but his own imagination.

The main details of Vālmīki's *Rāmāyaṇa* viz. the birth of the four sons of Daśaratha, Rāma's marriage with Sītā, the daughter of Janaka, his departure for the forest along with Lakṣmaṇa and Sītā, Rāvaṇa's kidnapping of Sītā, death of Jaṭāyu at Rāvaṇa's hands, Rāma's meeting with Sugrīva, Hanumat's departure for Laṅkā, his meeting with Sītā, the battle of Laṅkā, the rescue and ultimate banishment of Sītā are all described in Vimala's poem. But mere similarity of broad facts do not concern us much here. After a thorough examination of the entire Prakrit poem of Vimala[8] we have been able to find out a very good number of small yet important details which also occur in the original *Rāmāyaṇa*. We are giving below those details side by side from the two poems—

Paumacariyaṁ	*Rāmāyaṇa*
1. Description of Rājagṛha (2.8-14)	1. Description of Ayodhyā (I, ch. 5).
2. Rāvaṇa's encounter with Bālin and lifting of Kailāsa (9.24 ff.)	2. VII, ch. 34; VII. 16.25 ff.
3. Description of the Narmadā (10.29 ff.)	3. VII. 31.15 ff.
4. Sahasrakiraṇa's play in the water of the Narmadā (10.33 ff.).	4. VII. 32.2 ff. (in this epic he is called Arjuna of *sahasra* hands.
5. Rāvaṇa's worship of the Jina image near the bank of the Narmadā (10.45 ff).	5. VII. 31.37 ff. (he is shown as worshipping the Śiva-liṅga).
6. Nalakūbara-Uparambhā-Rāvaṇa affair (12.38 ff.)	6. VII, ch. 26 (the heroine is here Rambhā).
7. Indra-Rāvaṇa encounter (12.73 ff.)	7. VII, ch. 29.
8. Añjanā-Pavanañjaya love affair and birth of Hanumat (chs. 15-17).	8. VII, ch. 35.
9. Rāvaṇa-Varuṇa encounter (ch. 19).	9. VII, ch. 23.
10. Killing of Śambūka (43.48 ff.)	10. VII, ch. 76.
11. Khara-Dūṣana and their 14,000 associates (43.17; 44.11).	11. III. chs. 19-20.
12. Candranakhā's amorous advances (43.37 ff.)	12. Śūrpanakhā affair (III, ch. 17).
13 Rāma's lament (45.51 ff.)	13. III, chs. 62 f.
14. Sugrīva severely rebuked by Lakṣmaṇa (48.7 ff.)	14. IV, ch. 34.
15. Dadhimukha affair (ch. 49)	15. V, ch. 62.

Paumacariyaṁ	*Rāmāyaṇa*
16. Sītā gives Hanumat the *cūdāmaṇi* (53.72 ff.)	16. V, chs. 38 f.
17. Hanumat overpowered by Indrajit (53.118 f.)	17. V, ch. 48.
18. Hanumat returns to Rāma the *cūḍāmaṇi* given by Sītā (54.3 ff.)	18. V, ch. 65.
19. Indrajit's quarrel with Vibhīṣaṇa [55.8 ff.]	19. VI, ch. 15.
20. Rāvaṇa's quarrel with Vibhīṣaṇa [55.18 ff.]	20. VI, ch. 16.
21. Doubts raised in Rāma's camp about Vibhīṣaṇa. (55.29 ff.).	21 VI, ch. 17.
22. Rāma's lament (after Lakṣmaṇa was hit by Rāvaṇa's *śaktiśela* 62.4 ff).	22. VI, ch. 101.
23. Description of Mathurā (88.2 ff.)	23. VII. 70.9 ff.
24. Rāma becomes a target of hostile criticism at Ayodhyā [93.22 ff.]	24. VII. 43.16 ff.
25. Sītā's lament in the forest [94.87 ff.]	25. VII. 48 ff.

The above table shows that Vimala has very faithfully followed in his Prakrit poem the original *Rāmāyaṇa* including its First and Seventh Books, which are considered late additions to the original poem. A very good number of incidents, narrated in the Uttarakāṇḍa, have been recorded by the author of the *Paumacariyaṁ*. We have, for example, in this poem the story of Marutta's *yajña*, even the name Marutta's priest Saṁvarta is mentioned by Vimala (11.71). Vimala, to whom Rāvaṇa is a great Jain and Vidyādhara, has cleverly changed the passages of the Uttarakāṇḍa, which describe Rāvaṇa's discomfiture. As for example, in the Uttarakāṇḍa story Arjuna, king of Māhiṣmatī, is represented as having made Rāvaṇa his prisoner; but the *PC* just gives the opposite version. In another Uttarakāṇḍa story Rāvaṇa is shown as having suffered a humiliating defeat at the hands of Vālin; but in the *PC* Vālin appears as a Jain ascetic and is further shown as having pressed the mount Kailāsa with the finger of his feet when Rāvaṇa had lifted that mount. And Daśamukha, in utter distress, cried out and earned the name of Rāvaṇa. It is not little amusing to see how the Jain poet has cleverly assigned to Vālin the role of Śiva of the Uttarakāṇḍa (16.25-38). Let no one suppose from this that Vimala has here followed a different tradition, and not that recorded by the author of the *Rāmāyaṇa.*

The above discussion abundantly proves that the Jain author, writing in the 1st century A.D., has deliberately followed the original Rāma story, although here and there he has shown his Jain bias. Characters like Daśaratha, Bharata, Kumbhakarṇa, Indrajit and others are represented as embracing the ascetic life of Jain Munis. Rāvaṇa's killer, however, is not Rāma in this poem, but Lakṣmaṇa, who takes a more important part in the battle of Laṅkā than Rāma. But Vimala has done a grave injustice to this great brother of Rāma by representing him as a love-sick, sentimental hero.

Vimala according to his own testimony was a disciple of Vijaya and grand-disciple of Rāhu, who belonged to the Nāila or Nāgila *kula, which* according to the *Therāvalī*,[9] originated from the preceptor Ārya Vajrasena. Nothing is known regarding the home of Vimala, but from the detailed and eulogistic description of Mathurā, it appears, that he was a monk of that city.

The work of Vimala is the foundation on which later Jain writers built lofty edifices. We have the *Padma Purāṇa* of Digambara Raviṣeṇa, which will be discussed in the next chapter. A number of other writers including Svayambhū also wrote on the Rāma story and his work also will be noticed in the next chapter.

We should now turn our attention to the *Vasudevahiṇḍī*[10]

written by Saṅghadāsagaṇi Vācaka and Dharmasenagaṇi. This work according to the eminent Prakrit scholar Alsdorf[11] was written in all probability in the Gupta period as its Prakrit shows quite a number archaic forms and for the students of the Prakrit language this work offers a fruitful field of study. Only the first part of the work has so far been published and even that edition, according to Alsdorf,[12] is full of mistakes. The original work extends to 100 Lambakas and the first part which extends to 29 Lambakas is a continuous prose work of 370 quarto pages Let us remember that this work was known to both Jinabhadagraṇi,[13] who flourished in the 6th century A.D., and Jinadāsagaṇi Kṣamāśramaṇa[14]. There is therefore little doubt that this work was quite popular from the Gupta period.

The *Vasudevahiṇḍī* is probably the earliest imitation of the famous *Bṛhatkathā* written in the Śātavāhana period by Guṇāḍhya in the Paiśācī language. That work has not yet been discovered, but we have a number of Sanskrit versions. Vasudeva, the father of Kṛṣṇa, who is the romantic hero of this novel, evidently reminds us of Naravāhanadatta, the hero of Guṇāḍhya. Unlike the *Bṛhatkathā* it is written in the Mahārāṣṭrī Prakrit, the language in which the well-known *Aṅgavijjā* has been written. Besides the *Bṛhatkathā,* materials from the popular Vaiṣṇava Purāṇas including the *Harivaṁśa* and *Viṣṇu Purāṇa* have been incorporated. The language is heavily influenced by the canonical language and sometimes we have the entire passages from the *Samavāyāṅga* and *Sthānāṅga* which prove that the author had little originality.

After the Introduction we have the story of Dhammilla, the son of a merchant. A number of his adventures have been recorded including his passion for prostitutes. Vasantatilakā, the mistress of Dhammilla reminds us of Vasantasenā of the *Mṛcchakaṭika* of Sūdraka and *Cārudatta* of Bhāsa. It is interesting to note that there is a direct reference to the *Bhagavadgītā* in this section of the *Vasudevahiṇḍī*.[15] This, we believe, to be the earliest reference to that famous poem in a non-Brāhmaṇical text. The author shows his intimate acquaintance with various places of Western India. He refers to Kalyāṇa,[16] Bharukaccha,[17] Girinagara[18] and also Yavana-viṣaya.[19] He further mentions the well-known temple of Vāsupūjya[20] of

Campā. He quotes also a passage[21] from the *Arthaśāstra* of Kauṭilya and mentions a Nāga temple.[22]

In the section entitled Pīṭhikā[23] we have the story of the Vṛṣṇis of Dvārakā and here he has mainly followed the Vaiṣṇava Purāṇas. The highly poetical description of Kṛṣṇa[24] has a theistic ring. The author has competently described the rivalry between Rukmiṇī and Satyabhāmā. The story of Kṛṣṇa's elopement with Jāmbavatī and his son's love affair with Vaidarbhī are also given. Sāmba also appears here as a romantic hero as in the Vaiṣṇava works.

A number of sections or Lambakas of this work were evidently named in imitation of the *Bṛhatkathā*. We have, for example, Gandharvadattā, Vegavatī and a few other Lambakas. The text also refers to *dīnāra*[25] and *kārṣāpaṇa*[26] coins. There was a brisk commercial intercourse with Cīna, Suvarṇabhūmi and Yavadvīpa.[27] It also refers to the popular Indra festival.[28] The picture of the society, painted in this text, is not different from what we get in Bhāsa and Śūdraka.[29]

The story of Rāma, given in this text,[30] is almost entirely taken from the original *Rāmāyaṇa*, although like the *PC* the killer of Rāvana here is Lakṣmaṇa.[31] Some of the minor details of Vālmīki's *Rāmāyaṇa* are also to be found in this text. Even we have a reference to the *krodhāgāra*[32] of Kaikeyī. Unlike Vimala, the author of this text has not changed the name of Śūrpanakhā. The description of the rivalry between Vālin and Sugrīva[33] is evidently based on that of the Fourth Book of the *Rāmāyaṇa*.

In the present published edition of this text the Books 19-20 and a part of the Book 28 are missing. The Book 28 entitled Devakī Lambaka closely follows the *Harivaṁśa* and later Jain writers including the author of the Jain *Harivaṁśa* have followed the version given in the *Vasudevahiṇḍī*. The text also contains lives of the Tīrthaṅkaras like Kunthu and Arhanātha. Ṛṣabha also gets a very special treatment.[34]

The celebrated Haribhadra, who flourished in the middle of the 8th century, was not only a great philosopher, but also one of the finest literary figures of the early mediaeval period. However, not much is known about his personal life. We only know that he was a native of Citrakūṭa (Chitor) and was a Brāhmaṇa by caste. He informs us that he obeyed the command of Jinabhaṭa, a Śvetāmbara Ācārya, and was a pupil of Jinadatta, who belonged to the Vidyādhara *kula.* We further learn from the colophons of his works that he was a spiritual son of the nun Yākinī Mahattarā. From Udyotana's *Kuvalayamālā,*[35] which was written in Śaka 700 we learn that its author was taught the science of logic by Haribhadra, the author of several treatises. And this Haribhadra is no other than our Haribhadra, who was also a great logician, as we will see in a later chapter. Jacobi opines[36] that Haribhadra in later part of his life had migrated to Western Rajasthan and probably founded the clan of Porevals, who according to the *Neminăthacariya* originated at Śrīmāla (Bhinmal). That scholar further believes that Haribhadra, as a *yati,* probably wandered in various parts of India including the eastern regions and learnt the logical system of the Buddhists in the Buddhist schools of these regions.

According to the Jain tradition Haribhadra was the author of some 1440 works, which is clearly an absurd figure. The earliest writer that refers to this figure is Abhayadeva who finished his *Ṭīkā* on Haribhadra's *Pañcāśaka* in 1068 A.D. We have a list of 88 works of Haribhadra given by Muni Kalyāṇavijaya[37]. A sketch of Haribhadra's life has been given in the *Prabhāvakacarita* which is however not much reliable[38]. Rājaśekhara in his *Prabandhakośa*[39] also has given a sketch of his life.

Haribhadra's fame as a creative literary writer rests chiefly on his Prakrit *Samarāiccakahā*[40], a work which the author himself describes as *dharmakathā* and which Winternitz[41] fittingly terms as a religious novel. The fortune of the hero Samarāditya is traced through his nine births (*bhava*). Underlying all the narratives, there is the Jain doctrine of Karman. For the study of the cultural religious and economic history of Northern India of the 8th century A.D. the work offers a unique scope. In the First Book there is a reference to the well known Madana-festival. The second Book gives an interesting description of marriage of those days and mentions a Nāga temple. It further refers to the cloth of Cīna and Ardha-Cīna. The Third Book refers to the philosophy of Cārvāka and in the 4th Book we have not only a reference to Tāmralipta port but also to Kaṭāhadvīpa, which is also mentioned in the Cola inscriptions[42] and the *Kathāsaritsāgara*.[43] It appears from this Book of the *Samarāic-cakahā* that there was a brisk commerce between eastern India and the islands of East Indies in those days. The 5th Book refers to Suvarṇabhūmi and Mahākaṭāha. The 6th Book contains a wealth of information. Here we have the confirmation of the belief that the god Skanda was looked upon as the presiding god of thieves. We are told that Skanda-Rudra was the inventor of a thief's pill called Coragulivā which was used as *paradṛṣṭimohanī* (charmer of other's sight). There is also a detailed description of the temple of Kātyāyanī which had a four-armed icon of that goddess with the implements *kodaṇḍa*, *ghaṇṭā*, *khaḍga* and the tail of Mahiṣāsura. It further refers to the town of Devapura which was situated near China and also Suvarṇadvīpa and Ratnadvīpa. We come accross an interesting character in the figure of Ṭoppa, a merchant of Devapura. The town of Tagara is also mentioned. There are a few interesting geographical names in other Books including Madanapura of Kāmarūpa mentioned in the 9th Book.

That Haribhadra was a successful storyteller is also proved by his well-known satire *Dhūrtākhyāna*[44] which is also written in Prakrit. That there was an earlier Jain text of this name is proved by the evidence of the *Niśīthaviśeṣacūrṇī*[45]. The only purpose of Haribhadra was to ridicule the stories of the Hindu epics and Purāṇas and, in order to belittle them, he has told the tales of five rogues called Mūlaśrī, Kaṇḍarīka, Elāṣāḍha, Śasa and Khaṇḍapāṇā. Such a satire is expected from the pen of a writer, who was a renegade. However, it does not deserve the lavish praise bestowed on it by Upadhye[46] and the stories, told by the rogues, are only weak satires. It is a matter of regret the Jains, who have written so many works in imitation of the epics, should indulge in senseless condemnation of these two great poems. This once more proves our contention that the Jains like the Buddhists suffered from some sort of inferiority-complex from the very beginning of their career.

The next Śvetāmbara writer is Udyotanasūri, the author of the *Kuvalayamālā*, which was completed according to the colophon of the work in the last month of the year Śaka 700, which is equivalent to 779 A.D. at Jāvālipura, modern Jalor (Rajasthan), when Vatsarāja was the reigning sovereign[47]. The *Praśasti* given at the end of the work, as we have already pointed out has great historical value. His immediate *guru* was Tattvācārya and he was taught Siddhānta by Vīrabhadra and logic by Haribhadra. Vatsarāja, who is mentioned here, is the celebrated Pratīhāra king, a contemporary of Dharmapāla and Rāṣṭrakūṭa Dhruva. The same Pratīhāra king is also mentioned in the *Harivaṁśa* of Jinasena II as we will note in the next chapter.

The *Kuvalayamālā* is probably the most interesting and complex Jain literary text of the 8th century A.D. The poet has shown his great power of observation and learning in this exceedingly readable work, written in the Mahārāṣṭrī Prakrit. It has been argued that the author was influenced by Bāṇa and Haribhadra. He has shown his thorough acquintance with the works of previous writers by referring to them, among whom a few were Brāhmaṇical writers and a few Digambara poets. He has beautifully described the corrupt city life. It further appears from his text that cities of India enjoyed rare prosperity in the 8th century and in this connexion he has referred to the affluence enjoyed by the inhabitants of Pratiṣṭhāna. An interesting passage quoted by J. C. Jain in his work[48] throws a flood of light on the everyday religious life of those days. This passage alludes to the popularity of the *Bhagavadgītā* among the Vaiṣṇavas and also mentions the temples dedicated to Buddha, Jina, Śiva, Śakti (Koṭṭajjā) and Kārttikeya.

The poet has very successfully painted romantic love scenes and it is quite sure that he had first-hand experience of love and romance. In their descriptions of romantic episodes, the Jain writers could even put to shame the author of the *Śiśupālavadha*. And in this respect, as we will see afterwards, the Digambaras did not lag much behind. There is an interesting description of the life led by students in a large educational institution in which pupils from Lāṭa, Kannaḍa, Mālava, Kānyakubja, Golla, Marahaṭṭha, Ṭakka, Śrīkaṇṭha and Sindhudeśa pursued their study. In this institution the students were given lessons by expert teachers on almost all sciences and philosophies[49]. Not all the students were equally serious and there is a humorous picture of college life, which was not probably much different from what we find in modern college and university hostels. The poet has given us some idea regarding the characteristics of the peoples of different *janapadas*. The inhabitants of Golla (country around Godāvarī) were black, rude, licentious and shameless; those of Magadha were ugly, careless and knew no sexual restraints. The people of Antarvedī (the land between the Gaṅgā and Yamunā) were brown, having reddish-brown eyes and were fond of good food and table-talk. The people of Kīra (Himalayan regions) were tall, fair, having flat nose and could carry big loads. The inhabitants of Ṭakka (Punjab) were lacking in finer qualities and were close-fisted. They could not appreciate knowledge and were also not chivalrous. The Sindhu people were thoroughly well-bred and soft-spoken and at the same time had a passion for music. They were proud of their own country. The residents of the Maru country (Rajasthan) were crooked, foolish and were given to over-eating. The people of Gurjara country were fond of butter and ghee and were religious in temperament, and at the same time, were fond of both peace and war. The people of Lāṭa were fond of perfumes and were conscious about their dress. The Mālavas were of short stature and dark complexion. They were both conceited and wrathful. The Karṇāṭaka people were exceedingly proud, and at the same time, addicted to women. They too, were of violent temperament. The Tājikas (Muslims) were mainly non-vegetarians and knew only wine and women. The Kosalans possessed all the finer qualities of character and were easily excitable and proud. They were generally strongly built. The people of Mahārāṣṭra were tolerant and physically quite fit. However they were somewhat conceited and quarrelsome. The Āndhras were good fighters and were handsome, but they were fond of women and known for then extravagant food habits. Elsewhere the poet has praised the people of the Lāṭa country. We must remember that the original home of Udyotanasūri was situated not far from Lāṭadeśa and that explains why he had soft corner for that country.

Śīlāṅka's *Caupaṇṇmahāpurisacariyaṁ*[50] is the earliest Śvetāmbara work on the lives of 54 great men. This work is written in Prakrit and according to the *Bṛhaṭṭippanikā* the work was completed in the Vikrama Saṁvat 925 corresponding to 867 A.D. In his *Ācārāṅgaṭīkā* we have three dates for Śīlāṅka viz Śaka 772, 784 and 798. The earliest date for this writer is therefore 840 A.D.[51] and the latest 876 A.D. A few scholars[52] think that Śīlāṅka, the commentator of the *Ācārāṅga* and *Sūtrakṛtāṅga* should be distinguished from Śīlāṅka, the author of the *Caupaṇṇamahāpurisacariyaṁ*. But we should remember that both these Śīlāṅkas belonged to the Nivṛti *kula*[53] and lived in the middle of the 9th century A.D. Therefore there is no valid reason why these two Śīlāṅkas should not be regarded as identical. The *Ācārāṅgaṭīkā* has an additional name for Śīlāṅka viz. Tattvāditya and the *Caupaṇṇamahāpurisacariyaṁ* gives another name viz. Vimalamati. It appears that Vimalamati was his original name and Śīlāṅka or Śīlācārya the name given to him after he became a Jain *Sādhu*. The name Tattvāditya appears to be a title conferred upon him for his vast learning. His *guru* according to the *praśasti* of the *Caupaṇṇamahāpurisacariyaṁ* was Mānadeva.

The work runs to 10,800 *ślokas* and he has very skilfully utilised the earlier sources including the Āgamas and the available Śvetāmbara commentaries and other non-canonical texts including Vimala's *Paumacariyaṁ*. Among 54 characters only 19 have received extensive treatment. About 21 characters have been dismissed only in a few pages Characters like Ṛṣabha, Bharata, Śānti, Sumati, Mallī, Sagara, Neminātha, Pārśva, Baladeva and Vardhamāna have naturally been allotted much greater space. One interesting feature of the work is the drama *Vibudhānanda*[54] which has been inserted in the story of one of the former births of Ṛṣabha. We are told that king Mahābala (4th *bhava* of Ṛṣabha) was led to *vairāgya* after this dramatic performance. It appaers that Śīlāṅka got the idea of writing this play from a statement of Jinadāsa Mahattara.[55] The play is constructed in every respect upon the model of the Classical drama. However, the tragic end (viz. the death of the hero) violates the rule of the Sanskrit drama.

There are quite a few valuable cultural materials scattered in this vast work. The writer refers to an old Jain shrine at

Ānandapura (Vaḍnagar) of Gujarat.[56] He further informs us elsewhere that the court of Śālavāhana was graced by more than one hundred poets.[57] That the official religion of Ceylon was Buddhism was known to Śīlāṅka.[58] He refers to the great prosperity of the Kāśī kingdom.[59] In p. 38 he refers to the following texts—Pādalipta's *Taraṅgavatī,* Bharata's *Nāṭyaśāstra,* Samudra's *Puruṣalakṣaṇaśāstra,* Citraratha's *Saṅgītaśāstra,* Naggai's *Citrakalāśāstra,* Dhanvantari's *Āyurvedaśāstra,* Śālibhadra's *Aśvaśāstra,* Vihāṇa's *Dyūtaśāstra,* Bubbuha's *Hastiśāstra,* Aṅgirasa's *Yuddhaśāstra,* Śabara's *Indrajālaśāstra,* Kātyāyana's *Strīlakṣaṇaśāstra,* Senāpati's *Śakunaśāstra,* Gajendra's *Svapnalakṣaṇaśāstra,* Nala's *Pākaśāstra* and Vidyādhara's *Patrachedyaśāstra.* Śīlāṅka further refers to the worship of Kāmadeva[60] who was prapitiated by women desirous of good husband. The Yakṣa-worship was also popular[61] and there is a vivid description of a Kāpālika.[62] It has been argued[63] that even Hemacandra was inspired by Śīlāṅka's work when he wrote his famous *Triṣaṣṭiśalākāpuruṣacaritra.*

Another well-known Śvetāmbara work of the 9th century is Jayasiṁha's *Dharmopadeśamālā*[64] written according to the testimony of the poet himself in the Vikrama Saṁvat 915; and he gives the vital information that at this time king Bhoja was ruling the earth. There is absolutely no doubt that the poet has referred to the Pratīhāra king Bhoja for whom we have dates ranging from V.S. 893 to 936.[65] Vikrama Saṁvat 915 corresponds to 867 A.D. The work was composed in the Jain shrine of Nāgapura (i.e. Nagaur) which is in Rajasthan. He also gives some information regarding the activities of his spiritual predecessors.

The work has a number of *gāthās* written by Jayasiṁha and to illustrate the *gāthās* he has himself composed 156 stories, most of which are based on the earlier Jain literature. The style of Jayasiṁha is superior to most other Jain writers. It appears that the original home of this writer was at Vasantapura, which is mentioned more than 25 times in this work and which has yielded, as we have already seen, a 7th century Jain inscription and which is identified with the present Vasantagaḍh in Sirohi district of Rajasthan. Jayasiṁha, it is interesting to note, describes Mathurā as adorned with Jain temples.[66] He further refers to the town of Acalapura and its king Arikeśarī,[67] who is described as a devotee of the Digambaras. It further appears from this work[68] of Jayasiṁha that there was intense rivalry between the Śvetāmbaras and the Digambaras in the 9th century and this is also confirmed by the statements of the contemporary Digambara writers. Probably the earliest reference to the famous Śakunikāvihāra of Bhṛgukaccha, which was dedicated to Muni Suvrata, is to be found in this work.[69] It is apparent from this, that this famous temple of Suvrata at this well-known port was built much earlier. The author describes the popularity of the Jain religion at Ujjayinī.[70] The holy hill of Śatruñjaya has also been mentioned.[71] He also shows his acquaintance with the philosophy of Siddhasena Divākara.[72] There are also interesting stories about Subandhu, Cāṇakya, Śālibhadra, Mūladeva, Āryarakṣita and others. Some of these stories are also told in contemporary Digambara works.

Let us now turn our attention to one of the most interesting texts written in the beginning of the 10th century A.D. viz. the *Upamitibhavaprapañcākathā*.[73] This work was composed by Siddharṣi in the Vikrama Saṁvat 962 corresponding to 906 A.D. The *praśasti* of this work gives some valuable information about the spiritual predecessors of this writer. He at first mentions Sūryācārya of Nivṛtikula, who flourished in Lāṭadeśa. His disciple was Dellamahattara, who was an expert in astronomy and prognostics. His disciple was Durgasvāmin, a rich Brāhmaṇa, who had become a Jain monk and died, it is interesing to note, at Bhillamāla (Bhinmal). Durgasvāmin was the teacher of Siddharṣi and is praised by him chiefly on account of his exemplary piety. Both teacher and pupil had been ordained by Gargasvāmin, about whom we are not told anything more. But the highest praise is reserved for Haribhadra, who as we learn from the *praśasti* was the source of his inspiration. It must, however, not be supposed that Haribhadra was a contemporary of Siddharṣi. The former lived some two centuries earlier, as is indicated in the *Kuvalayamālā* written in the Śaka year 700.

In the *Prabhāvakacarita*[74] we have a romantic account of Siddharṣi's conversion from Buddhism which has, however, been rightly rejected by Jacobi.[75] That work further represents Siddharṣi as a cousin of Māgha, the author of the *Śiśupālavadha,* which is surely impossible, as Māgha lived in the middle of the 7th century A.D., since his grandfather served under king Varmalāta, who is definitely known from an inscription[76] to have flourished in 625 A.D.

The work of Siddharṣi is an elaborate and extensive allegory. Probably the earliest specimen of such an allegory is the unnamed play of Aśvaghoṣa, discovered from Central Asia.[77] However this work of Siddharṣi is the first extensive allegory in the Indian literature and it was followed two centuries later by Kṛṣṇa Miśra's great allegory *Prabodhacandrodaya.* Siddharṣi's work is a narrative consisting of series of birth stories i.e. the hero of all stories is the some person in different births. This is an ancient device known to the earlier Buddhist and Jain writers including Haribhadra whose *Samarāiccakahā* is openly acknowledged by Siddharṣi[78] as his model.

Siddharṣi proposes to explain the mundane career of the Soul (*Jīva*) under the name of Saṁsārijīva from the lowest stage of existence to the final liberation. However, only six births are narrated, a few more are sketched, and the rest is only summarily noticed. In the lives fully narrated, Saṁsārijīva is described as being under the influence of four cardinal passions (*krodha* in the 3rd Prastāva, *māna* in the 4th, *māyā* in the 5th and *lobha* in the 6th) ; and similarly he is governed by the five cardinal vices (*hiṁsā* in the 3rd, *anṛta* in the 4th, *steya* in the 5th, *abrahma* in the 6th, *parigraha* in the 7th). And in the Prastāvas are inserted allegorical stories which illustrate the baleful influence of the five senses viz. *sparśana, rasana, ghṛāṇa, dṛṣṭi* and *śruti.* The chief intention of the author was to illustrate the Jain religion, not as dogmatist, but as a moralist. The order followed by Siddharṣi is to be found also in the *Tattvārthādhigama Sūtra.*[79] The work has been compared with the *Pilgrim's Progress.*[80] The author deliberately uses Sanskrit and not Prakrit, because Sanskrit was the language of the educated people. However, his language is very easy to understand, and he does not care, like Dhanapāla or Somadeva, to imitate the style of Subandhu or Bāṇa.

Dhanapāla,[81] who flourished in the last quarter of the 10th century A.D. is the author of the *Tilakamañjarī*,[82] which was probably composed in the very beginning of the reign of Paramāra Bhoja. This author had written his Prakrit *Pāiyalacchī*[83] in the Vikrama year 1029 corresponding to 972 A.D., when Mānyakheṭa was sacked by the Mālava army. In the *Tilakamañjarī*[84] some extremely valuable information regarding the early kings of the Paramāra dynasty has been given. The author is a conscious imitator of Bāṇa, but he is only a very inferior imitator. The hero Harivāhana reminds us of Candrāpīḍa of the *Kādambarī* and his friend Samaraketu is modelled on Vaiśampāyana of Bāṇa's work. The heroine Tilakamañjarī instinctively reminds us of Kādambarī and Malayavatī is in every respect like Mahāśvetā, the immortal creation of Bāṇa. In Bāṇa's work the childless king Tārāpīḍa worships Śiva in the Mahākāla temple and here in the *Tilakamañjarī* Meghavāhana worships Jina in the temple of Śakrāvatāra Siddhāyatana of Ayodhyā for a son. It appears from Dhanapāla's work that this temple of Jina at Ayodhyā was established long before its composition. It is extremely interesting to note that this Jain shrine of Ayodhyā is mentioned in Jinaprabha's *Vividhatīrthakalpa*[85]. We should remember that the grandfather of the poet was originally a resident of Sāṅkāśya[86] and Dhanapāla himself probably had personally visited this shrine of Ayodhyā.

Dhanapāla, as we learn from later works like the *Prabhāvakacarita*[87] and *Prabandhacintāmaṇi*[88], received favours from both Muñja and Bhoja. This is also confirmed by his own work. A summary of this work entitled *Tilakamañjarīkathāsāra*[89] was written by another poet of the same name at Patan in V.S. 1261.

Dhanapāla's another work is the *Ṛṣabhapañcāśikā*[90] which is a poem of 50 stanzas. This is written in Prakrit and the first twenty verses contain allusions to the events of the life of the first Tīrthaṅkara; the remaining thirty stanzas are devoted exclusively to the praise of Ṛṣabha. This poem contains probably the earliest reference to chess-board[91].

Quite a few other works by Śvetāmbara writers were written before 1000 A.D. We should mention here the *Ajitaśāntistava*[92] (*Ajiyasantithaya*) by Nandiṣeṇa who lived before the 9th century.

This poem written in rare but artificial metres in Prakrit, glorifies Ajita, the second and Śāntinātha, the 16th Tīrthaṅkara. It is also probable that the original *Śatruñjayamāhātmya*[93] was written, as claimed by the poet, during the reign of one of the Śīlādityas of Valabhī and afterwards in the later period interpolations were made in the body of this Jain *Māhātmya.* If this is accepted, then we have to assign the original work before the last quarter of the 8th century, which is the date for the last king of Valabhī, bearing that name.

NOTES

1 P. 29 (SGJM, Vol. XII, Calcutta, 1940).

2 Pp. 11 ff

3 Verse No. 1508.

4 Edited in Nemivijñānagranthamālā Vikrama Saṁvat, 2000. It was translated in German by Leumann as *Die Nonne* in 1921 in *ZB*, Vol. III, 193 ff and 272 ff. A separate offprint was also published. A Gujarati translation was published from Ahmedabad in 1924.

5 See our paper in *Ancient Indian Literary and Cultural Tradition*, pp. 177 f.

6 *Loc. cit.*

7 Italics ours.

8 Ed. Jacobi, 1914 (Bhavnagar) ; recently Prakrit Text Society Varanasi has published the work in two parts.

9 *S.B.E.*, Vol. XXII. p. 293.

10 Edited in Ātmānanda Jain Granthamālā, 1930-31 (Bhavnagar). A Gujarati translation of this text was made by Prof. Sandeswara in V.S. 2003.

11 See his paper in *Bulletin of the School of Oriental Studies* (London), Vol. VIII (1935-37), pp. 319-333.

12 *Ibid.*, p. 320 fn. 1.

13 See Jain, *Prakrit Sāhitya kā itihāsa.* p. 381. The *Viśeṣaṇavatī* has been published by Ṛṣabhadeva Kesarīmala Saṁsthā, Ratlam, 1927.

14 See *Niś Cū*, Vol IV, p. 26 ; see also Āva Cū, Vol. I, pp. 164, 460 and Vol. II, p. 324.

15 P. 50 ; see also Gujarati translation, p. 60.

16 P. 66.

17 P. 74.

18 P. 50.

19 Pp. 38, 62.

20 P. 155.

21 P. 38.

22 P. 65.

23 Translation (Gujarati), pp. 92-130.

24 *Ibid.*. pp. 92-93.

25 *Ibid.*, p. 378.

26 *Ibid.*, p. 350.

27 *Ibid.*, p. 189.

28 *Ibid.*, p. 287.

29 See also *Introd.*, Gujarati translation, pp. 33 ff.

30 Trans., pp. 313 ff.

31 *Ibid.*, p. 319.

32 *Ibid.*, p. 314.

33 *Ibid.*, p. 317.

34 *Ibid.*, pp. 202 ff.

35 Ed. A. N. Upadhye, p. 282.

36 See his Introd., *Samarāiccakahā,* Vol. I. p. VI.

37 See his Sanskrit Introduction entitled *Granthakāraparicaya* in his edition of Haribhadra's *Dharmasaṅgrahiṇī*, Bombay, 1918.

38 IX, 48-206.

39 Pp. 24 ff.

40 Ed. by Jacobi, 1926 (Calcutta, Asiatic Society) ; afterwards it was edited in two parts by Bhagwandas with Sanskrit *chāyā* and published from Ahmedabad (1938, 1942). There is an abstract of this text which was compiled by Pradyumna in 1214 A.D. and edited by Jacobi, Ahmedabad, 1905.

41 *Hist. of Indian Lit.*, Vol. II, p. 523.

42 See Sastri, The *Coḷas,* p. 217.

43 Ed. Durgaprasad and Parab, XIII 74 ; for some useful information on Kaṭāha, see *The Ocean of Story* (Tawney and Penzer), Vol. I. p. 155 fn. 1. In this work Kaṭāha has been mentioned several times.

44 Ed. A N. Upadhye, Bombay, 1944.

45 See Pīṭhikā, p. 105.

46 See pp. 20 ff. of his 'Critical Study' of the *Dhūrtākhyāna* given in his edition of that text.

47 Edited in two Parts by A. N. Upadhye in Singhi Jain Granthamālā, Bombay, 1959 and 1970. There is a valuable introduction in the second part by the same scholar.

48 Jain, *op. cit.*, p. 420.

49 *Ibid.*, p. 423.

50 Prakrit Text Society, Varanasi, 1961.

51 The date 772 is actually given in some manuscripts in the Gupta Saṁvat, which according to Fleet is a mistake for the Ṣaka year; see *A Hist. of the Canonical Lit. of the Jainas* by Kapadia, p. 197.

52 See *Prastāvanā* in Hindi by A. M. Bhojak in the P.T.S. edition, pp. 54 ff; see also *Jaina Sāhitya kā Bṛhad itihāsa*, Vol. VI, p. 70.

53 In the concluding line of his *Ṭīkā* on the 1st Ṣrutaskandha of the *Ācārāṅga* we have the information that Ṣīlācārya belonged to the Nivṛti *kula*; see *Jaina Sāhitya kā bṛhad itihāsa*, Vol. III, p. 382 fn. 1.

54 Pp. 17-27.

55 See Introd. by Klaus Bruhn, p. 29.

56 P. 189.

57 P. 138.

58 P. 154.

59 P. 86.

60 P. 110.

61 P. 232.

62 P. 228.

63 Cf. Alsdorf's view quoted in Klaus Bruhn's Introduction, p. 9.

64 Singhi Jaina Granthamālā, Bombay, 1949 (ed. by L. B. Gandhi).

65 See D. R. Bhandarkar, *A List of the Inscriptions of Northern India*, Nos. 25, 28, 33 and 36.

66 P. 32.

67 P. 177.

68 Pp. 177-179

69 P. 160.

70 P. 148.

71 P. 220.

72 P. 37.

73 Edited in Bibliotheca Indica, 1914 by P. Peterson and Jacobi (Calcutta, Asiatic Society). For another edition see D.L.P. No. 46.

74 V. 22 ff.

75 See Preface, pp. XIII ff.

76 D.R. Bhandarkar, *List*, No. 11.

77 See Winternitz *H.I.L.* (Reprint), Vol. III, Part I, pp. 222 f

78 See p. 147.

79 VIII, 10; VII, 1, II. 20.

80 Jacobi, *op. cit.*, p. XVIII.

81 See the paper entitled 'Mahākavi Dhanapāla aur unkī *Tilaka-mañjarī*' in Guru Gopaladas Baraiya Smṛtigrantha, pp. 484-91. See Merutuṅga, *Prabandhacintāmaṇi*, pp. 36 ff.

82 Ed. Kāvyamālā Series, Bombay, 1938.

83 See Chowdhary, G. C. *P.H.N.I.* etc., p. 85.

84 *Ibid.*, pp. 85 ff.

85 Edited Jinavijaya, Santiniketan, 1934, p. 73.

86 See *Prabandhacintāmaṇi* (ed. Jinavijaya) p. 36.

87 See the Prabandha entitled 'Mahendrasūriprabandha'.

88 Pp. 36 ff.

89 Edited Ahmedabad, 1970.

90 Edited in Kāvyamālā Series Pt. VII; see also *Jinaratnakośa*, p. 3. A German translation along with the original text edited by Klatt was published in *Z.D.M.G.*, Vol. 33, pp. 445 ff.

91 See Klatt, *op. cit.*, pp. 465 f.

92 Ed. Viravijaya, Ahmedabad, V.S. 1992.

93 See *I.A.*, Vol. 30, pp. 239 ff; 288 ff.

CHAPTER XIII

The Literature of the Digambaras

The Digambaras, who formally separated themselves from the original Saṅgha in the early years of the 2nd century A.D., can rightly boast of an exceedingly rich literature. However, the so-called canonical texts of this sect, unlike the Śvetāmbara canon, is devoid of any interest for the students of history. The subject treated in these canonical works are technical in nature and will be liked only by the students of metaphysics. The canonical texts of the Digambaras were discovered from Muḍbidri in South Kanara district of Karnatak some fifty years back. The first part of the canon is known as the *Karmaprābhṛta* and also as the *Ṣaṭkhaṇḍāgama*. The earliest available commentary on it is the *Dhavalā* written by Vīrasena, who describes himself as a disciple of Āryanandin and a grand-disciple of Candrasena of the Pañcastūpānvaya and who had studied the Siddhānta under Elācārya. The commentary was completed in the Śaka year 738 corresponding 816 A.D., when Amoghavarṣa I was the reigning king.[1] That commentator gives us some information regarding the original authors of the *Karmaprābhṛta*.

According to Vīrasena,[2] after the death of Lohācārya, the 28th *guru* in succession of Mahāvīra, the knowledge of ancient scriptures became practically extinct. There was only one saint viz. Dharasena who had some knowledge regarding those ancient texts. This saint was originally a resident of Girinagara (Girnar). While he was engaged in penances in the Candragumphā Cave of Girnar hill, he decided to send a letter to the monks of Dakṣiṇāpatha warning them against the danger of complete extinction of the knowledge of early scriptures. The monks, on receipt of that letter sent two intelligent monks called Puṣpadanta and Bhūtabali to Dharasena who taught them ancient scriptures. These two monks afterwards composed the *Ṣaṭkhaṇḍāgama* and according to Vīrasena, that work was completed 683 years after the Nirvāṇa of Mahāvīra. We further learn that Puṣpadanta composed the first 20 cardinal Sūtras and the rest of the work running to 6000 Sūtras was completed by Bhūtabali.

The above discussion shows that the earliest Digambara canon, according to their own testimony, is not earlier than the 2nd century A.D. This indirectly supports the Śvetāmbara tradition regarding the date of the formal separation of the Digambaras from the original Saṅgha. We have already seen, that according to the Śvetāmbaras, the Digambaras separated 609 years after the Nirvāṇa of Mahāvīra. It is natural that after their separation they should be in search of a separate canon for themselves. The testimony of Vīrasena proves that the Digambara canon was originally compiled in Western India in which the monks of the South also took part. Although the Digambaras reject the authenticity of the Śvetāmbara sacred texts, their early writers do not hesitate to quote from the Svetāmbara canon. Even Vīrasena has shown complete acquaintance with a number of Śvetāmbara sacred texts[3].

Vīrasena further informs us that at the time of the compilation of the sacred texts, the Digambara monks of the South were assembled at the town of Mahimā which was situated on the bank of the river Veṇyā (modern Bena) in the Andhra country and which is identified with Mahimānagar in the district of Satara in present Maharashtra. The commentary written by Vīrasena runs to 72,000 *ślokas* and it was based, according to his own statement, on the earlier commentaries including that written by the celebrated Kundakunda. A number of earlier commentaries are also mentioned in Indranandi's *Śrutāvatāra*[4]. But none of these commentaries has survived. The *Dhavalā* commentary was written at Vāṭagrāmapura, which has not yet been properly identified[5].

The second part of the Digambara canon is known as the *Kaṣāyaprābhṛa*[6] which was written by one Guṇadhara Ācārya, who probably was a contemporary of Bhūtabali and Puṣpadanta.[7] The work runs into 233 verses of which probably the first 180 were written by Guṇadhara[8]. The earliest commentary on it is the *Cūrṇisūtra* of Yativṛṣabha, who as we will see afterwards, probably flourished in the last quarter of the 6th century A.D. Yativṛṣabha, we are told, followed the commentary of Ārya Maṅkhu and Nāgahastin[9]. Afterwards according to Indranandi two other commentators wrote their learned treatises on this work and finally Vīrasena composed the first 20,000 *ślokas* of his *Jayadhavalā,* which was afterwards completed in 60,000 *ślokas* by his disciple Jinasena. This great commentary[10] was completed in Śaka 759, when Amoghavarṣa I was the reigning king[11]. We should also refer to the last part of *Ṣaṭkhaṇḍāgama* called *Mahābandha* written by Bhūtabali[12] which runs to 40,000 *ślokas* and on which Vīrasena has not written any commentary.

We have already said that the Digambara Āgamic texts are devoid of any interest, at least for the historian. However students of Jain philosophy and metaphysics treat them as source-books. Later Jain philosophers have freely borrowed from these texts. Let us then turn our attention to a few other Digambara Jain texts, which also deal with abstruse points of Digambara philosophy. We will not discuss here the works of the celebrated Digambara philosophers, which we propose to do in the next chapter, but only refer to a few classics which deal with doctrinal matters.

The *Mūlācāra*[13] of Vaṭṭakera which runs to 1252 verses is one of the earliest non-canonical Digambara works dealing with various practices of Jain ascetics. The work is divided into 12 parts (*Adhikāra*). There are a few interesting stories for which the author is indebted to the earlier Śvetāmbara canon. Like the *Nandīsūtra* and *Anuyogadvāra* it condemns works like the *Rāmāyaṇa*, *Mahābhārata*, *Arthaśāstra* etc. Some of the rules for the Jain monks are directly taken from the Śvetāmbara canonical texts including the *Bṛhatkalpa* and a few of the verses remind us of the *Daśavaikālika*[14]. It has been claimed[15] that the author Vaṭṭakera should be identified with Kundakunda; but there is no genuine basis for such a suggestion. From the linguistic point of view the work should be assigned to the 5th century A.D.

The *Bhagavatī Ārādhanā*[16] appears to be a work of the

same period. It has little over 2,100 verses and its Prakrit bears close similarity with the Prakrit of the *Mūlācāra*[17]. It was composed, according to the colophon of the work, by Pāṇitala-bhojī Śivārya, who studied the Mūla Sūtras under the feet of Ārya Jinanandi Gaṇī, Ārya Śarvagupta Gaṇī and Arya Mitranandi Gaṇī. We have already seen in a previous chapter[18] that there was a Pāṇitalabhojī Digambara ascetic during the reign of Rāmagupta, who flourished in the 2nd half of the 4th century A.D. Prabhācandra, who wrote his *Kathākośa* during the reign of Jayasiṁha of Dhārā (middle of the 11th century A.D.) claims that this Śivārya (also called Śivakoṭi) was previously a king and later converted by the celebrated Samanta-bhadra[19]. We are further told by him that his work was based on the *Ārādhanā* of Lohācārya which ran to 84,000 verses. We must however note that Hariṣeṇa who wrote his *Kathākośa* much earlier, does not represent Śivārya as a disciple of the great Samantabhadra, although his work too, like that of Prabhā-candra, is based on the work written by Śivārya.

Śivārya refers to a number of Śvetāmbara texts including *Kalpa, Vyavahāra, Ācārāṅga* and *Jītakalpa.* This work, which deals with the conduct of Jain ascetics, has verses common with the *Mūlācāra* and a few Śvetāmbara canonical texts. A few scholars identify its author Śivārya with Śivabhūtī which can be rejected outright[20]. The probable date of Śivabhūti is 2nd century A.D., while Śivārya flourished in the Gupta period. There is a Sanskrit commentary on the *Ārādhanā* written by Aparājita called *Śrīvijayodayā.* This gentleman was a disciple of one Baladevasūrī and grand-disciple of Candranandi. He further tells us that he was inspired by Nāganandi. He also wrote, it is interesting to note, a commentary on the celebrated Śvetāmbara Āgamic poem *Daśavaikālika.* He shows his acquaintance with the philosophy of Pūjyapāda and the *Varāṅgacarita* of Jaṭā Siṁha-nandin. In all probability, Aparājita flourished in the 8th century A.D. A number of later commentaries are also known[21], which shows that *Ārādhanā* was looked upon as an extremely valuable work by the Digambara monks of later times. In the early 10th century Hariṣeṇa composed his *Bṛhatkathākośa,* which according to his own testimony was based on the original

Ārādhanā. This work will be discussed later in the present chapter.

The original *Lokavibhāga*[22], which is now lost, was written according to its translator Siṁhasūri in the Śaka year 380 corresponding to the 22nd year of king Siṁhavarman of Kāñcī. We are further told that its author was Sarvanandi, who was a resident of the village of Pāṭalika, which was situated in the Pāṇḍya kingdom. This shows that there existed a Digambara work on cosmography as early as the 5th century A.D. Yativṛṣabha in his *Tiloyapaṇṇatī* has repeatedly referred to this work.

We have already mentioned the fact that Yativṛṣabha had written a commentary (*Cūrṇī*) on the *Kāṣāyaprābhrta*. The same saint is the author of the famous work on Jain cosmography called *Tilovapaṇṇatī*[23]. Vīrasena in his *Dhavalā* frequently invokes him and quotes *gāthās* which are found with minor variations in the present edition of the work[24]. That the author flourished after 5th century A.D., is also proved by the fact that he mentions the *Lokavibhāga* several times. He also shows acquaintance with the *Mūlācāra*. It has been argued[25] that the *Lokavibhāga* was known to Jinabhadra Kṣamāśramaṇa, for whom we have a date Śaka 531 corresponding to 609 A.D. But he could not have flourished much earlier, since he refers to the duration of the Gupta rule as either 221[26] or 255[27]. It appears that the poet probably flourished in the last quarter of the 6th century A.D. He is the first writer to refer to the duration of the rule of the Imperial Guptas; and his testimony is strikingly confirmed by the evidence of Gupta inscriptions. It further appears that the earlier figure of 221 for the duration of the Gupta rule is more reasonable than the latter figure of 255[28]. We are also grateful to Yativṛṣabha for giving us an idea about post-Candragupta chronology. Incidentally he is the earliest author to mention that Chandragupta Maurya was a Jain[29]. Later writers including the author of the Jain *Harivaṁśa* were influenced by Yativṛṣabha. The *Tiloyapaṇṇatī* is divided into nine sections and runs to 8,000 verses. It gives a great deal of information on Jain doctrine and Purāṇic tradition about Tīrthaṅkaras. It has also been claimed that Yativṛṣabha was at home with the science of mathematics[30]. He also describes the five hills of Rājagṛha which is called by the name Paṁcaselaṇayara i.e. Pañcaśailanagara[31]. He further mentions a number of places which were regarded as sacred to the Jains. Yativṛṣabha is mentioned as an enemy of the Buddhists in the *Bṛhatkathākośa*[32] of Hariṣeṇa, which was written in 931 A.D.

The well known *Svāmikārttikeyānuprekṣā*[33] is a very important and popular work among the Digambara Jains. It explains the 12 Anuprekṣās or Meditations and has therefore altogether 12 chapters. These Anuprekṣās are recommended both for the monks and laymen. According to J. P. Jain this work was written in the early centuries of the Christian era[34]; and he further suggests that the author Svāmi Kumāra should be identified with Kumāranandin of a Mathurā inscription[35], dated Śaka 87. But there is little doubt that Kumāranandin of that inscription was a Śvetāmbara saint and this work is a typical Digambara product. Prof. A. N. Upadhye has shown that in no work before 13th century A.D., this text has been referred to[36]. He further argues that the author was acquainted with the *Gommaṭasāra* of Nemicandra, written in the 10th century A.D. Even if we reject this argument of Upadhye, we cannot suggest a much earlier date for this work. This author was clearly influenced by the views of Kundakunda and Śivārya Among other important didactic Digambara works of the 10th century we must mention the *Gommaṭasāra* and the works of Devasena. The Prakrit *Gommaṭasāra*[37] was written by Nemicandra, a close friend of the well-known Cāmuṇḍarāya, who flourished in the last quarter of the 10th century A.D. This work was also named after that great minister, whose original name was 'Gommaṭa'. Nemicandra is heavily indebted to earlier writers like Yativṛṣabha and Vīrasena. His work consists of two parts viz. Jīvakāṇḍa and Karmakāṇḍa "It is a kind of natural history of the living beings" and needless to say, this work is frankly unreadable. Devasena, was the author of the works *Ārādhanāsāra*[38] and *Darśanasāra*[39]. Luckily for us, in his *Darśanasāra* he has informed us that he was a resident of Dhārā and lived around 933 A.D. We are further told that this work was composed in the temple of Pārśvanātha which was situated at that town[40]. Devasena has given us some vital information regarding the origin of sects like Kāṣṭhāsaṅgha, Māthurasaṅgha, Drāviḍasaṅgha, and Yāpanīyasaṅgha.

Let us now turn our attention to the creative works of literature written by Digambara poets and writers. But before we do that, we have to refer to the Jainendra grammar. This work[41], which is ascribed to Devanandi Pūjyapāda has altogether five chapters and this is the reason why it is also known as the *Pañcādhyāyī*. Pūjyapāda refers to earlier Jain savents like Śrīdatta (1.4.34), Yaśobhadra (2.1.99), Bhūtabali (3.4.83), Prabhācandra (4.3.180), Siddhasena (5.1.7) and lastly Samantabhadra (5.4.140). Now, regarding the time of Pūjyapāda there is now no confusion. Devasena in his *Darśanasāra*[42] has clearly stated that Vajranandin, the disciple of Pūjyapāda founded the Drāviḍasangha at Southern Mathurā (i.e. Madura) in Vikrama Saṁvat 526 which corresponds to 468 A.D. Therefore the preceptor of Vajranandin, viz. Pūjyapada should be assigned to the first half of the 5th century A.D. It is interesting to note, and as pointed out by Premi[43], that Samantabhadra was a contemporary of Pūjyapāda, as he also was acquainted with Pūjyapāda's works. There are a number of early commentaries on Pūjyapāda's Grammar including one by Abhayanandi, and another by Prabhācandra. The latter was a contemporary of Paramāra Bhoja[44].

No Digambara literary work, written before the 7th century, is now available. The earliest datable work is the *Padma Purāṇa*[45] of Ācārya Raviṣeṇa which was written, according to the testimony of the poet himself, 1203½ years after Mahāvīra's Nirvāṇa. This suggests a date around 678 A.D. That poet further informs us that he was a disciple of Lakṣmaṇasena and granddisciple of Arhatmuni[46]. The latter, in turn, was a disciple of Divākara; Divākara's preceptor was Indra. We can, therefore assign the earliest *guru* Indra to the last quarter of the 6th century A.D.

The *Padma Purāṇa* or *Padmacarita* as we have already pointed out, is a free and direct Sanskrit translation of the Prakrit text of Vimala. However, nowhere in the text Raviṣeṇa cares to acknowledge his debt to the earlier and original poet.

He simply states[47] that he followed the work of Anuttaravāgmin who according to Svayambhū was identical with Kīrtidhara. But no work of Kīrtidhara is known. We can understand the reason why Raviṣeṇa has not mentioned Vimala in his work; the former was a diehard Digambara and the latter was a Śvetāmbara poet. It appears that before Raviṣeṇa, one Kīrtidhara made an attempt to translate in Sanskrit the Prakrit *kāvya* of Vimala. However, the popularity of Raviṣeṇa's work forced the poem of Kīrtidhara to disappear from the literary scene. Although Raviṣeṇa is a mere translator, we have to concede, that he was endowed with a genuine poetical fervour. The *Padma Purāṇa* is an exceedingly popular work among the Digambara Jains. That Raviṣeṇa was a learned poet is also evident from various chapters of his work. In chapter 24, in connexion with enumeration of Kaikeyī's skill, Raviṣeṇa has displayed his deep knowledge of various branches of learning. Like Vimala, he too, is thoroughly anti-Brāhmaṇical. Probably he was inspired by the style of Bāṇa. His descriptions of war-preparation (12.181 ff.) and love-scene (16.192 ff) remind us of Bāṇa's style. As Bāṇa flourished between 560-620 A.D., and Raviṣeṇa in the last quarter of the 7th century, there is nothing inherently improbable in Raviṣeṇa following the former. The easy, graceful style of Raviṣeṇa is also responsible for his extreme popularity. Later poets like Udyotanasūri, the author of the *Kuvalyamālā* (Śaka 700) and Jinasena, the author of the *Harivaṁśapurāṇa* (Śaka 705) refer to Raviṣeṇa with deference[48]. Since *Padma Purāṇa* is a mere translation of the *Paumacariyaṁ*, it is useless to discuss the contents of the poem. The present writer has elsewhere[49] tried to show that Raviṣeṇa had heard about the Muslims.

To the 7th century we can assign another poem written by a Digambara poet viz. the *Varāṅgacarita*[50] of Jaṭāsiṁhanandi. As late as 1933, it was believed that this work was composed by Raviṣeṇa. The two crucial verses referring to this work in the *Kuvalayamālā* and *Harivaṁśapurāṇa* were misunderstood by scholars[51]. But after the discovery of a number of manuscripts of this poem and the references to its author in various later works, all doubts disappeared regarding its actual authorship. As we have just now indicated, the earliest reference to the *Varāṅgacarita* is to be found in the work of Śvetāmbara Udyotanasūri, who wrote in Śaka 700. Five years later, Jinasena, in his *Harivaṁśa* has praised this work. But in the available manuscripts of this work, the name of its author has not been disclosed. But Udyotanasūri has referred to Jaṭila[52] and later writers like Cāmuṇḍrāya and Dhavala, the author of the Apabhraṁsa *Harivaṁśa*[53] have clearly mentioned him. The name Jaṭā Siṁhanandi is first found in the *Cāmuṇḍarāyapurāṇa*. As Upadhye rightly conjectures[54], Cāmuṇḍarāya calls him by that name in order to distinguish him from earlier Siṁhanandis.[55]. Still later writers like Nayasena, Pārśvapaṇḍita, Janna, and others show their acquintance with the *Varāṅgacarita* and its author Jaṭā Siṁhanandi.

An epigraph from the holy Kopbal area in Raichur district of Karnatak, as noted in a previous chapter,[56] refers to this poet, who was evidently looked upon as a great saint. It was probably inscribed a few centuries after the death of this savant. It therefore appears that Jaṭā Siṁhanandi became a celebrated figure after his demise in both North and South India.

The poem *Varāṅgacarita* runs to 31 chapters and describes the vicissitudes of the life of prince Varāṅga, the son of Dharmasena of Bhoja family, who ruled at Uttamapura in the territory of Vinītā (Ayodhyā). Some of the adventures of this prince remind us of those of Vasudeva as described in the Śvetāmbara work *Vasudevahiṇḍī*. However, being written in easy, graceful Sanskrit, it is a much more readable work. The poet uniformly calls it *dharmakathā,* which according to Haribhadra's definition is full of religious topics.[57] Varāṅga, the hero is represented as possessing great religious virtues. The poet, as shown by Upadhye,[58] was influenced by the views of Kundakunda, Umāsvāti, Samantabhadra, Siddhasena and others. In chapters XXIV-XXV he attacks the views of different Schools in an amateurish way and it appears from this apparent youngmanishness that he was a comparatively young man when he wrote this poem.

It appears from this poem that Jainism enjoyed rare prosperity during Jaṭila's time.[59] There are references to gorgeous

Jain temples with images of precious stones.[60] Elsewhere he has referred to the scenes of the Purāṇas which were painted or carved on the walls of the temples.[61] He also refers to the royal gifts of villages to the Jain temples.[62] A number of *janapadas* including Aṅga, Vaṅga, Magadha, Kaliṅga, Suhma, Puṇḍra, Kuru, Aśmaka, Ābhīra, Avanti, Kosala, Matsya, Saurāṣṭra, Vindhyapāla, Mahendra, Sauvīra, Saindhava, Kāśmīra, Oḍra, Vaidarbha, Vaidiśa, Pañcāla etc. are mentioned in one place of this poem.[63] Elsewhere Kāmboja, Bāhlīka, Simhala, Barbara, Kirāta, Gāndhāra, Pulinda are mentioned as non-Aryan peoples.[64] The poet was equally at home with Hindu Purāṇic stories.[65]

The well-known Dhanañjaya was the author of the *Rāghava-Pāṇḍavīya* or *Dvisandhāna*[66] which is an epic in eighteen cantos. Nothing practically is known about the personal life of the poet except that his father was one Vasudeva, and mother bore the name of Śrīdevī. Probably his *guru* was one Daśaratha. It has been suggested that he was probably not a monk but a Digambara layman.[67] This poem of Dhanañjaya has been praised by various poets including the famous Rājaśekhara who flourished around 900 A.D. The poem is based on the two Hindu epics viz. the *Rāmāyaṇa* and *Mahābhārata*, and unlike most Jain works, the characters are not represented as embracing the religion of the Jinas. He was inspired, it appears, by the writings of Kālidāsa, Bhāravi and Māgha. His other works are *Nāmamālā*, *Anekārtha-nāmamālā* and *Viṣāpahārastotra*. Even Vīrasena in his *Dhavalā*[68] has quoted a verse from the *Anekārthanāmamālā*. This shows that Dhanañjaya probably flourished in the 8th century A.D., if not earlier. N. Premi has shown[69] hat Jinasena I in his *Ādipurāṇa* has consciously imitated a particular verse from the *Viṣāpahā-rastotra*. That scholar has further drawn our attention to the fact that Somadeva (middle of the 10th century) in his famous *Yaśastilakacampū* writes a verse in imitation of the same poem of Dhanañjaya.[70] This proves that the Jain poets and philosophers from 800 A.D., were inspired by the writings of Dhanañjaya.

To the eighth century we can assign at least two poems, written by the Digambara poets. The first poem was written by Jinasena I and it was *Pārśvābhyudaya*.[71] Jinasena II in his well-known *Harivaṁśa,* which was completed in Śaka 705 refers to this poem of Jinasena I, who as we have already seen, was the famous disciple of the illustrious Vīrasena. It follows therefore that *Pārśvābhyudaya* was written before 783 A.D.

The poem runs to four cantos and has altogether 364 stanzas. It was written in imitation of the famous *Meghadūta* of Kālidāsa. Like the *Meghadūta* it is written in the Mandākrāntā metre. This is a poetical life-story of Pārśvanātha. In this poem the entire *Meghādūta* has been included by inserting one or two lines from that poem of Kālidāsa, whilst Jinasena I composed the rest. Needless to say, there is little similarity between the love-sick Yakṣa of Kālidāsa and the 23rd Tīrthaṅkara of the Jains. Yet Jinasena I, it appears, has acquitted himself creditably in this difficult and delicate task.

Probably the most remarkable Digambara poem of the second half of the 8th century is the *Harivaṁśapurāṇa*[72] of Jinasena II, written according to the colophon of the poem in Śaka 705 corresponding to 783 A.D. In a previous chapter we discussed the information supplied by Jinasena II on the political condition of his time. This poem, unlike many Jain works, give a very faithful account of the social, religious and cultural condition of India of the 8th century.[73] There is detailed list[74] of peoples which can be compared with the similar lists in the Purāṇas and other works. The only reference to the ancient town of Karṇasuvarṇa in Indian literature is to found in this work.[75] As we have already observed, the poet was influenced by Yativṛṣabha. He was also equally at home with Brāhmaṇical works including the Vaiṣṇava Purāṇas. As Premi has pointed out[76], Jinasena II is the only writer to give a continuous list of Jain teachers from the days of Lohārya (same as Lohācārya), who flourished 683 years after Mahāvīra's demise, to his own time i.e 783 A.D. There are altogether 29 preceptors between Lohārya and Jinasena II and the average comes to little over 21, which is quite reasonable. It should however, be remembered that the author belonged to the Punnāṭa Saṅgha, which originated in the ancient Punnāṭa country, which was another name of Karnatak.

The composition of the *Harivaṁśa* was started at the well-known ancient town of Vardhamāna in Gujarat and was completed at the town of Dostaṭikā (modern Dottāḍi)[77]. Vardhamāna is described as a prosperous city and a similar picture of this town is to be found in Hariṣeṇa's *Bṛhatkathākośa,*[78] which was completed in 931 A.D., some 150 years after the *Harivaṁśa.* Among the earlier poets and philosophers, mentioned by Jinasena II, the following deserve notice—Samantabhadra, Siddhasena, Devanandi, Vajrasūri (same as Vajranandi, the disciple of Devanandi-Pūjyapāda), Mahāsena (the author of the missing *Sulocanākathā*), Raviṣeṇa, Jaṭā Siṁhanandi, Śānta (probably same as Śāntiṣeṇa, about whom nothing is known), Viśeṣavādi (also mentioned by Vādirāja[79]), Kumārasena (whose fame was comparable to that of Prabhācandra[80]), Vīrasena, Jinasena I, and the unknown author of the *Vardhamāna Purāṇa.*[81]

Several great Digambara poets and writers of the 9th century enriched the Indian literature by their solid contributions. We should at first discuss the *Ādipurāṇa*[82] written by Jinasena I, whose *Pārśvābhyudaya* was written before 783 A.D., and who completed the *Jayadhavalā* of his *guru* in Śaka 759, corresponding to 838 A.D. There is little doubt that Jinasena I had a long life and his earliest poem *Pārśvābhyudaya* was probably written in his early youth. We further learn from his disciple Guṇabhadra that Jinesena I could not complete his *Ādipurāṇa,* and Guṇabhadra wrote the last 1620 *Ślokas* of this poem which runs to 12,000 verses. Jinasena I was the author of the first 42 chapters and the 3 verses of the 43rd chapter. The remaining portion of the 43rd chapter and the last four were written by Guṇabhadra.

The *Ādipurāṇa* is undoubtedly one of the finest poems written in the early mediaeval period. It was apparently written after the *Jayadhavalā* commentary, and he was naturally a man of advanced years at the time of its composition. The poem deals with the life of Ṛṣabha who is also known as Ādinātha. The poet calls it both 'Purāṇa' and 'Mahākāvya'. It has been called an encyclopaedia of the Digambara religion.[83] He started this poem in order to write the lives of 63 great men; but he could only complete the lives of the first Tīrthaṅkara and the first Cakravartin viz. Bharata. He knowledge of the writings of the Brāhmaṇas and of various Arts has not yet been equalled by any Jain writer. Being himself a Brāhmaṇa in his early life, he was acquainted with the Smṛti texts. His knowledge regarding the various *janapadas* is also remarkable.[84] In chapter 16 there is a short account of town-planning. A treatise on the duties of warriors and the Art of governing is to be found in the 42nd chapter. He has also poetically described the six seasons, the moonrise, sunrise etc.[85] Even the beauty of the female body has not escaped his notice.[86] The various love-scenes, portrayed by the poet, fully justify our contention that the Jain poets scrupulously followed the footsteps of earlier Hindu poets in their treatment of love, romance etc. The poet writes in an easy, limpid style and we will be fully justified if we call him the greatest Jain poet of all times.

Guṇabhadra, the great disciple of a great preceptor, as we have already said, is the author of the last portion of the *Ādipurāṇa* and the whole of the *Uttarapurāṇa*.[87] The two poems are together known as the *Mahāpurāṇa*. The *Uttarapurāṇa* runs to 8,000 verses and is therefore a shorter poem compared to the poem of Jinasena I. He had great respect for his preceptor.[88] It was formerly supposed that the *Uttarapurāṇa* was completed in Śaka 820, corresponding to 898 A.D. But Premi has shown[89] that the *Praśasti* of this poem was written by two poets viz. Guṇabhadra and his disciple Lokasena. The first 27 verses of the *Praśasti* was written by Guṇabhadra in which he has expressed the hope that the educated readers should pay all respect to this *Mahāpurāṇa* and make arrangements for a sufficient number of its copies. From verse No. 28 to the end the *Praśasti* was written by Lokasena. We are told by him that the work was consecrated at Baṅkāpura in Śaka 820 when Akālavarṣa i.e. Rāṣṭrakūṭa Kṛṣṇa II was on the throne and Sāmanta Lokāditya was governing the region around that town. Premi suggests[90] that Guṇabhadra was probably not alive at that time and the work was completed much earlier.

Like his *guru*, Guṇabhadra was also a very accomplished poet. In this work he has written about all the Tīrthaṅkaras except Ṛṣabha and other great men of Jain mythology. The story of Rāma as given in chapters 67-68 of this poem is a deliberate distortion of the story of Vālmīki. Daśaratha here like the *Daśaratha Jātaka* is painted as the king of Vārāṇasī. Sītā here is the daughter of Mandodarī, the wife of Rāvaṇa. Rāma's mother is here one Subālā and Lakṣmaṇa, the son of Kaikeyī. The story told in the *Adbhuta Rāmāyaṇa* is similar to the story told by Guṇabhadra. The author has also made several changes in his treatment of the story of the other Hindu epic viz. the *Mahābhārata*. Karṇa is here painted as the real son of Pāṇḍu, who, we are told, committed intercourse incognito with the virgin Kuntī (23. 109 ff.). Karṇa, who was abandoned by his mother, was later rescued by king Āditya (the name is significant), who afterwards asked his barren wife Rādhā to bring him up (23. 112). He further informs us that the system of *prājāpatya* marriage started in ancient India with the marriage of Pāṇḍu and Kuntī (23. 115). The examples of such distortions can easily be multiplied. But unlike other Jain poets, Guṇabhadra has the frankness to ask his readers to consult the original work for details (25. 117).[91] The story of Jīvandhara, as told in chapter 75, is quite interesting and later writers both in Sanskrit and Tamil wrote on it.

Svayambhū, like Vimala and Raviṣeṇa, wrote on the Rāma story. The name of his work is *Paumacariyu*[92] which is written in the Apabhraṁśa language. In the very opening stanza of the first Sandhi of his work the poet declares that he has taken on hand to narrate the Rāma story after keeping in view the *Ārṣa*. The colophons of all the Parvans of Raviṣeṇa's *Padmapurāṇa* begin with it—*ityārṣe Śrī Raviṣeṇācāryaprokte Padmapurāṇe*. This makes it clear that Svayambhū's reference pertains to that work. Elsewhere in Svayambhū's work (I. 2.9) we are told that he has embarked upon such a vast theme through the favour of Ācārya Raviṣeṇa.

The work is divided into five Books (called Kāṇḍas) viz. Vijjhāra, Ujjhā, Sundara, Jujjha and Uttara. The books are further divided into Sandhis. Now, the earliest writer to refer to Svayambhū directly is Puṣpadanta, who wrote in 959 A.D.

However as the editor Bhayani has shown[93], Svayambhū could not have written before the second half of the 9th century A.D., as he has referred[94] to Seuṇa-deśa, which was founded by Seuṇcandra I in the 1st half of the 9th century A.D. This country, according to the poet, was washed by the river Bhīmā (Bhīmarahī)[95]. It has been suggested that Svayambhū should be identified[96] with Śrīpāla mentioned by Jinesena I in his *Jayadhavalā* and *Ādipurāṇa*. But there is really no basis for such a surmise since Syayambhū flourished after Jinasena I.

The poet supplies us with some interesting information about the economic condition of India of his days. He mentions a number of countries with their spcial products[97]—betel-leaf of Deulvaḍaya i.e. Devakulapāṭaka, betel-nut of Cedi, *kañcuā* or *kañcuka* of Citrakūṭa, jewel of Ceylon, musk of Nepāla, molasses of Rāmapura, arrow of Pratiṣṭhāna, etc. Another list, preserved by Svayambhū[98], mentions various places along with the beautiful parts of the body for which their women were famous. Since the list is very interesting, we are reproducing it below—

Place	*Part of the body*
Paunāra . . .	Soles of feet
Cedi . . .	Nails
Golla . . .	Fingers
Mākandī . . .	Ankles
Śrīparvata . . .	Knees
Nepāla . . .	Thighs
Karahāṭaka . . .	Waist
Kāñcī . . .	Hips
Gambhīrā . . .	Navel
Siṅgāriya . . .	Back
Elāpura . . .	Breasts
Madhyadeśa . . .	Chest
Paścima-deśa . . .	Shoulders
Dvārakā . . .	Arms

Place	*Part of the body*
Sindhava . . .	Wrists
Kaccha . . .	Neck
Karṇāṭaka . . .	Teeth
Tuṅgaviṣaya . . .	Nose
Ujjayinī . . .	Eyes
Citrakūṭa . . .	Forehead
Kanauj . . .	Ears
Dakṣiṇadeśa . . .	Courteous manners

Svayambhū, elsewhere in his poem,[99] has given a list of peoples,[100] which is quite interesting from the point of view of historical geography.

There are indications in Svayambhū's text that he was helped by his son called Tribhuvana-Svayambhū, who was also known as Kavirāja Cakravartī.[101] It appears that the son had put a finishing touch to the works of his father. A second work written by Svyambhū and his son is known. This is the *Riṭṭhaṇemicariyu* or *Harivaṁśapurāṇa*. This work[102] runs to 18,000 verses and has altogether 112 Sandhis and 3 Books (*Kāṇḍas*) viz. Yādava, Kuru and Yuddha. A third work, written by the father and son called *Paṁcamicariyu* has not yet been discovered.[103]

Among other Digambara writers of the 9th century we can mention the names of Ugrāditya, Śākaṭāyana, Mahāvīrācārya and Amoghavarṣa I. Ugrāditya was the author of the *Kalyāṇakāraka*,[104] a medical treatise, written according to the testimony of the poet, during the reign of Amoghavarṣa I. We are further told that the author belonged to the Deśīgaṇa, Pustakagaccha, Pansogavalliśākhā of the Mūlasaṅgha of the line of Kundakunda. One Lalitakīrti Ācārya was his colleague, and his *guru* was Śrīnandī in whose establishment at Rāmagiri, which was situated in the level plains of Veṅgī in the country of Trikaliṅga, that Ugrāditya wrote his treatise, That monks belonging to the Deśīgaṇa resided in this part of India is proved by a 10th century inscription found from Udaygiri-Khaṇḍagiri, which has already been discussed.[105] The author further claims that the discourse on the uselessness of meat diet was delivered in the court of Śrī Nṛpatuṅga Vallabha Mahārājādhirāja, who was none other than Amoghavarṣa I.[106] A few scholars refuse to believe that this work was composed at such an early date[107]; but there is no genuine basis which can confirm their suspicion.

The work, written in Sanskrit, is divided into two parts with 25 chapters. It further appears that the author was acquainted with the earlier medical texts including those written by Hindu and Jain authorities. It further appears that the author was deeply indebted to the works of medicine, written by Samantabhadra and Pūjyapāda.

Śākaṭāyana, who was also a contemporary of Amoghavarṣa I was the author of the *Śabdānuśāsana* and its commentary *Amoghavṛtti*[108]. The work was certainly written in the second half of the 9th century. He belonged to the Yāpanīya Saṅgha as we learn from the commentary on *Nandīsūtra* by Malayagiri[109].

Mahāvīrācārya was the celebrated author of the *Gaṇitasārasaṅgraha*[110], which was written, according to the testimony of the writer, during the reign of Amoghavarṣa I, who is described by him as the follower of Syādvāda,[111] The author was acquainted with *Brāhmasphuṭasiddhānta* of Brahmagupta. It has been claimed[112] that he was much advanced in his field and his treatment of geometrical problems deserves special notice. The work was very much popular in South India and a Telegu translation appeared in the 11th century.[113]

Amoghavarṣa I, who had special love for the Jain religion, is the author of the *Praśnottara Ratnamālā*,[114] which also exists in Tibetan translation.[115] The work begins with an adoration to Vardhamāna[116] which shows that it is a Jain poem. The author displays typical Jain sentiment in his work, which is natural for a person with Jain leanings.

The most remarkable Digambara Jain author in the first half of the 10th century was Hariṣeṇa, the author of the *Bṛhatkathākośa*.[117] Fortunately for us, he not only states the year of its composition, but also refers to the king in whose kingdom, his work was composed. In the *Praśasti*[118] he gives the date both in the Śaka and Vikrama years. It was composed in Vikrama 989 or Śaka 853, corresponding to 931-932 A.D., when Vinayādikapāla was the ruling sovereign. The place of its composition is given as Vardhamāna, where Jinasena II had started the composition of his *Harivaṁśa.* Emperor Vinayādikapāla is to be identified with the Pratīhāra Vināyakapāla, who ruled according to his Asiatic Society plate in 931 A.D.[119] Several other inscriptions of this sovereign are known.[120] The kingdom of this king has been compared with that of Indra (*Śakropamānake*).[121] Hariṣeṇa's evidence proves that the Pratīhāra suzerainty was accepted in Gujarat as late as 931 A.D. The poet, like the author of the *Harivaṁśa* (783 A.D.), belonged to the Punnāṭa Saṅgha.

In the *Praśasti*[122] the poet thus gives his spiritual ancestry: There was that Maunibhaṭṭāraka, the full moon in the firmament of the Punnāṭa Saṅgha. His disciple was Śrīhariṣeṇa; the disciple of the latter was Bharatasena,, a man of encyclopaedic learning. And our author (who describes himself as devoid of learning and intelligence) was the disciple of this great Bharatasena. He further states that he has written his poem on the basis of the *Ārādhanā,*[123] which is surely the original work of Śivārya.

The *Bṛhatkathākośa* is an extremely informative work. The author not only shows his thorough acquaintance with the two epics,[124] but also with the original *Bṛhatkathā.*[125] It is also apparent that the poet was thoroughly at home with the earlier Digambara literature. There is an extremely interesting reference to the famous Sun-temple (*Ādityabhavana*) of Mūlasthāna or Multan (98.110), which was destroyed by the Muslims within 60 years of the composition of this poem. The author describes the great Bhadrabāhu as a resident of Devakoṭṭapura, which was situated in Puṇḍravardhana, which was also known as Varendra (131.1; 96.1). The city of Mathurā is described as abounding in Jain temples (2.1); a similar description of Ujjayinī is also to be found (3.2). He has also shown his acquaintance with the *Pañcatantra* and one story[126] including the verse (*aparīkṣitaṁ na kartavyaṁ* etc.) is taken directly from that work. The religious rivalry between the Jains and Buddhists are described in the story No. 12, where we have references to *Buddha-*

ratha and *Jinaratha* (12.116). Chariot-procession in honour of Buddha is referred to even by Fa-hien.[127] The Kāyasthas are ridiculed in story Nos. 23 and 25. They are denounced in a number of Brāhmaṇical works including the *Yājñavalkyasmṛti*.[128] Reference to 18 scripts is also found in this poem (22.4). This poem also contains one of the early references to 18 Purāṇas (126.175). There is an interesting story connected with Kārttikeya (No. 136) and like the *Mahābhārata* the town of Rohīṭeka (Rohītaka) is connected with the worship of that deity (136.23). Worship of Durgā was popular at Nasik 71.8 ff.) ; Rāmagiri is described as situated in the junction of Kaliṅgaviṣaya and Andhraviṣaya (59.194) and it is apparent that this Rāmagiri is to be identified with its namesake, mentioned in the *Kalyāṇakāraka*. There was great rivalry between Hinduism and Jainism (No. 33). In this connection there is a reference to *Brahmaratha* (33.9). We are also told the origin of Vindhyavāsinī by Hariṣeṇa (106.248 ff.) The Śvetāmbaras are denounced as holding false doctrine (131.69) and we are further told in this connexion that the Śvetāmbaras (*Ardhaphālakāḥ*) originated at Valabhī, which is described as situated in Saurāṣṭra.

The above discussion abundantly shows that this work of Hariṣeṇa is one of the representative Digambara Jain texts of the early mediaeval period. It is surely one of the important source-books for the historian of the Jain religion.

Let us now turn our attention to the two great Digambara literary luminaries of the second half of the 10th century A.D. The first was the celebrated Puṣpadanta and the second was Somadeva. Puṣpadanta is the author of the following three works—*Tisatthimahāpurisaguṇālaṅkāru* (*Triṣaṣṭimahāpuruṣaguṇālaṅkāra*), *Nāyakumāracariyu* (*Nāgakumāracarita*) and *Jasaharacariyu* (*Yaśodharacarita*), all of which were written in Apabhraṁśa.

The first work is also known as the *Mahāpurāṇa*.[129] It is divided into two parts viz. *Ādipurāṇa* and *Uttarapurāṇa*. The second part also includes the *Padmapurāṇa* and *Harivaṁsapurāṇa*. The entire work runs to some 20,000 verses and has altogether 142 Sandhis (chapters). The work, according to the testimony of the poet, was written under the patronage of Bharata, who was the minister of Kṛṣṇa III. The work was completed in Śaka 887 corresponding to 965 A.D. He was at that time a resident of Mānyakheṭa. Puṣpadanta was originally a Brahmin Saiva, but afterwards became a Digambara ascetic.[130]

Puṣpadanta was undoubtedly the greatest poet of the Apabhraṁśa language. He carries to perfection the possibilities of Apabhraṁśa as a vehicle of poetry. The *Mahāpurāṇa*, which delineates the lives of 63 great men, is undoubtedly one of the finest poems of the 10th century. In numerous places of this poem he shows his great poetic power and some of the verses praising Bharata, his patron, are written in chaste Sanskrit. We further learn from some of the subjective verses of the work that Puṣpadanta was a man of delicate temperament and health. He had several titles of which *Abhimānameru, Kāvyaratnākara, Kavikulatilaka, Sarasvatīnilaya* etc. deserve special mention. It has further been conjectured that that the poet in his earlier life had some bitter experience and had to leave his original home.[131] He was however cordially welcomed by the minister Bharata at Mānyakheṭa, where all his creative writings were produced.

The *Nāgakumāracarita*[132] is a short work consiting of nine Sandhis. It appears that even at the time of its composition Kṛṣṇa III was on the throne of Mānyakheṭa and this city still enjoyed rare prosperity. It was composed in the palace of Nanna, the son of Bharata, his earlier patron. The *Yaśodhara-carita*[133] is another beautiful work consisting of four Sandhis. The story of Yaśodhara was a favourite theme with the Jain poets and celebrated literary luminaries like Somadeva, Vādirāja and others have written on it. This poem was also written at the residence of Nanna, when Mānyakheṭa was virtually a ruined and deserted city. We must remember that according to Dhanapāla's *Pāiyalacchī* Mānyakheṭa was plundered by the Mālava army in V.S. 1029, corresponding to 972 A.D. Probably Khoṭṭiga was the reigning king when this calamity befell Mānyakheṭa, Even in the *Mahāpurāṇa* there is a verse[134] which refers to the sack of Mānyakheṭa by the king of Dhārā. This particular verse was probably composed seven years after the composition of the *Mahāpurāṇa*. We just do not know what happened to the poet or his new patron after the fall of Mānyakheṭa.[135]

The exact contemporary of Puṣpadanta was Somadeva, who as we have already noticed, in a previous chapter, is mentioned in an inscription of Śaka 888, when Kṛṣṇa III was the sovereign king.[136]

Three works of Somadeva have already been published. They are *Nītivākyāmṛta*, *Yaśastilakacampū* and *Adhyātmataraṅgiṇī*. The *Nītivākyāmṛta*,[137] according to its commentator,[138] was written at the request of Mahendrapāla, king of Kanauj. Raghavan proposed his identification with Mahendrapāla II, who is known from an inscription of V.S. 1003 corresponding to 946 A.D.[139] Now we definitely know from the *Yaśastilakacampū* that it was written in Śaka 881 corresponding to 949 A.D. It follows therefore that the *Nītivākyāmṛta* was written before he *Yaśastilakacampū*. However in the *Praśasti* of the *Nītivākyāmṛta* Somadeva is described as the author of the *Yaśodharacarita*. Raghavan and Premi[140] have opined that this *Praśasti* was added afterwards. It appears that Somadeva started his career at Kānyakubja and afterwards migrated to the South. We observed in a previous chapter that Somadeva was probably a Jain monk of Bengal, belonging to the Gauḍasaṅgha. Afterwards he lived in the Pratīhāra kingdom from there he migrated to the Sapādalakṣa country.

The *Nītivākyāmṛta* is largely based on the the *Arthaśāstra* of Kauṭilya and is written in prose. However it is surprising that nowhere in this work the author has cared to mention that great authority. Some earlier authorities like Śukra, Bhīṣma, Viśālākṣa etc., who are mentioned by Kauṭilya, are however referred to by Somadeva in this work. The language is attractive, which is but natural for a genius like Somadeva.

The *Yaśastilakacampū*[141] is one of the finest novels in the Sanskrit literature and, in some respects, it is similar to the *Kādambarī* of Bāṇa, which is a model for Somadeva. The conversion of the cruel king of the Yaudheyas viz. Māridatta, who is described as a devotee of the goddess Caṇḍamāri, to Jainism is the theme of the novel. It is basically based on a story of the *Uttarapurāṇa*. As we have already observed, he story of

Yaśodhara was extremely popular among the early Jain writers. The author of the *Kuvalayamālā*[142] is the first writer (Śaka 700) to refer to the story of this prince of Ujjayinī written by Pravañjana. Afterwards Haribhadra treated it in his 4th Book of his *Samarāiccakahā*. Hariṣeṇa and Puṣpadanta also wrote on Yaśodhara's adventures. However, there is little doubt that Somadeva is the most successful of those who have written on this subject. The work is also rich in culturai details and the students of social and cultural history of India can use this work with profit.[143] The third published work of Somadeva viz. the *Ādhyatmataraṅgiṇī*[144] is also known as the *Yogamārga,* and as the name indicates, it deals with spiritual matters. A commentary on it was written in the first half of the 12th century by Gaṇadharakīrti.

Among other prominent works which were written by the Digambara writers in the 10th century A,D., the folowing may be mentioned—*Neminirvāṇamahākāvya*[145] by Vāgbhaṭa, *Candraprabhacaritamahākāvya*[146] by Vīranandi, *Vardhamānacarita*[147] by Asaga, *Subhāṣitaratnasandoha*[148] by Amitagati, who was a contemporery of Muñja, *Jambudīvapaṇṇati*[149] by Padmanandi and *Pradyumnacaritakāvya*[150] by Mahāsena.

Several works were also written in our period by the Digambara writers in Tamil, Kannaḍa and other languages. The Tamil *Śīvaka-Śindāmani*[151] written by Tiruttakadeva in based on the *Uttarapurāṇa* of Guṇabhadra and was written in the 10th century. It is undoubtedly one of the finest poems written in that language. Several Digambara Jain writers been 850 and 1000 A.D., are known to have written in Kannaḍa. The earliest of these writers was Guṇavarma I who wrote his *Neminātha Purāṇa*[152] in the middle of the 9th century A.D. The three gems of the Kannaḍa literature of the 10th century were all Digambara Jains. They were Pampa, Ponna and Ranna. Pampa is the celebrated author of the *Ādi Purāṇa*[153], which is on the 1st Tīrthaṅkara, Ponna wrote the *Śānti Purāṇa*[154] (story of the 16th Tīrthaṅkara) and Ranna's fame rests on his *Ajita Purāṇa*[155] (life-story of the 2nd Tīrthaṅkara). A patron of Ranna was Cāmuṇḍa Rāya, the celebrated author of the *Cāmuṇḍarāya Purāṇa*[156].

NOTES

1 See the passage quoted in N. Premi's *Jaina Sāhitya aur itihāsa*, p. 147 fn 1. See also *Prastāvanā* to Vol. I *of Ṣaṭkhaṇḍāgama*; for a different view see J. P. Jain, *The Jain Sources* etc., pp. 186 ff.

2 *Ṣaṭkhaṇḍāgama*. Vol. I, pp. 67-72; this work has been published in 16 volumes from Amarāvatī (1939-1958) under the ediorship of H. L. Jain.

3 See J. C. Jain, *Prakrit Sāhitya kā itihāsa* p. 275.

4 See *Jaina Sāhitya kā bṛhad itihāsa*, Vol. IV, p. 60; see also *Prastāvanā*, *Ṣaṭkhaṇḍāgama*, Vol. I, pp. 46-53.

5 See in this connexion J. P. Jain, *Jain Sources etc.*, p. 188; see also *J. B. B. R. A. S.*, Vol. XVII p. 226; see for further details, Premi, *op. cit.*, pp. 143 f.

6 Edited with the *Cūrṇī* of Yativṛṣabha by H. L. Jain, Calcutta, 1955.

7 See *J. S. B. I.*, Vol. IV, p. 89.

8 *Loc. cit.*

9 *Ibid.*, pp. 91-1000,

10 Edited in several volumes from Mathurā, 1944-63.

11 For the relevant verse see Premi, *op. cit.*, p. 140 fn. 2.

12 Edited (Bhāratīya Jñānapīṭha), Varanasi, 1947-58.

13 Published in two parts (MDJM) from Bombay (Vikrama Saṁvat 1977 and 1980).

14 See Ghatge's paper in *I.H.Q.*, 1935: set also Jain, J. C., *op. cit.*, p. 311.

15 See Jain, *Jain Sources etc.*, p. 126; see also *Jain Antiquary*, Vol. XII, pp. 19-23; see in this connexion Winternitz, *H.I.L.*, Vol. II, p. 577 fn. 2

16 Edited with the commentaries of Aparājita and Āśādhara, Sholapur, 1935. An earlier edition was published from Bombay, V.S. 1989.

17 See Jain, J. C., *op. cit.*, p. 308.

18 See *supra*, p. 103.

19 Ed. Bhāratīya Jñānapīṭha, 1974, p. 14.

20 See H. L. Jain, *Nagpur University Journal*, No. 9; see also J. P. Jain, *op. cit.*, pp. 130 f.

21 See Premi, *op. cit.*, pp. 80 ff.

22 For the original verse see Premi, *op. cit.*, p. 2 fn. 4.

23 Edited in two volumes H. L. Jain and A. N. Upadhye, Sholapur, 1943, 1951.

24 See Upadhye, Introduction. Vol. II, p. 4.

25 *Ibid.*, p. 5.

26 IV. 1508.

27 IV. 1504.

28 See Chatterjee, A. K., *Ancient Indian Literary and Cultural Tradition*, pp. 100 f.

29 IV. 1481.

30 See J. P. Jain, *op. cit.*, p. 137.

31 I. 65

32 Story No. 156.

33 Edited by A. N. Upadhye, 1960 in Rājacandra Jaina Śāstramālā.

34 See *Jaina Sources* etc., p. 127.

35 See Lüders, *List*, No. 71.

36 Introd., p. 69.

37 Edited in 4 volumes with the commentaries of Abhayacandra and Keśavavarṇin, Calcutta, 1921. For other editions see *J. S. B. I.*, Vol. IV, p. 133 fn. 4.

38 Edited in M.D.J.M. series, Bombay, V.S. 1974.

39 Edited by Premi, Bombay, V.S. 1974.

40 Verses 49-50 which are quoted by Premi in his *Jaina Sāhitya* etc., p. 175 fn. 1

41 Edited and published with the commentary of Abhayanandi Muni in the Pandit, N.S., Vols. 31-34.

42 Quoted by Premi, *op. cit.*, p. 43 fn. 1.

43 Premi, *op. cit.*, pp. 45 f.

44 See *J.S.B.I.*, Vol. V, p. 11.

45 Edited in M.D.J.M. series, Nos., 29-31, Bambay, V.S. 1985. A new edition in three volumes was published by Bhāratīya Jñānapīṭha, Varanasi, 1958-59.

46 123. 167.

47 123. 166.

48 See Premi's Hindi Preface to Vol. I of *Padmacarita*, pp. 1-3.

49 See *A.I.L.C.T.*, pp. 99 f.

50 Edited by A. N. Upadhye in M.D.J.M. series (No. 40), Bombay, 1938.

51 See for example Premi's Introduction, *Padmacarita*, pp. 2 f.

52 The verse quoted by Upadhye in his Introduction to the *Varāṅgacarita*, p. 10.

53 *Ibid.*, pp. 10-11.

54 *Ibid.*, p. 12.

55 The earliest Siṁhanandi, as we have already noted in a previous chapter, was connected with the Western Gaṅgas. Another monk of that name is mentioned in an inscription from Śravaṇa Belgola dated Śaka 622, see *E.C.*, Vol. II, No. 32.

56 See *supra*, p. 195.

57 See *Samarāiccakahā*, p. 2.

58 Introduction, pp 20 ff.

59 See XV. 136 ff., see XII. 57 ff.

60 XV. 139.

61 XXII. 61 ff.
62 XXIII. 91.
63 XVI. 32 f.
64 VIII 3 f.
65 See ch. XXV.
66 Bhāratīya Jñānapīṭha edition, Varanasi, 1970.
67 See Premi, *op. cit.*, p. 109; see also *J.S.B.I.*, Vol. VI, p. 526.
68 See *J.S.B.I.*, Vol. VI, pp. 527 f; see also Premi, *op. cit.*, p. 111.
69 Premi, *op. cit.*, p. 112 fn. 1.
70 *Loc. cit.*
71 Edited with English translation, Bombay, 1965.
72 Bhāratīya Jñānapīṭha, Varanasi, 1962. An earlier edition was published from Bombay (M.D.J.M.), 1930.
73 See the present Author's 'Jain Harivaṁśa' included in his *A.I.L.C.T.*, pp. 89-107.
74 11.67 ff.
75 52.90.
76 Premi, *op. cit.*, p. 116.
77 66.53.
78 Edited by A. N. Upadhye, *Praśasti*, verse No. 4.
79 See Premi, *op. cit.*, p. 124.
80 Jinasena I has also mentioned Prabhācandra; for the relevant verse see Premi, *op. cit.*, p. 124 fn. 2.
81 The relevant verses regarding all these predecessors of Jinasena II are quoted in Premi's work, pp. 124 ff.
82 Bhāratīya Jñānapīṭha, Varanasi, 1951-54 (in three volumes).
83 See Winternitz *H.I.L.*, Vol. II, p. 498, also *J.S.B.I.*, Vol VI, p. 57.
84 The list quoted in the present Author's *A.I.L. C.T.*, p. 106.
85 9.11; 12.17; 26.148 etc.
86 See 6.69; 70.75.
87 Edited Bhāratīya Jñānapīṭha, Varanasi, 1954; an earlier edition was published from Indore in V.S. 1975.
88 See Premi, *op. cit.*, pp. 138-39.
89 *Ibid.*, pp. 141 f.
90 *Loc. cit.*
91 For further details see the Author's paper enttled 'The Bhārata Tradition in Jain Literature, *J.A.I.H.*, Vol. VII, pp. 159 ff.
92 Edited by H. Bhayani in three volumes 1953-54.
93 See his Introduction to Vol. III of his work, p. 41.
94 69. 63.
95 *Loc. cit.*
96 See J. P. Jain, *op. cit.*, pp. 201 f.
97 Vol. II, p. 192.
98 Vol. II, pp. 224-25.
99 82.6.1-6.

100 The list is quoted in the present Author's *A.I.L.C.T.*, p. 194.
101 See Premi, *op. cit.*, p. 198.
102 *Ibid.*, p. 201.
103 *Ibid.*, p. 203.
104 Published from Sholapur, 1940.
105 Set *supra*, p. 177.
106 The relevant line is quoted in J. P. Jain, *Jain Sources* etc., p. 206 fn. 1.
107 See *J.S.B.I.*, Vol. V, p. 231 ; see also Premi, *op. cit.*, p. 49 footnote.
108 See for further details *I.A.*, Vol. 43, pp. 205-212 ; Vol. 44, pp. 275-279 ; *A.B.O.R.I.*, Vol. I, pp. 7-12 ; and Premi, *op cit.*, pp. 155 ff.
109 Quoted in Premi's work, p. 157 fn. 1.
110 Published with an English translation by M. Rangacharya, Madras, 1912.
111 See Premi, *op. cit.*, p. 151 and footnote 6.
112 See *J.S.B.I.*, Vol. V, p. 161.
113 *Ibid.*, p. 162.
114 Edited by K. P. Pathak, Bombay.
115 Set Bhandarkar, *Early History of the Deccan*, p. 95 and Premi, *op. cit.*, p. 151.
116 The *śloka* quoted in Premi's work, p. 151 fn. 1.
117 Edited A. N. Upadhye, Bombay, 1943.
118 *Praśasti*, verses 11-12.
119 See *I.A.*, Vol. 15, pp. 138-41 ; see also H. C. Ray, *D.H.N.I.*, Vol. I, pp. 584-85.
120 See G. C. Choudhary, *P.H.N.I.* etc., pp. 43 f.
121 *Praśasti*, vs. 13.
122 Verses 3-7.
123 Verse No. 8.
124 Cf. the story Nos. 43, 58, 83, 84, 89, 96 and 122.
125 Cf. Nos. 143 and 153.
126 No. 102.2.
127 Legge's translation, p. 15.
128 I. 336—"*pīḍyamānāḥ prajā rakṣet Kāyasthaiśca ciśeṣataḥ*.
129 Edited in 3 Volumes by P. L. Vaidya, Bombay, 1937-41.
130 For further details are Premi, *op. cit.*, 225 ff.
131 See Premi, *op. cit.*, pp. 231 f.
132 Critically edited by H. L. Jain, Karanja, 1933.
133 Ed. P. L. Vaidya, Karanja, 1931.
134 See Premi, *op. cit.*, p. 250.
135 The evidence of the recently discovered *Dharmaparīkṣā* written by Pandit Hariṣeṇa in 987 A.D., proves that within a few years after the composition of the *Mahāpurāṇa* he became famous ; see Premi, *op. cit.*, p. 247.

136 See *supra*, p. 201.

137 Edited in *M.D.J.M.* V.S. 1979; an earlier edition was published by Nirnaysagar Press.

138 Quoted in Premi's work, pp. 180 f.

139 *E.I.*, Vol. 14, p. 176; see also Raghavan in *Jain Siddhānta Bhāskara*, Vol. X, part II.

140 See Premi, *op. cit.* p. 182.

141 Edited in Mahāvīra Jaina Granthamālā, Varanasi, in 2 volumes (1960, 1971); an earlier edition was published by Nirnaysagar Press, Bombay (1901-03).

142 P. 3 (*S.J.G.M.*).

143 For fuller treatment see K. K. Harndiqui, *Yaśastilaka and Indian Culture*, Sholapur, 1945; see also G. C. Jain, *Yaśastilaka kā sāṁskṛtik adhyayan*, Varanasi, 1967.

144 The text of this work is included in *M.D.J.M.*, Vol. XIII entitled *Tattvānuśāsnādisaṅgrahaḥ*, Bombay. V.S. 1975.

145 Nirnaysagar Press, Bombay, 1936.

146 Sholapur, 1970 (Jīvarāja Granthamālā).

147 Edited in 1931 (Sholapur).

148 Nirnaysagar Press, Bombay, 1909.

149 See. Premi, *op. cit.*, pp. 256 ff.

150 *M.D.J.M.*, Bombay, V.S. 1973.

151 See Sastri, *The Coḷas,* pp. 666 f.

152 See *The Age of Imperial Kanauj, pp.* 223 f.

153 *Loc. cit.*

154 *Loc. cit.*

155 *Loc. cit.*

156 See Premi, *op. cit.*, pp. 266 ff.

CHAPTER XIV

Jain Thinkers

The earliest Jain philosopher was Umāsvāti (called Umāsvāmin by the Digambaras), who was the celebrated author of the *Tattvārthādhigama Sūtra*[1], one of the most original works of philosophy, written by any thinker of ancient India. There is a great deal of controversy regarding his date; Satish Chandra Vidyabhusan assigns him to the first century A.D.[2], and frankly speaking, there is nothing in the body of the text, that goes against this date. The author also wrote a commentary[3], according to the Śvetāmbaras, although the Digambaras deny the authenticity of this *Bhāṣya*[4]. But there is irrefutable proof that this commentary was known to the Śvetāmbara monks even in the early 7th century A.D., if not earlier[5]. Both Siddhasena Gaṇi (*circa* 600 A.D.) and Haribhadra (middle of the 8th century) knew this *Bhāṣya*. According to the *Praśasti,* at the end of this *Bhāṣya*, Umāsvāti was a monk belonging to the Uccanāgarī *śākhā*, which according to the *Therāvalī* was a branch of the Koḍiya (Koḷiya) *gaṇa* and was quite popular in the Mathurā region, as we have already noted in a previous chapter. This *śākhā* originated, according to the testimony of that text in the 3rd century B.C. The reference to the *śākhā* of Umāsvāti goes far to destroy the Digambara claim that he was a thinker of that sect. In all probability, he wrote before the birth of the Digambara sect. We further learn from the same *Bhāṣya* that he was a resident of Kusumapura or Pāṭaliputra at the time of its composition. He was a Brāhmaṇa of the Kaubhīṣaṇi *gotra* and his father's name was Svāti and mother was called Vātsī. His preceptor in respect of initiation was Ghoṣanandi Kṣamāśramaṇa and grand-preceptor was Vācakamukhya Śivaśrī. His teacher in respect of education, according to the *Praśasti,* was Vācakācārya Mūla and grand-preceptor was Mahāvācaka Muṇḍpāda.

According to the Digambara *Paṭṭāvalīs*[6] Umāsvāmin was the 6th Digambara monk of the Sarasvatī *gccha*; according to another Digambara tradition he succeeded Kundakunda in 44 A.D.[7] But there is absolutely no doubt that not a single Digambara work or epigraph which makes him a successor of Kundakunda, is earlier than 1000 A.D.[8] As a matter of fact, it can be asserted with confidence, that Umāsvāti was the earlier philosopher and Kundakunda, who was a Southerner, could not have flourished before the 3rd century A.D. There is however nothing to show that Kundakunda was acquainted with the works of Umāsvāti.

The *Tattvārthādhigama Sūtra* has 357 verses and has altogether ten chapters and this is the reason why it is also known as the *Daśādhyāyī*. Writers belonging to both the Śvetāmbara and Digambara sects have written learned commentaries on this text. It is believed that the earliest commentary on this work of Umāsvāti was written by Samantabhadra[9] in 84,000 verses, which was known as the *Gandhahastimahābhāṣya;* it has further been contended that the earliest section of this work is the well-known *Āptamīmāṁsā* or *Devāgamastotra*[10]. But as Jugalkishore Mukhtar[11] has shown there is no proof that the *Gandhahasti* was a commentary on that philosophical treatise of Umāsvāti, and till now no such work has come to light. Therefore we should look upon the *Sarvārthasiddhi* of Pūjyapāda as its earliest available commentary. Several other celebrated savants also wrote commentaries of this treatise of Umāsvāti, which will be discussed afterwards.

It is difficult to make a correct assessment of the influence exercised by Umāsvāti on the Jain thinkers of later times. But it appears that not a single thinker, with the possible exception of Kundakunda and Samantabhadra, was immune from the all-pervading influence of this Brahmin savant. In the *Vividhatīrthakalpa*[12] Jinaprabha refers to Umāsvāti as a writer of 500 texts and a resident of Pāṭaliputra.

After Umāsvāti the most celebrated Jain philosopher was Kundakunda, who is probably the most controversial figure among the early Jain savants. Before we discuss his exact time, we have to refer to the works which are assigned to him, and all of which are very significantly written in the Prakrit language.

The *Ṣaṭkhaṇḍāgamaṭīkā* is assigned to Kundakunda by Indranandi in his *Śrutāvatāra.* This commentary was known as the *Parikarma* and is repeatadly mentioned by Vīrasena in his *Dhavalā.*[13] However, according to another authority this particular commentary was written by Kundakīrti, a disciple of Kundakunda. The work is now lost and Upadhye has doubts regarding Kundakunda's authorship of this commentary.[14]

The eight *Pāhuḍas*[15] which are ascribed to Kundakunda according to Upadhye[16] are quite in tune with the phrasiology of the *Pravacanasāra,* one of the representative works of that philosopher. The *Daṁsaṇapāhuḍa* has 36 verses, *Cāritta* 44, *Bodha* 62, *Bhāva* 163, *Sutta* 27, *Mokkha* 106, *Liṁga* 72 and *Sīla* has 40 verses. In the *Bhāvapāhuḍa,* it is interesting to note, Śivabhūti is mentioned (vs. 53) and this Śivabhūti seems to be identical with the person, who is represented in the Śvetāmbara texts as the founder of the Digambara sect. At the end of the *Bodhapāhuḍa,* we are told, that it is work of the disciple of Bhadrabāhu. However, we cannot identify this Bhadrabāhu with the celebrated contemporary of Candragupta Maurya.

The *Rayaṇasāra*[17] is also ascribed to Kundakunda, and has 162 verses. As Prof. Upadhye points out,[18] a few of the verses of this work are written in Apabhraṁśa, which probably shows that it is not a genuine work of Kundakunda. The *Bārasa-Aṇuvekkhā*[19] has 91 verses. As the name suggests, it deals with twelve reflections which should be cultivated for the stoppage of Karmic influx. It was a fascinating subject with the Jain authors of both the sects,[20] Some of the *gāthās* are common with the 8th chapter of the *Mūlācāra.* It has further been pointed out[21] that Pūjyapāda in his *Sarvārthasiddhi*[22] quotes five *gāthās* from this text of Kundakunda, which are found in the same order in the present text of that work. The *Niyamasāra*[23] seems to be a genuine work of Kundakunda and it has altogether 187 verses. It has a commentary by Padmaprabha, who flourished around 1000 A.D. This same commentator has quoted the verses of Amṛtacandra, who wrote commentaries on three *Pāhuḍas* of Kundakunda.[24] There is a discussion on the three jewels namely Right Faith, Right Knowledge and Right

Conduct in this work. The *Pañcāstikāyasāra*.[25] is preserved in two recensions, one by Amṛtacandra which has 173 verses, and the other by Jayasena which has 181 verses. As Upadhye[26] points out, this work is a mere compilation as its original name viz. *Paṁcatthiyasaṁgaha* suggests.

The finest and most popular work of Kundakunda appears to be the *Samayasāra*,[27] which has 415 verses, according to the earlier commentator Amṛtacandra (circa 10th century), and 439 *gāthās*, according to Jayasena, who flourished in the second half of the 12th century A.D. The Sāṅkhya doctrine is criticised in *gāthās* 117, 122 and 340; there is also reference to *Do-kiriyā-vāda* which was first preached by Ārya Gaṅga 228 years after Mahāvīra. The *Pravacanasāra*[28] has 275 *gāthās* according to Amṛtacandra, and 311 according ta Jayasena. It is a very important text of the Digambara Jains.

Kundakunda has almost become a legendary figure and hundreds of stories are told about him by the Digambara Jains. Various dates have been suggested for him and Upadhye, a very competent scholar, would place him in the 1st century A.D.[29] However, it appears that Upadhye has mainly relied on the evidence of the Mercara plates of Śaka 388 which are definitely spurious;[30] even if we accept it to be a genuine copy of an older record, we cannot assign the earliest of the six monks, mentioned here, before 325 A.D. (taking 25 years for each generation), who is delineated as belonging to the *anvaya* of Kundakunda. It is significant that in no genuine record of the early Gaṅgas, Kundakunda is mentioned by name. As a matter of fact, the *anvaya* of Kundakunda appears only in the records of South India, which were inscribed after 900 A.D. This however does not prove that Kundakunda never existed in reality. As we have already pointed out, Pūjyapāda definitely quotes a few verses from the *Bārasa-Anuvekkhā*; and the date of Pūjyapāda is fortunately now known. Devasena in his *Darśanasāra*[31] informs us that the Drāviḍa Saṅgha was founded by Vajranandi, the disciple of Pūjyapāda in the Vikrama year 526 corresponding to 468 A.D. Therefore, we have to assign Pūjyapāda, the teacher of Vajranandi in the first half of the

5th century A.D. And since Pūjyapāda knows Samantabhadra,[32] who probably flourished after Kundakunda, we have to assign the latter in the early 4th century A.D., which is the date suggested for him even by the writer of the Mercara plates. The present village of Koṇḍakunde[33], situated in the Anantapur district of Andhra Pradesh, may probably represent the original native-place of this Digambara savant.

Samantabhadra, like Kundakunda, is regarded as a great Digambara savant and one of the most powerful exponents of the doctrine of *Syādvāda*. But like Kundakunda his personal life is shrouded in obscurity. According to the colophons of a few manuscripts he was the son of the king of Uragapura (Tiruchirapalli), which is said to be included in the Phaṇimaṇḍala.[34] A few other manuscripts, call him by the name Śāntivarman[35] and it is tempting to identify him with his namesake of the Kadamba dynasty. However such speculations do not lead us anywhere and all we know about his personal achievements are to be found for the first time in the 11th century *Kathākośa*[36] of Prabhācandra, who was a contemporary of Jayasiṁha of Dhārā. In this work Samantabhadra is represented as calling himself the naked ascetic from Kāñcī. He is further shown as the preceptor of Śivakoṭi,[37] the author of the *Ārādhanā*. That work delineates him as visiting places like Puṇḍravardhana, Daśapura, Vārāṇasī, Pāṭaliputra, Kāñcī, Mālava, Sindhu, Ṭhakka (Punjab) and Karahāṭaka. It appears that Samantabhadra was an itinerant *sādhu* and was universally respected for his vast learning and mesmeric personality.

Regarding the date of Samantabhadra, this much is certain that he flourished before Pūjyapāda. Formerly scholars like Vidyabhusan or Winternitz were not aware of the evidence supplied by the *Darśanasāra* (933 A.D.) on Pūjyapāda's date and their chronology was therefore based on surmise. Now, happily we know the approximate wate of Pūjyapāda who emphatically mentions Samahtabhadra in his *Jainendra*.[38] The traditional Digambara chronology places him two generations before Devanandi Pūjyapāda[39] and we will be justified in placing Samantabhadra in the last quarter of the 4th century A.D.[40]

Among the works of Samantabhadra the most important and significant is the *Āptamīmāṁsā*,[41] which as we have already said, is also known as the *Devāgama*. This poem has 114 verses, each of which is a beauty in its own right. This work is replete with discussions on logical principles besides a review of the contemporary schools of philosophy including the Advaitavāda. This work, as noted by Vidyabhusan,[42] has been cited by the Hindu philosopher Vācaspati Miśra in explaining Śaṅkara's criticism of the Syādvāda. The earliest commentator of this great philosophical poem of Samantabhadra was Akalaṅka (8th century), followed by Vidyānanda and others. Several commentaries on this work also exist in Kannaḍa, Tamil and other Indian languages,[43] which show that it was looked upon as one of the most precious poems on philosophy by the later Jain thinkers. The second work of Samantabhadra is *Yuktyanuśāsana*[43A] which is a poem of 64 verses and has a Sanskrit commentary by Vidyānanda. It appears from the commentary[44] that this work was composed after the *Āptamīmāṁsā*. Like that poem it is also full of useful discussions. The *Svayambhūstotra*[45] is a poem of 143 verses and it contains *ślokas* in praise of various Tīrthaṅkaras. The highest number of verses (20) are reserved for Arhanātha and the second highest (10) for Neminātha. Mahāvīra has 8 and the others 5 each. The only commentary on it is by Prabhācandra. The 4th work of Samantabhadra is *Jinastutiśataka*[46] which has 116 verses and has a commentary by Narasiṁha Bhaṭṭa. It is a truly theistic poem and therefore very appealing. Nothing is known regarding the date of the commentator.

The *Ratnakaraṇḍakaśrāvakācāra*[47] which is also known as the *Upāsakādhyayana* is a manual of morals, as the name indicates, for the Jain layman. There is little doubt that it is one of the most popular Jain texts and in almost each Digambara Bhāṇḍār one or two copies of this work will be found. The only available Sanskrit commentary on it is by Prabhācandra, about whose exact date there is some doubt, as we have a formidable number of Jain scholars[48] bearing this name. The work has been highly praised by Vādirāja in his *Pārśvanāthacarita*[49], which was completed in Śaka 947 corresponding to 1025 A.D. The commentator Prabhācandra is also full of praise for this work[50]. Authors like Cāmuṇḍarāya and Padmaprabha have also freely used it[51].

Samantabhadra was looked upon as a model by later Jain savants including the great Jinasena I[52] That scholar represents him as a supreme poet, capable of destroying the dense darkness of ignorance by the lightning of his wisdom. Thinkers of later times also are full of praise for Samantabhadra and his works[53]. A number of Samantabhadra's works are now unfortunately lost.

Siddhasena Divākara is identified by some[54] with Kṣapaṇaka, traditionally regarded as one of the nine gems of the court of Vikramāditya. That he flourished in the Gupta period is indirectly proved by the fact that he is mentioned by Pūjyapāda (early 5th century) in his *Jainendra*[55]. He is claimed by both the Śvetāmbaras and Digambaras. According to a tradition, current with both the sects, Siddhasena Divākara performed a miracle during Vikramāditya's time in the celebrated Mahākāla temple of Ujjayinī. He is the author of the two well-known books viz. *Nyāyāvatāra*[56] and *Saṁmatitarka-Sūtra*[57]. Both the works deal with logic. The *Nyāyāvatāra* explains the doctrine of *pramāṇa* (source of valid knowledge) and *Naya* (the method of comprehending things from particular standpoint)[58]. Siddhasena also a wrote a commentary on the famous work of Umāsvāti[59]. This work has been quoted by Siddhasena II who flourished about 600 A.D.[60]. In the 7th-century *Cūrṇī* text viz. *Āvaśyakacūrṇī* of Jinadāsa, Siddhasena Divākara is mentioned[61]. Haribhadra (8th century) was also thoroughly acquainted with the philosophy of Siddhasena Divākara. According to the Śvetāmbaras Siddhasena Divākara was originally a Digambara thinker from Karṇāṭaka and afterwards was defeated and converted by the celebrated Vṛddhavādin[62]. It has also been demonstrated that he flourished before Jinabhadragaṇi[63].

Pūjyapāda, who was also known as Devanandi, as we have already noticed, definitely flourished in the first half of the 5th century. We have already referred to his grammar called *Jainendra.* His *Sarvārthasiddhi*[64] is undoubtedly the greatest and one of the earliest commentaries on the *Tattvārthādhigama Sūtra.* That he was an accomplished logician is evident from this commentary which has been highly praised by later writers. There are a few stories dealing with his life which are practically of no value for the serious historian.

Akalaṅka is undoubtedly one of the greatest names in the history of Indian logic. However, like majority of ancient authors, he gives practically no information regarding his personal life. Only in his *Tattavārtharājavārttika* he informs us that he was the son of the king Laghu Havva[65]. Regarding the identity of this king, nothing is known. However in the *Kathākośa* of Prabhācandra we are told that he was the son of the minister of king Śubhatuṅga of Mānyakheṭa[66] A number of writers beginning from Vādirāja and Prabhācandra refer to Akalaṅka's debating skill and his victory over the Buddhists. The earliest source that refers to this event is a 10th-century inscription of the reign of Būtuga II which has already been noticed[67]. Later Jain writers and authors of epigraphs have referred to this feat of Akalaṅka with evident pride. However regarding the name of the king, in whose reign this feat was accomplished, there is some confusion. As we have already noted, the patron of Akalanka, according to the *Kathākośa* of Prabhācandra was Śubhatuṅga, but the *Akalaṅkacarita*[68] mentions one Sāhasatuṅga in whose reign Akalaṅka defeated the Buddhists. Prabhācandra further informs us that the debate took place in the court of Himaśītala, who was evidently a contemporary of Śubhatuṅga. But the evidence of the *Akalaṅkacarita* is confirmed by the Śravaṇa Belgola inscription No. 67 which refers to Akalaṅka's patron as Sāhasatuṅga, who is generally identified with Dantidurga (middle of the 8th century)[69]. This date for Akalaṅka conflicts with the traditional date viz. Vikrama 700 given to him by later Jain writers[70]. But it appears that Akalaṅka was actually a contemporary of Dantidurga, and flourished in the middle of the 8th century A.D. This should be regarded as the latest date for Akalaṅka since he was known to both Haribhadra and Jinasena I. The suggestion that he was known also to Jinadāsa (7th century) seems gratuitous[71]. It has further been suggested that Himaśītala of Akalaṅka tradition should be identified with the king of Kaliṅga who was a contemporary of Yuan Chwang.[72] But this too is a mere surmise. Since Akalaṅka knows the Buddhist and

Brāhmaṇical scholars, who flourished even in the 7th century, we will be justified in placing him in the 8th century A.D.

Apart from his *Tattvārtharājavārtika*[73] which is a commentary on the famous book of Umāsvāti, Akalaṅka is the reputed author of the *Aṣṭaśatī*,[74] a precious work of Jain philosophy, in 800 verses dealing mainly with logic. It is a commentary on the *Āptamīmāṁsā* of Samantabhadra. Another well-known work on logic by him is the *Nyāyaviniścaya*[75]. His other works are *Laghīyastrayīprakaraṇa* and *Svarūpasambodhana*.[76] A treatise on expiatory rites called *Prāyaścittagrantha*[77] is also ascribed to him, but Akalaṅka's authorship of this work is extremely doubtful[78]. It has 90 *ślokas* and is called *Śrāvakācāra*[79]. The *Pramāṇasaṁgraha*[80] contains 87 *kārikās* and is also a work of logic. Another work called *Siddhiviniścaya* is also ascribed to Akalaṅka[81].

Haribhadra the great Śvetāmbara savant, was undoubtedly one of the greatest thinkers of the 8th century. He was not only a successful literary artist, but also, as Udyotana asserts, an authority on logic. Udyotana claims that he was taught logic by Haribhadra, and this information practically settles the date of Haribhadra. The *Kuvalayamālā*, from which this information has been obtained, was completed in Śaka 700. The earliest writer, who quotes from Haribhadra is the Buddhist Śāntarakṣita, who in his *Tattvasaṅgraha* (8th century) ascribes the verse to an Ācārya Sūri, who is no other than Haribhadra[82].

Haribhadra, as we have already said in a previous chapter, wrote in both Sanskrit and Prakrit. Being himself a Brāhmaṇa by birth, he was thoroughly well-acquainted with the Brāhmaṇical works of philosophy. His well-known commentary on Diṅnāga's *Nyāyapraveśa*[83] proves that he was equally at home with the Buddhist logic. As a matter of fact, because of Haribhadra's commentary this great work of the celebrated Diṅnāga, has survived in Sanskrit. His other works are only available in translations. Another well-known work of Haribhadra is the *Anekāntajayapatākā*[84]. It has altogether four chapters in which he refutes the doctrines of Buddhist and Brāhmaṇical schools. Since he refers to Mallavādin in this work, it appears, that it is one of his latest works[85]. The *Ṣaḍdarśanasamuccaya*[86], a summary of the six philosophical systems in 87 verses, is the first work dealing with the six philosophical systems viz. Bauddha, Nyāya, Sāṁkhya, Jaina, Vaiśeṣika, and Jaimini. There is a short section on Cārvāka's philosophy. Haribhadra emphatically says that Nyāya and Vaiśeṣika cannot be separated from one another, although he treats them separately. There is no discussion on the Yoga and Vedānta systems. Haribhadra, unlike many orthodox Jain philosophers, have discussed other systems with some amount of impartiality. In another work called *Lokatattvanirṇaya*[87], a work written in chaste Sanskrit, he shows his scholarship and depth of feeling. The works like *Yogabindu*[88], *Yogadṛṣṭisamuccaya*[89] and *Dharmabindu*[90] are written primarily for the Jains. The *Yogabindu* has 526 verses; the *Yogadṛṣṭisamuccaya* shows has depth as philosopher. The *Dharmabindu* has 8 chapters and has a commentary by Municandra. This work is a manual of morals and asceticism. The author deals with the duties of both layman and monk. In the last few verses of this work he describes the bliss of the perfect soul in Nirvāṇa. As Winternitz remarks "the title 'Drop of the Religion' is an expression of modesty. As the drop of water is to the ocean, so is this work to the religion of the Jinas"[91]. Another text dealing with doctrinal matters is the *Śāstravārtāsamuccaya*[92]. Here also he has referred to the views of Buddhist logicians. The *Lalitavistarā*[93], is said to have been composed for Siddharṣi[94], the author of the *Upamitibhavaprapañcākathā*, which is impossible. Siddharṣi, as we have already seen in a previous chapter, flourished long after Haribhadra. Another interesting work of Haribhadra is the *Upadeśapada*[95], which is written in Prakrit and has a commentary by Municandra.

Another Jain logician of the 8th century was Mallavādin who wrote a commentary called *Dharmottaraṭippanaka*[96] on the *Nyāyabindu* of Buddhist Dharmakīrti. This Mallavādin seems to be identical with his namesake mentioned in the Surat plates of Karka (821 A.D.)[97] and described as the grand-preceptor of Aparājita, the donee of the grant. If this is accepted, we have to assign Mallavādin in the first half of the 8th century and therefore it is not surprising that he is mentioned by Haribhadra, as noted above. It should also be remembered that the Śvetāmbara tradition makes him a nephew of the last Śilāditya of Valabhī (2nd half of the 8th century)

Vidyānanda, who lived in the 9th century, was a well-known logician of the early mediaeval period. According to a later writer[98] he was a resident of Pāṭaliputra. He was also known as Pātrakeśari. In the colophons of several of his works a number of Western Gaṅga kings ruling in the later part of the 8th century and the first half of the 9th century are mentioned[99] This shows that he lived around 800 A.D. Further, in his *Aṣṭa-sahasrī*[100] he admits that he was greatly helped by the advice of Kumārasena, who may be identical with the saint of the same name, mentioned in the *Harivaṁśa*[101] of Jinasena II (783 A.D.). We should also remember that Vidyānanda-Pātra-keśari is also mentioned by Jinasena I in his *Ādipurāṇa* [102].

The principal work of Vidyānanda is the *Āptamīmāṁsālaṁkṛti*[103] also called *Aṣṭaśatībhṣāya* and *Aṣṭasahasrī*. It contains an elaborate exposition of various logical principles. In the opening and closing lines of this text he makes an indirect reference to Samantabhadra and Akalaṅka respectively. In chapter X he openly says that he followed the *Aṣṭaśatī* of Akalaṅka in explaining the *Āptamīmāṁsā*. Another important work of Vidyānanda is the *Āptaparīkṣā*[104], which consists of 124 verses, is generally based on the *Āptaparīkṣā*. The *Pramāṇa-parīkṣā*[105] is a work in Sanskrit prose and it is definitely a contribution to Jain logic. The *Ślokavārttika*[106] is a commentary on Umāsvāti's famous work. Vidyānanda shows his thorough acquaintance with almost all Buddhist and Brāhmaṇical logicians. His other works include *Satyaśāsanaparīkṣā*[107] and *Vidyānanda-mahodaya*[108]. In the former Vidyānanda has made an examination of Indian philosophical systems.

Māṇikyanandi is the author of the *Parīkṣāmukhasūtra*[109] which has 207 Sūtras and is based on Akalaṅka's *Nyāyaviniścaya*. It has a commentary by Prabhācandra called *Prameyakamala-mārtaṇḍā*[110]. Vidyānanda, Māṇikyanandi and Prabhācandra are pronounced as contemporaries by K. B. Pathak[111]. But in the printed edition of the *Prameyakamalamārtaṇḍa,* we are told, that Prabhācandra, the disciple of Padmanandi Siddhānta composed it during the reign of Bhoja of Dhārā[112]. But this is quite puzzling as Jinasena I in his *Ādipurāṇa* mentions *Candrodaya* as the work of Prabhācandra and actually in his *Nyāyakumunda-candrodaya* Prabhācandra claims that he is also the author of the *Prameyakamalamārtaṇḍa*[113]. It therefore appears, and as suggested by Mukhtar[114] that the printed edition has referred to a commentator, bearing the same name. Let us further remember that in the Jain literature there are no less than 20 Prabhācandras[115]. The *Prameyakamalamārtaṇḍa* refers to a number of Buddhist logicians including Dharmakīrti, Diṅnāga and others. Amṛtacandra, who lived around 900 A.D. is the author of the *Tattvārthasāra*[116] and *Ātmakhyāti*[117]. The *Tattvārthasāra* has 618 verses and is divided into nine chapters. The seven *padārthas* are discussed in this work. The *Ātmakhyāti* is the name of the author's commentary on *Samayasāra* of Kundakunda.

Two great Śvetāmbara logicians flourished in the last quarter of the 10th century. One was Pradyumnasūri of Rājagaccha, who was eleventh in descent from Māṇikyacandra, the author of the *Pārśvanāthacaritra* (1219 A.D.). So we have to place Pradyumna in the 3rd quarter of the 10th century. In the *Pārśvanāthacaritra* we are told that Pradyumna defeated the Digambaras in debate at Veṅkapaṭṭa[118]. His disciple Abhayadeva, who flourished around 1000 A.D., is the author of the *vṛtti*[119] on *Saṁmatimahātarka* of Siddhasena Divākara. His another work is *Vādamahārṇava*[120], which is not available at present, but which is repeatedly mentioned by the writers of the Rājagaccha. "He is described as the lion that roared at ease in the wild forest of books on logic. That the rivers of various conflicting opinions might not sweep the path of the good, Abhayadeva wrote his *Vādamahārṇava*".[121]

The above discussion shows that a great number of Jain thinkers of both the sects wrote philosophical and logical texts and enriched the ancient Indian philosophical literature by their solid contributions. Even in the later medieval period Jain metaphysicans and logicians continued to write thought-provoking texts, which will be discussed in the next volume of the present work.

NOTES

1 Edited by J. L. Jaini, Arrah, 1920; for other editions see Winternitz, *H.I.L.*, Vol. II, p. 578 fn. 3.

2 *A History of Indian Logic*, Calcutta, p. 168.

3 This *Bhāṣya* is included in the edition published by the Asiatic Society, Calcutta (1903-05).

4 See in this connexion J. P. Jain, *Jain Sources* etc., p. 135.

5 As noted by Sukhlal (English translation of his Hindi work on *Tattvārthasūtra*), p. 21 even Jacobi (*Z.D.M.G.*, Vol. 60, pp. 287 ff) accepts the authenticity of this *Bhāṣya*; see also p. 34 of Sukhlal's work.

6 See Hoernle in *I.A.*, Vol. XX, 1891, p. 391.

7 See J. P. Jain, *op. cit.*, p. 136.

8 As noted by Sukhlal, *op. cit.*, p. 114, the earliest epigraph referring to Umāsvāti as belonging to the *anvaya* of Kundakunda is No. 47 dated Ṣaka 1047 from Ṣravaṇa Belgola. Premi also does not believe that Umāsvāti has anything to do with Kundakunda, see Sukhlal, pp. 111 ff. Elsewhere Premi has tried to show that Umāsvāti was probably a monk belonging to the Yāpanīya Saṅgha, see *Jaina Sāhitya aur itihāsa*, pp. 533 ff., which is clearly untenable.

9 See Vidyabhusan, *op. cit.*, p. 182.

10 See Winternitz, *op. cit.*, p. 581.

11 See his "Svāmī Samantabhadra" in Hindi included in his edition of the *Ratnakaraṇḍakaśrāvakācāra* (*M.D.J.M.*, No. 24), pp. 212 ff.

12 P. 69.

13 See *J.S.B.I.*, Vol. IV, p. 60.

14 See his Introduction to *Pravacanasāra*, Bombay, 1935. p. XVIII.

15 These *Pāhuḍas* are edited by P. L. Soni in *M.D.J.M.* (No. 17) Series, V.S. 1977. Of these, with the exception of *Limga* and *Sīlapāhuḍas* all others have commentaries by Ṣrutasāgara.

16 Upadhye, *op. cit.*, p. XXXVII.

17 This text is included in the M.D.J.M. (No. 17) edition which includes the *Pahuḍlas*.

18 See his Introduction to *Pravacanasāra*, p. XXXIX.

19 Included in the *M.D.J.M.* No. 17 edition.

20 See Upadhye, *op. cit.*, p. XXXIX footnote.

21 *Ibid.*, p. XXI.

22 Kolhapur edition, pp. 90 f.

23 Edited by Jaina Grantharatnākara Kāryālaya, Bombay. 1916.

24 See Jain, J. C., *Prakrit Sàhitya kā itihāsa*, p. 300.

25 Edited in *Sacred Books of the Jains* series, Vol. III by Prof. A. Chakravarti, Arrah, 1920; for other editions of this text see Upadhye, *op. cit.*, p. XLII fn. 4.

26 Upadhye, *op. cit.*, p. XLIV.

27 Edited by J. L. Jaini in *S.B.J.*, Vol. VIII, Lucknow, 1930; for other editions, see Upadhye, *op. cit.*, p. XLV fn. 1.

28 Edited A. N. Upadhye, Bombay, 1935.

29 *Ibid.*, pp. XIX, XXII.

30 See *Epigraphia Carnatica* (revised ed.). 1972, Vol. I, Introduction, pp. X f.

31 P. 24.

32 Cf. *Jainendra*, V. 4.140.

33 For details see Desai, *Jainism in South India* etc., pp. 152 ff.

34 See the life of Samantabhadra in Hindi by Jugalkishore Mukhtar included in his edition of the *Ratnakarṇḍakaśrāvakācāra*, p. 4.

35 *Ibid.*, pp. 5 ff.

36 Edited in Bhāratīya Jñānapīṭha, Varanasi, 1974, p. 13.

37 *Ibid.*, p. 14.

38 V. 4. 140.

39 See Jain, *Jain Sources etc.*, p. 145.

40 On the date of Samantabhadra see K. B. Pathak in *A.B.O.R.I.*, Vol. XI, 1930, pp. 149 ff; Pandit Jugalkishore Mukhtar in the same journal, Vol. XV, pp. 67 ff refutes the view of Pathak.

41 Edn. in Jain Grantha Ratnākara and Sanātana Jaina Granthamālā, 1905; for some more details on this see Mukhtar, *op. cit.*, pp. 197 ff.

42 Vidyabhusan, *op. cit.*, pp. 182 ff.

43 See Mukhtar, *op. cit.*, pp. 201 f.

43A Text edited with Vidyānanda's commentary in *M.D.J.M.*, No. 15.

44 See Mukhtar, *op. cit.*, p. 202.

45 For this text see Mukhtar, *op. cit.*, pp. 203 f.

46 *Ibid.*, pp. 204 f.

47 *M.D.J.M.*, No. 24 (edited by Jugalkishore Mukhtar), Bombay, Vikrama Saṁvat 1982. The commentary by Prabhācandra is also included in this edition.

48 See Mukhtar, *op. cit.*, *Prastāvanā*, pp. 53 ff.

49 For the relevant verses from the *Pārśvanāthacarita*, see Mukhtar, *op. cit.*, p. 11.

50 See the edition of Mukhtar, p. 100; set also his *Life* of Samantabhadra in the same work, p. 205.

51 Mukhtar's *Prastāvanā*, pp. 10-11.

52 See Mukhtar's *Life*, pp. 19, 21.

53 *Ibid.*, pp. 19 ff.

54 See Vidyabhusan, *op. cit.*, pp. 173 f; see also J. P. Jain, *op. cit.*, p. 150.

55 V. 1. 7.

56 Edited with English translation by S. C. Vidyabhusan, Calcutta, 1909.

57 Edited in Yaśovijaya Jaina Granthamālā, No. 13; another ed., Poona, 1926.

58 For further discussion, Vidyabhusan, *op. cit.*, pp. 174 ff.

59 The commentary *Tattvānusāriṇī Tattvārthaṭīkā* was printed in Ahmedabad.

60 See Vidyabhusan, *op. cit.,* p. 182 ; set also Winternitz, *op. cit.,* p. 580 fn 1.

61 Vol. I, p. 380

62 For details see *Prabandhakośa,* pp. 15 ff ; see also *Vividhatīrthakalpa,* p. 88.

63 Set Mukhtar quoted in Premi's *Jaina Sāhitya aur itihāsa,* p. 42.

64 Edited Kolhapur, 1904 ; see also Jacobi, *Z.D.M.G.*, Vol. 60, p. 290.

65 See J. P. Jain, *op. cit.*, p. 172 fn 1.

66 See Hiralal, *Catalogue,* Introduction, p. 26.

67 See *supra,* p. 188.

68 See *E.C.*, Vol. II, Introd. pp. 48 ff ; see Fleet, *Dynasties* etc., pp. 32-33 ; and J. P. Jain, *Jain Sources etc.*, p. 172.

69 See *supra,* p. 202.

70 See in this connexion *Life* of Samantabhadra by Mukhtar, p. 125 where the relevant verse from the *Akalaṁkacarita* has been quoted.

71 See in this connexion, J. P. Jain, *op. cit.*, p. 177.

72 See the same scholar in *J.U.P.H.S.*, Vol. III (N.S.), Part II, pp. 108-125.

73 Edited in Sanātana Jaina Granthamālā, Varanasi, 1915.

74 This commentary is published with *Āptamīmāṁsā* in Sanātana Jaina Granthamālā, No. 10 Varanasi, 1914.

75 *Jinaratnakośa,* p. 221.

76 These two works are edited in *M.D.J.M.*, No. 1. The *Laghīyastrayīprakaraṇa* is a work containing 78 *Kārikās,* divisible into three chapters on *Pramāṇa, Naya* and *Āgama* which give it the name *Laghīyastrayī.* This work is also edited in Singhi Jaina Series, No. 12, Ahmedabad, 1939. According to some others *Svārūpasambodhana* was written by Mahāsena, pupil of Nayasena ; for details see *Jinaratnakośa,* p. 458.

77 Edited in *M D.J.M.*, No. 18, Bombay, V.S. 1978.

78 See Introd. by Hiralal to his Catalogue, p. XXVI.

79 See *Jinaratnakośa,* p. 279.

80 Singhi Jaina Granthamālā, Ahmedabad, 1939.

81 See *Jinaratnakośa,* p. 441.

82 See Gaekwad Oriental Series, Vol. 30, Introd., p. lxxv.

83 Edited in *G.O.S.* by A. B. Dhruva, Baroda, 1930. In this edition of the *Nyāyapraveśa* both the commentaries of Haribhadra and Candrasūri have been included.

84 Published in Yaśovijayajī Jaina Granthamālā, No. 40, Vīra Saṁvat 2436-2439.

85 Since J. P. Jain, *Jain Sources* etc., p. 191 and footnote 4.

86 This text has several editions; the earliest one is published with Guṇaratna's commentary in the Bibliotheca Indica, Calcutta, 1905; for other editions see *Jinaratnakośa,* p. 402.

87 This text, which has 145 verses was published from Bhavnagar, V.S. 1958; an Italian translation was published by L. Suali in Florence, 1905.

88 Edited by L. Suali, Bhavnagar, 1911.

89 Edited by L. Suali from Bombay, 1913.

90 Edited by L. Suali, Calcutta, 1912; for other editions see *Jinaratnakośa,* p. 191.

91 See *H.I.L.*, Vol. II, p. 584 fn. 3.

92 Bombay, 1913.

93 This work is published with the *Caityavandanāsūtra* from Bombay, 1915.

94 See *Jinaratnakośa,* p. 125.

95 Edited Palitana, 1909; also Baroda, Vira Saṁvat, 2449.

96 Edited Stcherbatsky, St. Petersburg, 1909. For details see Vidyabhusan, *op. cit.*, pp. 194 f; also *Vienna Oriental Journal,* IV, p. 67.

97 See *supra,* p. 161.

98 Brahmanemidatta in his *Kathākośa* quoted by Vidyabhusan, *op. cit.*, p. 188.

99 See J. P. Jain in *Anekānta,* Vol. X, pp. 274-288; see also *Jain Sources* etc., pp. 199-200.

100 Colophon, verse 3 quoted in J. P. Jain, *op. cit.*, p. 199 fn. 3.

101 I. 38.

102 Quoted by K. B. Pathak in *J.B.B.R.A.S.*, 1892, p. 222.

103 Edited along with the *Āptamīmāṁsā* by N. R. Gandhi, Bombay, 1915.

104 Edited Varanasi, 1913.

105 Varanasi, 1914.

106 Edited along with the original text of Umāsvāti by M. L. Sastri, 1918.

107 See *Jinaratnakośa,* p. 412.

108 *Ibid.*, p. 355

109 Bombay, 1927; see also *Jinaratnakośa,* pp. 238-39.

110 Published along with the Bombay edition of the *Parīkṣāmukhasūtra;* another edition, Varanasi, 1928.

111 See *J.B.B.R.A.S.*, 1892, pp. 227, 229.

112 The relevant lines are quoted by Mukhtar in his Hindi Introd. to Samantabhadra's *Ratnakaraṇḍakaśrāvakācāra,* p. 59. See also Winternitz, *op. cit.*, Vol. II, p. 282 and footnote 6.

113 See Winternitz, *loc. cit.*

114 Mukhtar, *op. cit.*, p. 60.

115 *Ibid.*, pp. 57 ff.

116 Bombay, 1905.

117 See *Jinaratnakośa,* p. 26.
118 See Vidyabhusan, *op. cit.,* p. 196 fn. 2.
119 Ahmedabad, V. S. 1980-84 with the original text of Divākara.
120 See *Jinaratnakośa,* p. 348.
121 See Vidyabhusan, *op cit.,* pp. 196 f.

APPENDIX A

Ājīvikism and Gośāla

In the third chapter of the present work we discussed briefly the career of the Ājīvika philosopher Mokkhaliputta Gośāla. In this Appendix we will try to give a connected account of the origin of the Ājīvika religion and also of the principal events of the life of Gośāla, who like Lord Mahāvīra, was not the founder of his sect. In this connection we will endeavour to correlate the evidences supplied by the Pāli and Jain texts on Ājīvikism and Gośāla.

It is apparent from the Pāli texts that Ājīvikism was a living religion during the days of Buddha. The first Ājīvika whom Buddha met in his career was Upaka.[1] The story of ot this meeting is told in the *Ariyapariyesana Sutta* of the *Majjhima Nikāya*[2] and it appears to be one of the oldest parts of the Pāli canon. We are told here that Buddha had met this Ājīvika teacher immediately after his enlightenment, apparently near Gayā. Buddha was in his 36th year and according to our calculations this event took place in the 3rd quarter (or in the beginning of the 4th) of the sixth century B.C. It is interesting to note that the Ājīvika Upaka was in no mood to accept Buddha's claim that he was a *Jina* and left him quite coldly. This story is also repeated in a few other places of the Pāli canon.[3] Later Pāli commentators have given the romantic story of his marriage with one Cāpā and even affirm that he was converted to Buddhism in the later part of his life.[4] There is little doubt that the later stories were invented in order to show Buddha's greatness; in the original canon there is no indication that Upaka ever changed his faith.

We have already said that Buddha was a senior contemporary of Mahāvīra[5] and therefore Upaka should also be regarded as a senior contemporary of Gośāla, who according to the

Bhagavatī declared himself a *Jina* in the 6th year of Lord Mahāvīra's wanderings, or in other words, in Mahāvīra's 36th year. This suggests that the monks belonging to the Ājīvika religion wandered in Northern India before Gośāla, a conclusion which is strongly supported by the facts told about them in other places of Pāli and Ardhamāgadhī texts.

The Pāli texts repeatedly refer to the Ājīvikas, but never represent Gośāla as the founder of the sect. Several teachers like Nanda Vaccha,[6] Kisa Saṅkicca[7] and Paṇḍuputta[8] are mentioned in the Pāli canon and it appears that at least the first two viz. Nanda Vaccha and Kisa Saṅkicca were looked upon as important personalities in the days of Buddha. Pūraṇa Kassapa, who was one of the six great rivals of Buddha, had a great deference for these two teachers and also Gośāla[9], as he includes them in the 6th or the purest type (*parama-sukhābhijātas*) of men. Elsewhere Buddha[10] declares that although the Ājīvikas had *existed for a long time,*[11] they had only produced three distinguished teachers viz. Nanda Vaccha, Kisa Saṅkicca and Mokkhali Gośāla. This definitely shows that Ājīvikism is older than Buddhism and Gośāla was only one of the "distinguished teachers" of this religious sect.

The *Bhagavatīsūtra,* which is universally regarded as one of the oldest Jain canonical texts, also directly confirm the evidence of the Pāli canon regarding the antiquity of the Ājīvika religion. When challenged by Mahāvīra in Śrāvastī he declares that he is actually the 8th Ājīvika teacher and the first seven were the following—Udāi Kuṁḍiyāyaṇa, Eṇejja, Mallarāma, Maṇḍiya, Roha, Bhāradvāja and lastly Ajjuna Goyamaputta.[12] Basham, who has made a special study of the Ājīvika religion, remarks[13] in this connexion that the immediate predecessor of Gośāla viz. Ajjuna Goyamaputta is distinguished by a *gotra* name or patronymic as Udāi Kuṁḍiyāyaṇa, in whose body the migrant soul of Gośāla was originally born". He further notes that other five names have not been given any patronymics. From this he comes to the conclusion that the 1st and the 7th were "real" persons, and not figures of imagination. This is indeed a very strange logic! There is really no need for the Jain writer of the *Bhagavatī* to give the *gotra* names of all the predecessors of Gośāla in a passage, which was apparently written in haste and with the avowed intention to discredit the Ājīvika religion. The list of the seven predecessors of Gośāla should either be accepted in entirety or be summarily dismissed. Since the list occurs in a work, written by the stunch enemies of the Ājīvika religion, we have to accept it as genuine. Further, the Jain writer has also given, as noted by B. M. Barua,[14] the geographical centres of activities of all the seven predecessors of Gośāla, including the period of their missionary life. The earliest teacher viz. Udāi Kuṁḍiyāyaṇa was associated with the city of Rājagṛha and had preached for 22 years. This suggests that Udāi Kuṁḍiyāyaṇa was probably the founder of Ājīvikism and the celebrated Rājagṛha, the earlier capital of Magadha was the first centre of this new religion. Since the Ājīvikas went about naked, it is natural for them to choose a hilly place like Rājagṛha where they could easily get natural shelters. The next teacher was Eṇejja, who was associated with the town of Uddaṇḍapura (identification uncertain, but should be in eastern India) and had preached for 21 years. The third teacher of this sect was one Mallarāma, who spent his life at Campā and taught the principles of the Ājīvika religion for 20 years. The 4th prophet was Maṇḍiya, who was associated with the famous city of Vārāṇasī in which the celebrated Pārśvanātha was born. The missionary life of this gentleman, covered a total period of 19 years. The 5th teacher of this sect was one Roha, who preached at the town of Ālabhiyā (Āḷavī of the Pāli texts), which was not far from Śrāvastī,[15] taught for 18 years. Then came one Bhāradvāja, who belonged to the city of Śrāvastī and preached for 17 years. His successor was Ajjuna Goyamaputta, apparently of the same city, whose missionary life covered a period of 16 years.

A discerning reader of this passage will not fail to notice two special features regarding the list of the seven predecessors of Gośāla. The first, of course, is the progressive diminution by one year of the period of each reanimation and the second, which is more significant, is the gradual westward migration of this religion. In course of 133 years the Ājīvika religion gradually spread from Rājagṛha to Śrāvastī, a distance of nearly 300 miles. The progressive diminution of exactly one year seems somewhat artificial, but this cannot be the basis of the entire rejection of the complete list. The *Bhagavatī* passage indicates that the religion of the Ājīvikas was founded in the beginning of the 7th century B.C., probably 100 years after Pārśvanātha. Thus from point of chronology, Ājīvikism stands midway between Jainism and Buddhism.

Barua is of the view that the Ājīvikas even existed in the post-Vedic period,[16] which can, however, be rejected offhand. In no Vedic text there is even the remotest mention of the Ājīvika religion. It is also interesting to note, that like Buddhism and Jainism, the Ājīvika religion has been totally ignored in the two Indian epics, even in their latest sections. There is also no basis for V. S. Agrawala's surmise[17] that Ājīvikism was known to Pāṇini.

Basham is of the opinion that Pūraṇa Kassapa, one of the six great rivals of Buddha, was an Ājīvika teacher.[18] In support of his surmise he quotes from the Tamil poem *Nīlakeśī*. It is true that according to the malicious account,[19] left by Buddhaghoṣa, Pūraṇa went about naked. But in the *Sāmaññaphala Sutta*[20] of the *Dīgha Nikāya*, a clear distinction has been made between the doctrine of Gośāla and that of Kassapa. That Buddhaghoṣa was thoroughly biased is proved by the fact that he represents Pūraṇa as a slave, which is clearly wrong, as Kassapa is a Brahmin *gotra*. But it is quite likely that Gośāla and Pūraṇa had some respect for each other as the latter is represented in the *Aṅguttara Nikāya* as praising the three important Ājīvika teachers, a point which has already been noted.

Let us now try to have a close and hard look at the personality and career of Gośāla, probably the most controversial and enigmatic figure in the history of Indian philosophy. We should never forget that the texts, which deal with him, were all written by arch-enemies of the Ājīvikas, namely the Jains and Buddhists. Yet the life of this Ājīvika teacher, as painted in the *Bhagavatī*, the 5th Aṅga text of the Jains, is the only available source regarding his career. The references to him and the Ājīvikas in the Pāli *Tripiṭaka* often help us, but they are only incidental notices. The *Bhagavatī*[21] represents Gośāla as the son of one Maṅkhali by his spouse Bhadrā. This work further tells us that this Maṅkhali was a *maṅkha* which means a royal bard[22]. It appears from the *Bhagavatī* that Maṅkhali, the father of Gośāla was a poor, wandering poet or bard, who earned his livelihood by singing old, heroic ballads and exhibiting pictures (*cittaphalaga*) connected with his songs. The boy Gośāla was born in the cow-stall (*gośāla*) of a rich Brāhmaṇa called Gobahula, who was a resident of a village called Śaravana. That Makkhali was born in a cow-shed is also attested to by Buddhaghoṣa[23] in his *Sumaṅgalavilāsinī* and *Papañcasūdanī*. That writer also paints him as a servant of a rich man, and tells a ridiculous story to explain his name *makkhali*; however, the Jains do not confirm this story and, as we have already pointed out, a similar story is told by Buddhaghoṣa, that diehard Buddhist, regarding Pūraṇa Kassapa.

It appears from the *Bhagavatī* that Gośāla, after attaining manhood, accepted the professional life of his father. It further appears that from the very beginning of his career he developed some sort of repugnance against worldly life. When he met Mahāvīra at Nālandā near Rājagṛha for the first time, he was already a recluse. According to the writer of the *Bhagavatī*[24] Mahāvīra at first turned down Gośāla's request to make him his disciple. But afterwards accepted his second request at a place called Kollāga near Nālandā, and this event according to the *Bhagavatī* took place in the 2nd year of Mahāvīra's wanderings. The two naked ascetics spent six years together and a detailed description of their wanderings has been given by Jinadāsa Mahattara[25], who flourished in the 7th century and, needless to say, his account is largely based on imagination.

The *Bhagavatī* informs us that as a result of doctrinal difference Gośāla left Mahāvīra after six years and declared himself a *Jina* at Śrāvastī. But Mahāvīra had to wait for another six years for attaining the stage of perfection. Now, it is known to all students of religious history, that no religious leader (ancient or modern) in India has any respect for his opponent. Buddha looked upon Mahāvīra with contempt[26]. This is proved by Buddha's utterances regarding Mahāvīra after his death. Therefore we cannot expect the canonical writer of the *Bhagavatī* to accept Gośāla's claim of Jinahood before Mahāvīra. Had any Ājīvika canonical text survived, we would have come across similar refution of Mahāvīra's claim of attaining *kevalajñāna*. In the absence of such a text, the historian has no other alternative but to accept the fact that Gośāla became a *Jina*, at a time, when Mahāvīra was a mere learner. Further, nowhere in the Pāli canon Gośāla is represented as a pupil of Nāthaputta. It appears that the two teachers were good friends in their early career and because of serious doctrinal difference they not only parted company, but also developed deadly hatred against each other. We agree with Basham[27] when he declares that the *Bhagavatī* account is pervaded by deadly sectarian prejudice.

Gośāla was apparently in his late thirties when he established his own headquarters in Śrāvasti at the residence of the wealthy female potter Hālāhalā. He was recognised, as is evident from the *Bhagavatī*[28], as the head of the Ājīvikasaṅgha, which was established, as we have already noticed quite a few years earlier in that city by Bhāradvāja, the 6th Ājīvika teacher. Gośāla, it appears, not only succeeded in enlarging his circle of disciples in that city, but also converted quite a few important personalities of other places to his doctrine. One such person, according to the *Cullavagga*, was a highly official (*mahāmatta*). The *Vinaya Piṭaka* elsewhere[30] refers to a blood-relation of king Bimbisāra as embracing the Ājīvika religion and becoming a recluse of that Saṅgha. These two examples definitely prove the popularity of the Ājīvika religion among the aristocracy of those days. Probably such conversions of high officials to the religion of the Ājīvikas was not liked by Buddha, and this explains his outburts against Gośāla and his teachings. One such outburst is recorded in the *Aṅguttara Nikāya*[31] where Buddha calls the doctrine of Gośāla the 'meanest doctrine' and he is branded as a *moghapurisa*, which means a 'stupid fellow'. It is interesting to note that only Gośāla receives this epithet in the Pāli canon. But Gośāla not only succeeded in popularising his religion in different parts of Madhya-deśa and eastern India before long, but was also able to produce a number of remarkable Ājīvika teachers before his death.

The account of Gośāla's final meeting with Mahāvīra, as recorded in the *Bhagavatī*, deserves a close scrutiny. We are told that this meeting took place in the 24th years of Gośāla's ascetic-life, and 16 years before Mahāvīra's death. The place of this fateful meeting was the Koṣṭhaka shrine of the city of Śrāvastī[32]. Here we find Mahāvīra at first ridiculing Gośāla's claim that he was in possession of perfect knowledge. Gośāla simply denies that he was ever a disciple of Mahāvīra, and asserts, as we have already noted, that he is the 8th prophet of the Ājivika religion. One of Mahāvīra's disciples called Sunakṣatra, who tried to argue on behalf of his *guru* was consumed by Gośāla's *tejoleśyā* (anger). Lord Mahāvīra too, became a victim of Gośāla's spiritual power and the meeting ended abruptly. We are told that the debate was inconclusive and Mahāvīra, as is apparent from a passage of the text, did not succeed in his attempt to destroy the Ājīvika organisation of Śrāvastī. However, the *Bhagavatī* represents Gośāla as dying shortly after the meeting in Śrāvastī. There is little doubt that the account of Gośāla's death is highly exaggerated. And it is probable that his untimely demise promted the Jain canonical writer to devise this story.

That the account of his death is not based on facts will be clear from the contradictory and unhistorical statements in the account itself. We have already noted, that according to this account Gośāla died 16 years before the Nirvāṇa of Mahāvīra. Yet in another passage we are told that the death of Gośāla coincided with the Mahāśilākaṇṭaka war[33], which as we know from another passage of the *Bhagavatī*[34], was fought between Ajātaśatru on the one hand, and Nine Mallas and nine Licchavis on the other. Now, we definitely know that Ajātaśatru became king 8 years before Buddha's death, and less than 8 years before Mahāvīra's demise. Therefore, Gośāla, who according to the *Bhagavatī* died 16 years before Mahāvīra, was not alive when Kūṇika Ajātaśatru ascended the Magadhan throne and the passage which affirms that his death coincided with that famous war must be dismissed as a piece of poetic fancy. The same remark applies to another list of eight finalities, which coincided with Gośāla's death, viz. the last sprinkling-scent elephant (*gandhahastī*), which according to the *Nirayavalikā* was the cause of dispute between Ceṭaka and Ajātaśatru.

From the *Naṅguṭṭha Jātaka*[35] we learn that there was a group of Ājīvika ascetics living near Jetavana in Srāvastī, who were in the habit of performing difficult penances. That the Ājīvikas were respected for their austere life is clear from a number of passages in the Pāli canon. In an identical passage, preserved in the *Majjhima*[36] and *Saṁyutta*[37], Gośāla is praised by a *deva* for his perfect self-control. He is further delineated there as a speaker of truth and doer of no evil. Elsewhere in a Vinaya passage[38] we find the Ājīvikas condemning Buddhist monks for carrying parasols. These evidences strongly suggest that the Ājīvikas were respected for their strict and austere living.

It is surprising that the Ājīvikas, who could lead such an austere life should hold fatalistic views regarding life and nature. Their teaching as represented in the *Sāmaññaphalasutta* deny action (*kiriya*) endeavour (*viriya*) and result of action (*kamma*). According to Gośāla all beings attain perfection through *saṁsāra-śuddhi*. We can understand why Buddha could not tolerate the Ājīvikas, who were against all his ideas and ideals. "Like a fish-trap set at river-mouth, Makkhali was born into the world to be a man-trap for the distress and destruction of men"[39], Buddha declared. But in spite of such warnings, a number of respectable people of Buddha's own time chose this religion in preference to the teachings of Buddha and Mahāvīra.

In several places of the Jain canon we finds references to Ājīvika devotees and the Ājīvika doctrines. In the *Upāsakadaśā*[40] we have one Saddālaputta, who was a devotee of Gośāla. Another lay devotee called Ayaṁpula is mentioned in the *Bhagavatī*[41].

References in the later literature and epigraphs fully prove that Ājīvikisms survived upto the late mediaeval period. The inscriptions of Aśoka and his successor prove that the Ājīvikas were held in esteem in the Mauryan period. In the 7th Pillar Edict[42] they are mentioned after the Bauddhas and Brāhmaṇas, but before the Nirgranthas. In the Barabar Hill cave (Gayā district, Bihar) have been discovered inscriptions according to which Aśoka made a gift of several caves to the Ājīvikas in his 12th and 19th regnal years. Asoka's grandson Daśaratha was surely a patron of the Ājīvika religion. We have three short inscriptions[43] of this emperor in the Nāgārjuni Hill (Gayā district, Bihar) according to which he made gifts of cave-dwellings to the Ājīvikas.

In the *Arthaśāstra* (III. 20) of Kauṭilya and in the *Mahābhāṣya* (III. 96) of Patañjali the Ājīvikas are mentioned. In the latter work, Patañjali the author, shows his acquaintance with the principal doctrine of the Ājīvikas. Patañjali distinctly says that the Ājīvikas deny the freedom of the will. The *Mahāvaṁśa* (X. 102) informs us that the Ājīvikas could be seen in Ceylon during the reign of Pāṇḍukābhaya, who ruled in the 4th century B.C. This proves that after the death of Gośāla Ājīvikism penetrated into Southern India including Ceylon. This is proved by the references to the Ājīvikas in the Tamil Sangam literature. In a 5th century inscription[44] found from Nellore district (Andhra) of the reign of Siṁhavarman Pallava there is a reference to the Ājīvikas, which shows that monks belonging to this sect flourished in this part of India at that time. Varāhamihira (early 6th century) and his commentator Utpala (10th century) know the Ājīvikas[45]. On a basis of wrong statement of Utpala, D. R. Bhandarkar[46] came to the conclusion that, in the later days, the Ājīvikas weare identical with Vaiṣṇavas. But as Basham[47] has shown, this theory is purely speculative. The Ājīvikas were also known to Kumāradāsa[48] as is evident from his *Jānakīharaṇa*, which was composed probably during the closing years of the 7th century[49]. There are references to them in several South Indian inscriptions of a much later period. However by 1200 A.D., they disappeared completely from history[50].

NOTES

1 For details see Malalasekera, *D.P.P.N.*, Vol. I, pp. 385 f.

2 *Majjhima*, Vol. I, pp. 160-175; see also Malalasekera, *op. cit.*, Vol. I, pp. 179-80.

3 See *Jātaka,* I. 81 ; *Mahāvagga* (trans. I. B. Horner), p. 11.

4 See Malalasekera, *op. cit.,* Vol. I, p. 662 ; the *theri Cāpā* is mentioned in the *Therīgāthā* (see Nālandā edition *Khuddaka Nikāya,* Vol. II, pp. 441-443), but there the name of Upaka is conspicuously absent.

5 See *supra,* p. 31 fn. 3.

6 See Malalasekera, *op. cit.,* Vol. II, p. 14.

7 *Ibid.,* Vol. I, p. 609.

8 *Ibid.,* Vol. II, p. 123.

9 See *Aṅguttara,* Vol. III (translation), p. 273.

10 See *Majjhima, Sandakasutta* (No. 76) ; see also Malalasekera, *op. cit.,* Vol. II, p. 14 ; see also Hindi translation published by Mahābodhi Sabhā, p. 307.

11 Italics ours.

12 *Bhagavatī* (Sailana edition), Vol. V, pp. 2425-26.

13 *History and Doctrines of the Ājīvikas,* London, 1951, p. 32.

14 See *J.D.L.,* Vol. II, p. 5.

15 See *D.P.P.N.,* Vol. I, p. 295.

16 See *A.B.O.R.I.,* Vol. 8, pp. 183-84.

17 See the Hindi translation of his work entitled *Pāṇinikālin Bhāratavarṣa,* p. 370.

18 Basham, *op. cit.,* pp. 80 ff.

19 See *Sumaṅgavilāsinī,* Vol. I, p. 142.

20 *Dīgha,* No. 2

21 Vol. V, p. 2373.

22 See M. M. Williams, *S.E.D.,* p. 772.

23 See *Sumaṅgalavilāsinī,* Vol. I, pp. 143 f ; and *Pañcasudanī,* Vol. I, p. 422 ; see also Malalasekera, *op. cit.,* Vol. II, p. 400.

24 Vol. V, p. 2381.

25 See *Āvaśyakacūrṇī,* Vol. I, pp. 271, 282-84, 287-299.

26 See *Majjhima,* Vol. II, pp, 243f ; *Dīgha,* pp. 117, 210.

27 Basham, *op. cit.,* p. 66.

28 Vol. V, p. 2369.

29 Nālandā edition, p. 260.

30 See Nālandā ed. *Pācittiya,* p. 106.

31 See Nālandā ed. of *Aṅguttara,* Vol. I, p. 267.

32 Vol. V, p. 2418.

33 *Ibid.,* p. 2444.

34 *Ibid.,* Vol. III, pp. 1190 ff.

35 No. 144.

36 See Malalasekera, *D.P.P.N.,* Vol. I, p. 238 fn 1.

37 *Loc. cit.*

38 *Loc. cit.*

39 Nālandā edition, *Aṅguttara,* Vol. I, p. 267.

40 Pp. 114 ff (ed. N. A. Gore, Poona, 1953).

41 Vol. V, p. 2449.

42 See Bühler, *E.I.*, Vol. II, pp. 245 ff ; see also Sircar, *Sel. Ins* etc., pp. 62 ff.

43 See *I.A.*, Vol. 20, p. 364 ; Lüders, *List*, Nos. 954-956 ; see also Sircar, *op. cit.*, pp. 77 f.

44 *E.I.*, Vol. 24, pp. 296 ff.

45 See Basham, *op. cit.*, pp. 168 ff.

46 See *I.A.*, Vol. 41, pp. 286-290.

47 Basham, *op. cit.*, pp. 173 ff.

48 *Ibid.*, pp. 165 f.

49 See Winternitz, *H.I.L.*, Vol. III, Part I, p. 81.

50 Basham believes that the *nagnāṭakas*, who defiled Deva-temples during the region of Harṣa of Kashmir (last quarter of the 11th century), were probably the Ājīvikas ; see *op. cit.*, pp. 205 ff ; but this surmise seems to be entirely wrong.

APPENDIX B

Early Jainism and Yakṣa Worship

The early Vedic texts show some acquaintance with supernatural 'beings' or 'spirits' called Yakṣas. But compared with Rakṣas they are mentioned less freequently. Unlike Rakṣas and Piśācas, the Yakṣas are depicted in the early and later Vedic literature as less dangerous and malignant, although they too, sometimes are conceived as pure evil spirits. It is of great interest to note that Kubera, the leader of the Yakṣas of later literature, is delineated as the king (*rājan*) of Rakṣas and other evil-doers in such an old text as the *Satapatha Brāhmaṇa*.[1] He is further called by his other name Vaiśravaṇa in that text, A still earlier reference to him will be found in the *Atharvaveda*,[2] but there he is not connected with either the Yakṣas or Rakṣas. There are separate references[3] to the Yakṣas and Kubera in later Vedic literature, but Kubera as the king of the Yakṣas appears only in the post-Vedic literature. The term 'Yakṣa' also appears in the *Jaininīya Brāhmaṇa*[4] as the name of an unexplained being. But exactly at what time Kubera lost his position as the king of Rakṣas, it is not possible to say in the present state of our knowledge. But there is little doubt that he came to be associated with Yakṣas long before Mahāvīra and Buddha.

From the epics we learn a great deal about Yakṣas and some of their prominent leaders. In both the *Rāmāyaṇa* and *Mahābhārata* the Yakṣas, unlike other supernatural beings, appear as demi-gods. The interesting story told bout the struggle of the Yakṣas led by Kubera, and Rakṣas led by his younger broher Rāvaṇa in the Uttarakāṇḍa[5] of the *Rāmāyaṇa* shows that by the time that portion of the epic was composed, the Yakṣas were looked upon as somewhat benevolent beings, We should particularly take note of the epithet *mahātman* applied to Maṇibhadra and Kubera in that Book of the *Rāmāyaṇa*[6]. The famous

Yakṣa-Yudhiṣthira story told in the *Mahābhārata,*[7] also proves that the poet of that part of the great epic had real deference for Yakṣas. Another point that will have to be noted in this connexion that Kubera or Vaiśravaṇa, the lord of the Yakṣas in the epics, is conceived not only as an honourable member of the Brāhmaṇical pantheon but also as one of the four Lokapālas. We are told in the Uttarakāṇḍa[8] that formerly there were three Lokapālas and that Kubera or Vaiśravaṇa was installed as the fourth Lokapāla by Brahman after the former satisfied the latter by his penances. There is no doubt that Kubera was either a Rakṣa or Yakṣa before he was accepted in tht Indian pantheon and his elevation supports our contention that in the period of the composition of the epics, Yakṣas had their regular devotees among the local population, and this will be confirmed by our present discussion.

In the literature of both the Jains and Buddhists the Yakṣas play a very important role. But the early Jain canonical writers, even more than their Buddhist counter-parts, show a very intimate acquaintance not only with the Yakṣas, but also disclose the names of innumerable Yakṣa shrines of the Āryāvarta and Uttarāpatha. Any one who is even superficially acquainted with the Aṅgas and Upāṅgas know that one such Yakṣa shrine is mentioned almost in every *Sūtra* of these texts. There was hardly a city or town which had not a Yakṣa *āyatana* or *caitya.* We are giving below a list containing the names of some important shrines (majority of which were dedicated to Yakṣas) in the Jain texts.

Name of the city		*Name of the Shrine*
Vardhamānapura		Maṇibhadra
Kayaṁgalā	—	Chattapalāsa
Campā	—	Purṇabhadra and Aṅgamandira
Vāṇiyagāma (a suburb of Vaiśālī)	—	Suhamma

Name of the city		*Name of the Shrine*
Vaiśālī	—	Bahuputtiyā and Koṁdiyāyaṇa
Mithilā	—	Maṇibhadra
Ālabhiyā	—	Saṁkhavaṇa and Pattakālaga
Vārāṇasī	—	Koṭṭhaga and Ambasālavana
Kauśāmbī	—	Caṁdotaraṇa
Srāvastī	—	Koṭṭhaga
Mathurā	—	Sudarśana
Hastināpura	—	Sahasaṁbavana
Dvārāvatī	—	Surapriya

This list is, by no means, exhaustive and it is not difficult to mention, at least, another one hundred such shrines situated in various parts of Northern and Eastern India.

The Pāli Buddhist texts disclose the names of a good number of so-called Yakkha-cetiyas, most of which were situated in various parts of Eastern India. In the *Mahāparinibbāna Suttanta* of the *Dīgha Nikāya,* quite a few shrines situated in the celebrated city of Vaiśāli or Vesālī, are mentioned. They are—Sārandada, Cāpāla, Udena, Gotamaka, Bahuputta and Sattamba. From another Book of the *Dīgha Nikāya* viz. *Pātika Suttanta* we further learn that Udena was situated to the east, Gotamaka to the south, Sattamba to the west and Bahuputta to the north of this city. We have already seen that the shrine of Bahuputta is mentioned in the *Bhagavatī,*[9] the celebrated 5th Aṅga of the Jains from which we further learn that it was once visited by Mahāvīra. As a matter of fact, this is the only shrine that is mentioned both in the Jain and Buddhist texts. Another Bahuputta shrine was situated on the road between Rājagṛha and Nālandā, according to the *Saṁyutta Nikāya.*[10] In this shrine Buddha exchanged robes with Mahākassapa. We have also seen that a few Yakṣa shrines of Ālabhiyā are mentioned in the Jain texts. It is just possible that one of these Yakṣa shrines is repeatedly mentioned in the Pāli texts[11] as connected with the activities of Buddha and few of his disciples. The Pāli texts also disclose the names of a few other shrines of eastern India viz. Supatittha of Rājagṛha[12], Ānanda of Bhoganagara (in the Vajji territory)[13], Makuṭabandhana of the Mallas[14], and Ajakalāpa of Pātali or Pāvā[15].

It is, however, extremely doubtful whether all the *ceiyas* and *cetiyas or āyatanas* of the Jain and Buddhist texts were dedicated to the Yakṣas. Lea us first take up the case of the famous Bahuputta shrine situated in the northern part of Vaiśālī and which as we have already noted, was the only shrine of ancient India to be mentioned clearly in both the Ardha-māgadhi and Pāli canons. There is reason to believe that this shrine was named after the goddess Bahuputtiyā, whose story is told so beautifully and humourously in the Upāṅga text the *Nirayavalikā*. We learn from the 4th Adhyayana of that Jain text that the goddess (and not a female Yakṣa) Bahuputtiyā was intimately connected with the welfare of children. We however cannot be sure on this point since another Bahuputtiyā is mentioned in the *Bhagavatī*[16], *Sthānāṅga*[17] and *Nāyādhammakahāo*[18] as the wife of Yakṣa Pūrṇabhadra. The well-known Gotamaka shrine of the same city, was in all probability, not a Yakṣa temple. We invite, in this connexion, the attention of readers to a few *ślokas* of the Sabāparvan[19] of the *Mahābhārata* where we come across the name of one Gautamauka temple of Rājagṛha which according to these verses was named after the Ṛṣi Gautama. The Sanskrit word *gautamauka* is exactly the same as the Pāli *gotamaka.* Since the temple of Gautamauka at Rājagṛha was dedicated to Ṛṣi Gautama, it is reasonable to infer that the shrine of the same name situated at Vaiśālī was also named after that Vedic Ṛṣi. It is also interesting to note that a sect called Gotama-Goyama is mentioned both in the *Anuyogadvāra*[20] a Jain canonical text, and the *Aṅguttara*[21] a Pāli work. According to Hemacandra[22], the commentator of *Anuyogodvāra,* the mendicants belonging to that school, earned their livelihood by exhibiting young bulls, painted and decorated as well as by performing tricks. The worship of ancient Ṛṣis was not an uncommon thing in ancient India. We have the well known instance of Agastya worship. A shrine called Kāmamahāvana is mentioned in several Jain texts including the *Antagaḍadasāo*[23] and *Bhagavatī*[24] as situated at Vārāṇasī. It can, by no stretch of imagination, be called a Yakṣa shrine. It was serely dedicated to the Hindu god of love Kāmadeva, who was one of the most popular gods of ancient India and whose festivals were regularly held in almost all important cities of India during spring time. The Aṅgamandira[25] shrine of Campā, connected with the activities of the Ājīvika philosopher Makkhaliputta Gośāla was also probably a Brāhmaṇical temple. The is only *'ceiya'* of the Jain literature whose name has the significant ending *mandira* meaning probably a *devakula*. We should further note that the deities and even noble persons were often called 'Yakṣas' in ancient India. In the *Majjhima Nikāya*[26] and the *Petavatthu*[27] Indra is called a 'Yakṣa'. The famous city of gods Alakanandā is mentioned in the *Dīgha*[28] as the city of Yakṣas. Even Buddha is called a 'Yakṣa' in the *Majjhima Nikāya*[29]. The highly interesting Buddhist Sanskrit tert the *Mahāmāyūrī,* recently edited and translated by D. C. Sircar,[30] has a comprehensive list of the so-called Yakṣa shrines in which almost all the well known Hindu gods are called 'Yakṣas.' As for example, Viṣṇu of Dvārakā in verse No. 19, Śiva of Śivapura in verse 47 and Kārttikeya of Rohītaka in No. 35. We have already noted that the epics, the *Rāmāyaṇa* and *Mahābhārata* have nothing but deference for the Yakṣas, who were superior in character and demeanour, to the Rākṣasas and Piśācas. Even a person like Yudhiṣṭhira is delineated in the *Mahābhārata*[31] as worshipping Yakṣa Maṇibhadra whose shrine according to the Jain texts,[32] was situated both at Mithilā and Vardhamānapura of Bengal. This particular Yakṣa is mentioned elsewhere in the *Mahābhārata* as the presiding deity of travellers and traders[33] and a Buddhist canonical text[34] alludes to a shrine of the same Yakṣa at Gayā. Another Buddhist text[35] refers to the sects who apparently worshipped Maṇibhadra and Pūrṇabhadra both of whom are honourably mentioned in the Jain texts.

The list given above regarding some of the Yakṣa-cetiyas

shows that most of these shrines were situated in eastern India. There is no doubt that Yakṣa-worship was basically anti-Vedic in character. And only when the fusion of Aryans with non-Aryans was complete, that they were looked upon with veneration. It is also a fact that a few members of the Brāhmaṇical pantheon like Śiva, Gaṇapati, Skanda and Durgā were originally local deities, worshipped by non-Aryans, or to put it more correctly, un-Aryans. Both Jainism and Buddhism, which were basically anti-Vedic, naturally befriended popular and indigenous religious systems, which had a greater appeal for the masses. Pārśva, who may be called the real founder of Jainism, probably used to visit the well-known Yakṣa shrines of Vārāṇasī. His visit to the famous Pūrṇabhadra shrine of Campā is recorded in the *Nāyādhammakahāo*,[36] the 6th Aṅga text. Regarding his illustrious successor the lord Mahāvira, we can say with certainty that the Yakṣa shrines of eastern India were his most favourite resorts. In this connexion the following words of the Master found in the *Bhagavatī* may be reproduced here "I pass my nights in *devakulas, sabhās, pavās, ārāmas* and *ujjāṇas*." Most of the *ceiyas* of the Jain texts were situated in *ujjāṇas* meaning gardens, He also used to visit frequently shrines like Guṇaśila of Rājagṛha Pūrṇabhadra of Campā, Koṣṭhaka of Srāvastī etc. Quite a good number of his lectures were delivered according to the *Bhagavatī*, in the Guṇaśila shrine of Rājagṛha. A very vivid and useful description of the famous Yakṣa shrine of Pūrṇabhadra, situated to the north-east direction of Campā is given in the well-known Upāṅga text the *Aupapātika*.[37] The description there leaves no room to doubt that this particular shrine was one of the most prominent cultural and religious centres of that celebrated city, represented as the metropolis of Kūṇika-Ajātaśatru, the son of Śreṇika-Bimbisāra.

Although the *Bhagavatī* refers to Mahāvīra's visit to *devakulas*, very few *devakulas* are actually mentioned either in the Jain or Buddhist canonical texts. We have already referred to the temple of the god of Love situated at Vārāṇasī. There is little doubt that all the three teachers Pārśva, Mahāvīra and Buddha scrupulously and carefully avoided temples dedicated to Brāhmaṇical gods. But the *cetiya-ceiyas*, dedicated to Yakṣas, were favoured by them. In this connexion we can recall the following words spoken by Buddha to his followers in the *Aṅguttara Nikāya*,[38] "Vajjian shrines should be revered" By Vajjian he means the famous shrines of Vaiśālī and possibly also of Bhoganagara which was also situated in the Vajjī country. So it seems that both Mahāvīra and Buddha had some genuine deference for Yakṣa shrines, particularly of eastern India. Unlike Buddha, who spent the major part of his ascetic life in the luxurious Jetavana-vihāra of Śrāvastī and the Squirrels' feeding place of Rājagṛha, Mahāvīra, who wandered about absolutely naked, spent the major portion of his life in deserted caves and dilapidated shrines. Here we would like to draw the attention of readers to the fact that Mahāvīra became a Kevalin near a dilapidated shrine (*ceiya*).[39]

It is clear from the *Vipākaśruta*[40] and *Aupapātika*[41] that Yakṣas were worshipped like gods, with leaves, flowers incense and sandal etc. Just like gods they were worshipped for progeny, success etc.[42] These shrines invariably had an image[43] of the Yakṣa to whom it was dedicated. There is also reason to believe the image worship was originally a non-Aryan custom and it probably started with the worship of Yakṣa images. Image worship was also an integral part of Jain religion from the earliest times. Even in the most ancient texts of the Jains we have references to images and shrines dedicated to various Tīrthaṅkaras. If the evidence of the Hāthigumphā inscription is to be believed, a Nanda king of the 4th century B.C., took away a Jina image from Kaliṅga.[44] It is also possible that early Jain sculptors got inspiration from the Yakṣa images installed in various shrines. Even there is reason to believe that the association of every Tīrthaṅkara with a particular tree was due to the influence of Yakṣa worship which was often connected with *rukṣa* or tree worship. We should remember that the original Sanskrit word *caitya* also meant a sacred tree.[45] Further the commentary of the *Dhammapada* describes the Udena and Gotamaka shrines as *rukkhacetiyas*. This is not surprising since most of the Yakṣa shrines, according to the Jain canonical texts, were situated in the midst of big gardens (*ujjāṇa*)[46]

The intimate connexion of both Jainism and Buddhism with

Yakṣa worship is also proved by the fact that Vaiśravaṇa Kubera, the lord of Yakṣas, is probably the most prominent of the Hindu gods to be worshipped by the Jains and Buddhists alike. This is proved by the references to him in their canonical texts. He was popular even outside India.[47] As Jainism found favour with the traders from quite early times, it is natural that god of wealth Kubera, who was the supreme lord of the Yakṣas, should be popular among the devotees of Pārśva and Mahāvīra.

It is clear from the above discussion that early Jainism had close and intimate connexion with Yakṣa worship and gradually incorporated and absorbed some of its salient features. The Jains, it should be noted, had a very favourable attitude towards the so-called malignant spirits. This is proved by Vimala's treatment af some Rākṣasa characters of the *Rāmāyaṇa* in his celebrated *Paumacariyaṁ*. Characters like Rāvaṇa, Kumbhakarṇa and others are represented in this poem as vegetarian Vidyādharas, believing firmly in non-violence. Vimalasūri, who flourished in the 1st century (530 years after the Nirvāṇa of Mahāvīra) A.D., even takes the author of the *Rāmāyaṇa* to task, for delineating the Rākṣasas as cruel beings.[48] As firm believers in non-violence, the early Jain writers refused to believe that even supernatural beings or spirits could indulge in violence. It is, therefore, entirely natural that Yakṣas should get an honourable place in the early Jain canonical literature.

NOTES

1 XIII. 4.3.10.

2 VIII. 10.28.

3 *Mānava GS,* 11.14 ; *Śāṅ GS,* 1.1.7 ; *Hiraṇya GS,* II. 1.3.7 ; see also *SBE,* Vol. 29, p. 219.

4 II. 203, 272.

5 Chs. 14 f.

6 VII. 15.15, 29.

7 III, Chs. 312 ff.

8 3.11 ff.

9 Para. 617.

10 Vol. II, p. 149.

11 *Suttavibhaṅga,* Vol. I, p. 246 ; Vol. 2, pp. 71, 194 ; 223 ; *Aṅguttara,* Vol. IV, p. 147 ; *Saṁyutta,* 1, pp. 234, 275 ; etc.

12 *Mahāvagga,* p. 45.

13 *Aṅguttara,* Vol. II, p. 174.

14 *Mahāparinibbāna* of the *Dīgha.*

15 *Udāna,* p. 6.

16 Para. 406.

17 Para. 273.

18 Para. 153.

19 21. 5-8.

20 Para 20.

21 Vol. III, p. 200.

22 *Anuyogadvāra-vṛtti,* p. 25.

23 Para. 15.

24 Para 550 ; see also *Nāyā,* 151.

25 *Bhag,* 550.

26 I, p. 252.

27 II, 9.65 f

28 II, p. 170.

29 I, p. 386.

30 JAIH, Vol. V, pp. 262-328.

31 VIV. 65.7

32 *Jambudvīpaprajñapti,* 1.178 ; *Sūryaprajñapti,* 1-2 ; set also *Bhag,* 362.

33 III. 64.13 ; III, 65.22.

34 *Saṁyutta,* I, p. 266.

35 *Mahāniddesa,* pp. 89, 92 ; set also *Milindapañha,* p. 191.

36 Para 152.

37 Para 2

38 Vol. IV, p. 10.

39 See *Kalpasūtra,* 120 (*SBE.* Vol. XXII, p. 263) ; set also *Ācārāṅga,* 11. 15. 25.

40 See *Vipāka* (Kota, 1935), p. 248.

41 Para 2

42 *Vipāka,* p. 244.

43 Set *Ant.*, p. 86 (ed. L. D. Barnett) ; *Vipāka*, p. 86.

44 See Sircar, *Select Inscriptions* etc., p. 217.

45 Cf. *Mahābhārata*, I. 150. 33-
eko vṛkṣo hi yo grāme bhavet parṇaphalānvitaḥ
caityo bhavati nirjñātirarcanīyaḥ supūjitaḥ.

46 See especially *Aupapātika* (3) which describes a big garden just outside the Pūrṇabhadra *caitya* of Campā.

47 See *Yuan Chwang* (Watters), Vol. I, p. 108 ; See also *Mahāvaṁśa* X. 89.

48 See the paper on *Vimalasūri's Paumachriyaṁ* included in the present author's work entitled *Ancient Indian Literary and Cultural Tradition*, pp. 177-195.

SELECT BIBLIOGRAPHY

[For detailed information regarding the sources used in this work, consult the NOTES at the end of each Chapter]

Chapter I

1 Kalpasūtra, ed. H. Jacobi, Leipzig, 1879; translation by the same scholar *S.B.E,* Vol. 22.

2 Samavāyāṅga, edited along with the *vṛtti* by Abhayadeva, Āgamodaya Samiti, Bombay, 1918.

3 Sthānāṅga, Āgamodaya Samiti, Bombay, 1918-20.

4 Nāyādhammakahāo, Āgamodaya Samiti, Bombay, 1919.

5 Bhāgavata Purāṇa, Gītā Press edition, Gorakhpur.

6 M. L. Mehta and K. R. Chandra, Prakrit Proper Names, 2 Parts, Ahmedabad, 1970-72.

Chapter II

In addition to the texts mentioned for Chapter I consult the following—

1 Bhagavatī, Āgamodaya Samiti, Bombay, 1918-21.

2 Cambridge History of India, Vol. I (Cambridge, Reprint, 1935), Chapter VI.

3 M. Bloomfield, The Life and Stories of the Jain Savior Pārśvanātha, Baltimore, 1919.

Chapter III

In addition to the works recommended for the first two chapters, consult the following—

1 Suttāgame (collection of eleven Aṅga texts), ed. by Puppha bhikkhu, Gurgaon Cantt.

2 Dictionary of Pāli Proper Names in two Volumes by Malalasekera.

3 J. C. Jain, Life in Ancient India as depicted in Jain Canons, Bombay, 1947.

Chapter IV

In addition to the sources indicated in the *NOTES* of this chapter, no additional work is recommended here.

Chapter V

In addition to the sources indicated in the *NOTES,* consult the following—

1 Guérinot, A. Répertoire d' Epigraphie Jain, Paris, 1908.

2 C. L. Jain, Jaina Bibliography Calcutta, 1945. Some recent Jain inscriptions, discovered from Mathurā have been edited in *J.U.P.H.S.* and *Epigraphia Indica;* they have also been noticed in *Jaina Śilālekha Saṅgraha.*

Chapter VI

No additional work is recommended here.

Chapter VII

In addition to the *NOTES* consult the following—

1 G. C. Choudhary, Political History of Northern India from Jain Sources, Amritsar, 1963.

2 Shah, C. J., Jainism in North India, Bombay, 1932.

Chapter VIII

For detailed study consult the following modern works—

1 R. Ayyangar and B. Seshagiri, Studies in South Indian Jainism, Madras, 1922.

2 B. A. Saletore, Mediaeval Jainism, Bombay, 1938.

3 P. B. Desai, Jainism in South India and some Jaina Epigraphs, Sholapur, 1957.

Chapter IX

No additional text is recommended.

Chapter X

No additional text is recommended.

Chapter XI

The *NOTES* will be found sufficiently useful; for detailed Bibliography on the Śvetāmbara canonical texts consult the following works—

1 H. D. Velankar, Jinaratnakośa, Poona, 1944.

2 W. Schubring, The Doctrine of the Jains (translation of the original German work of the author), Delhi, 1962.

3 Doshi, Jain, Mehta and others, Jaina Sāhitya kā bṛhad itihāsa (first three volumes), Varanasi, 1966-67.

4 J. C. Jain, Prakrit Sāhitya kā itihāsa, Varanasi, 1961.

Chapter XII

The *NOTES* will be found sufficiently informative.

Chapters XIII and XIV

In addition to the sources indicated in the *NOTES* consult Velankar's *Jinaratnakośa* in which all published Jain works of literature are included.

Appendix A

1 B. M, Barua, The Ājīvikas, *J.D.L,* Vol. 2, pp. 1-80; see also his paper in *A.B.O.R.I.,* Vol. 8; the chapter on Gośāla in his classic work 'A History of Pre-Buddhistic Indian Philosophy' Calcutta, 1921, is also quite thought-provoking.

2 A. L. Basham, History and Doctrines of the Ājīvikas, London, 1951.

3 Two other relevant papers are by D. R. Bhandarkar (*I.A.*, Vol. 41, pp. 286-90) and A. S. Gopani (Bhāratīya Vidyā Vol. 2, pp. 201-10; Vol. 3, pp. 47-59).

Appendix B

1 J. Fergusson, Tree and Serpent Worship, London, 1873.

INDEX

Abaddhiya 104
Abhaya 250
Abhaya (disciple of Mahāvīra) 26
Abhayacandra 169, 317
Abhayadeva 236, 241, 244-46, 262, 264, 266, 268, 281
Abhayadeva (Rājagaccha) 332
Abhayadeva Sūri 233
Abhayanandi 300
Abhayanandi Bhaṭāra 138
Abhayanandi Muni 317
Abhidhānacintāmaṇi 63
Abhimānameru 313
Abhinandana 5
Ābhīra 303
Acalapura 287
Ācārāṅga 13, 17, 20-4, 31-2, 67, 78, 83, 101, 228-31, 233, 238, 261, 297, 357
Ācārāṅganiryukti 257-8
Ācārāṅgaṭīkā 285
Ācārāṅgavivaraṇa 261
Ācārāṅgavṛtti 93
Ācārya Ariṣṭanemi 194
Ācārya Āryanandin 193
Ācārya Guhanandin 105
Acchā 249
Acirāvatī 234
Adhicchatra 91
Adhyātmataraṅgiṇī 314, 315
Ādinātha 105, 124, 160, 305
Ādipurāṇa 106, 199, 303, 305-06, 312, 315, 331-32
Āditya 307
Āditya I 214-15
Ādityabhavana 311
Adur 181
Agāsavanā 110, 153
Agastyasiṁha 107, 261, 270
Aggoti 196
Aghama 56
Agnibhūti (disciple of Mahāvīra) 28
Agrawala, V. S. 58, 64, 66, 341
Āguptāyika 198
Ahariṣṭi 143
Ahicchatra 56, 66, 90-1, 93-5, 107, 168, 249
Aihole 177, 181
Airāṇi 256-57
Airāvata 274
Aitareya Brāhmaṇa 3, 88, 269
Aivarmalai 128-29, 217-18
Ajakalāpa 350
Ajātaśatru 26, 27, 31, 237, 239, 250; see also Kūṇika
Ajātaśatru (K of Kāśi) 11
Ajitā 5
Ajitanātha 4, 290
Ajita Purāṇa 315
Ajitaśāntistava 289
Ajitasenabhaṭṭāraka 190
Ajitatīrthakarapurāṇatilakam 209
Ājīvika 28-29, 41, 92, 118, 126-27, 146, 212, 233-34, 236, 238-40, 243-45, 248, 338-47, 351
Ājīvikasaṅgha 343
Ajjanandi 218-19
Ajjuna Goyamaputta 339-40
Akalaṅka 188, 202, 326, 328-29
Akalaṅkacarita 328, 335
Akālavarṣa 201, 306
Akālavarṣa Kannaradeva 208
Akṣayakīrti 194
Ālabhikā 24
Ālabhiyā 239, 340, 349-50

CORRECTIONS AND ADDITIONS

P. 8 We cannot entirely rule out the possibility of the identification of Ariṣṭanemi with Aranemi mentioned in the *Aṅguttara Nikāya* (see Nālandā edition of that text Vol. III, 83, 84, 256) where he is distinctly called *titthakara*.

P. 13 and elsewhere read '*Ācārāṅga*' for '*Ācāraṅga*'

P. 25 (line 4) and elsewhere read 'Sāketa' for 'Śāketa'

P. 44 (line 16)—read 'Magadha' for 'Maghadha'

P. 69 (No. 26)—read Gahapravika for Gahaprakiva

P. 80 (line 10)—read 'Arhats' for 'Arahats'

P. 84 (line 27)—read 'Puṣyamitra' for 'Puśyamitra'.

P. 85 (line 25)—add 'of' after 'character'

P. 88 (line 8)—read 'Udayagiri' for 'Udagiri'.

P. 90 A recently discovered bowl from Rajasthan (Bharatpur district) contains the word *negata* in early Brāhmī which may stand for *nigaṭha* (Jain); see *Indian Archaeology*, 1965-66, p. 67.

P. 96 Second para (last line)—read 'any' for 'and'.

P. 111 (Second para, line 5)—see in this connexion *A.S.W.I*, Vol. 3, p. 11; and *A.B.O.R.I*, Vol. 16, p. 7.

P. 112 Add a new footnote 11A with the following observation—From Kauśāmbī an icon of Padmaprabha, belonging to the early Gupta period, has been recently unearthed, see *Indian Archaeology*, 1953-54, p. 9. This surely proves the association of that Tīrthaṅkara with this ancient city.

P 116 Footnote 122 (line 7) read 'Jinaprabha' for 'Jinabhadra'.

P. 123 Second para (line 25) add 'also' after 'was'.

P. 129 First para (line 2) read 'Seṭṭipoḍavu' for 'Seṭṭipoḍanu'.

P. 141 Second para (line 7) read 'property' for 'propery'.
Same page (Third para)—see in this connexion N. Premi, *Jaina sāhitya aur itihāsa,* pp. 559 ff.

P. 143 Second line read '*ūrjas*' for '*orjas*'.
Same page, Third para (line 4) read 'different' for "dicerent'.

P. 144 Second line—delete 'The' before Harivarman
Same page, Second para (first line) read 'Kadamba' for 'kadamba'.

P. 157 Third para (first line) read 'Citrakūṭa' for 'Citraflūṭa'.

P. 167 Second para (line 4) read 'Vetravatī' for 'Vetravatī'.

P. 180 Third para (line 7) add 'of' after 'year'.

P. 192 Second para (last line) read 'These' for 'Therc'.

P. 222 Footnote 92 (line 3) read 'Kopaṇādri' for 'Kapaṇādri'.
Same page, same footnote (line 4) read '*Cāmuṇḍarāya*' for '*Cāmuṇḍrāya*'.

P. 228 Fourth para (line 6) read '*Niśītha*' for 'Niśītha'

P. 239 First para (last line) read 'Ambaḍa' for 'Ambada'.

P. 251 Second para (line 2) read '*Puṣpikā*' for '*Puṣpita*'.

P. 253 Second para (line 12) read 'Śayyambhava' for 'Sayyambhava'

P. 255 Third para (line 4) read 'Jinadāsagaṇi' for '*Jinadāsagaṇi*'

P. 256 Second para (line 9) read 'it' for 'if'.
Same page, same para (line 15) read '*suvarṇa*' for '*suvaṇa*'

P. 273 Second para (line 5) read Guṇāḍhya' for 'Gunāḍhya'.

P. 282 Second para (line 11) add 'that' after 'regret'

P. 284 Last line, read 'Caupaṇṇamahāpurisacariyam'

P. 288 Third para (line 12) read '*ghrāṇa*' for '*ghṛāṇa*'.

P. 308 Second para (line 5) read 'Deulavaḍaya' for Deulya-vaḍaya'.

P. 336 Footnote 86 (line 1) read 'was' for 'is'.